NETWORK SECURITY HACKS™

Other computer security resources from O'Reilly

Related titles
Wireless Hacks™
BSD Hacks™
Knoppix Hacks™
Ubuntu Hacks™
Linux Desktop Hacks™

Linux Server Hacks™
Linux Server Hacks™,
   Volume 2
Linux Multimedia Hacks™
Windows XP Hacks™
Windows Server Hacks™

Hacks Series Home
hacks.oreilly.com is a community site for developers and power users of all stripes. Readers learn from each other as they share their favorite tips and tools for Mac OS X, Linux, Google, Windows XP, and more.

Security Books Resource Center
security.oreilly.com is a complete catalog of O'Reilly's books on security and related technologies, including sample chapters and code examples.

oreillynet.com is the essential portal for developers interested in open and emerging technologies, including new platforms, programming languages, and operating systems.

Conferences
O'Reilly brings diverse innovators together to nurture the ideas that spark revolutionary industries. We specialize in documenting the latest tools and systems, translating the innovator's knowledge into useful skills for those in the trenches. Visit *conferences.oreilly.com* for our upcoming events.

Safari Bookshelf (*safari.oreilly.com*) is the premier online reference library for programmers and IT professionals. Conduct searches across more than 1,000 books. Subscribers can zero in on answers to time-critical questions in a matter of seconds. Read the books on your Bookshelf from cover to cover or simply flip to the page you need. Try it today for free.

SECOND EDITION

NETWORK SECURITY HACKS™

Andrew Lockhart

O'REILLY®

Beijing · Cambridge · Farnham · Köln · Paris · Sebastopol · Taipei · Tokyo

Network Security Hacks™, Second Edition

by Andrew Lockhart

Copyright © 2007, 2004 O'Reilly Media, Inc. All rights reserved.
Printed in the United States of America.

Published by O'Reilly Media, Inc., 1005 Gravenstein Highway North,
Sebastopol, CA 95472.

O'Reilly books may be purchased for educational, business, or sales promotional use. Online editions are also available for most titles (*safari.oreilly.com*). For more information, contact our corporate/institutional sales department: (800) 998-9938 or *corporate@oreilly.com*.

Editor: Brian Sawyer
Production Editor: Philip Dangler
Copyeditor: Rachel Wheeler
Indexer: Ellen Troutman-Zaig

Cover Designer: Karen Montgomery
Interior Designer: David Futato
Illustrators: Robert Romano
    and Jessamyn Read

Printing History:

April 2004:	First Edition.
November 2006:	Second Edition.

 This book uses RepKover™, a durable and flexible lay-flat binding.

ISBN 10: 0-596-52763-2
ISBN 13: 978-0-596-52763-1
[C]

Contents

Credits

About the Author

Andrew Lockhart is originally from South Carolina but currently resides in northern Colorado, where he spends his time trying to learn the black art of auditing disassembled binaries and trying to keep from freezing to death. He holds a BS in computer science from Colorado State University and has done security consulting for small businesses in the area. When he's not writing books, he's a senior security analyst with Network Chemistry, a leading provider of wireless security solutions. Andrew is also a member of the Wireless Vulnerabilities and Exploits project's (*http://www.wirelessve.org*) editorial board and regularly contributes to their wireless security column at Network-World (*http://www.networkworld.com/topics/wireless-security.html*). In his free time, he works on Snort-Wireless (*http://snort-wireless.org*), a project intended to add wireless intrusion detection to the popular open source IDS Snort.

Contributors

The following people contributed hacks, writing, and inspiration to this book:

- Oktay Altunergil is the founder of The Free Linux CD Project (*http://www.freelinuxcd.org*) and one of the maintainers of Turk-PHP.com (a Turkish PHP portal). He also works full-time as a Unix system administrator and PHP programmer.

- Michael D. (Mick) Bauer (*http://mick.wiremonkeys.org*) writes *Linux Journal*'s "Paranoid Penguin" security column. By day, he works to keep strangers out of banks' computer networks.

- Schuyler Erle (*http://nocat.net*) is a Free Software developer and activist. His interests include collaborative cartography, wireless networking, software for social and political change, and the Semantic Web. Schuyler is the lead developer of NoCatAuth, the leading open source wireless captive portal.

- Bob Fleck (*http://www.securesoftware.com*) is Director of Security Services at Secure Software. He consults in the fields of secure development and wireless security and is a coauthor of O'Reilly's *802.11 Security* book. The results of his more recent investigations into Bluetooth security can be found at *http://bluetooth.shmoo.com*.

- Rob Flickenger (*http://nocat.net*) is a writer and editor for O'Reilly's Hacks series. He currently spends his time hacking on various projects and promoting community wireless networking.

- Preston Gralla is the author of more than 30 books about computers and the Internet, which have been translated into 15 languages, including *Windows XP Hacks* (O'Reilly), *Internet Annoyances* (O'Reilly), and *Windows XP Power Hound* (Pogue Press). He has been writing about technology since the dawn of the PC age, and he has been an editor and columnist for many national newspapers, magazines, and web sites. He was the founding editor of *PC Week*; a founding editor, then editor, then editorial director of *PC/Computing*; and executive editor for ZDNet/CNet. Preston has written about technology for numerous magazines and newspapers, including *PC Magazine*, *Computerworld*, *CIO Magazine*, *Computer Shopper*, the *Los Angeles Times*, *USA Today*, the *Dallas Morning News* (where he was a technology columnist), and many others. He has been a columnist for ZDNet/CNet and is currently a columnist for TechTarget.com. His commentaries about technology have been featured on National Public Radio's "All Things Considered," and he has won the award for the Best Feature in a Computer Publication from the Computer Press Association. Under his editorship, *PC/Computing* was a finalist in the category of General Excellence for the National Magazine Awards. Preston is also the editor of O'Reilly's WindowsDevCenter.com site. He lives in Cambridge, MA, with his wife and two children—although his daughter has recently fled the nest for college. Between writing books, articles, and columns, he swims, plays tennis, goes to the opera, and contemplates the ram's skull hanging on the wall of his office.

- Michael Lucas (*http://www.blackhelicopters.org/~mwlucas/*) lives in a haunted house in Detroit, Michigan, with his wife Liz, assorted rodents, and a multitude of fish. He has been a pet wrangler, a librarian, and a security consultant, and he now works as a network engineer and system administrator with the Great Lakes Technologies Group. Michael is the author of *Absolute BSD*, *Absolute OpenBSD*, and *Cisco Routers for the Desperate* (all from No Starch Press), and he is currently preparing a book about NetBSD.

- Matt Messier (*http://www.securesoftware.com*) is Director of Engineering at Secure Software and a security authority who has been programming for nearly two decades. In addition to coauthoring the O'Reilly books *Secure Programming Cookbook for C and C++* and *Network Security with OpenSSL*, Matt coauthored the Safe C String Library (SafeStr), XXL, RATS, and EGADS.

- Ivan Ristic (*http://www.modsecurity.org*) is a web security specialist and the author of mod_security, an open source intrusion detection and prevention engine for web applications. He is a member of the OASIS Web Application Security Technical Committee, where he works on the standard for web application protection.

- Hans Schefske is a columnist on myITforum.com (*http://www.myitforum.com*) and has over eight years experience engineering and designing the architecture and implementation of Microsoft client/server-based network solutions. Consulting and leading projects in the IT industry, he has provided technical expertise in the areas of designing and implementing infrastructures for large enterprise-level companies such as Nabisco, Prudential, AIG, Simpson, Thatcher and Bartlett, Novartis, and Hoffman LaRoche Pharmaceuticals. In 2003, Hans was awarded a Microsoft Most Valuable Professional (MVP) Award for SMS for his outstanding technical skills and willingness to share knowledge with his peers. As a technical author at myITforum.com, he provides technical information, tools, scripts, and utilities for IT professionals and administrators to better assist them in managing their Microsoft-based solutions. Hans is currently a Senior Active Directory and SMS consultant at a large telecommunications company based in Atlanta, GA.

- Rod Trent, manager at myITforum.com (*http://www.myitforum.com*), is the leading expert on Microsoft Systems Management Server (SMS). He has over 18 years of IT experience, 8 of which have been dedicated to SMS. He is the author of such books as *Microsoft SMS Installer*, *Admin911: SMS*, and *Windows 2000 IIS 5.0: A Beginner's Guide* (all from McGraw-Hill) and has written thousands of articles on technology topics. myITforum.com is the central location for third-party SMS support and a well-known online gathering place for IT professionals and the IT community. Rod speaks at least three times a year at various conferences and is a principal at NetImpress, Inc. (*http://www.netimpress.com*).

- Mitch Tulloch (*http://www.mtit.com*) is President of MTIT Enterprises, an IT content development company based in Winnipeg, Canada. Prior to starting his own company in 1998, Mitch worked as a Microsoft Certified Trainer for Productivity Point International. Mitch is a widely recognized expert on Windows administration, networking, and security and has been awarded Most Valuable Professional (MVP) status by Microsoft for his outstanding contributions in supporting users who deploy Microsoft platforms, products, and solutions. Mitch is also currently a professor at Jones International University (JIU), where he teaches graduate-level courses in Information Security Management that he codeveloped with his wife, Ingrid Tulloch, for JIU's MBA program. Mitch is the author of 14 books, including *Windows Server Hacks* (O'Reilly), *Windows Server 2003 in a Nutshell* (O'Reilly), the *Microsoft Encyclopedia of Networking* (Microsoft Press), the *Microsoft Encyclopedia of Security* (Microsoft Press), and *IIS 6 Administration* (Osborne/ McGraw-Hill). Mitch has also written feature articles for industry magazines such as *NetworkWorld* and *Microsoft Certified Professional Magazine*, and he contributes articles regularly to O'Reilly's Windows-DevCenter.com, ITWorld.com, and WindowsNetworking.com. Mitch's articles have been widely syndicated on other IT sites, such as Computerworld.com, Smallbusiness.com, and even CNN.com.
- John Viega (*http://www.securesoftware.com*) is Chief Technology Officer and Founder of Secure Software. He is also the coauthor of several books on software security, including *Secure Programming Cookbook for C and C++* (O'Reilly) and *Building Secure Software* (Addison-Wesley). John is responsible for numerous software security tools, and he is the original author of Mailman, the GNU mailing list manager.

Acknowledgments

Once again I have to thank Karen (a.k.a. DJ Jackalope for Defcon attendees) for her constant support and encouragement, and for putting up with the many hours spent in toil.

Also, thanks go out to Brian Sawyer for his patience throughout this whole process, and to all of the other wonderful people at O'Reilly who worked hard to make this book a tangible reality. I'd also like to thank John Hoopes for providing the technical review for this edition. John's advice was instrumental in making this a better book.

Finally, I'd like to thank my parents for their continued encouragement.

Preface

Nowhere is the term *hacker* more misconstrued than in the network security field. This is understandable because the very same tools that network security professionals use to probe the robustness of their own networks also can be used to launch attacks on any machine on the Internet. The difference between system administrators legitimately testing their own machines and system crackers attempting to gain unauthorized access isn't so much a question of techniques or tools, but a matter of intent. After all, as with any powerful piece of technology, a security tool isn't inherently good or bad—this determination depends entirely on how it is used. The same hammer can be used to either build a wall or knock it down.

The difference between "white hat" and "black hat" hackers lies not in the tools or techniques they use (or even the color of their hats), but in their intentions. The difference is subtle but important. White hat hackers find that building secure systems presents an interesting challenge, and the security of such systems can be truly tested only through a thorough knowledge of how to subvert them. Black hat hackers (more appropriately called *crackers*) pursue precisely the same knowledge, but without regard for the people who built the systems or the servers they attack. They use their knowledge to subvert these systems for their own personal gain, often to the detriment of the systems they infiltrate.

Of course, tales of daring international techno-robberies and black-clad, cigarette-smoking, laptop-wielding evil masterminds tend to sell better than simple tales of engineers who build strong networks, so the term *hacking* has gained a bad reputation in the popular press. They use it to refer to individuals who break into systems or who wreak havoc using computers as their weapon. Among people who solve problems, though, the term *hack* refers to a "quick-and-dirty" solution to a problem, or a clever way to get something done. And the term *hacker* is taken very much as a compliment, referring to someone as being *creative*, i.e., having the technical chops to get things done. The Hacks series is an attempt to reclaim this word, document the ways people are hacking (in a good way), and pass the hacker ethic of creative participation on to the uninitiated. Seeing how others approach systems and problems is often the quickest way to learn about a new technology. Only by openly discussing security flaws and implementations can we hope to build stronger systems.

Why Network Security Hacks?

This second edition of *Network Security Hacks* is a grimoire of 125 powerful security techniques. This volume demonstrates effective methods for defending your servers and networks from a variety of devious and subtle attacks. Within this book are examples of how to detect the presence (and track every keystroke) of network intruders, methods for protecting your network and data using strong encryption, and even techniques for laying traps for would-be system crackers. Many important security tools are presented, as well as clever methods for using them to reveal real, useful information about what is happening on your network.

How This Book Is Organized

Although each hack is designed to stand on its own, this book makes extensive use of cross-referencing between hacks. If you find a reference to something you're interested in while reading a particular hack, feel free to skip around and follow it (much as you might while browsing the Web). The book itself is divided into several chapters, organized by subject:

Chapter 1, *Unix Host Security*

As the old saying goes, Unix was designed to share information, not to protect it. This old saw is no longer true with modern operating systems, where security is an integral component to any server. Many new programs and kernel features have been developed that provide a much higher degree of control over what Unix-like operating systems can do. Chapter 1 demonstrates advanced techniques for hardening your Linux, FreeBSD, or OpenBSD server.

Chapter 2, *Windows Host Security*

Microsoft Windows is used as a server platform in many organizations. As the Windows platform is a common target for various attacks, administering these systems can be challenging. This chapter covers many important steps that Windows administrators often overlook, including tightening down permissions, auditing all system activity, and eliminating security holes that are present in the default Windows installation.

Chapter 3, *Privacy and Anonymity*

These days, controlling the information trail left online is more important than ever. As more of our lives are conducted online, our information becomes easier to access by both friend and foe. This chapter discusses several ways to protect oneself online by offering solutions for encrypting email, remaining anonymous, and managing passwords for web sites.

Chapter 4, *Firewalling*

Firewalls are a key technology in the realm of network security. Without them, the world of network security would be quite different. This chapter shows how to set up firewalls under various operating systems, such as Linux, OpenBSD, FreeBSD, and Windows. Different filtering and firewall testing techniques are also covered in this chapter.

Chapter 5, *Encrypting and Securing Services*

Limiting how services can affect the system on which they're running is a key aspect of server security. It's also vital that traffic between the service and the clients connecting to it remain confidential in order to protect data and users' authentication credentials. This chapter shows how to do that for several popular services, such as SMTP, IMAP, POP3, Apache, and MySQL.

Chapter 6, *Network Security*

Regardless of the operating system your servers use, if your network is connected to the Internet, it uses TCP/IP for communications. Networking protocols can be subverted in a number of powerful and surprising ways, leading to attacks that can range from simple denial of service to unauthorized access with full privileges. This chapter demonstrates some tools and techniques used to attack servers using the network itself, as well as methods for preventing these attacks.

Chapter 7, *Wireless Security*

Wireless networks have become a common sight on the home network landscape and continue to gain traction in enterprise networks. However, warding off unauthorized users and attackers poses a greater challenge in a wireless network. While this chapter includes only a handful of hacks, what can be learned from them is invaluable. Whether you want to share your network with others (but still maintain a semblance of security) or lock down your wireless network with fine-grained authentication, this chapter has something for you.

Chapter 8, *Logging*

Network security administrators live and die by the quality of their logs. If too little information is tracked, intrusions can slip by unnoticed. If too much is logged, attacks can be lost in the deluge of irrelevant information. This chapter shows you how to balance the need for information with the need for brevity by automatically collecting, processing, and protecting your system logs.

Chapter 9, *Monitoring and Trending*

As useful as system logs and network scans can be, they represent only a single data point of information, relevant only to the instant that the events were recorded. Without a history of activity on your network, you have no way to establish a baseline for what is "normal," nor any real way to determine if something fishy is going on. This chapter presents a number of tools and methods for watching your network and services over time, allowing you to recognize trends that will aid in future planning and enable you to tell at a glance when something just isn't right.

Chapter 10, *Secure Tunnels*

How is it possible to maintain secure communications over networks as untrustworthy as the Internet? The answer nearly always involves powerful encryption and authentication techniques. Chapter 10 shows you how to implement powerful VPN technologies, including IPSec, PPTP, and OpenVPN. You will also find techniques for protecting services using SSL, SSH, and other strong encryption tools.

Chapter 11, *Network Intrusion Detection*

How do you know when your network is under attack? While logs and historical statistics can show you if something is out of sorts, there are tools designed to notify you (or otherwise take action) immediately when common attacks are detected. This chapter centers on the tremendously popular NIDS tool Snort and presents many techniques and add-ons that unleash this powerful tool's full potential. Also presented are methods for setting up your own "honeypot" network to attract and confuse would-be system crackers.

Chapter 12, *Recovery and Response*

Even the most competent and careful network administrator will eventually have to deal with successful security incidents. This chapter contains suggestions on how to verify your system's integrity, preserve evidence for later analysis, and track down the human being at the other end of undesirable network traffic.

Conventions Used in This Book

The following typographical conventions are used in this book:

Italic

Indicates new terms, URLs, email addresses, filenames, file extensions, pathnames, directories, daemons, programs, and Unix utilities

Constant width

> Indicates commands, options, switches, variables, attributes, keys, functions, types, classes, namespaces, methods, modules, properties, parameters, values, objects, events, event handlers, XML tags, HTML tags, macros, the contents of files, and the output from commands

Constant width bold

> Shows commands or other text that should be typed literally by the user

Constant width italic

> Shows text that should be replaced with user-supplied values

Gray type

> Used to indicate a cross-reference within the text

You should pay special attention to notes set apart from the text with the following icons:

> This is a tip, suggestion, or general note. It contains useful supplementary information about the topic at hand.

> This is a warning or note of caution, often indicating that your money or your privacy might be at risk.

The thermometer icons, found next to each hack, indicate the relative complexity of the hack:

 beginner   moderate   expert

Safari® Enabled

 When you see a Safari® Enabled icon on the cover of your favorite technology book, that means the book is available online through the O'Reilly Network Safari Bookshelf.

Safari offers a solution that's better than e-books. It's a virtual library that lets you easily search thousands of top tech books, cut and paste code samples, download chapters, and find quick answers when you need the most accurate, current information. Try it for free at *http://safari.oreilly.com*.

Using Code Examples

This book is here to help you get your job done. In general, you may use the code in this book in your programs and documentation. You do not need to contact us for permission unless you're reproducing a significant portion of the code. For example, writing a program that uses several chunks of code from this book does not require permission. Selling or distributing a CD-ROM of examples from O'Reilly books *does* require permission. Answering a question by citing this book and quoting example code does not require permission. Incorporating a significant amount of example code from this book into your product's documentation *does* require permission.

We appreciate, but do not require, attribution. An attribution usually includes the title, author, publisher, and ISBN. For example: "*Network Security Hacks, Second Edition,* by Andrew Lockhart. Copyright 2007 O'Reilly Media, Inc., 978-0-596-52763-1."

If you suspect your use of code examples falls outside fair use or the permission given here, feel free to contact us at *permissions@oreilly.com*.

How to Contact Us

Please address comments and questions concerning this book to the publisher:

O'Reilly Media, Inc.
1005 Gravenstein Highway North
Sebastopol, CA 95472
800-998-9938 (in the United States or Canada)
707-829-0515 (international or local)
707-829-0104 (fax)

We have a web page for this book, where we list errata, examples, and any additional information. You can access this page at:

http://www.oreilly.com/catalog/netsechacks2/

To comment or ask technical questions about this book, send email to:

bookquestions@oreilly.com

For more information about our books, conferences, Resource Centers, and the O'Reilly Network, see our web site at:

http://www.oreilly.com

Got a Hack?

To explore Hacks books online or to contribute a hack for future titles, visit:

http://hacks.oreilly.com

## CHAPTER ONE

Unix Host Security

Hacks 1–22

Networking is all about connecting computers together, so it follows that a computer network is no more secure than the machines that it connects. A single insecure host can make lots of trouble for your entire network, because it can act as a tool for reconnaissance or a strong base of attack if it is under the control of an adversary. Firewalls, intrusion detection mechanisms, and other advanced security measures are useless if your servers offer easily compromised services. Before delving into the network part of network security, you should first make sure that the machines you are responsible for are as secure as possible.

This chapter offers many methods for reducing the risks involved in offering services on a Unix-based system. Even though each of these hacks can stand on its own, it is worth reading through this entire chapter. If you implement only one type of security measure, you run the risk of all your preparation being totally negated once an attacker figures out how to bypass it. Just as Fort Knox isn't protected by a regular door with an ordinary dead bolt, no single security feature can ultimately protect your servers. And the security measures you may need to take increase proportionally to the value of what you're protecting.

As the old saying goes, *security* isn't a noun, it's a verb. That is, security is an active process that must be constantly followed and renewed. Short of unplugging it, there is no single action you can take to secure your machine. With that in mind, consider these techniques as a starting point for building a secure server that meets your particular needs.

H A C K
1

Secure Mount Points

Use mount options to help prevent intruders from further escalating a compromise.

The primary way of interacting with a Unix machine is through its filesystem. Thus, when an intruder has gained access to a system, it is desirable to limit what he can do with the files available to him. One way to accomplish this is with the use of restrictive mount options.

A *mount option* is a flag that controls how the filesystem may be accessed. It is passed to the operating system kernel's code when the filesystem is brought online. Mount options can be used to prevent files from being interpreted as device nodes, to disallow binaries from being executed, and to disallow the SUID bit from taking effect (by using the nodev, noexec, and nosuid flags). Filesystems can also be mounted read-only with the ro option.

These options are specified from the command line by running mount with the -o flag. For example, if you have a separate partition for */tmp* that is on the third partition of your first IDE hard disk, you can mount with the nodev, noexec, and nosuid flags, which are enabled by running the following command:

```
# mount -o nodev,noexec,nosuid /dev/hda3 /tmp
```

An equivalent entry in your */etc/fstab* would look something like this:

```
/dev/hda3    /tmp    ext3    defaults,nodev,noexec,nosuid    1 2
```

By carefully considering your requirements and dividing up your storage into multiple filesystems, you can utilize these mount options to increase the work that an attacker will have to do in order to further compromise your system. A quick way to do this is to first categorize your directory tree into areas that need write access for the system to function and those that don't. You should consider using the read-only flag on any part of the filesystem where the contents do not change regularly. A good candidate for this might be */usr*, depending on how often updates are made to system software.

Obviously, many directories (such as */home*) will need to be mounted as read/write. However, it is unlikely that users on an average multiuser system will need to run SUID binaries or create device files within their home directories. Therefore, a separate filesystem, mounted with the nodev and nosuid options, could be created to house the users' home directories. If you've determined that your users will not need to execute programs stored in their home directories, you can use the noexec mount option as well. A similar solution could be used for */tmp* and */var*, where it is highly unlikely that any process will legitimately need to execute SUID or non-SUID binaries or access device files. This strategy would help prevent the possibility of an attacker leaving a Trojan horse in a common directory such as */tmp* or a user's home directory. The attacker may be able to install the program, but it will not be able to run, with or without the proper chmod bits.

> Services running in a sandboxed environment [Hack #10] might be broken if nodev is specified on the filesystem running in the sandbox. This is because device nodes such as */dev/log* and */dev/null* must be available within the chroot( ) environment.

There are a number of ways that an attacker can circumvent these mount restrictions. For example, the noexec option on Linux can be bypassed by using */lib/ld-linux.so* to execute binaries residing on a filesystem mounted with this option. At first glance, you'd think that this problem could be remedied by making *ld-linux.so* nonexecutable, but this would render all dynamically linked binaries nonexecutable.

So, unless all of the programs you rely on are statically linked (they're probably not), the noexec option is of little use in Linux. In addition, an attacker who has already gained root privileges will not be significantly hampered by filesystems mounted with special options, since these can often be remounted with the -o remount option. But by using mount flags, you can easily limit the possible attacks available to a hostile user before he gains root privileges.

Scan for SUID and SGID Programs

HACK #2

Quickly check for potential root-exploitable programs and backdoors.

One potential way for a user to escalate her privileges on a system is to exploit a vulnerability in an SUID or SGID program. SUID and SGID are legitimately used when programs need special permissions above and beyond those that are available to the user who is running them. One such program is *passwd*. Simultaneously allowing a user to change her password while not allowing any user to modify the system password file means that the *passwd* program must be run with root privileges. Thus, the program has its SUID bit set, which causes it to be executed with the privileges of the program file's owner. Similarly, when the SGID bit is set, the program is executed with the privileges of the file's group owner.

Running ls -l on a binary that has its SUID bit set should look like this:

```
-r-s--x--x   1 root     root        16336 Feb 13  2003 /usr/bin/passwd
```

Notice that instead of an execute bit (x) for the owner bits, it has an s. This signifies an SUID file.

Unfortunately, a poorly written SUID or SGID binary can be used to quickly and easily escalate a user's privileges. Also, an attacker who has already gained root access might hide SUID binaries throughout your system in order to leave a backdoor for future access. This leads us to the need for scanning systems for SUID and SGID binaries. This is a simple process and can be done with the following command:

```
# find / \( -perm -4000 -o -perm -2000 \) -type f -exec ls -la {} \;
```

One important thing to consider is whether an SUID program is in fact a shell script rather than an executable, since it's trivial for someone to change an otherwise innocuous script into a backdoor. Most operating systems ignore any SUID or SGID bits on a shell script, but if you want to find all SUID or SGID scripts on a system, change the argument to the -exec option in the last command and add a pipe so that the command reads:

```
# find / \( -perm -4000 -o -perm -2000 \) -type f \
-exec file {} \; | grep -v ELF
```

Now, every time an SUID or SGID file is encountered, the file command will run and determine what type of file is being examined. If it's an executable, grep will filter it out; otherwise, it will be printed to the screen with some information about what kind of file it is.

Most operating systems use ELF-format executables, but if you're running an operating system that doesn't (older versions of Linux used a.out, and AIX uses XCOFF), you'll need to replace the ELF in the previous grep command with the binary format used by your operating system and architecture. If you're unsure of what to look for, run the file command on any binary executable, and it will report the string you're looking for.

For example, here's an example of running file on a binary in Mac OS X:

```
$ file /bin/sh
/bin/sh: Mach-O executable ppc
```

To go one step further, you could even queue the command to run once a day using cron and have it redirect the output to a file. For instance, this crontab entry would scan for files that have either the SUID or SGID bits set, compare the current list to the one from the day before, and then email the differences to the owner of the crontab (make sure this is all on one line):

```
0 4 * * * find / \( -perm -4000 -o -perm -2000 \) -type f \
> /var/log/sidlog.new && \
diff /var/log/sidlog.new /var/log/sidlog && \
mv /var/log/sidlog.new /var/log/sidlog
```

This example will also leave a current list of SUID and SGID files in */var/log/ sidlog*.

HACK #3 Scan for World- and Group-Writable Directories

Quickly scan for directories with loose permissions.

World- and group-writable directories present a problem: if the users of a
system have not set their umasks properly, they will inadvertently create insecure files, completely unaware of the implications. With this in mind, it
seems it would be good to scan for directories with loose permissions. As in
"Scan for SUID and SGID Programs" [Hack #2], this can be accomplished with
a find command:

```
# find / -type d \( -perm -g+w -o -perm -o+w \) -exec ls -lad {} \;
```

Any directories that are listed in the output should have the sticky bit set,
which is denoted by a t in the directory's permission bits. Setting the sticky
bit on a world-writable directory ensures that even though anyone may create files in the directory, they may not delete or modify another user's files.

If you see a directory in the output that does not contain a sticky bit, consider whether it really needs to be world-writable or whether the use of
groups or ACLs [Hack #4] will work better for your situation. If you really do
need the directory to be world-writable, set the sticky bit on it using chmod
+t.

To get a list of directories that don't have their sticky bit set, run this command:

```
# find / -type d \( -perm -g+w -o -perm -o+w \) \
-not -perm -a+t -exec ls -lad {} \;
```

If you're using a system that creates a unique group for each user (e.g., you
create a user *andrew*, which in turn creates a group *andrew* as the primary
group), you may want to modify the commands to not scan for group-writable directories. (Otherwise, you will get a lot of output that really isn't pertinent.) To do this, run the command without the -perm -g+w portion.

HACK #4 Create Flexible Permissions Hierarchies with POSIX ACLs

When Unix mode-based permissions just aren't enough, use an ACL.

Most of the time, the traditional Unix file permissions system fits the bill
just fine. But in a highly collaborative environment with multiple people
needing access to files, this scheme can become unwieldy. *Access control
lists*, otherwise known as *ACLs* (pronounced to rhyme with "hackles"), are a
relatively new feature of open source Unix operating systems, but they have
been available in their commercial counterparts for some time. While ACLs
do not inherently add "more security" to a system, they do reduce the

complexity of managing permissions. ACLs provide new ways to apply file and directory permissions without resorting to the creation of unnecessary groups.

ACLs are stored as extended attributes within the filesystem metadata. As the name implies, they allow you to define lists that either grant or deny access to a given file or directory based on the criteria you provide. However, ACLs do not abandon the traditional permissions system completely. ACLs can be specified for both users and groups and are still separated into the realms of read, write, and execute access. In addition, a control list may be defined for any user or group that does not correspond to any of the other user or group ACLs, much like the "other" mode bits of a file.

Access control lists also have what is called an *ACL mask*, which acts as a permission mask for all ACLs that specifically mention a user and a group. This is similar to a umask, but not quite the same. For instance, if you set the ACL mask to r--, any ACLs that pertain to a specific user or group and are looser in permissions (e.g., rw-) will effectively become r--. Directories also may contain a default ACL, which specifies the initial ACLs of files and subdirectories created within them.

Enabling ACLs

Most filesystems in common use today under Linux (Ext2/3, ReiserFS, JFS, and XFS) are capable of supporting ACLs. If you're using Linux, make sure one of the following kernel configuration options is set, corresponding to the type of filesystem you're using:

```
CONFIG_EXT2_FS_POSIX_ACL=y
CONFIG_EXT3_FS_POSIX_ACL=y
CONFIG_REISERFS_FS_POSIX_ACL=y
CONFIG_JFS_POSIX_ACL=y
CONFIG_FS_POSIX_ACL=y
CONFIG_XFS_POSIX_ACL=y
```

To enable ACLs in FreeBSD, mount any filesystems you want to use them on with the acls mount option:

```
# mount -o acls -u /usr
# mount
/dev/ad0s1a on / (ufs, local)
devfs on /dev (devfs, local)
/dev/ad0s1e on /tmp (ufs, local, soft-updates)
/dev/ad0s1f on /usr (ufs, local, soft-updates, acls)
/dev/ad0s1d on /var (ufs, local, soft-updates)
```

The -u option updates the mount, which lets you change the mount options for a currently mounted filesystem. If you want to undo this, you can disable

ACLs by using the noacls option instead. To enable ACLs automatically at boot for a filesystem, modify the filesystem's */etc/fstab* entry to look like this:

```
/dev/ad0s1f          /usr          ufs     rw,acls          2          2
```

Managing ACLs

Once they've been enabled, ACLs can be set, modified, and removed using the setfacl command. To create or modify an ACL, use the -m option, followed by an ACL specification and a filename or list of filenames. You can delete an ACL by using the -x option and specifying an ACL or list of ACLs.

There are three general forms of an ACL: one for users, another for groups, and one for others. Let's look at them here:

```
# User ACL
u:[user]:<mode>
# Group ACL
g:[group]:<mode>
# Other ACL
o:<mode>
```

Notice that in user and group ACLs, the actual user and group names that the ACL applies to are optional. If these are omitted, it means that the ACL will apply to the base ACL, which is derived from the file's mode bits. Thus, if you modify these, the mode bits will be modified, and vice versa.

See for yourself by creating a file and then modifying its base ACL:

```
$ touch myfile
$ ls -l myfile
-rw-rw-r--    1 andrew    andrew          0 Oct 13 15:57 myfile
$ setfacl -m u::---,g::---,o:--- myfile
$ ls -l myfile
----------    1 andrew    andrew          0 Oct 13 15:57 myfile
```

From this example, you can also see that multiple ACLs can be listed by separating them with commas.

You can also specify ACLs for an arbitrary number of groups or users:

```
$ touch foo
$ setfacl -m u:jlope:rwx,g:wine:rwx,o:--- foo
$ getfacl foo
# file: foo
# owner: andrew
# group: andrew
user::rw-
user:jlope:rwx
group::---
group:wine:rwx
mask::rwx
other::---
```

Now if you changed the mask to r--, the ACLs for *jlope* and *wine* would effectively become r-- as well:

```
$ setfacl -m m:r-- foo
$ getfacl foo
# file: foo
# owner: andrew
# group: andrew
user::rw-
user:jlope:rwx               #effective:r--
group::---
group:wine:rwx               #effective:r--
mask::r--
other::---
```

As mentioned earlier, a directory can have a default ACL that will automatically be applied to files that are created within that directory. To designate an ACL as the default, prefix it with a d::

```
$ mkdir mydir
$ setfacl -m d:u:jlope:rwx mydir
$ getfacl mydir
# file: mydir
# owner: andrew
# group: andrew
user::rwx
group::---
other::---
default:user::rwx
default:user:jlope:rwx
default:group::---
default:mask::rwx
default:other::---

$ touch mydir/bar
$ getfacl mydir/bar
# file: mydir/bar
# owner: andrew
# group: andrew
user::rw-
user:jlope:rwx               #effective:rw-
group::---
mask::rw-
other::---
```

As you may have noticed from the previous examples, you can list ACLs by using the getfacl command. This command is pretty straightforward and has only a few options. The most useful is the -R option, which allows you to list ACLs recursively and works very much like ls -R.

Protect Your Logs from Tampering

HACK #5

Use file attributes to prevent intruders from removing traces of their break-ins.

In the course of an intrusion, an attacker will more than likely leave telltale signs of his actions in various system logs. This is a valuable audit trail that should be well protected. Without reliable logs, it can be very difficult to figure out how the attacker got in, or where the attack came from. This information is crucial in analyzing the incident and then responding to it by contacting the appropriate parties involved [Hack #125]. However, if the break-in attempt is successful and the intruder gains root privileges, what's to stop him from removing the traces of his misbehavior?

This is where file attributes come in to save the day (or at least make it a little better). Both Linux and the BSDs have the ability to assign extra attributes to files and directories. This is different from the standard Unix permissions scheme in that the attributes set on a file apply universally to all users of the system, and they affect file accesses at a much deeper level than file permissions or ACLs [Hack #4]. In Linux, you can see and modify the attributes that are set for a given file by using the lsattr and chattr commands, respectively. Under the BSDs, you can use ls -lo to view the attributes and use chflags to modify them.

One useful attribute for protecting log files is append-only. When this attribute is set, the file cannot be deleted, and writes are only allowed to append to the end of the file.

To set the append-only flag under Linux, run this command:

```
# chattr +a filename
```

Under the BSDs, use this:

```
# chflags sappnd filename
```

See how the +a attribute works by creating a file and setting its append-only attribute:

```
# touch /var/log/logfile
# echo "append-only not set" > /var/log/logfile
# chattr +a /var/log/logfile
# echo "append-only set" > /var/log/logfile
bash: /var/log/logfile: Operation not permitted
```

The second write attempt failed, since it would overwrite the file. However, appending to the end of the file is still permitted:

```
# echo "appending to file" >> /var/log/logfile
# cat /var/log/logfile
append-only not set
appending to file
```

Obviously, an intruder who has gained root privileges could realize that file attributes are being used and just remove the append-only flag from the logs by running `chattr -a`. To prevent this, you'll need to disable the ability to remove the append-only attribute. To accomplish this under Linux, use its capabilities mechanism. Under the BSDs, use the securelevel facility.

The Linux capabilities model divides up the privileges given to the all-powerful root account and allows you to selectively disable them. To prevent a user from removing the append-only attribute from a file, you need to remove the `CAP_LINUX_IMMUTABLE` capability. When present in the running system, this capability allows the append-only attribute to be modified. To modify the set of capabilities available to the system, use a simple utility called *lcap* (*http://snort-wireless.org/other/lcap-0.0.6.tar.bz2*).

To unpack and compile the tool, run this command:

```
# tar xvfj lcap-0.0.6.tar.bz2 && cd lcap-0.0.6 && make
```

Then, to disallow modification of the append-only flag, run:

```
# ./lcap CAP_LINUX_IMMUTABLE
# ./lcap CAP_SYS_RAWIO
```

The first command removes the ability to change the append-only flag, and the second command removes the ability to do raw I/O. This is needed so that the protected files cannot be modified by accessing the block device on which they reside. It also prevents access to */dev/mem* and */dev/kmem*, which would provide a loophole for an intruder to reinstate the `CAP_LINUX_IMMUTABLE` capability.

To remove these capabilities at boot, add the previous two commands to your system startup scripts (e.g., */etc/rc.local*). You should ensure that capabilities are removed late in the boot order, to prevent problems with other startup scripts. Once `lcap` has removed kernel capabilities, you can only reinstate them by rebooting the system.

The BSDs accomplish the same thing through the use of *securelevels*. The securelevel is a kernel variable that you can set to disallow certain functionality. Raising the securelevel to 1 is functionally the same as removing the two previously discussed Linux capabilities. Once the securelevel has been set to a value greater than 0, it cannot be lowered. By default, OpenBSD will raise the securelevel to 1 when in multiuser mode. In FreeBSD, the securelevel is −1 by default.

To change this behavior, add the following line to */etc/sysctl.conf*:

```
kern.securelevel=1
```

Before doing this, you should be aware that adding append-only flags to your log files will most likely cause log rotation scripts to fail. However, doing this will greatly enhance the security of your audit trail, which will prove invaluable in the event of an incident.

HACK #6 Delegate Administrative Roles

Let others do your work for you without giving away root privileges.

The *sudo* utility can help you delegate some system responsibilities to other people, without having to grant full root access. *sudo* is a setuid root binary that executes commands on an authorized user's behalf, after she has entered her current password.

As root, run */usr/sbin/visudo* to edit the list of users who can call *sudo*. The default *sudo* list looks something like this:

```
root ALL=(ALL) ALL
```

Unfortunately, many system administrators tend to use this entry as a template and grant unrestricted root access to all other admins unilaterally:

```
root ALL=(ALL) ALL
rob ALL=(ALL) ALL
jim ALL=(ALL) ALL
david ALL=(ALL) ALL
```

While this may allow you to give out root access without giving away the root password, this method is truly useful only when all of the *sudo* users can be completely trusted. When properly configured, the *sudo* utility provides tremendous flexibility for granting access to any number of commands, run as any arbitrary user ID (UID).

The syntax of the *sudo* line is:

```
user machine=(effective user) command
```

The first column specifies the *sudo* user. The next column defines the hosts in which this *sudo* entry is valid. This allows you to easily use a single *sudo* configuration across multiple machines.

For example, suppose you have a developer who needs root access on a development machine, but not on any other server:

```
peter beta.oreillynet.com=(ALL) ALL
```

The next column (in parentheses) specifies the effective user who may run the commands. This is very handy for allowing users to execute code as users other than root:

```
peter lists.oreillynet.com=(mailman) ALL
```

Finally, the last column specifies all of the commands that this user may run:

```
david ns.oreillynet.com=(bind) /usr/sbin/rndc,/usr/sbin/named
```

If you find yourself specifying large lists of commands (or, for that matter, users or machines), take advantage of *sudo*'s alias syntax. An alias can be used in place of its respective entry on any line of the *sudo* configuration:

```
User_Alias ADMINS=rob,jim,david
User_Alias WEBMASTERS=peter,nancy
Runas_Alias DAEMONS=bind,www,smmsp,ircd
Host_Alias WEBSERVERS=www.oreillynet.com,www.oreilly.com,www.perl.com
Cmnd_Alias PROCS=/bin/kill,/bin/killall,/usr/bin/skill,/usr/bin/top
Cmnd_Alias APACHE=/usr/local/apache/bin/apachectl
WEBMASTERS WEBSERVERS=(www) APACHE
ADMINS ALL=(DAEMONS) ALL
```

It is also possible to specify a system group instead of a user, to allow any user who belongs to that group to execute commands. Just prefix the group name with a %, like this:

```
%wwwadmin WEBSERVERS=(www) APACHE
```

Now any user who is part of the *wwwadmin* group can execute *apachectl* as the *www* user on any of the web server machines.

One very useful feature is the NOPASSWD: flag. When present, the user won't have to enter a password before executing the command. For example, this will allow the user *rob* to execute *kill*, *killall*, *skill*, and *top* on any machine, as any user, without entering a password:

```
rob ALL=(ALL) NOPASSWD: PROCS
```

Finally, *sudo* can be a handy alternative to *su* for running commands at startup out of the system *rc* files:

```
(cd /usr/local/mysql; sudo -u mysql ./bin/safe_mysqld &)
sudo -u www /usr/local/apache/bin/apachectl start
```

For that to work at boot time, the default line root ALL=(ALL) ALL must be present.

Use *sudo* with the usual caveats that apply to setuid binaries. Particularly if you allow *sudo* to execute interactive commands (like editors) or any sort of compiler or interpreter, you should assume that it is possible that the *sudo* user will be able to execute arbitrary commands as the effective user. Still, under most circumstances this isn't a problem, and it's certainly preferable to giving away undue access to root privileges.

—*Rob Flickenger*

Automate Cryptographic Signature Verification

HACK #7

Use scripting and key servers to automate the chore of checking software authenticity.

One of the most important things you can do for the security of your system is to make yourself familiar with the software you are installing. You probably will not have the time, knowledge, or resources to go through the source code for all of the software that you install. However, verifying that the software you are compiling and installing is what the authors intended can go a long way toward preventing the widespread distribution of Trojan horses.

Recently, Trojaned versions of several pivotal pieces of software (such as *tcpdump*, *libpcap*, *sendmail*, and OpenSSH) have been distributed. Since this is an increasingly popular attack vector, verifying your software is critically important.

Why does this need to be automated? It takes little effort to verify software before installing it, but either through laziness or ignorance, many system administrators overlook this critical step. This is a classic example of "false" laziness, since it will likely lead to more work for the sysadmin in the long run.

This problem is difficult to solve, because it relies on the programmers and distributors to get their acts together. Then there's the laziness aspect. Software packages often don't even come with a signature to use for verifying the legitimacy of what you've downloaded, and even when signatures are provided with the source code, to verify the code you must hunt through the software provider's site for the public key that was used to create the signature. After finding the public key, you have to download it, verify that the key is genuine, add it to your keyring, and finally check the signature of the code.

Here is what this would look like when checking the signature for Version 1.3.28 of the Apache web server using GnuPG (*http://www.gnupg.org*):

```
# gpg -import KEYS
# gpg -verify apache_1.3.28.tar.gz.asc apache_1.3.28.tar.gz
gpg: Signature made Wed Jul 16 13:42:54 2003 PDT using DSA key ID 08C975E5
gpg: Good signature from "Jim Jagielski <jim@zend.com>"
gpg:                     aka "Jim Jagielski <jim@apache.org>"
gpg:                     aka "Jim Jagielski <jim@jaguNET.com>"
gpg: WARNING: This key is not certified with a trusted signature!
gpg:          There is no indication that the signature belongs to the
owner.
Fingerprint: 8B39 757B 1D8A 994D F243  3ED5 8B3A 601F 08C9 75E5
```

As you can see, it's not terribly difficult to do, but this step is often over-looked when people are in a hurry. This is where this hack comes to the rescue. We'll use a little bit of shell scripting and what are known as *key servers* to reduce the number of steps required to perform the verification process.

Key servers are a part of a public-key cryptography infrastructure that allows you to retrieve keys from a trusted third party. A nice feature of GnuPG is its ability to query key servers for a key ID and to download the result into a local keyring. To figure out which key ID to ask for, we rely on the fact that the error message generated by GnuPG tells us which key ID it was unable to find locally when trying to verify the signature.

In the previous example, if the key that GnuPG was looking for had not been imported prior to verifying the signature, it would have generated an error like this:

```
gpg: Signature made Wed Jul 16 13:42:54 2003 PDT using DSA key ID 08C975E5
gpg: Can't check signature: public key not found
```

The following script takes advantage of that error:

```
#!/bin/sh
VENDOR_KEYRING=vendors.gpg
KEYSERVER=search.keyserver.net
KEYID="0x`gpg --verify $1 $2 2>&1 | grep 'key ID' | awk '{print $NF}'`"
gpg --no-default-keyring --keyring $VENDOR_KEYRING --recv-key \
  --keyserver $KEYSERVER $KEYID
gpg --keyring $VENDOR_KEYRING --verify $1 $2
```

The first line of the script specifies the keyring in which the result from the key server query will be stored. You could use *pubring.gpg* (which is the default keyring for GnuGP), but using a separate file will make managing vendor public keys easier. The second line of the script specifies which key server to query (the script uses *search.keyserver.net*; another good one is *pgp. mit.edu*). The third line attempts (and fails) to verify the signature without first consulting the key server. It then uses the key ID it saw in the error, prepending an 0x in order to query the key server on the next line. Finally, GnuPG attempts to verify the signature and specifies the keyring in which the query result was stored.

This script has shortened the verification process by eliminating the need to search for and import the public key that was used to generate the signature. Going back to the example of verifying the Apache 1.3.28 source code, you can see how much more convenient it is now to verify the package's authenticity:

```
# checksig apache_1.3.28.tar.gz.asc apache_1.3.28.tar.gz
gpg: requesting key 08C975E5 from HKP keyserver search.keyserver.net
gpg: key 08C975E5: public key imported
gpg: Total number processed: 1
```

```
gpg:                    imported: 1
gpg: Warning: using insecure memory!
gpg: please see http://www.gnupg.org/faq.html for more information
gpg: Signature made Wed Jul 16 13:42:54 2003 PDT using DSA key ID 08C975E5
gpg: Good signature from "Jim Jagielski <jim@zend.com>"
gpg:                    aka "Jim Jagielski <jim@apache.org>"
gpg:                    aka "Jim Jagielski <jim@jaguNET.com>"
gpg: checking the trustdb
gpg: no ultimately trusted keys found
gpg: WARNING: This key is not certified with a trusted signature!
gpg:            There is no indication that the signature belongs to the
owner.
Fingerprint: 8B39 757B 1D8A 994D F243  3ED5 8B3A 601F 08C9 75E5
```

This small, quick script has reduced both the number of steps and the amount of time needed to verify a source package. As with any good shell script, it should help you to be lazy in a good way: by doing more work properly, but with less effort on your part.

Check for Listening Services
#8

Find out whether unneeded services are listening and looking for possible backdoors.

One of the first things you should do after a fresh operating system install is see what services are running and remove any unneeded services from the system startup process. You could use a port scanner (such as Nmap [Hack #66]) and run it against the host, but if one didn't come with the operating system install, you'll likely need to connect your fresh (and possibly insecure) machine to the network to download one.

Also, Nmap can be fooled if the system is using firewall rules. With proper firewall rules, a service can be completely invisible to Nmap unless certain criteria (such as the source IP address) also match. When you have shell access to the server itself, it is usually more efficient to find open ports using programs that were installed with the operating system. One option is *netstat*, a program that will display various network-related information and statistics.

To get a list of listening ports and their owning processes under Linux, run this command:

```
# netstat -luntp
Active Internet connections (only servers)
Proto Recv-Q Send-Q Local Address Foreign Address  State   PID/Program name
tcp       0      0 0.0.0.0:22    0.0.0.0:*        LISTEN  1679/sshd
udp       0      0 0.0.0.0:68    0.0.0.0:*                1766/dhclient
```

From the output, you can see that this machine is probably a workstation, since it just has a DHCP client running along with an SSH daemon for remote access. The ports in use are listed after the colon in the Local Address column (22 for *sshd* and 68 for *dhclient*). The absence of any other listening processes means that this is probably a workstation, not a network server.

Unfortunately, the BSD version of *netstat* does not let us list the processes and the process IDs (PIDs) that own the listening port. Nevertheless, the BSD netstat command is still useful for listing the listening ports on your system.

To get a list of listening ports under FreeBSD, run this command:

```
# netstat -a -n | egrep 'Proto|LISTEN'
Proto Recv-Q Send-Q  Local Address        Foreign Address      (state)
tcp4      0      0  *.587                *.*                  LISTEN
tcp4      0      0  *.25                 *.*                  LISTEN
tcp4      0      0  *.22                 *.*                  LISTEN
tcp4      0      0  *.993                *.*                  LISTEN
tcp4      0      0  *.143                *.*                  LISTEN
tcp4      0      0  *.53                 *.*                  LISTEN
```

Again, the ports in use are listed in the Local Address column. Many seasoned system administrators have memorized the common port numbers for popular services and will be able to see at a glance that this server is running SSHD, SMTP, DNS, IMAP, and IMAP+SSL services. If you are ever in doubt about which services typically run on a given port, either eliminate the -n switch from the netstat command (which tells *netstat* to use names but can take much longer to run when looking up DNS addresses) or manually grep the */etc/services* file:

```
# grep -w 993 /etc/services
imaps           993/udp    # imap4 protocol over TLS/SSL
imaps           993/tcp    # imap4 protocol over TLS/SSL
```

The */etc/services* file should only be used as a guide. If a process is listening on a port listed in the file, it doesn't necessarily mean that the service listed in */etc/services* is what it is providing.

Also notice that, unlike in the output of netstat on Linux, with the BSD version you don't get the PIDs of the daemons themselves. You might also notice that no UDP ports were listed for DNS. This is because UDP sockets do not have a LISTEN state in the same sense that TCP sockets do. In order to display UDP sockets, you must add udp4 to the argument for egrep, thus making it 'Proto|LISTEN|udp4'. However, due to the way UDP works, not all UDP sockets will necessarily be associated with a daemon process.

Under FreeBSD, there is another command that will give us just what we want. The sockstat command performs only a small subset of what netstat can do and is limited to listing information on Unix domain sockets and Inet sockets, but it's ideal for this hack's purposes.

To get a list of listening ports and their owning processes with `sockstat`, run this command:

```
# sockstat -4 -l
USER     COMMAND    PID    FD PROTO  LOCAL ADDRESS       FOREIGN ADDRESS
root     sendmail   1141    4 tcp4   *:25                *:*
root     sendmail   1141    5 tcp4   *:587               *:*
root     sshd       1138    3 tcp4   *:22                *:*
root     inetd      1133    4 tcp4   *:143               *:*
root     inetd      1133    5 tcp4   *:993               *:*
named    named      1127   20 tcp4   *:53                *:*
named    named      1127   21 udp4   *:53                *:*
named    named      1127   22 udp4   *:1351              *:*
```

Once again, you can see that SSHD, SMTP, DNS, IMAP, and IMAP+SSL services are running, but now you have the process that owns the socket plus its PID. You can now see that the IMAP services are being spawned from inetd instead of standalone daemons, and that sendmail and named are providing the SMTP and DNS services.

For most other Unix-like operating systems, you can use the *lsof* utility (*http://ftp.cerias.purdue.edu/pub/tools/unix/sysutils/lsof/*). *lsof* is short for "list open files" and, as the name implies, it allows you to list files that are open on a system, in addition to the processes and PIDs that have them open. Since sockets and files work the same way under Unix, *lsof* can also be used to list open sockets. This is done with the `-i` command-line option.

To get a list of listening ports and the processes that own them using *lsof*, run this command:

```
# lsof -i -n | egrep 'COMMAND|LISTEN'
COMMAND   PID   USER FD   TYPE      DEVICE SIZE/OFF NODE NAME
named     1127 named 20u  IPv4  0xeb401dc0      0t0  TCP *:domain (LISTEN)
inetd     1133  root  4u  IPv4  0xeb401ba0      0t0  TCP *:imap (LISTEN)
inetd     1133  root  5u  IPv4  0xeb401980      0t0  TCP *:imaps (LISTEN)
sshd      1138  root  3u  IPv4  0xeb401760      0t0  TCP *:ssh (LISTEN)
sendmail  1141  root  4u  IPv4  0xeb41b7e0      0t0  TCP *:smtp (LISTEN)
sendmail  1141  root  5u  IPv4  0xeb438fa0      0t0  TCP *:submission (LISTEN)
```

Again, you can change the argument to `egrep` to display UDP sockets. However, this time use UDP instead of udp4, which makes the argument `'COMMAND|LISTEN|UDP'`. As mentioned earlier, not all UDP sockets will necessarily be associated with a daemon process.

Prevent Services from Binding to an Interface
Keep services from listening on a port instead of firewalling them.

Sometimes, you might want to limit a service to listen on only a specific interface. For instance, Apache [Hack #55] can be configured to listen on a

specific interface as opposed to all available interfaces. You can do this by
using the Listen directive in your configuration file and specifying the IP
address of the interface:

```
Listen 192.168.0.23:80
```

If you use VirtualHost entries, you can specify interfaces to bind to on a per-
virtual-host basis:

```
<VirtualHost 192.168.0.23>
...
</VirtualHost>
```

You might even have services that are listening on a TCP port but don't
need to be. Database servers such as MySQL are often used in conjunction
with Apache and are frequently set up to coexist on the same server when
used in this way. Connections that come from the same machine that
MySQL is installed on use a domain socket in the filesystem for communications. Therefore, MySQL doesn't need to listen on a TCP socket. To keep it
from listening, you can either use the --skip-networking command-line
option when starting MySQL or specify it in the [mysqld] section of your
my.cnf file:

```
[mysqld]
...
skip-networking
...
```

Another program that you'll often find listening on a port is your X11 server,
which listens on TCP port 6000 by default. This port is traditionally used to
enable remote clients to connect to your X11 server so they can draw their
windows and accept keyboard and mouse input; however, with the advent
of SSH and X11 forwarding, this really isn't needed anymore. With X11 forwarding enabled in *ssh*, any client that needs to connect to your X11 server
will be tunneled through your SSH connection and will bypass the listening
TCP port when connecting to your X11 server.

To get your X Windows server to stop listening on this port, all you need to
do is add -nolisten tcp to the command that is used to start the server. This
can be tricky, though—figuring out which file controls how the server is
started can be a daunting task. Usually, you can find what you're looking for
in */etc/X11*.

If you're using *gdm*, open *gdm.conf* and look for a line similar to this one:

```
command=/usr/X11R6/bin/X
```

Then, just add -nolisten tcp to the end of the line.

If you're using *xdm*, look for a file called *Xservers* and make sure it contains a line similar to this:

```
:0 local /usr/X11R6/bin/X -nolisten tcp
```

Alternatively, if you're not using a managed display and instead are using startx or a similar command to start your X11 server, you can just add -nolisten tcp to the end of your startx command. To be sure that it is passed to the X server process, start it after an extra set of hyphens:

```
$ startx -- -nolisten tcp
```

Once you start X, fire up a terminal and see what is listening using lsof or netstat [Hack #8]. You should no longer see anything bound to port 6000.

Restrict Services with Sandboxed Environments

Mitigate system damage by keeping service compromises contained.

Sometimes, keeping up with the latest patches just isn't enough to prevent a break-in. Often, a new exploit will circulate in private circles long before an official advisory is issued, during which time your servers might be open to unexpected attack. With this in mind, it's wise to take extra preventative measures to contain the possible effects of a compromised service. One way to do this is to run your services in a *sandbox*. Ideally, this minimizes the effects of a service compromise on the overall system.

Most Unix and Unix-like systems include some sort of system call or other mechanism for sandboxing that offers various levels of isolation between the host and the sandbox. The least restrictive and easiest to set up is a chroot( ) environment, which is available on nearly all Unix and Unix-like systems. FreeBSD also includes another mechanism called jail( ), which provides some additional restrictions beyond those provided by chroot( ).

> If you want to set up a restricted environment but don't feel that you need the level of security provided by a system-call-based sandboxed environment, see "Restrict Shell Environments" [Hack #20].

Using chroot( )

chroot( ) very simply changes the root directory of a process and all of its children. While this is a powerful feature, there are many caveats to using it. Most importantly, there should be no way for anything running within the sandbox to change its effective user ID (EUID) to 0, which is root's UID. Naturally, this implies that you don't want to run anything as root within the jail.

There are many ways to break out of a chroot( ) sandbox, but they all rely on being able to get root privileges within the sandboxed environment. Possession of UID 0 inside the sandbox is the Achilles heel of chroot( ). If an attacker is able to gain root privileges within the sandbox, all bets are off. While the attacker will not be able to directly break out of the sandboxed environment, he may be able to run functions inside the exploited processes' address space that will let him break out.

There are a few services that support chroot( ) environments by calling the function within the program itself, but many services do not. To run these services inside a sandboxed environment using chroot( ), you need to make use of the chroot command. The chroot command simply calls chroot( ) with the first command-line argument and attempts to execute the program specified in the second argument. If the program is a statically linked binary, all you have to do is copy the program to somewhere within the sandboxed environment; however, if the program is dynamically linked, you will need to copy all of its supporting libraries to the environment as well.

See how this works by setting up *bash* in a chroot( ) environment. First try to run chroot without copying any of the libraries *bash* needs:

```
# mkdir -p /chroot_test/bin
# cp /bin/bash /chroot_test/bin/
# chroot /chroot_test /bin/bash
chroot: /bin/bash: No such file or directory
```

Now find out what libraries *bash* needs by using the ldd command. Then copy the libraries into your chroot( ) environment and attempt to run chroot again:

```
# ldd /bin/bash
libtermcap.so.2 => /lib/libtermcap.so.2 (0x4001a000)
libdl.so.2 => /lib/libdl.so.2 (0x4001e000)
libc.so.6 => /lib/tls/libc.so.6 (0x42000000)
/lib/ld-linux.so.2 => /lib/ld-linux.so.2 (0x40000000)
# mkdir -p chroot_test/lib/tls && \
> (cd /lib; \
> cp libtermcap.so.2 libdl.so.2 ld-linux.so.2 /chroot_test/lib; \
> cd tls; cp libc.so.6 /chroot_test/lib/tls)
# chroot /chroot_test /bin/bash
bash-2.05b#
bash-2.05b# echo /*
/bin /lib
```

Setting up a chroot( ) environment mostly involves trial and error in getting the permissions right and getting all of the library dependencies in place. Be sure to consider the implications of having other programs such as *mknod* or *mount* available in the chroot( ) environment. If these are available, the attacker may be able to create device nodes to access memory directly or to remount filesystems, thus breaking out of the sandbox and gaining total control of the overall system.

This threat can be mitigated by putting the directory on a filesystem mounted with options that prohibit the use of device files [Hack #1], but that isn't always convenient. It is advisable to make as many of the files and directories in the chroot( )-ed directory as possible owned by root and writable only by root, in order to make it impossible for a process to modify any supporting files (this includes files such as libraries and configuration files). In general, it is best to keep permissions as restrictive as possible and to relax them only when necessary (for example, if the permissions prevent the daemon from working properly).

The best candidates for a chroot( ) environment are services that do not need root privileges at all. For instance, MySQL listens for remote connections on port 3306 by default. Since this port is above 1024, *mysqld* can be started without root privileges and therefore doesn't pose the risk of being used to gain root access. Other daemons that need root privileges can include an option to drop these privileges after completing all the operations for which they need root access (e.g., binding to a port below 1024), but care should be taken to ensure that the programs drop their privileges correctly. If a program uses seteuid( ) rather than setuid( ) to drop its privileges, an attacker can still exploit it to gain root access. Be sure to read up on current security advisories for programs that will run only with root privileges.

You might think that simply not putting compilers, a shell, or utilities such as *mknod* in the sandbox environment might protect them in the event of a root compromise within the restricted environment. In reality, attackers can accomplish the same functionality by changing their code from calling system("/bin/sh") to calling any other C library function or system call that they desire. If you can mount the filesystem the chroot( )-ed program runs from using the read-only flag [Hack #1], you can make it more difficult for attackers to install their own code, but this is still not quite bulletproof. Unless the daemon you need to run within the environment can meet the criteria discussed earlier, you might want to look into using a more powerful sandboxing mechanism.

Using FreeBSD's jail( )

One such mechanism is available under FreeBSD and is implemented through the jail( ) system call. jail( ) provides many more restrictions in isolating the sandbox environment from the host system and offers additional features, such as assigning IP addresses from virtual interfaces on the host system. Using this functionality, you can create a full virtual server or just run a single service inside the sandboxed environment.

Just as with chroot( ), the system provides a jail command that uses the jail( ) system call. Here's the basic form of the jail command, where *ipaddr* is the IP address of the machine on which the jail is running:

```
jail new root hostname ipaddr command
```

The hostname can be different from the main system's hostname, and the IP address can be any IP address that the system is configured to respond to. You can actually give the appearance that all of the services in the jail are running on a separate system by using a different hostname and configuring and using an additional IP address.

Now, try running a shell inside a jail:

```
# mkdir -p /jail_test/bin
# cp /stand/sh /jail_test/bin/sh
# jail /jail_test jail_test 192.168.0.40 /bin/sh
# echo /*
/bin
```

This time, no libraries need to be copied, because the binaries in */stand* are statically linked.

On the opposite side of the spectrum, you can build a jail that can function as a nearly fully functional virtual server with its own IP address. The steps to do this basically involve building FreeBSD from source and specifying the jail directory as the install destination. You can do this by running the following commands:

```
# mkdir /jail_test
# cd /usr/src
# make world DESTDIR=/jail_test
# cd etc && make distribution DESTDIR=/jail_test
# mount_devfs devfs /jail_test/dev
# cd /jail_test && ln -s dev/null kernel
```

However, if you're planning to run just one service from within the jail, this is definitely overkill. (Note that in the real world you'll probably need to create */dev/null* and */dev/log* device nodes in your sandbox environment for most daemons to work correctly.)

To start your jails automatically at boot, you can modify */etc/rc.conf*, which provides several variables for controlling a given jail's configuration:

```
jail_enable="YES"
jail_list=" test"
ifconfig_lnc0_alias0="inet 192.168.0.41 netmask 255.255.255.255"
jail_test_rootdir="/jail_test"
jail_test_hostname="jail_test"
```

```
jail_test_ip="192.168.0.41"
jail_test_exec_start="/bin/sh /etc/rc"
jail_test_exec_stop="/bin/sh /etc/rc.shutdown"
jail_test_devfs_enable="YES"
jail_test_fdescfs_enable="NO"
jail_test_procfs_enable="NO"
jail_test_mount_enable="NO"
jail_test_devfs_ruleset="devfsrules_jail"
```

Setting `jail_enable` to YES will cause /etc/rc.d/jail start to execute at
startup. This in turn reads the rest of the `jail_X` variables from *rc.conf*, by
iterating over the values for `jail_list` (multiple jails can be listed, separated
by spaces) and looking for their corresponding sets of variables. These variables are used for configuring each individual jail's root directory, hostname, IP address, startup and shutdown scripts, and what types of special
filesystems will be mounted within the jail.

For the jail to be accessible from the network, you'll also need to configure a
network interface with the jail's IP address. In the previous example, this is
done with the `ifconfig_lnc0_alias0` variable. For setting IP aliases on an
interface to use with a jail, this takes the form of:

```
ifconfig_<iface>_alias<alias number>="inet <address> netmask 255.255.255.255"
```

So, if you wanted to create a jail with the address 192.168.0.42 and use the
same interface as above, you'd put something like this in your *rc.conf*:

```
ifconfig_lnc0_alias1="inet 192.168.0.42 netmask 255.255.255.255"
```

One thing that's not entirely obvious is that you're not limited to using a different IP address for each jail. You can specify multiple jails with the same IP
address, as long as you're not running services within them that listen on the
same port.

By now you've seen how powerful jails can be. Whether you want to create
virtual servers that can function as entire FreeBSD systems within a jail or
just to compartmentalize critical services, they can offer another layer of
security in protecting your systems from intruders.

Use proftpd with a MySQL Authentication Source

H A C K #11

Make sure that your database system's OS is running as efficiently as
possible with these tweaks.

proftpd is a powerful FTP daemon with a configuration syntax much like
Apache. It has a whole slew of options not available in most FTP daemons,
including ratios, virtual hosting, and a modularized design that allows people to write their own modules.

One such module is *mod_sql*, which allows *proftpd* to use a SQL database as its backend authentication source. Currently, *mod_sql* supports MySQL and PostgreSQL. This can be a good way to help lock down access to your server, as inbound users will authenticate against the database (and therefore not require an actual shell account on the server). In this hack, we'll get *proftpd* authenticating against a MySQL database.

First, download and build the source to *proftpd* and *mod_sql*:

```
~$ bzcat proftpd-1.2.6.tar.bz2 | tar xf -
~/proftpd-1.2.6/contrib$ tar zvxf ../../mod_sql-4.08.tar.gz
~/proftpd-1.2.6/contrib$ cd ..
~/proftpd-1.2.6$ ./configure --with-modules=mod_sql:mod_sql_mysql \
--with-includes=/usr/local/mysql/include/ \
--with-libraries=/usr/local/mysql/lib/
```

> Substitute the path to your MySQL install, if it isn't in */usr/local/mysql/*.

Now, build the code and install it:

```
rob@catlin:~/proftpd-1.2.6$ make && sudo make install
```

Next, create a database for *proftpd* to use (assuming that you already have MySQL up and running):

```
$ mysqladmin create proftpd
```

Then, permit read-only access to it from *proftpd*:

```
$ mysql -e "grant select on proftpd.* to proftpd@localhost \
identified by 'secret';"
```

Create two tables in the database, with this schema:

```
CREATE TABLE users (
userid varchar(30) NOT NULL default '',
password varchar(30) NOT NULL default '',
uid int(11) default NULL,
gid int(11) default NULL,
homedir varchar(255) default NULL,
shell varchar(255) default NULL,
UNIQUE KEY uid (uid),
UNIQUE KEY userid (userid)
) TYPE=MyISAM;

CREATE TABLE groups (
groupname varchar(30) NOT NULL default '',
gid int(11) NOT NULL default '0',
members varchar(255) default NULL
) TYPE=MyISAM;
```

One quick way to create the tables is to save this schema to a file called *proftpd.schema* and run a command like `mysql proftpd < proftpd.schema`.

Now, you need to tell *proftpd* to use this database for authentication. Add the following lines to your */usr/local/etc/proftpd.conf* file:

```
SQLConnectInfo proftpd proftpd secret
SQLAuthTypes crypt backend
SQLMinUserGID 111
SQLMinUserUID 111
```

The `SQLConnectInfo` line takes the form *database user password*. You could also specify a database on another host (even on another port) with something like this:

```
SQLConnectInfo proftpd@dbhost:5678 somebody somepassword
```

The `SQLAuthTypes` line lets you create users with passwords stored in the standard Unix crypt format, or MySQL's `PASSWORD()` function. Be warned that if you're using *mod_sql*'s logging facilities, the password might be exposed in plain text, so keep those logs private.

The `SQLAuthTypes` line as specified won't allow blank passwords; if you need that functionality, also include the empty keyword. The `SQLMinUserGID` and `SQLMinUserUID` lines specify the minimum group and user ID that *proftpd* will permit on login. It's a good idea to make this greater than 0 (to prohibit root logins), but it should be as low as you need to allow proper permissions in the filesystem. On this system, we have a user and a group called *www*, with both the user ID (UID) and the group ID (GID) set to 111. As we'll want web developers to be able to log in with these permissions, we'll need to set the minimum values to 111.

Finally, you're ready to create users in the database. The following line creates the user *jimbo*, with effective user rights as *www/www*, and dumps him in the */usr/local/apache/htdocs* directory at login:

```
mysql -e "insert into users values ('jimbo',PASSWORD('sHHH'),'111', \
    '111', '/usr/local/apache/htdocs','/bin/bash');" proftpd
```

The password for *jimbo* is encrypted with MySQL's `PASSWORD()` function before being stored. The /bin/bash line is passed to *proftpd* to pass *proftpd*'s `RequireValidShell` directive. It has no bearing on granting actual shell access to the user *jimbo*.

At this point, you should be able to fire up *proftpd* and log in as user *jimbo*, with a password of *sHHH*. If you are having trouble getting connected, try running *proftpd* in the foreground with debugging on, like this:

```
# proftpd -n -d 5
```

Watch the messages as you attempt to connect, and you should be able to track down the problem. In my experience, it's almost always due to a failure to set something properly in *proftpd.conf*, usually regarding permissions.

The *mod_sql* module can do far more than I've shown here; it can connect to existing MySQL databases with arbitrary table names, log all activity to the database, modify its user lookups with an arbitrary WHERE clause, and much more.

See Also

- The *mod_sql* home page at *http://www.lastditcheffort.org/~aah/proftpd/mod_sql/*
- The *proftpd* home page at *http://www.proftpd.org*

—Rob Flickenger

HACK #12   Prevent Stack-Smashing Attacks

Learn how to prevent stack-based buffer overflows.

In C and C++, memory for local variables is allocated in a chunk of memory called the *stack*. Information pertaining to the control flow of a program is also maintained on the stack. If an array is allocated on the stack and that array is overrun (that is, more values are pushed into the array than the available space allows), an attacker can overwrite the control flow information that is also stored on the stack. This type of attack is often referred to as a *stack-smashing attack*.

Stack-smashing attacks are a serious problem, since they can make an otherwise innocuous service (such as a web server or FTP server) execute arbitrary commands. Several technologies attempt to protect programs against these attacks. Some are implemented in the compiler, such as IBM's ProPolice patches for GCC (*http://www.trl.ibm.com/projects/security/ssp/*). Others are dynamic runtime solutions, such as LibSafe. While recompiling the source gets to the heart of the buffer overflow attack, runtime solutions can protect programs when the source isn't available or recompiling simply isn't feasible.

All of the compiler-based solutions work in much the same way, although there are some differences in the implementations. They work by placing a *canary* (which is typically some random value) on the stack between the control flow information and the local variables. The code that is normally generated by the compiler to return from the function is modified to check the value of the canary on the stack; if it is not what it is supposed to be, the program is terminated immediately.

The idea behind using a canary is that an attacker attempting to mount a stack-smashing attack will have to overwrite the canary to overwrite the control flow information. Choosing a random value for the canary ensures that the attacker cannot know what it is and thus cannot include it in the data used to "smash" the stack.

When a program is distributed in source form, the program's developer cannot enforce the use of ProPolice, because it's a nonstandard extension to the GCC compiler (although ProPolice-like features have been added to GCC 4. x, that version of GCC isn't in common use). Using ProPolice is the responsibility of the person compiling the program. ProPolice is available with some BSD and Linux distributions out of the box. You can check to see if your copy of GCC contains ProPolice functionality by using the -fstack-protector option to GCC. If your GCC is already patched, the compilation should proceed normally. Otherwise, you'll get an error like this:

```
cc1: error: unrecognized command line option "-fstack-protector"
```

When ProPolice is enabled and an overflow is triggered and detected in a program, rather than receiving a SIGSEGV, the program will receive a SIGABRT and dump core. In addition, a message will be logged informing you of the overflow and the offending function in the program:

```
May 25 00:17:22 zul vulnprog: stack overflow in function Get_method_from_
request
```

For Linux systems, Avaya Labs's LibSafe technology is not implemented as a compiler extension, but instead takes advantage of a feature of the dynamic loader that preloads a dynamic library with every executable. Using LibSafe does not require the source code for the programs it protects, and it can be deployed on a system-wide basis.

LibSafe replaces the implementation of several standard functions that are vulnerable to buffer overflows, such as gets( ), strcpy( ), and scanf( ). The replacement implementations attempt to compute the maximum possible size of a statically allocated buffer used as a destination buffer for writing, using a GCC built-in function that returns the address of the frame pointer. That address is normally the first piece of information on the stack following local variables. If an attempt is made to write more than the estimated size of the buffer, the program is terminated.

Unfortunately, there are several problems with the approach taken by LibSafe. First, it cannot accurately compute the size of a buffer; the best it can do is limit the size of the buffer to the difference between the start of the buffer and the frame pointer. Second, LibSafe's protections will not work with programs that were compiled using the -fomit-frame-pointer flag to GCC, an optimization that causes the compiler not to put a frame pointer on the stack. Although relatively useless, this is a popular optimization for programmers to employ. Finally, LibSafe does not work on SUID binaries without static linking or a similar trick. Still, it does provide at least some protection against conventional stack-smashing attacks.

The newest versions of LibSafe also provide some protection against *format-string attacks*. The format-string protection also requires access to the frame pointer because it attempts to filter out arguments that are not pointers into either the heap or the local variables on the stack.

In addition to user-space solutions, you can opt to patch your kernel to use nonexecutable stacks and detect buffer overflow attacks [Hack #13].

HACK #13 Lock Down Your Kernel with grsecurity

Harden your system against attacks with the grsecurity kernel patch.

Hardening a Unix system can be a difficult process that typically involves setting up all the services that the system will run in the most secure fashion possible, as well as locking down the system to prevent local compromises. However, putting effort into securing the services that you're running does little for the rest of the system and for unknown vulnerabilities. Luckily, even though the standard Linux kernel provides few features for proactively securing a system, there are patches available that can help the enterprising system administrator do so. One such patch is grsecurity (*http://www.grsecurity.net*).

grsecurity started out as a port of the OpenWall patch (*http://www.openwall.com*) to the 2.4.x series of Linux kernels. This patch added features such as nonexecutable stacks, some filesystem security enhancements, restrictions on access to */proc*, as well as some enhanced resource limits. These features helped to protect the system against stack-based buffer overflow attacks, prevented filesystem attacks involving race conditions on files created in */tmp*, limited users to seeing only their own processes, and even enhanced Linux's resource limits to perform more checks.

Since its inception, grsecurity has grown to include many features beyond those provided by the OpenWall patch. grsecurity now includes many additional memory address space protections to prevent buffer overflow exploits from succeeding, as well as enhanced chroot( ) jail restrictions, increased randomization of process and IP IDs, and increased auditing features that enable you to track every process executed on a system. grsecurity also adds a sophisticated access control list system that makes use of Linux's capabilities system. This ACL system can be used to limit the privileged operations that individual processes are able to perform on a case-by-case basis.

> The *gradm* utility handles configuration of ACLs. If you already have grsecurity installed on your machine, feel free to skip ahead to "Restrict Applications with grsecurity" [Hack #14].

Patching the Kernel

To compile a kernel with grsecurity, you will need to download the patch that corresponds to your kernel version and apply it to your kernel using the *patch* utility. For example, if you are running Linux 2.6.14.6:

```
# cd /usr/src/linux-2.6.14.6
# zcat ~andrew/grsecurity-2.1.8-2.6.14.6-200601211647.patch.gz | patch -p1
```

While the command is running, you should see a line for each kernel source file that is being patched. After the command has finished, you can make sure that the patch applied cleanly by looking for any files that end in .*rej*. The *patch* program creates these when it cannot apply the patch cleanly to a file. A quick way to see if there are any .*rej* files is to use the find command:

```
# find ./ -name \*.rej
```

If there are any rejected files, they will be listed on the screen. If the patch applied cleanly to all files, you should be returned to the shell prompt without any additional output.

After the patch has been applied, you can configure the kernel to enable grsecurity's features by running make config to use text prompts, make menuconfig for a curses-based interface, or make xconfig to use a QT-based GUI (use gconfig for a GTK-based one). If you went the graphical route and used make xconfig, expand the Security options tree and you should see something similar to Figure 1-1.

There are now two new subtrees: PaX and Grsecurity. If you ran make menuconfig or make config, the relevant kernel options have the same names as the menu options described in this example.

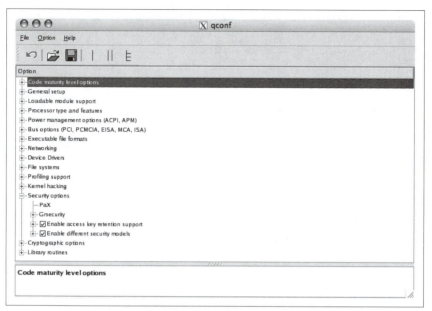

Figure 1-1. New sections added by the grsecurity patch

Configuring Kernel Options

To enable grsecurity and configure which features will be enabled in the kernel, expand the Grsecurity subtree and click the checkbox labeled Grsecurity. You should see the dialog shown in Figure 1-2.

After you've done that, you can enable predefined sets of features under the Security Level subtree, or set it to Custom and go through the menus to pick and choose which features to enable.

Low security. Choosing Low is safe for any system and should not affect any software's normal operation. Using this setting will enable linking restrictions in directories with mode 1777. This prevents race conditions in /tmp from being exploited, by only following symlinks to files that are owned by the process following the link. Similarly, users won't be able to write to FIFOs that they do not own if they are within a directory with permissions of 1777.

In addition to the tighter symlink and FIFO restrictions, the Low setting increases the randomness of process and IP IDs. This helps to prevent attackers from using remote detection techniques to correctly guess the operating system your machine is running [Hack #65], and it also makes it difficult to guess the process ID of a given program.

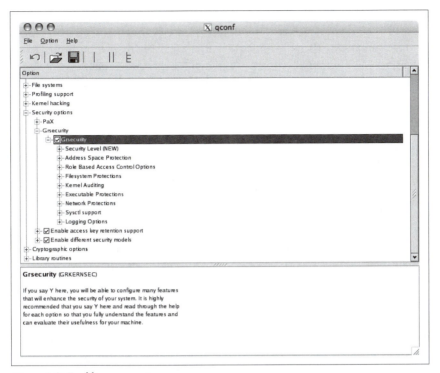

Figure 1-2. Enabling grsecurity

The Low security level also forces programs that use chroot( ) to change their current working directory to / after the chroot( ) call. Otherwise, if a program left its working directory outside of the chroot( ) environment, it could be used to break out of the sandbox. Choosing the Low security level also prevents non-root users from using *dmesg*, a utility that can be used to view recent kernel messages.

Medium security. Choosing Medium enables all of the same features as the Low security level, but this level also includes features that make chroot( )-based sandboxed environments more secure. The ability to mount filesystems, call chroot( ), write to sysctl variables, or create device nodes within a chroot( )-ed environment are all restricted, thus eliminating much of the risk involved in running a service in a sandboxed environment under Linux. In addition, the Medium level randomizes TCP source ports and logs failed fork( ) calls, changes to the system time, and segmentation faults.

Enabling the Medium security level also restricts total access to */proc* to those who are in the *wheel* group. This hides each user's processes from other users and denies writing to */dev/kmem*, */dev/mem*, and */dev/port*. This makes it more difficult to patch kernel-based root kits into the running kernel. The Medium level also randomizes process memory address space layouts, making it harder for an attacker to successfully exploit buffer overrun attacks, and removes information on process address space layouts from */proc*. Because of these */proc* restrictions, you will need to run your *identd* daemon (if you are running one) as an account that belongs to the *wheel* group. According to the grsecurity documentation, none of these features should affect the operation of your software, unless it is very old or poorly written.

High security. To enable nearly all of grsecurity's features, you can choose the High security level. In addition to the features provided by the lower security levels, this level implements additional */proc* restrictions by limiting access to device and CPU information to users who are in the *wheel* group. The High security level further restricts sandboxed environments by disallowing chmod to set the SUID or SGID bit when operating within such an environment.

Additionally, applications that are running within such an environment will not be allowed to insert loadable modules, perform raw I/O, configure network devices, reboot the system, modify immutable files, or change the system's time. Choosing this security level also lays out the kernel's stack randomly, to prevent kernel-based buffer overrun exploits from succeeding. In addition, it hides the kernel's symbols—making it even more difficult for an intruder to install Trojan code into the running kernel—and logs filesystem mounting, remounting, and unmounting.

The High security level also enables grsecurity's PaX code, which enables nonexecutable memory pages, among other things. Enabling this causes many buffer overrun exploits to fail, since any code injected into the stack through an overrun will be unable to execute. It is still possible to exploit a program with buffer overrun vulnerabilities, although this is made much more difficult by grsecurity's address space layout randomization features. However, some programs—such as XFree86, *wine*, and Java virtual machines—expect that the memory addresses returned by malloc( ) will be executable. Since PaX breaks this behavior, enabling it will cause those programs and others that depend on it to fail.

Luckily, PaX can be disabled on a per-program basis with the *paxctl* utility (*http://pax.grsecurity.net*). For instance, to disable nonexecutable memory for a given program, you can run a command similar to this one:

```
# paxctl -ps /usr/bin/java
```

Other programs also make use of special GCC features, such as trampoline functions, which allow a programmer to define a small function within a function so that the defined function is visible only to the enclosing function. Unfortunately, GCC puts the trampoline function's code on the stack, so PaX will break any programs that rely on this. However, PaX can provide emulation for trampoline functions, which can be enabled on a per-program basis with paxctl by using the -E switch.

Customized security settings. If you do not like the sets of features that are enabled with any of the predefined security levels, you can just set the kernel option to Custom and enable only the features you need.

After you've set a security level or enabled the specific options you want to use, just recompile your kernel and modules as you normally would:

```
# make clean && make bzImage
# make modules && make modules_install
```

Then, install your new kernel and reboot with it. In addition to the kernel restrictions already in effect, you can now use gradm to set up ACLs for your system [Hack #14].

As you can see, grsecurity is a complex but tremendously useful modification of the Linux kernel. For more detailed information on installing and configuring the patches, consult the extensive documentation at *http://www. grsecurity.net/papers.php*.

 Restrict Applications with grsecurity

Use Linux capabilities and grsecurity's ACLs to restrict applications on your system.

Now that you have installed the grsecurity patch [Hack #13], you'll probably want to make use of its flexible Role-Based Access Controls (RBAC) system to further restrict the privileged applications on your system, beyond what grsecurity's kernel security features provide.

 If you're just joining us and are not familiar with grsecurity, read "Lock Down Your Kernel with grsecurity" [Hack #13] first.

To restrict specific applications, you will need to make use of the *gradm* utility, which can be downloaded from the main grsecurity site (*http:// www.grsecurity.net*). You can compile and install it in the usual way: unpack the source distribution, change into the directory that it creates, and then run make && make install. This command installs *gradm* in */sbin*, creates the *letc/grsec* directory containing a default policy, and installs the manual page.

As part of running make install, you'll be prompted to set a password that will be used for *gradm* to authenticate itself with the kernel. You can change the password later by running gradm with the -P option:

```
# gradm -P
Setting up grsecurity RBAC password
Password:
Re-enter Password:
Password written to /etc/grsec/pw.
```

You'll also need to set a password for the admin role:

```
# gradm -P admin
Setting up password for role admin
Password:
Re-enter Password:
Password written to /etc/grsec/pw.
```

Then, use this command to enable grsecurity's RBAC system:

```
# /sbin/gradm -E
```

Once you're finished setting up your policy, you'll probably want to add that command to the end of your system startup. Add it to the end of *letc/rc.local* or a similar script that is designated for customizing your system startup.

The default policy installed in *letc/grsec/policy* is quite restrictive, so you'll want to create a policy for the services and system binaries that you want to use. For example, after the RBAC system has been enabled, ifconfig will no longer be able to change interface characteristics, even when run as root:

```
# /sbin/ifconfig eth0:1 192.168.0.59 up
SIOCSIFADDR: Permission denied
SIOCSIFFLAGS: Permission denied
SIOCSIFFLAGS: Permission denied
```

The easiest way to set up a policy for a particular command is to specify that you want to use grsecurity's learning mode, rather than specifying each one manually. If you've enabled RBAC, you'll need to temporarily disable it for your shell by running gradm -a admin. You'll then be able to access files within *letc/grsec*; otherwise, the directory will be hidden to you.

Add an entry like this to *letc/grsec/policy*:

```
subject /sbin/ifconfig  l
        /               h
        /etc/grsec      h
        -CAP_ALL
```

This is about the most restrictive policy possible, because it hides the root directory from the process and removes any privileges that it may need. The 1 next to the binary that the policy applies to says to use learning mode.

After you're done editing the policy, you'll need to disable RBAC and then re-enable it with learning mode:

```
# gradm -a admin
Password:
# gradm -D
# gradm -L /etc/grsec/learning.logs -E
```

Now, try to run the ifconfig command again:

```
# /sbin/ifconfig eth0:1 192.168.0.59 up
# /sbin/ifconfig eth0:1
eth0:1    Link encap:Ethernet  HWaddr 08:00:46:0C:AA:DF
          inet addr:192.168.0.59  Bcast:192.168.0.255  Mask:255.255.255.0
          UP BROADCAST RUNNING MULTICAST  MTU:1500  Metric:1
```

When the command succeeds, grsecurity will create learning log entries. You can then use gradm to generate an ACL for the program based on these logs:

```
# gradm -a admin
Password:
# gradm -L /etc/grsec/learning.logs -O stdout
Beginning full learning object reduction for subject /sbin/ifconfig...done.
### THE BELOW SUBJECT(S) SHOULD BE ADDED TO THE DEFAULT ROLE ###
subject /sbin/ifconfig {
user_transition_allow root
group_transition_allow root


         /                        h
         /sbin/ifconfig           rx
         -CAP_ALL
         +CAP_NET_ADMIN
         +CAP_SYS_ADMIN
}
```

Now, you can replace the learning policy for /sbin/ifconfig in /etc/grsec/policy with this one, and ifconfig should work. You can then follow this process for each program that needs special permissions to function. Just make sure to try out anything you will want to do with those programs, to ensure that grsecurity's learning mode will detect that it needs to perform a particular system call or open a specific file.

Using grsecurity to lock down applications can seem like tedious work at first, but it will ultimately create a system that gives each process only the permissions it needs to do its job—no more, no less. When you need to build a highly secured platform, grsecurity can provide finely grained control over just about everything the system can possibly do.

Restrict System Calls with systrace

HACK #15

Keep your programs from performing tasks they weren't meant to do.

One of the more exciting features in NetBSD and OpenBSD is *systrace*, a system call access manager. With *systrace*, a system administrator can specify which programs can make which system calls, and how those calls can be made. Proper use of *systrace* can greatly reduce the risks inherent in running poorly written or exploitable programs. *systrace* policies can confine users in a manner completely independent of Unix permissions. You can even define the errors that the system calls return when access is denied, to allow programs to fail in a more proper manner. Proper use of *systrace* requires a practical understanding of system calls and what functionality programs must have to work properly.

First of all, what exactly are system calls? A *system call* is a function that lets you talk to the operating-system kernel. If you want to allocate memory, open a TCP/IP port, or perform input/output on the disk, you'll need to use a system call. System calls are documented in section 2 of the manual pages.

Unix also supports a wide variety of C library calls. These are often confused with system calls but are actually just standardized routines for things that could be written within a program. For example, you could easily write a function to compute square roots within a program, but you could not write a function to allocate memory without using a system call. If you're in doubt whether a particular function is a system call or a C library function, check the online manual.

You might find an occasional system call that is not documented in the online manual, such as break( ). You'll need to dig into other resources to identify these calls.

> break( ) is a very old system call used within *libc*, but not by programmers, so it seems to have escaped being documented in the manpages.

systrace denies all actions that are not explicitly permitted and logs the rejections using *syslog*. If a program running under *systrace* has a problem, you can find out which system call the program wants to use and decide whether you want to add it to your policy, reconfigure the program, or live with the error.

systrace has several important pieces: policies, the policy-generation tools, the runtime access management tool, and the sysadmin real-time interface.

This hack gives a brief overview of policies; "Create systrace Policies Automatically" **[Hack #16]** shows how to use the *systrace* tools.

The systrace(1) manpage includes a full description of the syntax used for policy descriptions, but I generally find it easier to look at some examples of a working policy and then go over the syntax in detail. Since *named*, the name server daemon, has been a subject of recent security discussions, let's look at the policy that OpenBSD provides for *named*.

Before reviewing the *named* policy, let's review some commonly known facts about its system-access requirements. Zone transfers and large queries occur on port 53/TCP, while basic lookup services are provided on port 53/UDP. OpenBSD chroots *named* into */var/named* by default and logs everything to */var/log/messages*.

Each *systrace* policy file is in a file named after the full path of the program, replacing slashes with underscores. The policy file *usr_sbin_named* contains quite a few entries that allow access beyond binding to port 53 and writing to the system log. The file starts with:

```
# Policy for named that uses named user and chroots to /var/named
# This policy works for the default configuration of named.
Policy: /usr/sbin/named, Emulation: native
```

The Policy statement gives the full path to the program this policy is for. You can't fool *systrace* by giving the same name to a program elsewhere on the system. The Emulation entry shows which Application Binary Interface (ABI) this policy is for. Remember, BSD systems expose ABIs for a variety of operating systems. *systrace* can theoretically manage system-call access for any ABI, although only native and Linux binaries are supported at the moment.

The remaining lines define a variety of system calls that the program may or may not use. The sample policy for *named* includes 73 lines of system-call rules. The most basic look like this:

```
native-accept: permit
```

When */usr/sbin/named* tries to use the accept( ) system call to accept a connection on a socket, under the native ABI, it is allowed. Other rules are far more restrictive. Here's a rule for bind( ), the system call that lets a program request a TCP/IP port to attach to:

```
native-bind: sockaddr match "inet-*:53" then permit
```

sockaddr is the name of an argument taken by the accept( ) system call. The match keyword tells *systrace* to compare the given variable with the string inet-*:53, according to the standard shell pattern-matching (globbing) rules. So, if the variable sockaddr matches the string inet-*:53, the connection is

accepted. This program can bind to port 53, over both TCP and UDP protocols. If an attacker had an exploit to make *named* attach a command prompt
on a high-numbered port, this *systrace* policy would prevent that exploit from
working.

At first glance, this seems wrong:

```
native-chdir: filename eq "/" then permit
native-chdir: filename eq "/namedb" then permit
```

The eq keyword compares one string to another and requires an exact
match. If the program tries to go to the root directory, or to the directory /
namedb, *systrace* will allow it. Why would you possibly want to allow *named*
to access the root directory? The next entry explains why:

```
native-chroot: filename eq "/var/named" then permit
```

We can use the native chroot( ) system call to change our root directory to /
var/named, but to no other directory. At this point, the /*namedb* directory is
actually /*var/named/namedb*. We also know that *named* logs to *syslog*. To do
this, it will need access to /*dev/log*:

```
native-connect: sockaddr eq "/dev/log" then permit
```

This program can use the native connect( ) system call to talk to /*dev/log* and
only /*dev/log*. That device hands the connections off elsewhere.

We'll also see some entries for system calls that do not exist:

```
native-fsread: filename eq "/" then permit
native-fsread: filename eq "/dev/arandom" then permit
native-fsread: filename eq "/etc/group" then permit
```

systrace aliases certain system calls with very similar functions into groups.
You can disable this functionality with a command-line switch and only use
the exact system calls you specify, but in most cases these aliases are quite
useful and shrink your policies considerably. The two aliases are fsread and
fswrite. fsread is an alias for stat( ), lstat( ), readlink( ), and access( ),
under the native and Linux ABIs. fswrite is an alias for unlink( ), mkdir( ),
and rmdir( ), in both the native and Linux ABIs. As open( ) can be used to
either read or write a file, it is aliased by both fsread and fswrite, depending on how it is called. So *named* can read certain /*etc* files, it can list the
contents of the root directory, and it can access the groups file.

systrace supports two optional keywords at the end of a policy statement:
errorcode and log. The errorcode is the error that is returned when the program attempts to access this system call. Programs will behave differently
depending on the error that they receive. *named* will react differently to a
"permission denied" error than it will to an "out of memory" error. You can
get a complete list of error codes from the errno manpage. Use the error

---

name, not the error number. For example, here we return an error for non-existent files:

```
filename sub "<non-existent filename>" then deny[enoent]
```

If you put the word log at the end of your rule, successful system calls will be logged. For example, if you wanted to log each time *named* attached to port 53, you could edit the policy statement for the bind( ) call to read:

```
native-bind: sockaddr match "inet-*:53" then permit log
```

You can also choose to filter rules based on user ID and group ID, as the example here demonstrates:

```
native-setgid: gid eq "70" then permit
```

This very brief overview covers the vast majority of the rules you will see. For full details on the *systrace* grammar, read the *systrace* manpage. If you want some help with creating your policies, you can also use *systrace*'s automated mode [Hack #16].

The original article that this hack is based on is available online at *http://www.onlamp.com/pub/a/bsd/2003/01/30/Big_Scary_Daemons.html*.

—*Michael Lucas*

HACK #16 Create systrace Policies Automatically
Let systrace's automated mode do your work for you.

In a true paranoid's ideal world, system administrators would read the source code for each application on their system and be able to build system-call access policies by hand, relying only on their intimate understanding of every feature of the application. Most system administrators don't have that sort of time, though, and would have better things to do with that time if they did.

Luckily, *systrace* includes a policy-generation tool that will generate a policy listing for every system call that an application makes. You can use this policy as a starting point to narrow down the access you will allow the application. We'll use this method to generate a policy for *inetd*.

Use the -A flag to systrace, and include the full path to the program you want to run:

```
# systrace -A /usr/sbin/inetd
```

To pass flags to *inetd*, add them at the end of the command line.

Then use the program for which you're developing a policy. This system has ident, daytime, and time services open, so run programs that require those services. Fire up an IRC client to trigger ident requests, and telnet to ports 13 and 37 to get time services. Once you have put *inetd* through its paces, shut it down. *inetd* has no control program, so you need to kill it by using the process ID.

Checking the process list will show two processes:

```
# ps -ax | grep inet
24421 ??  Ixs    0:00.00 /usr/sbin/inetd
12929 ??  Is     0:00.01 systrace -A /usr/sbin/inetd
```

Do not kill the *systrace* process (PID 12929 in this example); that process has all the records of the system calls that *inetd* has made. Just kill the *inetd* process (PID 24421), and the *systrace* process will exit normally.

Now check your home directory for a *.systrace* directory, which will contain *systrace*'s first stab at an *inetd* policy. Remember, policies are placed in files named after the full path to the program, replacing slashes with underscores.

Here's the output of `ls`:

```
# ls .systrace
usr_libexec_identd    usr_sbin_inetd
```

systrace created two policies, not one. In addition to the expected policy for */usr/sbin/inetd*, there's one for */usr/libexec/identd*. This is because *inetd* implements time services internally, but it needs to call a separate program to service other requests. When *inetd* spawned *identd*, *systrace* captured the *identd* system calls as well.

By reading the policy, you can improve your understanding of what the program actually does. Look up each system call the program uses, and see if you can restrict access further. You'll probably want to look for ways to further restrict the policies that are automatically generated. However, these policies make for a good starting point.

Applying a policy to a program is much like creating the *systrace* policy itself. Just run the program as an argument to systrace, using the -a option:

```
# systrace -a /usr/sbin/inetd
```

If the program tries to perform system calls not listed in the policy, they will fail. This may cause the program to behave unpredictably. *systrace* will log failed entries in */var/log/messages*.

To edit a policy, just add the desired statement to the end of the rule list, and it will be picked up. You could do this by hand, of course, but that's the hard way. *systrace* includes a tool to let you edit policies in real time, as the system call is made. This is excellent for use in a network operations center environment, where the person responsible for watching the network monitor can also be assigned to watch for system calls and bring them to the attention of the appropriate personnel. You can specify which program you wish to monitor by using systrace's -p flag. This is called *attaching* to the program.

For example, earlier we saw two processes containing *inetd*. One was the actual *inetd* process, and the other was the *systrace* process managing *inetd*. Attach to the *systrace* process, not the actual program (to use the previous example, this would be PID 12929), and give the full path to the managed program as an argument:

```
# systrace -p 12929 /usr/sbin/inetd
```

At first nothing will happen. When the program attempts to make an unauthorized system call, however, a GUI will pop up. You will have the option to allow the system call, deny the system call, always permit the call, or always deny it. The program will hang until you make a decision, however, so decide quickly.

Note that these changes will only take effect so long as the current process is running. If you restart the program, you must also restart the attached *systrace* monitor, and any changes you previously set in the monitor will be gone. You must add those rules to the policy if you want them to be permanent.

> The original article that this hack is based on is available online at *http://www.onlamp.com/pub/a/bsd/2003/02/27/Big_Scary_Daemons.html.*

—Michael Lucas

Control Login Access with PAM
HACK #17

Seize fine-grained control of when and from where your users can access your system.

Traditional Unix authentication doesn't provide much granularity in limiting a user's ability to log in. For example, how would you limit the hosts that users can come from when logging into your servers? Your first thought might be to set up TCP wrappers or possibly firewall rules [Hack #44].

But what if you want to allow some users to log in from a specific host, but disallow others from logging in from it? Or what if you want to prevent some users from logging in at certain times of the day because of daily maintenance, but allow others (e.g., administrators) to log in at any time they wish? To get this working with every service that might be running on your system, you would traditionally have to patch each of them to support this new functionality. This is where pluggable authentication modules (PAM) enters the picture.

PAM allows for just this sort of functionality (and more) without the need to patch all of your services. PAM has been available for quite some time under Linux, FreeBSD, and Solaris and is now a standard component of the traditional authentication facilities on these platforms. Many services that need to use some sort of authentication now support PAM.

Modules are configured for services in a stack, with the authentication process proceeding from top to bottom as the access checks complete successfully. You can build a custom stack for any service by creating a file in */etc/pam.d* with the same name as the service. If you need even more granularity, you can include an entire stack of modules by using the pam_stack module. This allows you to specify another external file containing a stack. If a service does not have its own configuration file in */etc/pam.d*, it will default to using the stack specified in */etc/pam.d/other*.

There are several types of entries available when configuring a service for use with PAM. These types allow you to specify whether a module provides authentication, access control, password change control, or session setup and teardown. Right now, we are interested in only one of the types: the account type. This entry type allows you to specify modules that will control access to accounts that have been authenticated.

In addition to the service-specific configuration files, some modules have extended configuration information that can be specified in files within the */etc/security* directory. For this hack, we'll mainly use two of the most useful modules of this type: pam_access and pam_time.

Limiting Access by Origin

The pam_access module allows you to limit where a user or group of users may log in from. To make use of it, you'll first need to configure the service with which you want to use the module. You can do this by editing the service's PAM config file in */etc/pam.d*.

Here's an example of what */etc/pam.d/login* might look like:

```
#%PAM-1.0
auth       required      pam_securetty.so
auth       required      pam_stack.so service=system-auth
auth       required      pam_nologin.so
```

```
account     required     pam_stack.so service=system-auth
password    required     pam_stack.so service=system-auth
session     required     pam_stack.so service=system-auth
session     optional     pam_console.so
```

Notice the use of the pam_stack module; it includes the stack contained within the *system-auth* file. Let's see what's inside */etc/pam.d/system-auth*:

```
#%PAM-1.0
# This file is auto-generated.
# User changes will be destroyed the next time authconfig is run.
auth        required     /lib/security/$ISA/pam_env.so
auth        sufficient   /lib/security/$ISA/pam_unix.so likeauth nullok
auth        required     /lib/security/$ISA/pam_deny.so
account     required     /lib/security/$ISA/pam_unix.so
password    required     /lib/security/$ISA/pam_cracklib.so retry=3 type=
password    sufficient   /lib/security/$ISA/pam_unix.so nullok use_authtok
md5 shadow
password    required     /lib/security/$ISA/pam_deny.so
session     required     /lib/security/$ISA/pam_limits.so
session     required     /lib/security/$ISA/pam_unix.so
```

To add the pam_access module to the login service, you could add another account entry to the login configuration file, which would, of course, just enable the module for the login service. Alternatively, you could add the module to the *system-auth* file, which would enable it for most of the PAM-aware services on the system.

To add pam_access to the login service (or any other service, for that matter), simply add a line like this to the service's configuration file after any preexisting account entries:

```
account     required     pam_access.so
```

Now that you've enabled the pam_access module for our services, you can edit */etc/security/access.conf* to control how the module behaves. Each entry in the file can specify multiple users, groups, and hostnames to which the entry applies, and specify whether it's allowing or disallowing remote or local access. When pam_access is invoked by an entry in a service configuration file, it looks through the lines of *access.conf* and stops at the first match it finds. Thus, if you want to create default entries to fall back on, you'll want to put the more specific entries first, with the general entries following them.

The general form of an entry in *access.conf* is:

```
permission
   : users
   : origins
```

where *permission* can be either + or -. This denotes whether the rule grants or denies access, respectively.

The *users* portion allows you to specify a list of users or groups, separated by whitespace. In addition to simply listing users in this portion of the entry, you can use the form *user@host*, where *host* is the local hostname of the machine being logged into. This allows you to use a single configuration file across multiple machines, but still specify rules pertaining to specific machines.

The *origins* portion is compared against the origin of the access attempt. Hostnames can be used for remote origins, and the special LOCAL keyword can be used for local access. Instead of explicitly specifying users, groups, or origins, you can also use the ALL and EXCEPT keywords to perform set operations on any of the lists.

Here's a simple example of locking out the user *andrew* (Eep! That's me!) from a host named colossus:

```
- : andrew : colossus
```

Note that if a group that shares its name with a user is specified, the module will interpret the rule as applying to both the user and the group.

Restricting Access by Time

Now that we've covered how to limit where a user may log in from and how to set up a PAM module, let's take a look at how to limit what time a user may log in by using the pam_time module. To configure this module, you need to edit */etc/security/time.conf*. The format for the entries in this file is a little more flexible than that of *access.conf*, thanks to the availability of the NOT (!), AND (&), and OR (|) operators.

The general form for an entry in *time.conf* is:

```
services;devices;users;times
```

The *services* portion of the entry specifies what PAM-enabled service will be regulated. You can usually get a full list of the available services by looking at the contents of your */etc/pam.d* directory.

For instance, here are the contents of */etc/pam.d* on a Red Hat Linux system:

```
$ ls -1 /etc/pam.d
authconfig
chfn
chsh
halt
internet-druid
kbdrate
login
neat
other
```

```
passwd
poweroff
ppp
reboot
redhat-config-mouse
redhat-config-network
redhat-config-network-cmd
redhat-config-network-druid
rhn_register
setup
smtp
sshd
su
sudo
system-auth
up2date
up2date-config
up2date-nox
vlock
```

To set up pam_time for use with any of these services, you'll need to add a line like this to the file in */etc/pam.d* that corresponds to the service you want to regulate:

```
account     required     /lib/security/$ISA/pam_time.so
```

The *devices* portion specifies the terminal device from which the service is being accessed. For console logins, you can use !ttyp*, which specifies all TTY devices except for pseudo-TTYs. If you want the entry to affect only remote logins, use ttyp*. You can restrict it to all users (console, remote, and X11) by using tty*.

For the *users* portion of the entry, you can specify a single user or a list of users, separated with | characters.

Finally, the *times* portion is used to specify the times when the rule will apply. Again, you can stipulate a single time range or multiple ranges, separated with | characters. Each time range is specified by a combination of one or more two-character abbreviations denoting the day or days that the rule will apply, followed by a range of hours for those days.

The abbreviations for the days of the week are Mo, Tu, We, Th, Fr, Sa, and Su. For convenience, you can use Wk to specify weekdays, Wd to specify the weekend, or Al to specify every day of the week. If using the latter three abbreviations, bear in mind that repeated days will be subtracted from the set of days to which the rule applies (e.g., WkSu would effectively be just Sa). The range of hours is simply specified as two 24-hour times, minus the colons, separated by a dash (e.g., 0630-1345 is 6:30 A.M. to 1:45 P.M.).

If you wanted to disallow access to the user *andrew* from the local console on weekends and during the week after hours, you could use an entry like this:

```
system-auth;!ttyp*;andrew;Wk1700-0800|Wd0000-2400
```

Or perhaps you want to limit remote logins through SSH during a system maintenance window lasting from 7 P.M. Friday to 7 A.M. Saturday, but you want to allow a sysadmin to log in:

```
sshd;ttyp*;!andrew;Fr1900-0700
```

As you can see, there's a lot of flexibility for creating entries, thanks to the logical Boolean operators that are available. Just make sure that you remember to configure the service file in */etc/pam.d* for use with pam_time when you create entries in */etc/security/time.conf*.

HACK #18 Restrict Users to SCP and SFTP

Provide restricted file-transfer services to your users without resorting to FTP.

Sometimes, you'd like to provide file-transfer services to your users without setting up an FTP server. This leaves the option of letting them transfer files to and from your server using SCP or SFTP. However, because of the way OpenSSH's *sshd* implements these subsystems, it's usually impossible to do this without also giving the user shell access to the system. When an SCP or SFTP session is started, the daemon executes another executable to handle the request using the user's shell, which means the user needs a valid shell.

One way to get around this problem is to use a custom shell that is capable of executing only the SCP and SFTP subsystems. One such program is *rssh* (*http://www.pizzashack.org/rssh/*), which has the added benefit of being able to chroot( ), enabling you to limit access to the server's filesystem as well.

Setting Up rssh

To set up *rssh*, first download the compressed archive from program's web site and unpack it. Then, run the standard ./configure and make:

```
$ tar xfz rssh-2.3.2.tar.gz
$ cd rssh-2.3.2
$ ./configure && make
```

Once *rssh* has finished compiling, become root and run make install. You can now create an account and set its shell to *rssh*. Try logging into it via

SSH. You'll notice that the connection is closed before you're able to completely log in. You should also see this before the connection is closed:

```
This account is restricted by rssh.
This user is locked out.

If you believe this is in error, please contact your system administrator.
```

You should get similar results if you try to access the account with *scp* or *sftp*, because *rssh*'s default configuration locks out everything. To enable SFTP and SCP, add the following lines to your *rssh.conf* file (the file should be located in */usr/local/etc* or somewhere similar):

```
allowsftp
allowscp
```

Now, try accessing the account with sftp:

```
$ sftp rssh_test@freebsd5-vm1
Connecting to freebsd5-vm1...
Password:
sftp>
```

Configuring chroot( )

This has been easy so far. Now comes the hard part: configuring chroot( ). Here you have two options: you can specify a common environment for all users that have been configured to use *rssh*, or you can create user-specific chroot( ) environments.

To create a global environment, you just need to specify the directory to chroot( ) by using the chrootpath configuration directive. For instance, to have *rssh* chroot( ) to */var/rssh_chroot*, set up a proper environment there and add the following line to your *rssh.conf* file:

```
chrootpath=/var/rssh_chroot
```

Setting up *rssh* to use chroot( ) has one major caveat, though. Supporting chroot( ) requires the use of an SUID helper binary to perform the chroot( ) call for the user that has logged in. This is because only the root user can issue a chroot( ) call. This binary is extremely limited; all it does is perform the chroot( ) and take steps to ensure that it can only be executed by *rssh*. However, it's something to keep in mind if you consider this a risk.

For a user-specific chroot( ) environment, you can add a line like this:

```
user=rssh_test:077:00011:/var/rssh_chroot
```

The first set of numbers after the username is the umask. The second set of digits is actually a bit-vector specifying the allowed means of access. From left to right, these are Rsync, Rdist, CVS, SFTP, and SCP. In the previous example, only SFTP and SCP are allowed.

Finally, the last portion of the line specifies which directory to chroot( ) to. One thing allowed by this configuration syntax that isn't immediately obvious is the ability to specify per-user configurations without a directory to chroot( ) to: simply omit the directory. So, if you just want to allow one user to use only SCP but not SFTP (so they can't browse the filesystem), you can add a line similar to this one:

```
user=rssh_test:077:00001
```

Now, all you need to do is set up the sandbox environment. Create a *bin* directory within the root directory of your sandbox and copy */bin/sh* into it. Then, copy all of the requisite libraries for it to their proper places:

```
# cd /var/rssh_chroot
# mkdir bin && cp /bin/sh bin
# ldd bin/sh
bin/sh:
        libedit.so.4 => /lib/libedit.so.4 (0x2808e000)
        libncurses.so.5 => /lib/libncurses.so.5 (0x280a1000)
        libc.so.5 => /lib/libc.so.5 (0x280e0000)
        # mkdir lib
        # cp /lib/libedit.so.4 /lib/libncurses.so.5 /lib/libc.so.5 lib
```

Now, copy your *scp* and *sftp* binaries and all of their requisite libraries to their proper locations. Here is an example of doing so for *scp* (*sftp* should require the same libraries):

```
# ldd usr/bin/scp
usr/bin/scp:
        libssh.so.2 => /usr/lib/libssh.so.2 (0x2807a000)
        libcrypt.so.2 => /lib/libcrypt.so.2 (0x280a9000)
        libcrypto.so.3 => /lib/libcrypto.so.3 (0x280c1000)
        libz.so.2 => /lib/libz.so.2 (0x281b8000)
        libc.so.5 => /lib/libc.so.5 (0x281c8000)
        libgssapi.so.7 => /usr/lib/libgssapi.so.7 (0x282a2000)
        libkrb5.so.7 => /usr/lib/libkrb5.so.7 (0x282b0000)
        libasn1.so.7 => /usr/lib/libasn1.so.7 (0x282e8000)
        libcom_err.so.2 => /usr/lib/libcom_err.so.2 (0x28309000)
        libmd.so.2 => /lib/libmd.so.2 (0x2830b000)
        libroken.so.7 => /usr/lib/libroken.so.7 (0x28315000)
# cp /lib/libcrypt.so.2 /lib/libcrypto.so.3 /lib/libz.so.2 \
/lib/libc.so.5 /lib/libmd.so.2 lib
# mkdir -p usr/lib
# cp /usr/lib/libssh.so.2 /usr/lib/libgssapi.so.7 /usr/lib/libkrb5.so.7 \
/usr/lib/libasn1.so.7 /usr/lib/libcom_err.so.2 \
/usr/lib/libroken.so.7 usr/lib/
```

Next, copy *rssh_chroot_helper* to the proper place and copy your dynamic linker (the program that is responsible for issuing the chroot( ) call):

```
# mkdir -p usr/local/libexec
# cp /usr/local/libexec/rssh_chroot_helper usr/local/libexec
# mkdir libexec && cp /libexec/ld-elf.so.1 libexec/
```

This example is for FreeBSD. For Linux, you'll likely want to use */lib/ld-linux.so.2*.

Then, recreate */dev/null* in your chroot( ) environment:

```
# ls -la /dev/null
crw-rw-rw- 1 root  wheel    2,   2 Apr 10 16:22 /dev/null
# mkdir dev && mknod dev/null c 2 2 && chmod a+w dev/null
```

Now create a dummy password file:

```
# mkdir etc && cp /etc/passwd etc
```

Edit the password file to remove all the entries for other accounts, leaving only the accounts that will be used in the jail.

Now, try connecting with sftp:

```
$ sftp rssh_test@freebsd5-vm1
Connecting to freebsd5-vm1...
Password:
sftp> ls /etc
/etc/.
/etc/..
/etc/passwd
```

All that's left to do is to create a */dev/log* and change your *syslogd* startup options to listen for log messages on the */dev/log* in your chroot( ) environment. Using the -a option and specifying additional log sockets will usually take care of this:

```
# /sbin/syslogd -a /home/rssh_test/dev/log
```

rssh is an incredibly useful tool that can remove the need for insecure legacy services. In addition to supporting SCP and SFTP, it supports CVS, Rdist, and Rsync. Check out the rssh(1) and rssh.conf(5) manual pages for more information on setting those up.

 ## Use Single-Use Passwords for Authentication

HACK
#19   Use one-time passwords to access servers from possibly untrustworthy computers and to limit access to accounts.

Generally, it's best not to use untrusted computers to access a server. The pitfalls are plentiful. However, you can mitigate some part of the risk by using *one-time passwords* (OTPs) for authentication. An even more interesting use for them, though, is to limit access to accounts used for file transfer.

That is, if you want to provide a file to someone or allow someone to upload a file only once, you can set up an account to use OTPs. Once the person you've given the password to has done her thing (and disconnected), she no longer has access to the account. This works well with rssh **[Hack #18]**, since it prevents the user from accessing the system outside of a specified directory and from generating additional OTPs.

For this purpose, FreeBSD provides *One-time Passwords in Everything* (OPIE), which is thoroughly supported throughout the system. OpenBSD uses a similar system called *S/Key*.

OPIE Under FreeBSD

Setting up an account to use OPIE under FreeBSD is fairly simple. First, run opiepasswd to create an entry in */etc/opiepasswd* and to seed the OTP generator:

```
$ opiepasswd -c
Adding andrew:
Only use this method from the console; NEVER from remote. If you are using
telnet, xterm, or a dial-in, type ^C now or exit with no password.
Then run opiepasswd without the -c parameter.
Using MD5 to compute responses.
Enter new secret pass phrase:
Again new secret pass phrase:

ID andrew OTP key is 499 fr8266
HOVE TEE LANG FOAM ALEC THE
```

The 499 in the output is the OTP sequence, and fr8266 is the seed to use with it in generating the OTP. Once the sequence reaches 0, you'll need to run opiepasswd again to reseed the system.

The -c option tells it to accept password input directly. Needless to say, you shouldn't be setting this up over insecure channels; if you do, you'll defeat the purpose of OTP. Run this from the local console or over an SSH connection only!

Then, try logging into the system remotely:

```
$ ssh freebsd5-vm1
otp-md5 497 fr8266 ext
Password:
```

The first line of output is the arguments to supply to opiekey, which is used to generate the proper OTP to use. otp-md5 specifies the hashing algorithm that has been used. As before, 497 specifies the OTP sequence, and fr8266 is the seed.

Now, generate the password:

```
$ opiekey 497 fr8266
Using the MD5 algorithm to compute response.
Reminder: Don't use opiekey from telnet or dial-in sessions.
```

```
Enter secret pass phrase:
DUET SHAW TWIT SKY EM CITE
```

To log in, enter the passphrase that was generated. Once you've logged in, you can run opieinfo and see that the sequence number has been decremented:

```
$ opieinfo
496 fr8266
```

It's also possible to generate multiple passwords at the same time with opiekey:

```
$ opiekey -n 5 496 fr8266
Using the MD5 algorithm to compute response.
Reminder: Don't use opiekey from telnet or dial-in sessions.
Enter secret pass phrase:
492: EVIL AMID EVEN CRAB FRAU NULL
493: GEM SURF LONG TOOK NAN FOUL
494: OWN SOB AUK RAIL SEED HUGE
495: GAP THAT LORD LIES BOMB ROUT
496: RON ABEL LIE GWYN TRAY ROAR
```

You might want to do this before traveling, so you can print out the passwords and carry them with you.

> Be sure not to include the hostname on the same sheet of paper. If you do and you lose it, anyone who finds it can easily gain access to your system.

If you have a PDA, another option is to use PilOTP (*http://astro.uchicago.edu/home/web/valdes/pilot/pilOTP/*), an OTP generator for Palm OS devices, which supports both OPIE and S/Key systems.

S/Key Under OpenBSD

Setting up S/Key under OpenBSD is similar to setting up OPIE. First, the superuser needs to enable it by running skeyinit -E. Then, as a normal user, run skeyinit again. It will prompt you for your system password and then ask you for a password to initialize the S/Key system:

```
$ skeyinit
Reminder - Only use this method if you are directly connected
          or have an encrypted channel.  If you are using telnet,
          hit return now and use skeyinit -s.
Password:
[Adding andrew with md5]
Enter new secret passphrase:
Again secret passphrase:

ID andrew skey is otp-md5 100 open66823
Next login password: DOLE WALE MAKE COAT BALE AVID
```

To log in, you need to append :skey to your username:

```
$ ssh andrew:skey@puffy
otp-md5 99 open66823
S/Key Password:
```

Then, in another terminal, run skey and enter the password you entered when you ran skeyinit:

```
$ skey -md5 99 open66823
Reminder - Do not use this program while logged in via telnet.
Enter secret passphrase:
SOME VENT BUDD GONG TEAR SALT
```

Here's the output of skeyinfo after logging in:

```
$ skeyinfo
98 open66823
```

Although it's not wise to use untrusted computers to access your systems, you can see that one-time passwords can help mitigate the possible ill effects. Additionally, they can have other uses, such as combining them with other components to allow a user to access a protected resource only a limited number of times. With a little ingenuity, you can come up with some other uses, too.

HACK #20 Restrict Shell Environments

Keep your users from shooting themselves (and you) in the foot.

Sometimes a sandboxed environment [Hack #10] is overkill for your needs. But if you want to set up a restricted environment for a group of users that allows them to run only a few particular commands, you'll have to duplicate all of the libraries and binaries for those commands for each user. This is where restricted shells come in handy. Many shells include such a feature, which is usually invoked by running the shell with the -r switch. While not as secure as a system-call-based sandboxed environment, a restricted shell can work well if you trust your users not to be malicious (but worry that some might be curious to an unhealthy degree).

Some common features of restricted shells are the abilities to prevent a program from changing directories, to allow the execution of commands only using absolute pathnames, and to prohibit executing commands in other subdirectories. In addition to these restrictions, all of the command-line redirection operators are disabled. With these features, restricting the commands a user can execute is as simple as picking and choosing which commands should be available and making symbolic links to them inside the user's home directory. If a sequence of commands needs to be executed, you can also create shell scripts owned by another user. These scripts will execute in an unrestricted environment and can't be edited within the restricted environment by the user.

Let's try running a restricted shell and see what happens:

```
$ bash -r
bash: SHELL: readonly variable
bash: PATH: readonly variable
bash-2.05b$ ls
bash: ls: No such file or directory
bash-2.05b$ /bin/ls
bash: /sbin/ls: restricted: cannot specify `/' in command names
bash-2.05b$ exit
$ ln -s /bin/ls .
$ bash -r
bash-2.05b$ ls -la
total 24
drwx------    2 andrew    andrew       4096 Oct 20 08:01 .
drwxr-xr-x    4 root      root         4096 Oct 20 14:16 ..
-rw-------    1 andrew    andrew         18 Oct 20 08:00 .bash_history
-rw-r--r--    1 andrew    andrew         24 Oct 20 14:16 .bash_logout
-rw-r--r--    1 andrew    andrew        197 Oct 20 07:59 .bash_profile
-rw-r--r--    1 andrew    andrew        127 Oct 20 07:57 .bashrc
lrwxrwxrwx    1 andrew    andrew          7 Oct 20 08:01 ls -> /bin/ls
```

Restricted *ksh* is a little different in that it will allow you to run scripts and binaries that are in your PATH, which can be set before entering the shell:

```
$ rksh
$ ls -la
total 24
drwx------    2 andrew    andrew       4096 Oct 20 08:01 .
drwxr-xr-x    4 root      root         4096 Oct 20 14:16 ..
-rw-------    1 andrew    andrew         18 Oct 20 08:00 .bash_history
-rw-r--r--    1 andrew    andrew         24 Oct 20 14:16 .bash_logout
-rw-r--r--    1 andrew    andrew        197 Oct 20 07:59 .bash_profile
-rw-r--r--    1 andrew    andrew        127 Oct 20 07:57 .bashrc
lrwxrwxrwx    1 andrew    andrew          7 Oct 20 08:01 ls -> /bin/ls
$ which ls
/bin/ls
$ exit
```

This worked because */bin* was in the PATH before we invoked *ksh*. Now let's change the PATH and run *rksh* again:

```
$ export PATH=.
$ /bin/rksh
$ /bin/ls
/bin/rksh: /bin/ls: restricted
$ exit
$ ln -s /bin/ls .
$ ls -la
total 24
```

```
drwx------    2 andrew    andrew      4096 Oct 20 08:01 .
drwxr-xr-x    4 root      root        4096 Oct 20 14:16 ..
-rw-------    1 andrew    andrew        18 Oct 20 08:00 .bash_history
-rw-r--r--    1 andrew    andrew        24 Oct 20 14:16 .bash_logout
-rw-r--r--    1 andrew    andrew       197 Oct 20 07:59 .bash_profile
-rw-r--r--    1 andrew    andrew       127 Oct 20 07:57 .bashrc
lrwxrwxrwx    1 andrew    andrew         7 Oct 20 08:01 ls -> /bin/ls
```

Restricted shells are incredibly easy to set up and can provide minimal restricted access. They might not be able to keep out determined attackers, but they certainly make a hostile user's job much more difficult.

H A C K   Enforce User and Group Resource Limits
#21   Make sure resource-hungry users don't bring down your entire system.

Whether it's through malicious intent or an unintentional slip, having a user bring your system down to a slow crawl by using too much memory or CPU time is no fun at all. One popular way of limiting resource usage is to use the ulimit command. This method relies on a shell to limit its child processes, and it is difficult to use when you want to give different levels of usage to different users and groups. Another, more flexible way of limiting resource usage is with the PAM module pam_limits.

pam_limits is preconfigured on most systems that have PAM [Hack #17] installed. All you should need to do is edit */etc/security/limits.conf* to configure specific limits for users and groups.

The *limits.conf* configuration file consists of single-line entries describing a single type of limit for a user or group of users. The general format for an entry is:

```
domain    type    resource    value
```

The *domain* portion specifies to whom the limit applies. You can specify single users here by name, and groups can be specified by prefixing the group name with an @. In addition, you can use the wildcard character * to apply the limit globally to all users except for root. The *type* portion of the entry specifies whether it is a soft or hard resource limit. The user can increase soft limits, whereas hard limits can be changed only by root.

You can specify many types of resources for the *resource* portion of the entry. Some of the more useful ones are cpu, memlock, nproc, and fsize. These allow you to limit CPU time, total locked-in memory, number of processes, and file size, respectively. CPU time is expressed in minutes, and sizes are in kilobytes. Another useful limit is maxlogins, which allows you to specify the maximum number of concurrent logins that are permitted.

One nice feature of pam_limits is that it can work together with ulimit to allow the user to raise her limit from the soft limit to the imposed hard limit.

Let's try a quick test to see how it works. First, we'll limit the number of open files for the *guest* user by adding these entries to *limits.conf*:

```
guest           soft    nofile          1000
guest           hard    nofile          2000
```

Now the *guest* account has a soft limit of 1,000 concurrently open files and a hard limit of 2,000. Let's test it out:

```
# su - guest
$ ulimit -a
core file size      (blocks, -c) 0
data seg size       (kbytes, -d) unlimited
file size       (blocks, -f) unlimited
max locked memory   (kbytes, -l) unlimited
max memory size     (kbytes, -m) unlimited
open files          (-n) 1000
pipe size       (512 bytes, -p) 8
stack size      (kbytes, -s) 8192
cpu time        (seconds, -t) unlimited
max user processes      (-u) 1024
virtual memory      (kbytes, -v) unlimited
$ ulimit -n 2000
$ ulimit -n
2000
$ ulimit -n 2001
-bash: ulimit: open files: cannot modify limit: Operation not permitted
```

There you have it. In addition to open files, you can create resource limits for any number of other resources and apply them to specific users or entire groups. As you can see, pam_limits is quite powerful and useful in that it doesn't rely upon the shell for enforcement.

HACK #22 Automate System Updates

Patch security holes in a timely manner to prevent intrusions.

Updating and patching your systems in a timely manner is one of the most important things you can do to help protect them from the deluge of newly discovered security vulnerabilities. Unfortunately, this task often gets pushed to the wayside in favor of "more pressing" issues, such as performance tuning, hardware maintenance, and software debugging. In some circles, it's viewed as a waste of time and overhead that doesn't contribute to the primary function of a system. Coupled with management demands to maximize production, the task of keeping a system up-to-date is often pushed even further down on the to-do list.

Automate System Updates

Updating a system can be very repetitive and time-consuming if you're not using scripting to automate it. Fortunately, most Linux distributions make their updated packages available for download from a standard online location, and you can monitor that location for changes and automatically detect and download the new updates when they're made available. To demonstrate how to do this on an RPM-based distribution, we'll use AutoRPM (*http://www.autorpm.org*).

AutoRPM is a powerful Perl script that allows you to monitor multiple FTP sites for changes. It will automatically download new or changed packages and either install them automatically or alert you so that you may do so. In addition to monitoring single FTP sites, you can also monitor a pool of mirror sites, to ensure that you still get your updates if the FTP server is busy. AutoRPM will monitor busy FTP servers and keep track of how many times connections to them have been attempted. Using this information, it assigns internal scores to each of the FTP sites configured within a given pool, with the outcome that the server in the pool that is available most often will be checked first.

To use AutoRPM, download the latest package and install it like this:

```
# rpm -ivh autorpm-3.3.3-1.noarch.rpm
```

Although a tarball is also available, installation is a little trickier than the typical make; make install, so it is recommended that you stick to installing from the RPM package.

By default AutoRPM is configured to monitor for updated packages for Red Hat's Linux distribution, but you'll probably want to change this to use Fedora or another RPM-based distribution. To do this, open the AutoRPM configuration file, */etc/autorpm.d/autorpm.conf*, and find the following section:

```
######################### BEGIN Red Hat Linux
#################################
# This automatically determines the version of Red Hat Linux
# You have... you can comment this out and define it yourself
# if you want to
Eval_Var("RHVersion", "sed 's/\(Red Hat Linux \)\?release \([^ ]*\) (.*)/\2/
' /etc/redhat-release");
#Set_Var("RHVersion", "9.0");

# Look for official Red Hat updates
# (won't automatically install anything unless you edit the file)
Config_File("/etc/autorpm.d/redhat-updates.conf");
######################### END Red Hat Linux
#################################
```

Comment out the Eval_var, Set_Var, and Config_File lines. In the next section, uncomment the Eval_Var and Config_File lines to make it like this:

```
######################### BEGIN Fedora Linux
##################################
# This automatically determines your version of Fedora Linux
Eval_Var("FedoraVersion", "rpm -q fedora-release | awk -F'-' {'print $3'}");

# Look for official Fedora updates
# (won't automatically install anything unless you edit the file)
Config_File("/etc/autorpm.d/fedora-updates.conf");
######################### END Fedora Linux
##################################
```

After you've done that, you can add a crontab entry for */etc/autorpm.d/ autorpm.cron* to schedule AutoRPM to run at a regular interval. When it runs, it will automatically download any pending updates.

Another way to perform automatic updates is to use the *yum* program. By default, *yum* both downloads and installs updates, but you can change this behavior by installing the *downloadonly* plug-in (*http://linux.duke.edu/ projects/yum/download/yum-utils/*), causing *yum* to skip the installation step. You can then use the following command to download any updates that are available:

```
# yum --downloadonly -y update
```

Put this command in a crontab entry so that it will run at a regular interval. Then, when you've reviewed the updates that you've downloaded, you can use the usual yum update command to install them.

You can achieve similar results on Debian-based systems with apt-get -d -y upgrade. This command downloads any pending updates to packages that you have installed. When you've decided to install them, you can do so by running apt-get upgrade.

As you can see, there are many ways that you can keep a system updated with the latest fixed packages. Whatever you decide to do, it's important to stay current with operating system patches because of the security fixes they contain. If you fall behind, you're a much easier target for an attacker.

## CHAPTER TWO

Windows Host Security
Hacks 23–36

This chapter shows some ways to keep your Windows system up-to-date and secure, thereby making your network a safer place to work (and have fun). Although many may scoff at the mention of Windows and security in the same sentence, you actually can make a Windows system fairly secure without too much effort.

One of the main reasons that Windows gets a bad rap is the poorly administered state in which Windows machines seem to be kept. The recent deluge of worm and virus attacks that have brought down many a network shows this to hold true. A lot of this can be traced back to the "ease" of administration that Windows seems to provide by effectively keeping the Windows administrator out of the loop about the inner workings of her environment (and wresting control from her hands).

This chapter seeks to remedy that problem to some degree by showing you ways to see exactly what your server is really doing. While this might seem like old hat to a Unix sysadmin, getting details on open ports and running services is often a new concept to the average Windows administrator.

In addition, this chapter shows how to disable some Windows "features," such as sharing out all your files automatically and truncating log files. You'll also learn how to enable some of the auditing and logging features of Windows, to give you early warning of possible security incidents (rather than waiting for the angry phone call from someone at the wrong end of a denial-of-service attack originating from your network).

This chapter also covers how to use and manage the Windows Encrypting File System (EFS) for encrypting files and folders, how to configure automatic updates on a network of computers, and how to check for accounts that have passwords that never expire.

Check Servers for Applied Patches

HACK

#23

Make sure your Windows servers have the latest patches installed.

Keeping a network of systems patched and up-to-date is hard enough in Unix, but it can be even more difficult with Windows systems. A lack of robust built-in scripting and remote access capabilities makes Windows unsuitable for automation. Nevertheless, before you even attempt to update your systems, you need to know which updates have been applied to each system; otherwise, you might waste time and effort updating systems that don't need it.

Clearly, this problem gets more difficult as the number of systems that need to be managed increases. You can avoid much of the extra work of manually updating systems by using the *HFNetChk* tool, which was originally a standalone program from Shavlik Technologies. It is now a part of Microsoft's Baseline Security Analyzer (*http://www.microsoft.com/technet/security/tools/mbsa1/default.mspx*) and is available through its command-line interface, *mbsacli.exe*.

Not only can *HFNetChk* remotely check the status of Windows Server 2003 and Windows XP/2000/NT, but it can also check whether critical updates for IIS, SQL Server, Exchange Server, Media Player, and Internet Explorer have been applied. Although it can only check the update status of a system (and won't actually bring the system up-to-date), it is still an invaluable timesaving tool.

HFNetChk works by downloading a signed and compressed XML file from Microsoft that contains information on all currently available updates. This information includes checksums and versions of files covered by each update, as well as the Registry keys modified by each update. Additional dependency information is also included.

When scanning a system, *HFNetChk* first scans the Registry for the keys that are associated with the most current set of updates available for the current system configuration. If any of these Registry keys are missing or do not match what is contained in the XML file, it flags the update as not having been installed. If the Registry key for an update is present and matches the information in the XML file, *HFNetChk* then attempts to verify whether the files specified in the update information are present on the system and whether their versions and checksums match.

If any of the checks fails, *HFNetChk* flags the update. All flagged updates are then displayed in a report, along with a reference to the Microsoft Knowledge Base article with more information on the specific update.

Using HFNetChk

To install *HFNetChk* on your system, you first need to download and install the Microsoft Baseline Security Analyzer. To run *HFNetChk*, open a command prompt and change to the directory that was created during the install (*C:\Program Files\Microsoft Baseline Security Analyzer* is the default).

To check the update status of the local system, run this command:

```
C:\Program Files\Microsoft Baseline Security Analyzer>mbsacli /hf
Microsoft Baseline Security Analyzer
Version 1.2.1 (1.2.4013.0)
(C) Copyright 2002-2004 Microsoft Corporation. All rights reserved.
HFNetChk developed for Microsoft Corporation by Shavlik Technologies, LLC.
(C) Copyright 2002-2004 Shavlik Technologies, LLC. www.shavlik.com


Please use the -v switch to view details for
Patch NOT Found, Warning and Note messages

Scanning BLACKBIRD
Attempting to get CAB from http://go.microsoft.com/fwlink/?LinkId=18922
XML successfully loaded.

Done scanning BLACKBIRD
---------------------------
BLACKBIRD (192.168.0.67)
---------------------------

         * WINDOWS XP PROFESSIONAL SP2

         Note            MS05-009     887472
         Patch NOT Found MS06-021     916281
         Patch NOT Found MS06-022     918439
         Patch NOT Found MS06-025     911280
         Patch NOT Found MS06-032     917953
```

The first column tells why the check for a particular update failed. The second column shows which update failed the check, and the third column lists a Microsoft Knowledge Base (*http://support.microsoft.com*) article number that you can refer to for more information on the issue fixed by that particular update.

If you want more information on why a particular check failed, you can run the command with the -v (verbose) switch. Here are the results of the previous command, this time with the verbose switch:

```
C:\Program Files\Microsoft Baseline Security Analyzer>mbsacli /hf -v
Microsoft Baseline Security Analyzer
Version 1.2.1 (1.2.4013.0)
(C) Copyright 2002-2004 Microsoft Corporation. All rights reserved.
```

```
HFNetChk developed for Microsoft Corporation by Shavlik Technologies, LLC.
(C) Copyright 2002-2004 Shavlik Technologies, LLC. www.shavlik.com

Scanning BLACKBIRD
Attempting to get CAB from http://go.microsoft.com/fwlink/?LinkId=18922
XML successfully loaded.

Done scanning BLACKBIRD
--------------------------
BLACKBIRD (192.168.0.67)
--------------------------


        * WINDOWS XP PROFESSIONAL SP2

        Note            MS05-009        887472
        Please refer to 306460 for a detailed explanation.

        Patch NOT Found MS06-021         916281
        File version is less than expected.
        [C:\WINDOWS\system32\browseui.dll, 6.0.2900.2861 < 6.0.2900.2904]

        Patch NOT Found MS06-022         918439
        File version is less than expected.
        [C:\WINDOWS\system32\jgdw400.dll, 82.0.0.0 < 106.0.0.0]

        Patch NOT Found MS06-025         911280
        File version is less than expected.
        [C:\WINDOWS\system32\rasmans.dll, 5.1.2600.2180 < 5.1.2600.2908]

        Patch NOT Found MS06-032         917953
        File version is less than expected.
        [C:\WINDOWS\system32\drivers\tcpip.sys, 5.1.2600.2827 <
        5.1.2600.2892]
```

After applying the listed updates, you should see something like this:

```
Scanning BLACKBIRD
..............................
Done scanning BLACKBIRD
--------------------------
PLUNDER(192.168.0.67)
--------------------------


        * WINDOWS XP PROFESSIONAL SP2

        Information
        All necessary hotfixes have been applied.
```

You need Administrator privileges to scan the local system. Likewise, to scan a remote machine, you will need Administrator privileges on that machine. There are several ways to scan remote machines. To scan a single remote system, you can specify a NetBIOS name with the -h switch or an IP address with the -i switch.

For example, to scan the machine *PLUNDER* from another machine, use either of these two commands:

```
mbsacli /hf -h PLUNDER
mbsacli /hf -i 192.168.0.65
```

You can also scan a handful of additional systems by listing them on the command line, with commas separating each NetBIOS name or IP address.

Note that, in addition to having Administrator privileges on the remote machine, you must also ensure that you have not disabled the default shares [Hack #32]. If the default administrative shares have been disabled, *HFNetChk* will not be able to check for the proper files on the remote system and, consequently, will not be able to determine whether an update was applied.

If you want to scan a large group of systems, you have several options. Using the -fh option, you can specify a file containing up to 256 NetBIOS hostnames (one on each line) to be scanned. You can do the same thing with IP addresses, using the -fip option. You can also specify ranges of IP addresses by using the -r option.

For example, you could run a command like this to scan systems with IP addresses in the range 192.168.1.23 to 192.168.1.172:

```
mbsacli /hf -r 192.168.1.123 - 192.168.1.172
```

All of these options are very flexible, and you can use them in any combination to specify which remote systems will be scanned.

In addition to specifying remote systems by NetBIOS name and IP address, you can scan systems by domain name by using the -d option, or you can scan your entire local network segment by using the -n command-line option.

When scanning systems from a personal workstation, the -u and -p options can prove useful. These allow you to specify a username and password to use when accessing the remote systems. These switches are particularly handy if you don't normally log in using the Administrator account. (The account that is specified with the -u option will, of course, need to have Administrator privileges on the remote machines being scanned.)

Also, if you're scanning a large number of systems, you might want to use the -t option. This allows you to specify the number of threads used by the scanner, and increasing this value generally speeds up scanning. Valid values are from 1 to 128; the default value is 64.

If you are scanning more than one machine, a huge amount of data will simply be dumped to the screen. Use the -f option to specify a file to store the results of the scan in, and view it at your leisure using a text editor.

HFNetChk is a flexible tool and can be used to check the update statuses of a large number of machines in a very short amount of time. It is especially useful when a new worm has come onto the scene and you need to know if all of your systems are up-to-date on their patches.

See Also

* Frequently Asked Questions about the Microsoft Network Security Hotfix Checker (*Hfnetchk.exe*) Tool: Knowledge Base Article 305385, at *http://support.microsoft.com/default.aspx?scid=kb;EN-US;*

Use Group Policy to Configure Automatic Updates

Use Group Policy to simplify the configuration of Automatic Updates in an Active Directory environment.

Configuring Automatic Updates is a lot of work if you have to do it separately on every machine on your network. Fortunately, in an Active Directory environment, you can use Group Policy to simplify the job.

First, open an existing Group Policy Object (GPO), such as the Default Domain Policy, or create a new GPO and link it to the appropriate domain, organizational unit (OU), or site. Then, add the *wuau.adm* template to the GPO so that the Group Policy settings for Automatic Updates will be added to your GPO. This is done as follows.

These steps are unnecessary if you have Windows Server 2003.

Begin by expanding Computer Configuration to show Administrative Templates. Next, right-click on Administrative Templates, select Add/Remove Template, click Add, select *wuau.adm* from the list of templates in the *%Windir%\Inf* folder, click Open, and then click Close.

Now, configure the GPO settings for Automatic Updates by expanding Computer Configuration → Administrative Templates → Windows Components and selecting Windows Update in the pane on the left, as shown in Figure 2-1.

Let's dig into what the various settings in Figure 2-1 mean. The first setting, "Configure Automatic Updates," lets you perform basic configuration of Automatic Updates for computers in the domain, OU, or site to which the GPO is linked. The options here are the same as the options available when you manually configure the feature using the Control Panel's Automatic

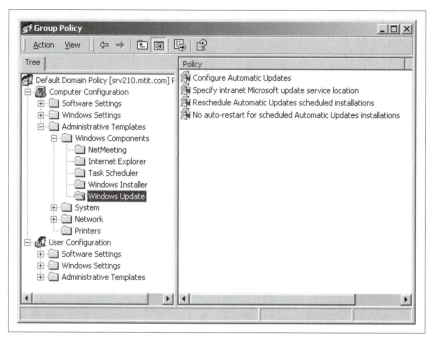

Figure 2-1. Using Group Policy to configure Automatic Updates

Updates utility (Windows 2000) or System utility (Windows Server 2003 and Windows XP). The next setting, "Specify intranet Microsoft update service location," applies only if you plan on using Software Update Services (SUS) to deploy updates.

The "Reschedule Automatic Updates schedule installations" option determines how long Automatic Updates will wait after the computer restarts before installing updates that have already been downloaded and are past the scheduled time for installation. The value ranges from 1 to 60 (minutes); the default is 1 if the setting is not configured and 5 when the policy is enabled. Disabling this policy defers the installation of overdue updates until the next scheduled installation day and time.

Finally, "No auto-restart for scheduled Automatic Updates installations" determines whether the logged-on user will be forcibly logged off in order to complete the installation process when a reboot is required. Enabling this policy means that machines will not be forcibly rebooted. While this might seem like a good idea (so users won't lose their work), it does have a downside: Automatic Updates won't be able to check the Windows Update web site for new updates until the machine is rebooted.

Enabling these policy settings will override any configuration of Automatic Updates that was done locally using the Control Panel and will prevent you from making such changes locally, even as an administrator. However, changing these policy settings back to Not Configured will restore the manual settings previously configured for Automatic Updates (though a reboot is required). And while changes made to these policies are automatically applied to client computers every 90 minutes (plus a random offset of up to 30 minutes), you can test the settings immediately by forcing a policy refresh with the command secedit /refreshpolicy machine_policy on Windows 2000 or gpupdate /force on Windows Server 2003.

Some Recommendations

If you want to configure different Automatic Updates policies for different users or computers, you have two options: (1) create multiple GPOs, link each to a different OU, and place users and computers into these OUs accordingly; or (2) filter the GPO settings to prevent their inheritance by specific users, computers, or groups.

You can also check the Security log in the Event Viewer if you want to see whether the machine has been rebooted to install scheduled updates. Look for the following Event IDs:

Event ID 21
    "Restart Required: To complete the installation of the following updates, the computer must be restarted. Until this computer has been restarted, Windows cannot search for or download new updates."

Event ID 22
    "Restart Required: To complete the installation of the following updates, the computer will be restarted within five minutes. Until this computer has been restarted, Windows cannot search for or download new updates."

Digging Deeper

There's another policy that controls how Automatic Updates works, but it's not found under Computer Configuration. Instead, it's found at User Configuration → Administrative Templates → Windows Components → Windows Update → "Remove access to use all Windows Update features."

This policy prevents the currently logged-on user from opening the Windows Update web site in Internet Explorer, in order to manually download and install updates on his machine. When the user attempts to access the URL *http://windowsupdate.microsoft.com*, an "Access Denied" page appears, explaining that a policy is preventing him from using the site. Enabling this policy also has the effect of preventing Automatic Updates from notifying users when new updates are ready to install. In other words, no notification icon will appear in the status area to inform the logged-on user that updates are ready to install. Even local administrators on the machine are affected by this policy, as are domain administrators.

So, why would you want to use this policy? While it prevents users from visiting or interacting with the Windows Update site, it doesn't prevent Automatic Updates from operating if the feature has been configured at the computer level using the policies discussed in the previous section. This is because this setting is a per-user policy, not a per-machine one. In other words, it affects only users; it doesn't affect configuration done at the machine level.

Enabling this policy might be a good idea, because it prevents users from trying to download and install updates on their own, even if they have administrative privileges.

> Microsoft says that this policy works only on Windows XP and Windows Server 2003, but in my experience it also works on Windows 2000.

While this policy prevents users from using the Windows Update site, it still leaves the Windows Update icon in the Start menu, tempting users to explore and see what it does. You can remove this icon from the Start menu by enabling another policy: User Configuration → Administrative Templates → Start Menu & Taskbar ⟩ "Disable and remove links to Windows Update."

This removes all temptation for users to try to keep their machines up-to-date by themselves. Administrators would do well to use such policies and to explore similar restrictions on user activity provided by Group Policy.

—Mitch Tulloch

List Open Files and Their Owning Processes

#25

Look for suspicious activity by monitoring file accesses.

Suppose you're looking at the list of processes in the task manager one day after noticing some odd behavior on your workstation, and you notice a process you haven't seen before. Well, what do you do now? If you were running something other than Windows, you might try to determine what the process is doing by looking at the files it has open. But Windows doesn't provide a tool to do this.

Fortunately, a third-party solution exists. Sysinternals makes an excellent tool called Handle, which is available for free at *http://www.sysinternals.com/ Utilities/Handle.html*. Handle is a lot like lsof **[Hack #8]**, but it can list many other types of operating resources, including threads, events, and semaphores. It can also display open Registry keys and IOCompletion structures.

Running handle without any command-line arguments lists all open file handles on the system. You can also specify a filename, which lists the processes that are currently accessing it, by typing this:

```
C:\> handle filename
```

Or you can list only files that are opened by a particular process—in this case, Internet Explorer:

```
C:\> handle -p iexplore
Handle v2.10
Copyright (C) 1997-2003 Mark Russinovich
Sysinternals - www.sysinternals.com

------------------------------------------------------------------
IEXPLORE.EXE pid: 688 PLUNDER\andrew
   98: Section       \BaseNamedObjects\MTXCOMM_MEMORY_MAPPED_FILE
   9c: Section       \BaseNamedObjects\MtxWndList
  12c: Section       \BaseNamedObjects\__R_0000000000d4_SMem_    _
  18c: File          C:\Documents and Settings\andrew\Local Settings\
Temporary Internet
Files\Content.IE5\index.dat
  198: Section       \BaseNamedObjects\C:_Documents and Settings_andrew_
Local
Settings_Temporary Internet Files_Content.IE5_index.dat_3194880
  1a0: File          C:\Documents and Settings\andrew\Cookies\index.dat
  1a8: File          C:\Documents and Settings\andrew\Local Settings\
History\History.IE5\
index.dat
  1ac: Section       \BaseNamedObjects\C:_Documents and Settings_andrew_
Local
Settings_History_History.IE5_index.dat_245760
  1b8: Section       \BaseNamedObjects\C:_Documents and
Settings_andrew_Cookies_index.dat_81920
  228: Section       \BaseNamedObjects\UrlZonesSM_andrew
  2a4: Section       \BaseNamedObjects\SENS Information Cache
  540: File          C:\Documents and Settings\andrew\Application
Data\Microsoft\SystemCertificates\My
  574: File          C:\Documents and Settings\All Users\Desktop
  5b4: Section       \BaseNamedObjects\mmGlobalPnpInfo
  5cc: File          C:\WINNT\system32\mshtml.tlb
  614: Section       \BaseNamedObjects\WDMAUD_Callbacks
  640: File          C:\WINNT\system32\Macromed\Flash\Flash.ocx
  648: File          C:\WINNT\system32\STDOLE2.TLB
  6a4: File          \Dfs
  6b4: File          C:\Documents and Settings\andrew\Desktop
  6c8: File          C:\Documents and Settings\andrew\Local Settings\
```

```
Temporary Internet Files\Content.IE5\Q5USFSTO\softwareDownloadIndex[1].htm
   70c: Section        \BaseNamedObjects\MSIMGSIZECacheMap
   758: File           C:\WINNT\system32\iepeers.dll
   75c: File           C:\Documents and Settings\andrew\Desktop
   770: Section        \BaseNamedObjects\RotHintTable
```

If you want to find the Internet Explorer process that owns a resource with a partial name of handle, you can type this:

```
C:\> handle -p iexplore handle
Handle v2.10
Copyright (C) 1997-2003 Mark Russinovich
Sysinternals - www.sysinternals.com

IEXPLORE.EXE        pid: 1396   C:\Documents and Settings\andrew\Local
Settings\Temporary
Internet Files\Content.IE5\H1EZGFSH\handle[1].htm
```

Additionally, if you want to list all types of resources, you can use the -a option. Handle is quite a powerful tool, and you can mix together any of its command-line options to quickly narrow your search and find just what you want.

List Running Services and Open Ports

#26 Check for remotely accessible services the Windows way.

Unix makes it quick and easy to see which ports on a system are open, but how can you do that on Windows? Well, with FPort from Foundstone (*http://www.foundstone.com/resources/proddesc/fport.htm*), it's as quick and easy as running good old netstat.

FPort has a few command-line options, which deal mostly with specifying how you'd like the output sorted. For instance, if you want the output sorted by application name, you can use /a; if you want it sorted by process ID, you can use /i. While it might not be as full of features as the Unix version of *netstat* [Hack #8], FPort definitely gets the job done.

To get a listing of all ports that are open on your system, simply type fport. If you want the list to be sorted by port number, use the /p switch:

```
C:\> fport /p
FPort v2.0 - TCP/IP Process to Port Mapper
Copyright 2000 by Foundstone, Inc.
http://www.foundstone.com

Pid   Process       Port  Proto Path
432   svchost    -> 135   TCP   C:\WINNT\system32\svchost.exe
8     System     -> 139   TCP
8     System     -> 445   TCP
672   MSTask     -> 1025  TCP   C:\WINNT\system32\MSTask.exe
```

```
8       System      ->  1028  TCP
8       System      ->  1031  TCP
1116    navapw32    ->  1035  TCP   C:\PROGRA~1\NORTON~1\navapw32.exe
788     svchost     ->  1551  TCP   C:\WINNT\system32\svchost.exe
788     svchost     ->  1553  TCP   C:\WINNT\system32\svchost.exe
788     svchost     ->  1558  TCP   C:\WINNT\system32\svchost.exe
1328    svchost     ->  1565  TCP   C:\WINNT\System32\svchost.exe
8       System      ->  1860  TCP
1580    putty       ->  3134  TCP   C:\WINNT\putty.exe
772     WinVNC      ->  5800  TCP   C:\Program Files\TightVNC\WinVNC.exe
772     WinVNC      ->  5900  TCP   C:\Program Files\TightVNC\WinVNC.exe

432     svchost     ->  135   UDP   C:\WINNT\system32\svchost.exe
8       System      ->  137   UDP
8       System      ->  138   UDP
8       System      ->  445   UDP
256     lsass       ->  500   UDP   C:\WINNT\system32\lsass.exe
244     services    ->  1027  UDP   C:\WINNT\system32\services.exe
688     IEXPLORE    ->  2204  UDP   C:\Program Files\Internet Explorer\
IEXPLORE.EXE
1396    IEXPLORE    ->  3104  UDP   C:\Program Files\Internet Explorer\
IEXPLORE.EXE
256     lsass       ->  4500  UDP   C:\WINNT\system32\lsass.exe
```

Notice that some of the processes listed—such as navapw32, putty, and IEXPLORE—don't appear to be services. These show up in the output because FPort lists all open ports, not just opened ports that are listening.

Though fport is not as powerful as some of the commands available under other operating systems, it is still a valuable, quick, and easy-to-use tool, and a great addition to Windows.

HACK #27 Enable Auditing

Log suspicious activity to help spot intrusions.

Windows includes some powerful auditing features, but unfortunately, they are not always enabled. Using these capabilities, you can monitor failed log-ins, account-management events, file accesses, privilege use, and more. You can also log security policy changes as well as system events.

To enable auditing in any one of these areas, locate and double-click the Administrative Tools icon in the Control Panel. Now find and double-click the Local Security Policy icon. Expand the Local Policies tree node, and you should see a screen like the one shown in Figure 2-2.

You can go through each of the audit policies and check whether to log suc-cesses or failures for each type. To do this, double-click the policy you wish to modify, located in the right pane of the window. After double-clicking, you should see a dialog similar to Figure 2-3.

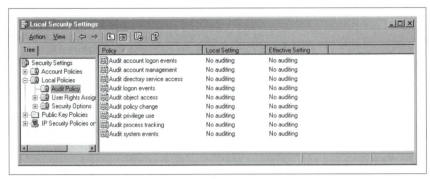

Figure 2-2. Audit Policy settings in the Local Security Settings applet

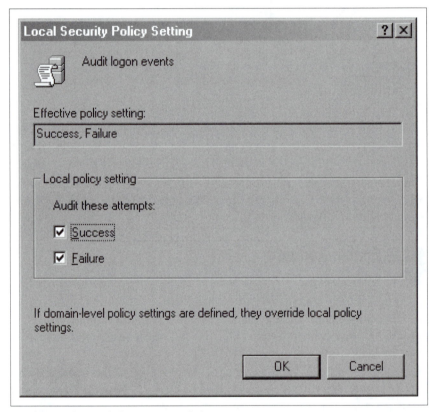

Figure 2-3. The "Audit logon events" dialog

Leaving auditing off is akin to not logging anything at all, so you should enable auditing for all policies. Once you've enabled auditing for a particular policy, you should begin to see entries in the event logs for when a particular audit event occurs. For example, once you have enabled logon event auditing, you should begin to see entries for logon successes and failures in the system's security event log.

Enumerate Automatically Executed Programs

HACK #28

Take control of your system by finding programs that Windows starts automatically.

One of the many problems Windows users face is being able to keep track of all the methods Windows uses to automatically start programs at system boot and when a user logs in. Of course, any programs in a user's *Startup* folder are automatically launched when the user logs in. The Registry keys that control system services, scheduled tasks, and Internet Explorer add-ons are just a few of the other things that can cause a program to be started automatically.

The onslaught of spyware has made it important to be able to find out exactly what's being automatically launched on your system and what's causing it to be launched. At the very least, finding out why a program is started automatically can be a minor annoyance. Many software packages install add-on utilities that start up automatically, and disabling these is usually easy to do so. However, spyware can be much more difficult to deal with, as it often uses more obscure Registry locations to launch itself.

Because spyware packages often launch via more than one avenue, they can be difficult to remove. If you notice something odd in one place and remove it, you'll often find that there's an entry buried somewhere else deep within the system Registry that either undoes your attempts to remove the software or attempts to start the offending piece of software. To completely rid yourself of the spyware, you need to remove all traces of it in one shot.

You've probably gotten the idea by now, but completely removing a spyware package can be difficult because all of these different avenues are buried deep within the system Registry. This problem is compounded by the fact that mistakes made when editing the Registry can often leave a system either partially or wholly inoperable. Luckily, some programs can help you track down all of the programs that are executed automatically and show you the Registry locations that are causing them to be executed.

One such program is Autoruns (*http://www.sysinternals.net/Utilities/Autoruns.html*). Not only does it let you find the programs, but it also lets you easily disable them. To install Autoruns, download the *.zip* archive from the Sysinternals site and then extract its contents to a suitable directory (e.g., *C:\Program Files\Autoruns*).

Then, launch *autoruns.exe*. After accepting the license agreement, you should see the window shown in Figure 2-4.

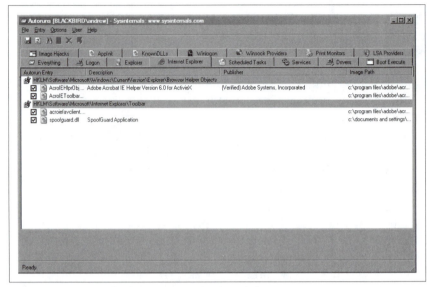

Figure 2-4. Autoruns displaying Internet Explorer helpers

As you can see, the Autoruns interface is fairly simple. The tabs at the top of the window allow you to filter by method of automatic execution. The Everything tab, of course, shows all automatically executed items, while the Logon tab shows items that are executed when you log in. Figure 2-4 displays the contents of the Internet Explorer tab, which shows the helper plug-ins loaded by Internet Explorer. The Internet Explorer tab is especially useful for tracking down browser toolbars and other pieces of software that can be used to monitor your web browsing.

If you feel that you're staring at too much information, you can ignore any standard items that are legitimate Microsoft programs. Just choose Options → Hide Microsoft Signed Entries to display only third-party programs. Make sure to choose File → Refresh to update the display.

If you want to disable an item, simply uncheck the box next to it. Autoruns will make a backup of the information, so that you can re-enable it later if you need to (simply recheck the entry). Also, if you're not quite sure what a program is, you can click on the item and choose Entry → Google to launch your web browser with search results for the item.

Secure Your Event Logs

HACK #29

Keep your system's logs from being tampered with.

Windows has some powerful logging features. Unfortunately, if you're still running an older Windows system, such as a variety of Windows 2000, by default the event logs are not protected against unauthorized access or modification. You might not realize that even though you have to view the logs through the Event Viewer, they're simply regular files just like any others. To secure them, all you need to do is locate them and apply the proper ACLs.

Unless their locations have been changed through the Registry, you should be able to find the logs in the *%SystemRoot%\system32\config* directory. The three files that correspond to the Application Log, Security Log, and System Log are *AppEvent.Evt*, *SecEvent.Evt*, and *SysEvent.Evt*, respectively.

Now, apply ACLs to limit access to only Administrator accounts. You can do this by bringing up the Properties dialog for the files and clicking the Security tab. After you've done this, remove any users or groups other than Administrators and SYSTEM from the top pane.

Change Your Maximum Log File Sizes

HACK #30

Change your log properties so that they see the whole picture.

From a security point of view, logs are one of the most important assets contained on a server. After all, without logs, how will you know if or when someone has gained access to your machine? Therefore, it is imperative that your logs not miss a beat. If you're trying to track down the source of an incident, having missing log entries is not much better than having no logs at all.

One common problem is that the maximum log size is set too low; depending on the version of Windows, the default can be as measly as 512 KB. To change this, go to the Administrative Tools control panel and open the Event Viewer. You should see the screen shown in Figure 2-5.

Right-click one of the log files in the left pane of the Event Viewer window and select the Properties menu item to bring up the Security Log Properties dialog, shown in Figure 2-6.

Now, locate the text input box with the label "Maximum log size." You can type in the new maximum size directly, or you can use the arrows next to the text box to change the value. What size is appropriate depends on how often you want to review and archive your logs. Anything above 1 MB is good. However, keep in mind that while having very large log files won't

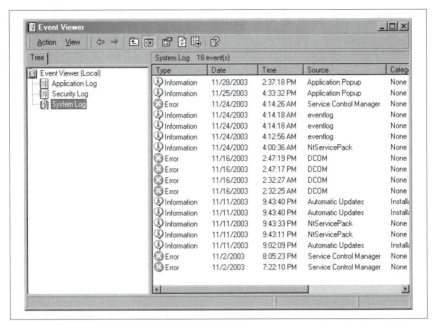

Figure 2-5. The Windows Event Viewer

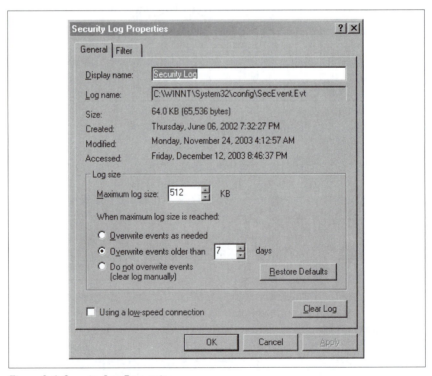

Figure 2-6. Security Log Properties

inherently slow down the machine, it can slow down the Event Viewer when you're trying to view the logs.

While you're here, you may also want to change the behavior for when the log file reaches its maximum size. By default, it will start overwriting log entries that are older than seven days with newer log entries. It is recommended that you change this value to something higher—say, 31 days. Alternatively, you can elect not to have entries overwritten automatically at all, in which case you'll need to clear the log manually.

Back Up and Clear the Event Logs

HACK
#31

Here's a nifty script you can use to back up and clear the Event logs on your servers.

Managing Event logs is an essential part of a system administrator's job. These logs are useful for a number of purposes, including troubleshooting system problems, verifying that services are functioning properly, and detecting possible intrusion attempts. While you can use the Event Viewer to save and clear these logs, it would be handy to have a script that would back up your Windows Event Logs and then clear the information contained within them.

This hack provides a script to do just that. You can run it manually (by double-clicking on a desktop shortcut) or automatically at different times (by adding a task to the *Scheduled Tasks* folder).

The Code

Type the following script into Notepad (make sure you have Word Wrap disabled), and save it as *archivelogs.vbs*:

```
Option Explicit
On Error Resume Next
Dim numThreshold
Dim strMachine
Dim strArchivePath
Dim strMoniker
Dim refWMI
Dim colEventLogs
Dim refEventLog

If WScript.Arguments.Count < 2 Then
WScript.Echo _
"Usage: archivelogs.vbs <machine> <archive_path> [threshold]"
WScript.Quit
End If
```

```
If WScript.Arguments.Count = 2 Then
numThreshold = 0
Else
numThreshold = WScript.Arguments(2)
If Not IsNumeric(numThreshold) Then
WScript.Echo "The third parameter must be a number!"
WScript.Quit
End If

If numThreshold < 0 OR numThreshold > 100 Then
WScript.Echo "The third parameter must be in the range 0-100"
WScript.Quit
End If
End If

strMachine = WScript.Arguments(0)
strArchivePath = WScript.Arguments(1)

strMoniker = "winMgmts:{(Backup,Security)}!\\" & strMachine
Set refWMI = GetObject(strMoniker)
If Err <> 0 Then
WScript.Echo "Could not connect to the WMI service."
WScript.Quit
End If

Set colEventLogs = refWMI.InstancesOf("Win32_NTEventLogFile")
If Err <> 0 Then
WScript.Echo "Could not retrieve Event Log objects"
WScript.Quit
End If

For Each refEventLog In colEventLogs
'if shouldAct( ) returns non-zero attempt to back up
If shouldAct(refEventLog.FileSize,refEventLog.MaxFileSize) <> 0 Then
If refEventLog.ClearEventLog( _
makeFileName(refEventLog.LogfileName)) = 0 Then
WScript.Echo refEventLog.LogfileName & _
" archived successfully"
Else
WScript.Echo refEventLog.LogfileName & _
" could not be archived"
End If
Else
WScript.Echo refEventLog.LogfileName & _
" has not exceeded the backup level"
End If
Next
Set refEventLog = Nothing
Set colEventLogs = Nothing
Set refWMI = Nothing

Function shouldAct(numCurSize, numMaxSize)
If (numCurSize/numMaxSize)*100 > numThreshold Then
shouldAct = 1
```

```
Else
  shouldAct = 0
  End If
End Function

Function makeFileName(strLogname)
  makeFileName = strArchivePath & "\" & _
  strMachine & "-" & strLogname & "-" & _
  Year(Now) & Month(Now) & Day(Now) & ".evt"
End Function
```

Running the Hack

To run the script, use *Cscript.exe*, the command-line script engine of the Windows Script Host (WSH). The script uses the following command-line syntax:

```
archivelogs.vbs machine archive_path [threshold]
```

where *machine* is the name of the server and *archive_path* is the path to where you want to save the backup. *threshold* is an optional parameter that checks the size (in MB) of the logs: if the logs are above the threshold value you specify, the script will back them up; otherwise, it will skip them.

The following example shows how to run the script and provides typical output when the script is executed against a domain controller (the archive directory *C:\Log Files* must first be created on the machine on which you run the script):

```
C:\>cscript.exe archivelogs.vbs srv210 "C:\Log Archive"
Microsoft (R) Windows Script Host Version 5.6
Copyright (C) Microsoft Corporation 1996-2001. All rights reserved.

Security archived successfully
System archived successfully
Directory Service archived successfully
DNS Server archived successfully
File Replication Service archived successfully
Application archived successfully

C:\>
```

The result of running the script is a set of files in *C:\Log Files* of the form *srv210-Application-20031217.evt*, *srv210-Security-20031217.evt*, and so on. Note that each archive file is named according to the server, event log, and current date.

If you plan on using the Backup utility instead to back up the Event log files on your Windows 2000 servers, it might surprise you to know that being part of the Backup Operators group will not allow you to back up or restore these Event log files; this right is available to only local or domain administrators!

—*Rod Trent*

Disable Default Shares

#32 Stop sharing all your files with the world.

By default, Windows enables sharing for each logical disk on your system (e.g., C$ for the C: drive) in addition to another share called ADMIN$ for the *%SystemRoot%* directory (e.g., *C:\WINNT*). Although the shares are accessible only to Administrators it is wise to disable them if possible, as they present a potential security hole.

To disable these shares, open the Registry by running *regedit.exe* and then find the HKey_Local_Machine\SYSTEM\CurrentControlSet\Services\lanmanserver\ parameters key.

If you're using Windows 2000 Workstation, add an AutoShareWks DWORD key with the value of 0 (as shown in Figure 2-7) by clicking Edit → New → DWORD Value. For Windows 2000 Server, add an AutoShareServer key with a value of 0. When you're done editing the Registry, restart Windows for the change to take effect.

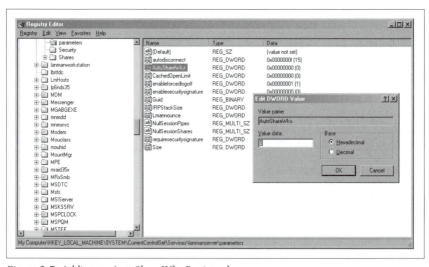

Figure 2-7. Adding an AutoShareWks Registry key

After Windows has finished loading, you can verify that the default shares no longer exist by running net share:

```
C:\>net share

Share name   Resource                       Remark
-------------------------------------------------------------------------
IPC$         Remote IPC
The command completed successfully.
```

Before doing this, you should be sure that disabling these shares will not negatively affect your environment. Lack of these shares can cause some system management software, such as HFNetChk **[Hack #23]** or System Management Server, to not work. This is because such software depends on remote access to the default administrative shares in order to access the contents of the systems disks.

HACK #33 Encrypt Your Temp Folder
Keep prying eyes out of your temporary files.

Many Windows applications create intermediary files while they do their work. They typically store these files in a temporary folder within the current user's settings directory. These files are usually created world-readable and aren't always cleaned up when the program exits. How would you like it if your word processor left a copy of the last document you were working on for anyone to come across and read? Not a pretty thought, is it?

One way to guard against this situation is to encrypt your temporary files folder. Open an Explorer window and go to the *C:\Documents and Settings\ <username>\Local Settings* folder, where you should see another folder called *Temp*. This is the folder that holds the temporary files. Right-click the folder and bring up its Properties dialog. Make sure the General tab is selected, and click the button labeled Advanced. This will bring up an Advanced Attributes dialog, as shown in Figure 2-8. Here you can choose to encrypt the folder.

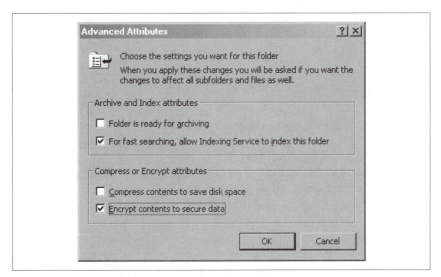

Figure 2-8. The Temp folder's Advanced Attributes dialog

Check the "Encrypt contents to secure data" box and click the OK button. When you have done that, click the Apply button in the Properties dialog. Another dialog (shown in Figure 2-9) opens, asking you whether you would like the encryption to apply recursively.

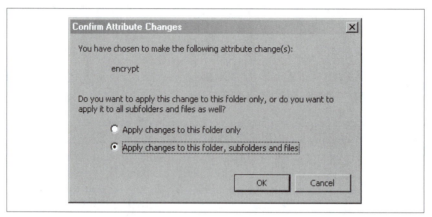

Figure 2-9. Confirming the choice of encryption and making it recursive

To apply the encryption recursively, choose the "Apply changes to this folder, subfolders and files" option. This automatically creates a public-key pair if you have never encrypted any files before. Otherwise, Windows will use the public key that it generated for you previously.

When decrypting, Windows ensures that the private keys are stored in non-paged kernel memory, so that the decryption key will never be left in the paging file. If you're using an older version of Windows, beware. Windows 2000 uses the DESX algorithm, which is almost useless. However, versions from Windows XP SP1 onward support both 3DES and the much stronger AES.

HACK #34 Back Up EFS

Backing up EFS recovery keys is essential if you want to be able to recover encrypted documents after a disaster.

The Encrypting File System (EFS) lets you encrypt files so that unauthorized individuals can't read them. Normally, this is a good thing, because it helps secure data stored on a machine's hard drive. However, this hack is concerned with what happens when something goes wrong—for example, if a user's machine becomes toast, taking her EFS private key and certificate to Never-Never Land.

The key to being able to recover encrypted files when something goes wrong is having a designated recovery agent already in place. Then, if you lose your EFS private key, the recovery agent can decrypt your encrypted files in an emergency. Every time you encrypt a file, EFS generates a unique *File Encryption Key* (FEK) that it uses to encrypt only that file. In other words, each encrypted file has its own unique FEK.

In addition, the FEK is itself encrypted using your own EFS public key and incorporated into the header of the file. Later, if you want to read the encrypted file, EFS automatically uses your EFS private key to decrypt the FEK for the file and then uses the FEK to decrypt the file itself. The FEK is thus used for both encrypting and decrypting the file (a process known as *symmetric encryption*), while your EFS public/private key pair is used for encrypting and decrypting the FEK (known as *asymmetric encryption*). This combination of symmetric (or secret-key) encryption and asymmetric (public-key) encryption is the basis of how EFS works.

But what happens if you lose your EFS private key? This might happen if your machine has two drives: a system drive (*C:*) and a data drive (*D:*), where encrypted files are stored. By default, your EFS keys are stored on your system drive, so if *C:* becomes corrupted, the encrypted files on *D:* will be inaccessible, right? That's where the recovery agent comes in. Each time you encrypt a file, the FEK is encrypted with both your own EFS public key and the EFS public key of the recovery agent. That means that the recovery agent can always decrypt the FEK by using its EFS private key and thus decrypt the file when something goes wrong and your own private key is lost or corrupted.

What are these recovery agents? By default, on standalone Windows 2000 machines, the built-in local administrator account is designated as a recovery agent, so you can always log on as Administrator and decrypt any encrypted files stored on the machine. You can add other users as recovery agents by using the Local Security Policy console, which you can open by using Start → Run → secpol.msc. Then, expand Security Settings → Public Key Policies → Encrypted Data Recovery Agents, right-click on that node, and select Add to start the Add Recovery Agent Wizard. Any user accounts that already have X.509v3 certificates on the machine can then be added as recovery agents.

 On standalone Windows Server 2003 machines, the built-in Administrator account is not a designated recovery agent. In fact, there are no default recovery agents in Windows Server 2003 in a workgroup environment. You must designate an account for this role.

In a domain environment, things are a little different. The built-in Domain Administrator account is the default recovery agent for all machines in the domain, and you can specify additional recovery agents by using Group Policy. Open the Group Policy Object for the domain, OU, or site in which the intended recovery agent account resides, and navigate to Computer Configuration → Windows Settings → Security Settings → Public Key Policies → Encrypted Data Recovery Agents. Right-click on this node and select Add to start the same Add Recovery Agent Wizard as before, but this time browse the directory to locate the account you want to add.

Once Group Policy refreshes, your new recovery agent will be able to decrypt files encrypted by other users, but only if the users encrypted the file after the new recovery agent was designated. This is because files encrypted previously have no information about this new recovery agent in their headers and therefore can't be decrypted yet by the new recovery agent. Fortunately, if the user who encrypted the file simply opens and then closes it, this alone is sufficient for EFS to add the new recovery agent to the encrypted file's header.

The moral of the story is that you should think before you implement EFS, and designate recovery agents before you allow users to start encrypting files. Otherwise, you might find yourself sending out an unusual email to everyone saying, "Please open and then close all files you have encrypted on your machines" or something similar.

Backing Up Encrypted Data and EFS Keys

Backing up files that have been encrypted using EFS is easy: simply use the Backup utility to back them up like any other files. What's really important is that you also back up the EFS certificate and public/private key pair for each user who stores data on the machine. Since EFS is implemented on a per-user basis, you have to back up this information for each user individually.

Fortunately, as this information is stored in the user profile for each user, by simply backing up user profiles you also back up the users' EFS certificates and keys. More specifically, a user's EFS private key is stored in the \Application Data\Microsoft\Crypto\RSA subfolder within that user's profile, while the user's EFS public key certificate and public key are stored in the \Application Data\Microsoft\SystemCertificates\My Certificates\My folder under the subfolders \Certificates and \Keys.

You can back up users' EFS certificates and key pairs as part of your regular backup program, and if you have roaming user profiles configured, you can do this centrally from the file server where such profiles are stored. If you don't have roaming profiles implemented and users store important documents on their own machines, it might be necessary to have users back up their own profiles locally by using Backup to back up to file instead of tape. Unfortunately, this guards against profile corruption only, and it might not help if a disk failure causes the backed-up profile to be lost as well.

A better alternative is to have each user export his EFS certificate and private key to a floppy and store it somewhere safe. That way, if a user's system drive crashes, he can still decrypt information on his data drive by importing his previously exported EFS certificate and private key.

The steps to export a user's EFS certificate and private key are quite straightforward and can be done easily by any user. Simply open Internet Explorer, select Tools → Internet Options, switch to the Content tab, click the Certificates button, and select the Personal tab, as shown in Figure 2-10.

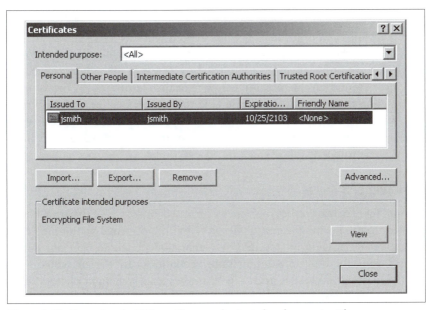

Figure 2-10. Exporting the EFS certificate and private key for user jsmith

Then, select the certificate you want to export (the correct certificate will display "Encrypting File System" beneath "Certificate intended purposes," near the bottom of the properties page) and click Export to begin the Certificate Export Wizard. Choose the option to include the user's private key in the export (the public key is automatically included in the certificate), specify a password to protect your export file, and choose a name and destination for your export file. The result of this export process will be a Personal Information Exchange (*.pfx*) file, located in the target folder or media.

As mentioned previously, users will typically export their EFS keys to a floppy, but you could burn them to a CD or even store them on a secure network share if you prefer. The important thing is, wherever you export this information, keep it safe so that no one except the user and trusted administrators can access it. Anyone who gets their hands on the export file and cracks the password can use it to decrypt any encrypted files they can access.

If a user's EFS keys later become corrupted and the need arises to reinstall these keys, this can be done either by repeating the previous process (but clicking Import instead of Export in Figure 2-10) or, more simply, by double-clicking on the *.pfx* file itself to start the Certificate Import Wizard. This wizard is smart enough to figure out that the EFS certificate and private key stored in the *.pfx* file should be imported into the user's personal certificate store.

An interesting option to consider when exporting a user's EFS certificate and private key is to delete the user's private key from his profile during the process. This option is labeled "Delete the private key if the export is successful" and is found on the penultimate page of the Certificate Export Wizard. If you choose this option, you'll be able to encrypt files by using EFS, but you won't be able to decrypt them unless you supply the private key on some medium—something that might be an option to consider in a high-security environment.

Restoring EFS Keys

If a user's EFS private key becomes corrupted or lost and the user hasn't backed up the key to a floppy as described in the previous section, it's time for the recovery agent to step in. On a standalone machine, you can simply log on using the built-in Administrator account, locate the encrypted folders the user can no longer access in Windows Explorer, right-click on each folder, select Properties, click Advanced, and clear the "Encrypt contents to secure data" checkbox for each folder. This decrypts the files within the folders and enables the user to read them again.

In a domain environment, you typically don't want to log onto a user's machine as a domain administrator and see a local user profile being created for your account as a result. Instead, simply instruct the user to use the Backup utility to back up to file any encrypted volumes or folders on her machine. The resulting backup (*.bkf*) file processes files it backs up as a data stream and preserves their encrypted status. Then, have the user copy her *.bkf* file to a network share where you, as domain administrator, can access the backup file, restore it to another folder, decrypt any files the user needs, and copy these files to the share where the user can access them.

While this is the most common solution, there's another approach that's worth considering: unite the user with her EFS keys again. Even if the user hasn't previously exported her keys to a floppy for safekeeping, chances are, in a domain environment, that you make regular backups of users' profiles (assuming roaming profiles are enabled). By simply restoring a user's profile from backup you restore her EFS certificate and keys, allowing her to read her encrypted files again. Then, tell her politely but firmly to immediately export her certificate and keys to a floppy, because you don't want to have to go through this again!

If EFS is being used to encrypt files on a file server where multiple users store their files, this process can become complicated if you've designated different recovery agents for different groups of users. In particular, you might need to determine which recovery agents are designated for any encrypted files that users can no longer access. To do this, you can use the *efsinfo* command-line utility included in the Windows 2000 Server Resource Kit. This handy little utility can tell you who originally encrypted a file and who the designated recovery agents for the file are. Just type `efsinfo/r /ufilename`, where `filename` includes the path to the encrypted file. Once you know any recovery agent for the file, you can proceed to decrypt it as shown previously.

What if the individual who can't access her encrypted files is your boss and she needs access to her files immediately? Export your own EFS certificate and private key to floppy as a domain administrator or other recovery agent, walk the floppy over to your boss's office, insert the floppy into her machine, import the certificate and private key, and decrypt her files. Then, delete the certificate and key from her machine. When she tries to encrypt a file again, a new EFS certificate and private key will automatically be generated. Smile, because you've acted like Superman, and send her an email later asking for a raise.

But what if your own EFS certificate and private key as domain administrator or recovery agent is lost or corrupted?

Backing Up Recovery Agent Keys

Obviously, it's a good idea for administrators and other recovery agents to also make backup copies of their own EFS certificates and private keys. Otherwise, a point of failure exists in this whole recovery process, and users' encrypted files could be lost forever and unrecoverable.

If you're operating in a workgroup environment, recall that the built-in local Administrator account is the default recovery agent in Windows 2000. This means you have to back up the EFS certificate and private key of the Administrator account, so log onto the machine using this account and use Start → Run → secpol to open Local Security Policy as before. Select the Encrypted Data Recovery Agents node under Public Key Policies in the left pane, right-click the EFS certificate in the right pane, and select All Tasks → Export to start the Certificate Export Wizard. Choose the option to export the private key as well, specify a password to protect the export file, and specify a filename and destination to export the information to—typically, some form of removable media, such as a floppy. Keep that floppy safe.

In a domain environment, the built-in Domain Administrator account is the default recovery agent and the EFS certificate and private key are located on the first domain controller in the domain (the one that created the domain when you ran dcpromo on it). Log onto this machine using that account, use Start → Run → dompol.msc to open the Domain Security Policy, select Encrypted Data Recovery Agents in the left pane, right-click the EFS certificate in the right pane, again select All Tasks → Export to start the Certificate Export Wizard, and proceed as before. If you are not given the option to export the private key, you might not be logged onto the right domain controller, so change machines and try again.

Another method for exporting certificates and keys is to use the Certificates snap-in. Open a blank MMC console, add this snap-in while logged on as Administrator, expand Certificates → Current User → Personal → Certificates, and find the certificate you want to back up by looking under the Intended Purposes column, as shown in Figure 2-11. The power of this approach is that you can also use it to back up and restore other sorts of certificates and keys, including EFS keys.

Now that you've backed up your recovery agent's EFS certificate and keys, you're ready for the worst—unless your dog eats your floppy!

—Mitch Tulloch

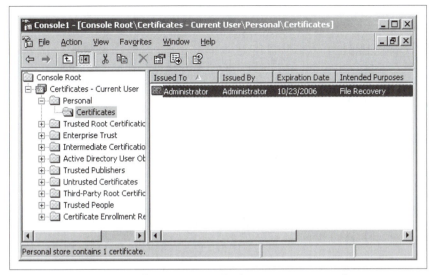

Figure 2-11. Using the Certificates snap-in to back up a recovery agent key

Clear the Paging File at Shutdown

Prevent information leaks by automatically clearing the swap file before shutting down.

Virtual memory management (VMM) is truly a wonderful thing. It protects programs from one another and lets them think that they have more memory available than is physically in the system. To accomplish this, VMM uses what is called a *paging file*.

As you run more and more programs over the course of time, you'll begin to run out of physical memory. Since things can start to go awry when this happens, the memory manager will look for the least frequently used pieces of memory owned by programs that aren't actively doing anything at the moment and write the chunks of memory out to the disk (i.e., the virtual memory). This is known as *swapping*.

However, there is one possibly bad side effect of this feature: if a program containing confidential information in its memory space is running, the memory containing such information may be written out to disk. This is fine when the operating system is running and there are safeguards to prevent the paging file from being read, but what about when the system is off or booted into a different operating system?

This is where this hack comes in handy. What we're going to do is tell the operating system to overwrite the paging file with zeros when it shuts down. Keep in mind that this will not work if the cord is pulled from the system or the system is shut down improperly, since this overwrite will only be done during a proper shutdown.

To enable this feature of Windows, you must edit the system Registry. Open the Registry and find the HKEY_LOCAL_MACHINE\SYSTEM\CurrentControlSet\ Control\Session Manager\Memory Management key. You should now see the screen shown in Figure 2-12.

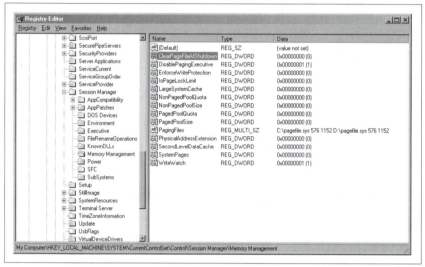

Figure 2-12. The Memory Management Registry key

Locate the ClearPageFileAtShutdown entry in the right pane of the window and change its value to 1. Now, restart Windows for the change to take effect, and your swap file will be cleared at shutdown.

The only side effect of enabling this is that Windows may take longer to shut down. However, this is very much dependent on your hardware (e.g., disk controller chipset, disk drive speed, processor speed, etc.), since that's what will govern how long it will take to overwrite your paging file with zeros.

HACK #36   Check for Passwords That Never Expire

Here's a handy script that makes it simple to find user accounts with nonexpiring passwords.

User accounts set to never expire are sometimes used for permanent employees of a company, while temporary employees are assigned accounts that expire after a specified period of time. Ever wish you could quickly and simply find out which user accounts have their passwords set to never expire, along with the dates the flags were set? Here is a sample script that accomplishes this and more.

This script prompts for the desired domain, checks all user accounts in the domain to see if their passwords are set to never expire, and reports the date the flags were set. It then writes the output to a comma-separated values (CSV) file called *PWDNeverExpired.csv*, creating this file in the same directory where the script itself is located. For each password that is not set to expire the script records a Yes. If the password is set to expire, the script instead records a No and the date the password will expire.

The Code

To use the script, type it into Notepad (with Word Wrap turned off) and save it as *PWDNeverExpired.vbs*:

```
' Set WshShell
Set WshShell = WScript.CreateObject("WScript.Shell")
strVer = "Ver 1.0 "
Set FileSystem = WScript.CreateObject("Scripting.FileSystemObject")
Set oFile = FileSystem.CreateTextFile("PWDNeverExpired.csv", true)

' Pull Environment variables for domain/user
strDomain = WshShell.ExpandEnvironmentStrings("%USERDOMAIN%")
strUserName = WshShell.ExpandEnvironmentStrings("%USERNAME%")
strOS = WshShell.ExpandEnvironmentStrings("%OS%")

strMessage = strMessage & "Hit Cancel or enter a blank to quit"
strTitle = "Domain to Search"
'get resource domain name, domain default
UserDomain = InputBox(strMessage, strTitle, strDomain)
strMessage = ""
strTitle = ""

'strMessage = "Please enter the USER Login ID" & vbCrLf & vbCrLf & _
'"Default is: " & strUserName & vbCrLf & vbCrLf
'strMessage = strMessage & "Hit Cancel or enter a blank to quit"
'strTitle = "USER Login ID"
'get resource domain name, domain default via input box
'objUserName = InputBox(strMessage, strTitle, strUserName)

' Display Just a minute!
strMessage = "This may take a few seconds. . ."
WshShell.Popup strMessage,2,"One moment please. . . "
strMessage = ""

Set ObjDomain = GetObject("WinNT://" & UserDomain)
ObjDomain.Filter = Array("User")
For Each ObjUser In ObjDomain
```

```
' Attempt to bind to the user
'Set objUser = GetObject("WinNT://"& UserDomain &"/"& objUser.Name, user)
Set UserName = GetObject("WinNT://" & UserDomain & "/" & ObjUser.Name & _
",User")

' Is password set to NEVER expire?
objPwdExpires = UserName.Get("UserFlags")
If (objPwdExpires And &H10000) <> 0 Then
objPwdExpiresTrue = "Yes"
strPwdExpires = "Date Set: "
msgPwdExpires = "Password Set to Never Expire: "
Else objPwdExpiresTrue = "No"
strPwdExpires = "Password Expires: "
msgPwdExpires = "Password Set to Never Expire: "
End If
oFile.WriteLine (UserName.fullname & "," & UserName.name & ","
& _ msgPwdExpires & objPwdExpiresTrue & "," & strPwdExpires & _
objUser.PasswordExpirationDate)
'Wscript.Echo "Full Name: " & UserName.fullname & vbCrlf &
'"Account Name: " & UserName.name & vbCrlf &
'msgPwdExpires & objPwdExpiresTrue & vbCrlf &
'strPwdExpires & objUser.PasswordExpirationDate & vbCrlf
Set UserName = Nothing
Next
Wscript.Echo "Done Checking Accounts"
```

Running the Hack

To run this hack, simply create a shortcut to the script and double-click on the shortcut. Figure 2-13 shows a sample CSV output file for the script, viewed in Excel.

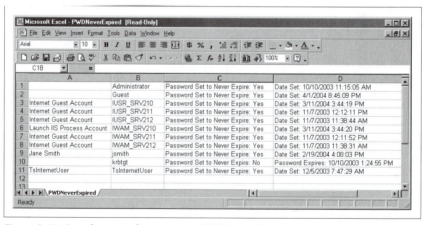

Figure 2-13. Sample output from running PWDNeverExpired.vbs

—*Hans Schefske*

Privacy and Anonymity
Hacks 37–43

It's been said before, but it's truer now than ever: the Internet can be a scary place. Performing banking transactions, filing taxes, paying bills, and buying and selling goods online—all of these things were unheard of in the early days of the Internet. However, as people and businesses have become increasingly savvy in the electronic world, so have the crooks that prey on them. In addition, the increased scrutiny of people's online identities by governments, employers, and other organizations might make you think twice about what you say the next time you post on a public message board.

Because of this, it's important to take precautions to safeguard your identity and take control of your information online. This chapter provides you with a few ways to do just that. In this chapter, you'll learn how to protect your privacy and remain anonymous while using the Internet. You'll also learn how to encrypt your files and email using strong encryption. Finally, you'll learn how to guard against phishing attacks and how to easily use different passwords for each web site you use without struggling to keep track of them.

HACK #37

Evade Traffic Analysis

Use transparent onion routing to evade traffic analysis and protect your privacy.

Privacy is something most people value, or at least think they do, but in our ever-connected world it's becoming quite a rare commodity. Every packet your computer sends out onto the Internet is ultimately traceable back to you (the Internet wouldn't work properly if it weren't), but that's just the tip of the iceberg. Since all your traffic must flow through your ISP, it's possible for them to build a complete picture of you from the web sites you visit.

One way to guard against traffic analysis is to use The Onion Router, Tor (*http://tor.eff.org*).

Onion Routing

Onion routing is a technique for anonymous communication that involves randomly building a virtual circuit through several routers to obfuscate the connection's source. Thus, someone monitoring your traffic will just see you communicating with the first hop in the circuit, and the final destination will think that it's communicating with the last hop in the circuit.

Before the data is transmitted, though, Tor negotiates encryption keys with each hop in the circuit to protect your data along the way. It then encrypts the packet with the key for the last hop in the circuit, then the next to last, and so on until the packet is encrypted with the key for the first hop in the circuit. This process creates a packet encapsulated in multiple layers of encryption.

This is what makes the onion metaphor apropos for describing this technique. As the packet passes through each hop of the circuit, the outermost encrypted layer is peeled off. This also has the nice side effect of each hop in the circuit not having a complete picture of the circuit. An individual hop knows about only the previous hop and the next hop.

Installing Tor

Before compiling Tor, you'll need to have Zlib and OpenSSL installed on your system. (Most systems should have Zlib and OpenSSL already.) Tor also requires *libevent* (*http://monkey.org/~provos/libevent/*), which you can install by simply downloading the tarball, unpacking it, and doing the standard `./configure && make` and running `make install` as root. Once those prerequisites are out of the way, you can install Tor.

Before doing anything else, add a user and group to run Tor as. Then, run `./configure` and specify the user and group that you created:

```
$ ./configure --with-tor-user=tor --with-tor-group=tor
```

As the script executes, you might see the following error:

```
checking whether we need extra options to link libevent... configure: error:
Found linkable libevent in (system), but it doesn't run, even with -R.
Maybe specify another using --with-libevent-dir?
```

If you do encounter this, run `./configure` again and tell it where to find *libevent*:

```
$ ./configure --with-tor-user=tor --with-tor-group=tor --with-libevent-dir=/
usr/local
```

Once the *configure* script completes, run make, become root, and run make install.

You'll now need to create a directory for Tor to store its data in. For example:

```
# mkdir /var/run/tor && chown tor:tor /var/run/tor
```

Installing Privoxy

If you plan to use Tor with a web browser, you should also install Privoxy (*http://www.privoxy.org*). Most web browsers support only SOCKS4 or SOCKS5, which use IP addresses to initiate connections through the proxy. This means that your web browser will have to perform name lookups using your normal DNS server, which can reveal your web-browsing activities to others. Using an HTTP proxy such as Privoxy to browse the Web fixes this problem, by forwarding the DNS requests and traffic through Tor.

To install Privoxy, first unpack the tarball and change into the directory that it creates. Then, run the following command:

```
$ autoheader && autoconf
```

You can safely ignore most of the warnings you'll see in the output. Just make sure that the *./configure* file exists after autoconf finishes executing.

Now you'll need to create a user and group to run Privoxy under (e.g., *privoxy*). Then, you can run ./configure:

```
$ ./configure --with-user=privoxy --with-group=privoxy
```

Once the *configure* script has finished, run make, become root, and run make install.

Configuring Privoxy for Tor

Now all that's standing between you and a working Tor installation is the task of configuring Privoxy. To do this, add the following line at the beginning of the */usr/local/etc/privoxy/config* file:

```
forward-socks4a / localhost:9050 .
```

This line tells Privoxy to forward all requests to a SOCKS4a proxy at 127.0.0.1:9050, which Tor has been configured to act as.

Privoxy will log all requests by default, so you'll also want to disable logging. You can do this by locating and removing the following lines:

```
logfile logfile
jarfile jarfile
```

Now, start Privoxy and Tor:

```
# /usr/local/sbin/privoxy --user privoxy privoxy /usr/local/etc/privoxy/
config
Apr 10 00:26:10 Privoxy(-1208432960) Info: loading configuration file '/usr/
local/etc/privoxy/config':
```

```
Apr 14 00:26:10 Privoxy(-1208432960) Info: Privoxy version 3.0.3
Apr 10 00:26:10 Privoxy(-1208432960) Info: Program name: /usr/local/sbin/
privoxy
Apr 10 00:26:10 Privoxy(-1208432960) Info: Listening on port 8118 for local
connections only
# /usr/local/bin/tor --user tor --group tor --datadirectory /var/run/tor
Apr 10 00:27:50.023 [notice] Tor v0.1.1.18-rc. This is experimental
software. Do not rely on it for strong anonymity.
Apr 10 00:27:50.024 [notice] Configuration file "/usr/local/etc/tor/torrc"
not present, using reasonable defaults.
Apr 10 00:27:50.027 [notice] Initialized libevent version 1.1a using method
epoll. Good.
Apr 10 00:27:50.027 [notice] connection_create_listener( ): Opening Socks
listener on 127.0.0.1:9050
Apr 10 00:27:56.626 [notice] We now have enough directory information to
build circuits.
Apr 10 00:28:01.463 [notice] Tor has successfully opened a circuit. Looks
like client functionality is working.
```

You can now configure your web browser to use Privoxy as its HTTP proxy.
When doing this, specify *localhost* as the hostname and port 8118. You can
then test out your Tor setup by visiting the Tor test page (*http://serifos.eecs.
harvard.edu/cgi-bin/ipaddr.pl?tor=1*). If you're connecting to it through Tor,
you should see something similar to Figure 3-1.

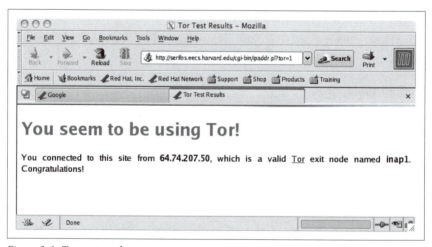

Figure 3-1. Tor test results

Tor can be used for much more than just anonymizing web browsing,
though. You can tunnel SSH through Tor [Hack #38] and use Tor with IRC clients, IM, and anything else that supports SOCKS. However, keep in mind
that Tor does not provide end-to-end encryption. Any unencrypted traffic
sent through Tor will only be protected until it exits the Tor network.

See Also

- "Tunnel SSH Through Tor" [Hack #38], for information on using Tor to anonymize SSH connections
- "Block Tor" [Hack #53], for information on blocking Tor for users on your network

Tunnel SSH Through Tor

Ensure your privacy when accessing shell accounts remotely.

"Evade Traffic Analysis" [Hack #37] shows how to set up Tor and Privoxy, with a focus on using Tor to anonymize web-browsing traffic. In this hack, we'll look at using Tor to anonymize SSH connections. This is useful if you have shell access to any Internet-facing servers but don't want the server operators to be able to build a profile of locations you might be coming from.

This hack makes use of SSH's little-used ProxyCommand option, which lets you specify a program to proxy connections though. When using this option, SSH will tunnel all traffic through to the program's standard input and output. The option takes the following form:

```
ProxyCommand <program> <args>
```

When specifying the arguments, you can make use of the %h and %p macros. SSH will expand these to be the host and port that you are connecting to when executing the command. One nice thing about implementing proxying this way is that it is incredibly flexible. Simply drop in a program that can connect to whatever type of proxy you're interested in using.

One simple program that can perform this task is *connect.c* (available at *https://savannah.gnu.org/maintenance/connect.c*), which can be used with SSH's ProxyCommand to direct SSH connections through a proxy server. Download it and compile it:

```
$ gcc -o connect connect.c
```

If that produces any errors, check the comments at the beginning of *connect.c* for tips on getting it to compile. Once you've done that, copy it to an appropriate place. Now, to use it with SSH to connect through Tor, run a command like this:

```
$ ssh -o ProxyCommand="/home/andrew/bin/connect -S localhost:9050 %h %p" \
10.0.0.23
```

Replace *localhost* with the address or hostname of your Tor server, if you're not running one on your local machine. Also note that the previous example command uses an IP address, instead of a hostname, to specify the server to connect to. This prevents *ssh* from resolving the IP address using your name server before passing it to the *connect* program. If you were to let *ssh* do the resolving, it might reveal the location you are connecting to, since Tor wouldn't protect the name resolution traffic.

So, what do you do if you don't know the IP address of the host to which you want to connect? There's an easy solution. Included with the Tor distribution is a program called *tor-resolve*. Its purpose is to resolve hostnames to IP addresses by making DNS queries through the Tor network.

The program takes only two arguments: the hostname to resolve and the SOCKS proxy connection information (i.e., the address and port on which your Tor proxy is listening). So, if your Tor proxy is running locally, you'd use something like this to resolve *www.google.com*:

```
$ tor-resolve www.google.com localhost:9050
64.233.161.99
```

Then, you can use the IP address returned by tor-resolve when running ssh.

See Also

- "Evade Traffic Analysis" [Hack #37], for information on setting up Tor and Privoxy
- "Block Tor" [Hack #53], for information on blocking Tor for users on your network

HACK #39   Encrypt Your Files Seamlessly

Use TrueCrypt to protect your data.

"Encrypt Your Temp Folder" [Hack #33] showed how to encrypt files using the Windows EFS, but it also touched on some problems with EFS, such as lack of support for the same algorithms across all versions of Windows on which it's available. One other big caveat is that the keys used by EFS are attached to your user account, so it leaves you unable to access the files on another system unless you decrypt them before moving them there.

Another good solution for seamless file encryption under Windows is True-Crypt (*http://www.truecrypt.org*). With TrueCrypt, you can choose either to create an encrypted disk volume (a container file) or to actually encrypt a whole disk device (USB memory drives are especially good for this). In addition, TrueCrypt supports a wide variety of encryption and hashing algorithms. What's more, it runs under Linux and it's free.

To set up TrueCrypt, download the *.zip* file from the project's download page, unzip the archive, and launch the installer: *TrueCrypt Setup.exe*. The installer features all of the options that you'd expect. You can choose whether to install it for your own account or for all users on the system, whether to create Start menu and desktop icons for it, where to install it, and a variety of other options.

After you've installed it, launching TrueCrypt brings up the window shown in Figure 3-2.

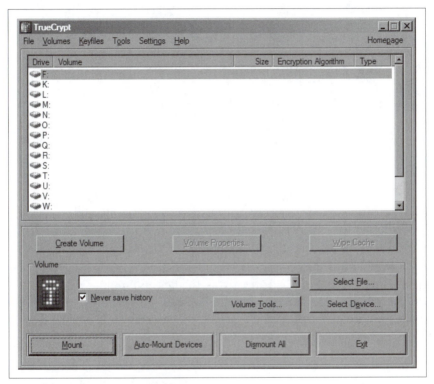

Figure 3-2. TrueCrypt's main window

This window lists all currently mounted TrueCrypt volumes. Since you've just installed it, you won't have any, so now it's time to create one. Click the Create Volume button to launch the Volume Creation Wizard. You should see the window shown in Figure 3-3.

The first option you'll be presented with is whether to create a *hidden volume*—one of the coolest features TrueCrypt has to offer. A hidden volume allows you to create an encrypted disk volume (the outer volume) with one password and hide another volume (with a different password) within the free space of the outer volume. This allows you to disclose the key to the outer volume if you're compelled to do so, but still leave the hidden volume

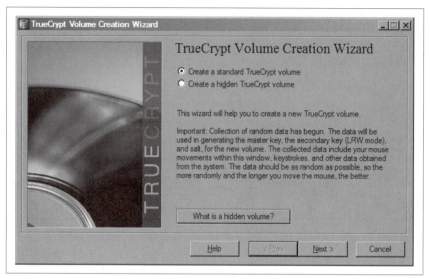

Figure 3-3. Creating a volume

undetected. The only major drawback to doing this is that the outer volume must be formatted using the FAT filesystem. However, the hidden volume can be formatted as either FAT or NTFS.

If you choose to create a hidden volume, you can either do so within a FAT-formatted volume that already exists, or choose to create a new outer volume and hidden volume. Whatever you decide, you'll still be going through the same volume-creation process used for standard volumes (you'll just do it twice in the latter case), so we'll cover creating a standard volume here.

Select the "Create a standard TrueCrypt volume" radio button and click Next. You should now see the dialog shown in Figure 3-4.

Here is where you can select the location of the container file where you want to store the encrypted disk image or which partition you want to encrypt. For now, try out a container file. Enter a name for your container file, and click Next.

You'll be presented with options for what algorithm to use for encryption and which hashing algorithm to use for generating the encryption key. In this example, Figure 3-5 shows that AES will be used for encryption and RIPEMD-160 will be used to generate the key.

If you want to see what encryption algorithm will likely yield the highest performance, click the Benchmark button. After the benchmarking window pops up, click the Benchmark button to display the screen shown in Figure 3-6.

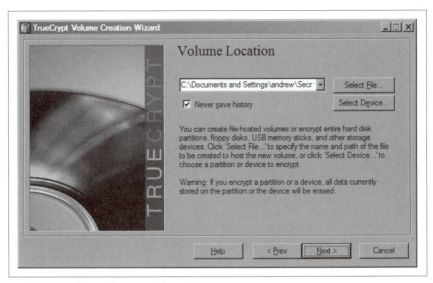

Figure 3-4. Selecting the image file or device to encrypt

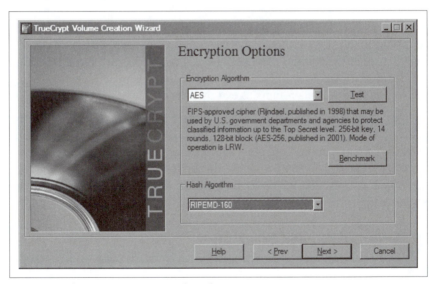

Figure 3-5. Choosing an encryption algorithm

On the system used here, it might be worthwhile to choose Blowfish instead of AES, because Blowfish is significantly faster at decryption. Once you've chosen which algorithms to use, click Next. You'll then be able to specify the size of the encrypted volume. Of course, if you're creating a hidden volume, you won't be able to make it any larger than the outer volume in which it's located.

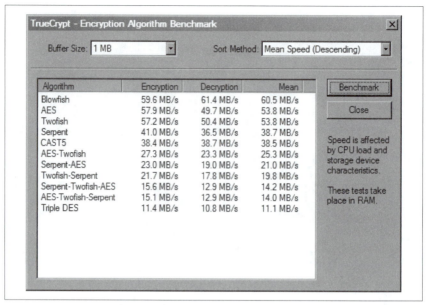

Figure 3-6. Encryption algorithm benchmarks

After specifying the size, you'll be prompted to set a password. Then it's time to format the volume. Choose either NTFS or FAT and specify the cluster size to use, and then click Format. After TrueCrypt finishes formatting the volume, follow the prompts to exit the wizard.

You can now go back to the main TrueCrypt window and select the encrypted container file or the device that you encrypted. Once you do that, click the Mount button. You'll be prompted for your password. If your password is accepted, you should see the details of the volume listed in the topmost pane of the window. Just double-click the drive letter to open it in the Explorer shell.

HACK #40 Guard Against Phishing

Protect your users from phishing attacks by deploying SpoofGuard.

Internet scams that use fraudulent web sites and emails to gain sensitive information, known as *phishing scams*, have become quite the epidemic in the past few years. And, with ever more sophisticated techniques such as *IDN spoofing*, it has become increasingly harder for the average end user to tell a fake web site from its legitimate counterpart.

To combat phishing, you need to know the signs to look out for. However, even with the best advice on how to spot a phishing scam, if you don't have foundational knowledge in how the Web operates it can be difficult to remember and spot all the warning signs.

One thing that would certainly help is to have an expert watch over your shoulder while you're surfing the Web, though that's obviously infeasible. The next best thing might be to use something like SpoofGuard (*http://crypto.stanford.edu/SpoofGuard/*).

SpoofGuard

SpoofGuard is an extension to Internet Explorer produced by the Security Lab at Stanford University. It allows users to spot suspicious sites easily by displaying a simple traffic signal indicator (e.g., green is safe, yellow is suspicious, and red is unsafe) that shows the safety level of the current site.

For example, Figure 3-7 shows the legitimate PayPal site (notice the green light on the toolbar), while Figure 3-8 shows a spoofed PayPal site.

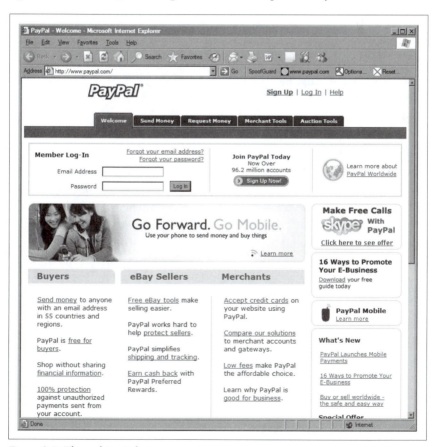

Figure 3-7. The real PayPal site

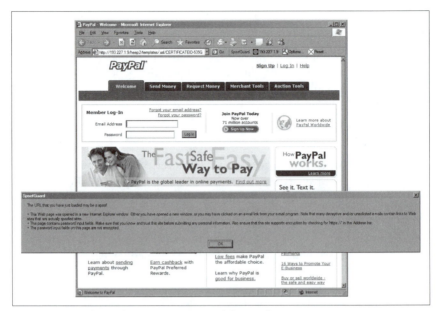

Figure 3-8. SpoofGuard's warning on a spoofed PayPal site

Aside from the URL, the spoofed site looks very convincing. However, notice that the light on the toolbar is now red and SpoofGuard has kindly popped up a warning that explains why it thinks that this site is a scam.

Installing SpoofGuard

Installing SpoofGuard is easy. Simply go to the download page, where both Default and Light versions are available. The Default version will report information back to the team at Stanford to help them gauge what methods are most effective in detecting spoofed web sites. If you don't want to do this, download the Light version, which doesn't report anything.

Once you've downloaded the installer, execute it and restart Internet Explorer. You should now see a toolbar like one shown earlier. If you don't, choose View → Toolbars → WarnBar Class.

You can begin configuring SpoofGuard by clicking the Options toolbar button, which brings up the window shown in Figure 3-9.

SpoofGuard works by performing a series of checks on the URL and the contents of the web page you are viewing. You can configure each of these tests with a weight in the Options window. When one of the tests returns positive, its weight is added to the total score for the page. If the page's score exceeds the Total Alert Level you've configured, SpoofGuard will warn you.

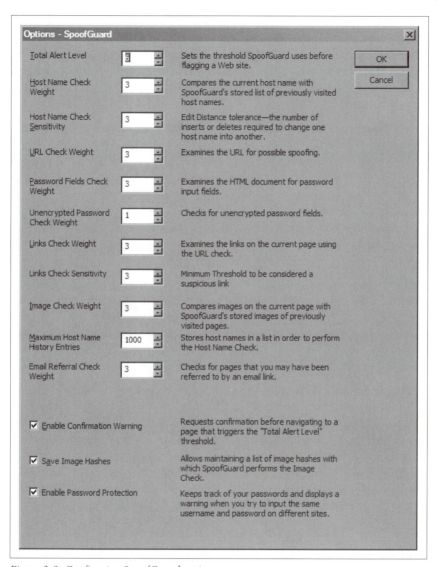

Figure 3-9. Configuring SpoofGuard options

How SpoofGuard Works

The first three tests are performed before the browser has even made the page request. When navigating to a site, SpoofGuard first checks the domain to see if it is similar to any domains in the browser history. It does this by computing the distances between the domain of the site being navigated to and the domains of sites in the browser history.

The *distance* is the number of changes that are required to transform one string into another one. For instance, *google.com* and *googIe.com* might appear to be the same in your address bar or on a web page, depending on what font is being used. The distance between these two domain names would be one, so the smaller the distance, the more similar it is to the legitimate site's domain.

Next, SpoofGuard checks the URL to make sure it does not have a suspicious username embedded in it (e.g., *http://www.paypal.com@10.0.0.1/...*), because such tricks are often used to fool users into thinking they're accessing a legitimate web site. In addition, SpoofGuard searches the URL for elements common to hostnames, such as *www* and commercially used TLDs to ensure that the domain of the site isn't obscured. Next, it checks to make sure that the URL refers to commonly used port numbers (e.g., port 80 for HTTP and 443 for HTTPS).

The other thing that SpoofGuard checks before loading the page is the referrer field. If this field is blank, either the user has entered the URL manually or she's followed it from an external application (e.g., an email client). SpoofGuard also checks to see if the referrer is a known web-based email site. If these checks cause SpoofGuard to flag the site as possibly being unsafe, you can choose to be alerted that the site might be unsafe and given the option to block it from loading.

Once a page finishes loading, SpoofGuard then performs a series of checks on the content of the page. It first looks for password fields and, if the page isn't secured with SSL, displays a warning if it finds one. Next, it analyzes all links on the page, looking for suspicious URLs according to the same criteria it uses for analyzing the page URL before it is loaded. Finally, Spoof-Guard generates hashes for the images on the current page and then looks through your browser cache and compares them to images on previously visited sites. If an image on the current page matches one on another site, a warning flag is raised.

In addition to all of these checks, you can configure SpoofGuard to monitor for usernames and passwords being used on more than one web site. Spoof-Guard monitors forms for elements that look like usernames and passwords and then combines them to generate a hash. It then compares the hash of the username and password on the page that you're visiting with previously generated values.

While SpoofGuard is a very powerful tool, it's not foolproof. Make sure that you educate your users to look out for signs of phishing. With some education and tools like SpoofGuard, they might just stand a chance.

Use the Web with Fewer Passwords

Help your users stay more secure by giving them fewer passwords to remember.

At first glance, this hack might seem counterintuitive. Shouldn't you be using strong passwords that are unique to every account? Well, yes you should, but let's face it: that's hard to do. IT security professionals should try to practice what they preach, but it can be unrealistic to expect the average corporate or home user to follow such practices, especially since nearly everything seems to require user registration these days. Unfortunately, this makes the issue much more problematic, because if the user is using the same password for multiple online accounts, discovery of that password can jeopardize all of them.

PwdHash

One tool that helps to improve this situation is PwdHash (*http://crypto. stanford.edu/PwdHash/*), from the Security Lab at Stanford University. PwdHash is an extension (available for Internet Explorer, Firefox, and Opera) that enables a user to easily use strong passwords that are unique to each web site with which they register.

PwdHash does this by reading any password fields in a web form and dynamically replacing them with a unique strong password. It generates the password by combining the user-specified password with the domain name of the web site and then generating a one-way hash from it. This also alleviates the users' worries about the security of their browsers' password stores: they no longer need to have their browsers remember their passwords, because in their minds, they each only have one password.

In addition, using PwdHash can help mitigate the result of phishing attacks [Hack #40]. If a user clicks on a link purporting to be a legitimate web site and ignorantly enters his password, PwdHash will replace it with its generated hash. Unless the phishers actually managed to take control of the legitimate site's domain, the phisher's domain used to compute the hash will be different, so the hash will be too.

Installing PwdHash is easy: just go to the site and click on the installer corresponding to the browser with which you want to use it. Depending on your browser's security systems, you might need to allow *crypto.stanford.edu* to install extensions. Once you've installed the extension, restart your browser. PwdHash is selectively triggered for password fields by either prefixing the password you enter with @@ or pressing the F2 key.

Remote PwdHash

One problem that implementing PwdHash locally presents is what to do when you're away from your computer. Remote PwdHash (*http://crypto. stanford.edu/PwdHash/RemotePwdHash/*), shown in Figure 3-10, solves this problem.

Figure 3-10. Remote PwdHash

Remote PwdHash is a web-based implementation of PwdHash's hashing algorithm. It's done in JavaScript and executed only within your browser, so you can rest assured that the password you enter won't be transmitted or stored anywhere. Enter the domain of the web site you want to access, along with the password, and it will generate the proper hash for you.

Though PwdHash and its remote cousin are incredibly simple, they're extremely powerful tools. PwdHash exhibits one of the main hallmarks of good security: usability. If the security policies you make aren't followed in spirit (as many password policies aren't), they're no good. This tool goes a long way toward keeping both administrators and end users happy.

HACK #42 Encrypt Your Email with Thunderbird

Use strong encryption with Mozilla's Thunderbird to protect your email from electronic eavesdroppers.

With the growth of the Internet, email has become ubiquitous. You would have to look very hard to find anyone that uses a computer but doesn't have an email address. However, as with any form of interpersonal communication, certain information shared between parties might be of a sensitive nature. Because of this, it's a wonder that most email is sent as unencrypted clear-text.

One way to get started easily with encrypted email is to use the Mozilla Foundation's Thunderbird email client (*http://www.mozilla.com/thunderbird/*) with the Enigmail extension (*http://enigmail.mozdev.org*). This extension enables Thunderbird to integrate strong encryption almost seamlessly by using powerful public-key encryption based on the OpenPGP standard.

Setting Up Thunderbird

Of course, the first thing you'll need to do, if you haven't already, is install Thunderbird and configure it to access your email account. The next step is to download GnuPG for Windows (*http://www.gnupg.org/download/index.html*). Once you've done that, launch the installer and follow the prompts presented by the installation wizard until it has completed installation.

Then, download the Enigmail extension (*http://enigmail.mozdev.org/download.html*) by right-clicking and saving it.

 If you're running Firefox and don't choose to save the extension, Firefox will incorrectly attempt to install it as a Firefox extension.

After you've done that, start Thunderbird, go to the Tools menu, and click Extensions. You should now see a window like the one shown in Figure 3-11.

Figure 3-11. The Thunderbird Extensions window

Click the Install button to open a file-selection dialog. Locate the file you just downloaded and click Open. You'll be presented with a dialog like the one shown in Figure 3-12.

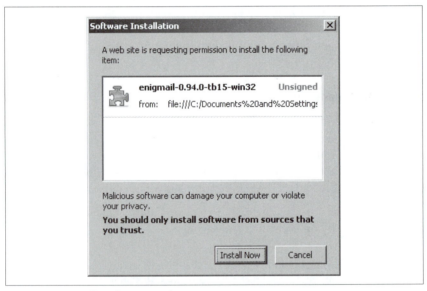

Figure 3-12. Installing the Enigmail extension

Click Install Now, and you should see Enigmail listed in the Extensions window.

To load the extension, restart Thunderbird. You should now see a new OpenPGP menu, as shown in Figure 3-13.

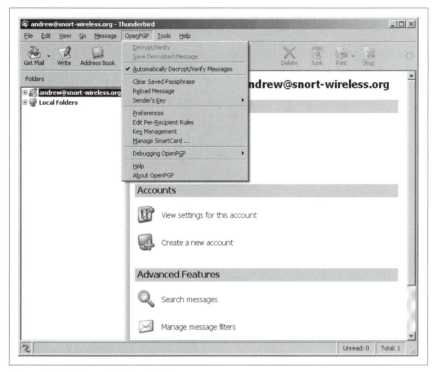

Figure 3-13. Enigmail's OpenPGP menu

Now you need to tell Enigmail where to find the GnuPG installation. Open the OpenPGP menu and choose Preferences. You should now see the dialog box shown in Figure 3-14.

Click the Browse button next to the "GnuPG executable path" item, locate the *gpg* executable (e.g., *C:\Program Files\GNU\GnuPG\gpg.exe*), and click OK.

Providing a Public/Private Key Pair

Now, you'll need to provide Enigmail with a *public/private key pair*. The public key is what others use to send encrypted email to you. Data encrypted with your public key can only be decrypted with your private key. Likewise, you can sign an email by encrypting it with your private key, so that others can decrypt it only with your public key. Since only you know your private key, this assures the receiver that the email is truly from you.

When using Enigmail you have the choice of importing an existing key pair or generating a new one.

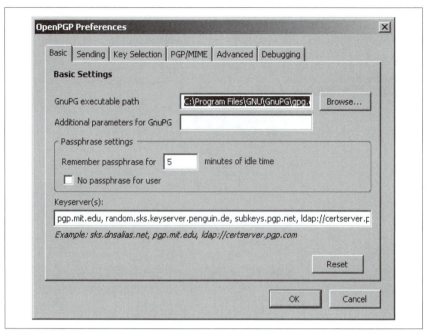

Figure 3-14. Telling Enigmail where gpg.exe is located

Importing an existing key pair. To import an existing key pair, open the Open-PGP menu and choose Key Management to bring up the window shown in Figure 3-15.

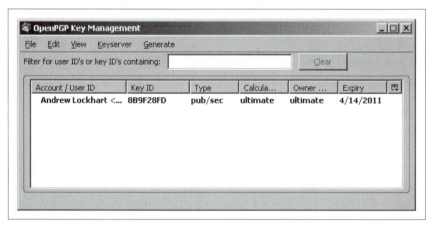

Figure 3-15. The key management window

Choose File → Import Keys From File and locate your key files in the file dialog that appears. After you import the key, you should see it listed in the key management window.

Generating a new key pair. If you need to generate a new key, go to the Open-PGP menu and choose Key Management. In the key management window, select Generate → New Key Pair. After doing so, you should see the dialog box shown in Figure 3-16.

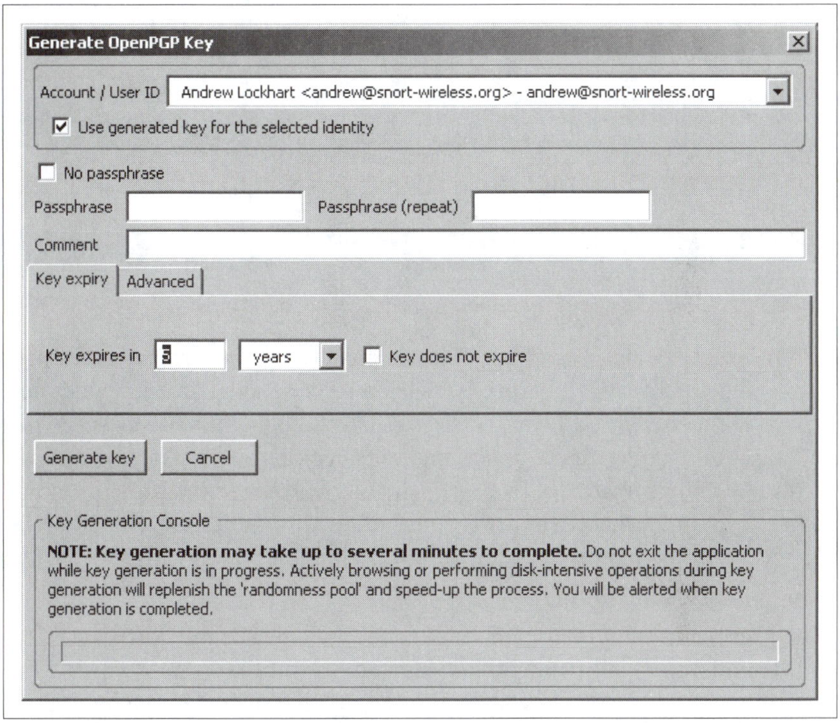

Figure 3-16. Generating a new key pair

In this menu, enter a password to protect your private key and indicate how long the key should be valid before it expires. Once you're done setting your password and expiration info, click the "Generate key" button. After the key is generated, it should appear in the list of keys displayed in the OpenPGP Key Management window.

Sending and Receiving Encrypted Email

You should now see an OpenPGP menu, as shown in Figure 3-17, when composing messages.

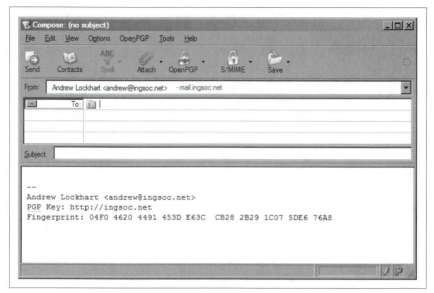

Figure 3-17. Composing an encrypted message in Thunderbird

Sign messages by clicking OpenPGP → Sign Message and encrypt messages by clicking OpenPGP → Encrypt Message. Before sending an encrypted message to someone, you'll need to import that person's public key into your keyring. You can do this by following the same method for importing your own public and private key pair (i.e., clicking File → Import Keys From File in the key management window). After you've imported the public key for the recipient, it will automatically be used for encrypting the message when you send it.

When receiving encrypted mail, all you need to do is click on the message and Thunderbird will prompt you for your private key's password. After accepting your password, it will display the unencrypted message for you.

HACK #43 Encrypt Your Email in Mac OS X

Use strong encryption to protect your email when using a Mac.

"Encrypt Your Email with Thunderbird" [Hack #42] shows how to set up GPG with Mozilla's Thunderbird by using the Enigmail extension. While Thunderbird is cross-platform and will run under Mac OS X, it might not be your cup of tea. This hack shows how to set up GPG with Apple's *Mail.app*, the default mail application included with Mac OS X.

Installing GPG

The first thing to do is to install a copy of GPG, a program that uses strong public-key encryption to protect your data. Simply download Mac GPG from *http://macgpg.sourceforge.net* and open the disk image. You should see the window shown in Figure 3-18.

Figure 3-18. Mac GPG installation window

Launch the installer by double-clicking on the *.mpkg* file. Follow the prompts, and be sure to choose your boot volume when presented with the choice of where to install GnuPG.

Creating a GPG Key

Before installing GPGMail, you'll need to create a public and private key pair, if you don't have one already. The public key is what others use to send encrypted email to you. Public keys can be decrypted with your private key. Likewise, you can sign an email by encrypting it with your private key, so that others can decrypt it only with your public key. Since only you know your private key, this assures the receiver that the email is truly from you.

You can do this by running the following command from the command line, which can be accessed by opening *Terminal.app*:

```
$ gpg --gen-key
```

Then, just follow the prompts. The default choices should generally be okay.

Alternatively, you can create a GPG key using GPG Keychain Access, which is available from the Mac GPG site. Just download it and launch the application bundle. You'll be presented with a dialog like the one shown in Figure 3-19.

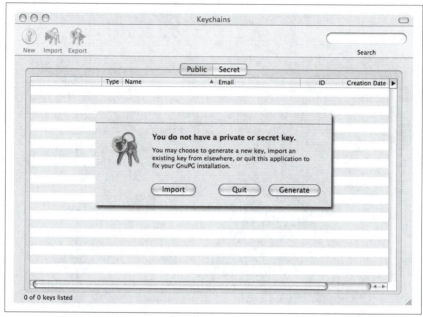

Figure 3-19. Creating a GPG key

When you click the Generate button, Mac GPG will walk you through the rest of the process.

Installing GPGMail

Now that you have a key, you can install GPGMail. Download it from *http://www.sente.ch/software/GPGMail/* and open the disk image file. Then, double-click the Install GPGMail icon. This AppleScript will copy the *GPGMail.mailbundle* file to the *Library/Mail/Bundles* folder in your home directory and then enable plug-in support for *Mail.app*.

The next time you launch *Mail.app*, you should see a new section called PGP in its Preferences panel, as shown in Figure 3-20.

Make sure that the key that you created appears in the drop-down list. For everything else, the default configuration should work fine. Now, find a friend with a GPG or PGP key to exchange encrypted email with, so that you can test it out.

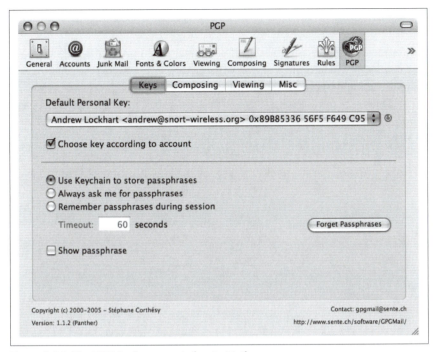

Figure 3-20. The PGP Preferences window in Mail.app

Sending and Receiving Encrypted Email

When composing messages, you'll now see two additional checkboxes, one for signing the message and another for encrypting it, as shown in Figure 3-21.

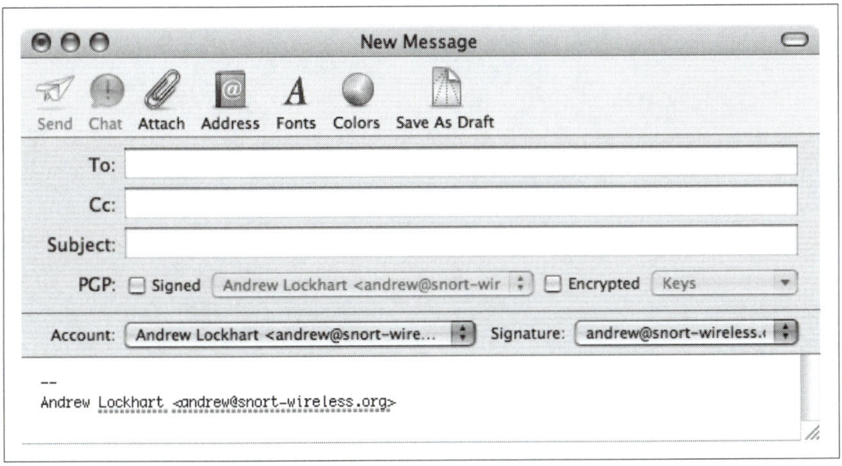

Figure 3-21. Composing an encrypted message in Mail.app

The drop-down boxes next to the checkboxes should automatically select the appropriate key for you.

When receiving encrypted mail, all you need to do is click on the message and *Mail.app* will prompt you for your private key's password. Then it will display the unencrypted message for you.

## CHAPTER FOUR

Firewalling
Hacks 44–53

When designing a network, it's often desirable to define policies governing how and where certain vital network services can be accessed. The *firewall* is a key technology that is instrumental in enforcing these policies and can allow network administrators to delineate trust relationships between networks and hosts with a fine grain of detail.

By instituting a firewall, you can prevent unauthorized access to services at the network level before an attacker is given the chance to attempt to exploit them. You can use a firewall not only to limit what information flows into a network, but also to prevent the egress of information. Doing so aids in preventing worm propagation and helps stop important confidential information from leaving an enterprise. Additionally, firewall logs can be excellent tools to help you understand where the threats to your network originate.

A variety of firewalls are available today. In addition to the many firewall appliances that are available, Linux, BSD, and Windows all include some form of firewalling support. This chapter shows how to set up firewalls with Linux, FreeBSD, OpenBSD, and Windows, as well as how to test your firewall rulesets. You'll also see how to perform MAC address filtering and how to create a gateway that will authenticate machines based on login credentials. Finally, you'll learn a few additional tricks to keep certain types of traffic from exiting your network.

 HACK #44

Firewall with Netfilter

Protect your network with Linux's powerful firewalling features.

Linux has long had the capability for filtering packets, and it has come a long way since the early days in terms of both power and flexibility. The first generation of packet-filtering code, called *ipfw* (for "IP firewall"), provided basic filtering capability. Since it was somewhat inflexible and inefficient for complex configurations, *ipfw* is rarely used now. The second generation of IP filtering was called *IP chains*. It improved greatly on *ipfw* and is still in common use. The latest generation of filtering, called *Netfilter*, is manipulated with the `iptables` command and used exclusively with the 2.4.x and later series of kernels. Although Netfilter is the kernel component and *iptables* is the user-space configuration tool, these terms are often used interchangeably.

An important concept in Netfilter is the *chain*, which consists of a list of rules that are applied to packets as they enter, leave, or traverse the system. The kernel defines three chains by default, but new chains of rules can be specified and linked to the predefined chains. The INPUT chain applies to packets that are received by and destined for the local system, and the OUTPUT chain applies to packets that are transmitted by the local system. Finally, the FORWARD chain applies whenever a packet will be routed from one network interface to another through the system. It is used whenever the system is acting as a router or gateway, and it applies to packets that are neither originating from nor destined for the local system.

The `iptables` command makes changes to the Netfilter chains and rulesets. Using `iptables`, you can create new chains, delete chains, list the rules in a chain, flush chains (i.e., remove all rules from a chain), and set the default action for a chain. `iptables` also allows you to insert, append, delete, and replace rules in a chain.

Setting the Filtering Policy

Before we get started with some example rules, it's important to set a default behavior for all the chains. To do this, use the -P (which stands for "policy") command-line switch:

```
# iptables -P INPUT DROP
# iptables -P FORWARD DROP
```

This ensures that only those packets covered by subsequent rules that you specify will make it past your firewall. After all, with the relatively small number of services that your network will likely provide, it is far easier to explicitly specify all the types of traffic that you want to allow than it is to specify all the traffic that you don't.

Note that you don't specify a default policy for the OUTPUT chain. This is because you'll want to allow traffic to proceed out of the firewall itself in a normal manner.

With the default policy set to DROP, you'll specify what is actually allowed. Here's where you'll need to figure out what services will have to be accessible to the outside world. For the rest of these examples, assume that eth0 is the external interface on the firewall and eth1 is the internal one. The sample network will contain a web server (192.168.1.20), a mail server (192.168.1.21), and a DNS server (192.168.1.18)—a fairly minimal setup for a self-managed Internet presence.

We'll begin specifying rules momentarily, but first, remove filtering from the loopback interface:

```
# iptables -A INPUT -i lo -j ACCEPT
# iptables -A OUTPUT -o lo -j ACCEPT
```

Rule Examples

Now, let's construct some rules to allow this traffic through. First, make a rule to allow traffic on TCP port 80—the standard port for web servers—to pass to the web server unfettered by the firewall:

```
# iptables -A FORWARD -m state --state NEW -p tcp \
-d 192.168.1.20 --dport 80 -j ACCEPT
```

And now for the mail server, which uses TCP port 25 for SMTP:

```
# iptables -A FORWARD -m state --state NEW -p tcp \
-d 192.168.1.21 --dport 25 -j ACCEPT
```

You might also want to allow remote POP3, IMAP, and IMAP+SSL access:

POP3
```
# iptables -A FORWARD -m state --state NEW -p tcp \
-d 192.168.1.21 --dport 110 -j ACCEPT
```

IMAP
```
# iptables -A FORWARD -m state --state NEW -p tcp \
-d 192.168.1.21 --dport 143 -j ACCEPT
```

IMAP+SSL
```
# iptables -A FORWARD -m state --state NEW -p tcp \
-d 192.168.1.21 --dport 993 -j ACCEPT
```

Finally, allow DNS access via port 53:

```
# iptables -A FORWARD -m state --state NEW -p tcp \
-d 192.168.1.21 --dport 53 -j ACCEPT
```

Unlike the other services, DNS can use both TCP and UDP port 53. Using a default deny policy makes it slightly more difficult to use UDP for DNS. This is because the policy relies on the use of state-tracking rules, and since UDP is a stateless protocol, there is no way to track it. In this case, you can configure the DNS server either to use only TCP, or to use a UDP source port of 53 for any response that it sends back to clients that were using UDP to query the name server.

If the DNS server is configured to respond to clients using UDP port 53, you can allow this traffic through with the following two rules:

```
# iptables -A FORWARD -p udp -d 192.168.1.18 --dport 53 -j ACCEPT
# iptables -A FORWARD -p udp -s 192.168.1.18 --sport 53 -j ACCEPT
```

The first rule allows traffic destined for the DNS server into your network, and the second rule allows responses from the DNS server to leave the network.

A Word About Stateful Inspection

You might be wondering what the -m state and --state arguments are about. These two options allow us to use Netfilter's stateful packet-inspection engine. Using these options tells Netfilter that you want to allow only new connections to the destination IP and port pairs that you have specified. When these rules are in place, the triggering packet is accepted and its information is entered into a state table.

Now, you can specify that you want to allow any outbound traffic that is associated with these connections by adding a rule like this:

```
# iptables -A FORWARD -m state --state ESTABLISHED,RELATED -j ACCEPT
```

The only thing left now is to allow traffic from machines behind the firewall to reach the outside world. To do this, use a rule like the following:

```
# iptables -A FORWARD -m state --state NEW -i eth1 -j ACCEPT
```

This rule enters any outbound connections from the internal network into the state table. It works by matching packets coming into the internal interface of the firewall that are creating new connections. If you were setting up a firewall that had multiple internal interfaces, you could have used a Boolean NOT operator on the external interface (e.g., -i ! eth0). Now, any traffic that comes into the firewall through the external interface that corresponds to an outbound connection will be accepted by the preceding rule, because this rule will have put the corresponding connection into the state table.

Ordering Rules

In these examples, the order in which the rules were entered does not really matter. Since you're operating with a default DENY policy, all your rules have an ACCEPT target. However, if you had specified targets of DROP or REJECT as arguments to the -j option, you would have had to take a little extra care to ensure that the order of those rules would result in the desired effect.

Remember that the first rule that matches a packet is always triggered as the rule chains are traversed, so rule order can sometimes be critically important.

It should also be noted that rule order can have a performance impact in some circumstances. For example, the rule shown earlier that matches ESTABLISHED and RELATED states should be specified before any of the other rules, since that particular rule will be matched far more often than any of the rules that will match only on new connections. Putting that rule first will prevent any packets that are already associated with a connection from having to traverse the rest of the rule chain before finding a match.

To complete the firewall configuration, you'll want to enable packet forwarding. Run this command:

```
# echo 1 > /proc/sys/net/ipv4/ip_forward
```

This tells the kernel to forward packets between interfaces whenever appropriate. To have this done automatically at boot time, add the following line to */etc/sysctl.conf*:

```
net.ipv4.ip_forward=1
```

If your system doesn't support */etc/sysctl.conf*, you can put the preceding echo command in one of your startup *rc* scripts, such as */etc/rc.local*.

Another useful kernel parameter is rp_filter, which helps prevent IP spoofing. Running the following command enables source address verification by checking that the IP address for any given packet has arrived on the expected network interface:

```
# echo 1 > /proc/sys/net/ipv4/conf/default/rp_filter
```

You can also enable source address verification by editing */etc/sysctl.conf* on systems that support it, or else putting the changes in your *rc.local*. To enable rp_filter in your *sysctl.conf*, add the following line:

```
net.ipv4.conf.all.rp_filter=1
```

To save all of the rules, either write them to a shell script or use your Linux distribution's particular way of saving them. Do this in Red Hat by running the following command:

```
# /sbin/service iptables save
```

This saves all currently active filter rules to */etc/sysconfig/iptables*. To achieve the same effect under Debian, edit */etc/default/iptables* and set enable_iptables_initd=true.

After doing this, run the following command:

```
# /etc/init.d/iptables save_active
```

When the machine reboots, your *iptables* configuration will automatically be restored.

Firewall with OpenBSD's PacketFilter
#45   Use OpenBSD's firewalling features to protect your network.

PacketFilter, commonly known as *PF*, is the firewalling system available in OpenBSD. While it is a relatively new addition to the operating system, it has already surpassed IPFilter, the system it replaced, in both features and flexibility and has even become a part of FreeBSD as of 5.3-RELEASE. PF shares many features with Linux's Netfilter, and while Netfilter is more easily extensible with modules, PF outshines it in its traffic normalization capabilities and enhanced logging features.

OpenBSD supports PF out of the box. However, under FreeBSD, you'll need to enable at minimum the following kernel configuration options:

```
device pf
device pflog
```

If you don't have these options enabled, add them in and rebuild and reinstall your kernel. For more information on how to do that, see the "Building and Installing a Custom Kernel" section of the FreeBSD Handbook.

To communicate with the kernel portion of PF, you'll need to use the `pfctl` command. Unlike the `iptables` command that is used with Linux's Netfilter, `pfctl` is not used to specify individual rules, but instead uses its own configuration and rule specification language. To actually configure PF, you must edit */etc/pf.conf*.

Configuring PF

PF's rule specification language is actually very powerful, flexible, and easy to use. The *pf.conf* file is split up into seven sections, each of which contains a particular type of rule. You don't need to use all of the sections; if you don't need a specific type of rule, you can simply omit that section from the file.

The first section is for macros. In this section, you can specify variables to hold either single values or lists of values for use in later sections of the configuration file. Like an environment variable or a programming-language identifier, a macro must start with a letter and may contain digits and underscores.

Here are some example macros:

```
EXT_IF="de0"
INT_IF="de1"
RFC1918="{ 192.168.0.0/16, 172.16.0.0/12, 10.0.0.0/8 }"
```

You can reference a macro later by prefixing it with the $ character:

```
block drop quick on $EXT_IF from any to $RFC1918
```

The second section allows you to specify tables of IP addresses to use in later rules. Using tables for lists of IP addresses is much faster than using a macro, especially for large numbers of IP addresses, because when a macro is used in a rule, it will expand to multiple rules, with each one matching on a single value contained in the macro. Using a table adds just a single rule when it is expanded.

Thus, rather than using the macro from the previous example, you could define a table to hold the nonroutable RFC 1918 IP addresses:

```
table <rfc1918> const { 192.168.0.0/16, 172.16.0.0/12, 10.0.0.0/8 }
```

The const keyword ensures that this table cannot be modified once it has been created. Specify tables in a rule in the same way that they were created:

```
block drop quick on $EXT_IF from any to <rfc1918>
```

You can also load a list of IP addresses into a table by using the file keyword:

```
table <spammers> file "/etc/spammers.table"
```

If you elect not to use the const keyword, you can add addresses to a table by running a command such as this:

```
pfctl -t spammers -T add 10.1.1.1
```

Additionally, you can delete an address by running a command like this:

```
pfctl -t spammers -T delete 10.1.1.1
```

To list the contents of a table, you can run this command:

```
pfctl -t spammers -T show
```

In addition to IP addresses, you can also specify hostnames. In this case, all valid addresses returned by the resolver will be inserted into the table.

Global Options

The next section of the configuration file contains options that affect the behavior of PF. By modifying options, you can control session timeouts, defragmentation timeouts, state-table transitions, statistic collection, and other behaviors. Specify options by using the set keyword. The available options are too numerous to discuss all of them in any meaningful detail; however, we will discuss the most pertinent and useful ones.

One of the most important options is block-policy. This option specifies the default behavior of the block keyword and can be configured to silently drop matching packets by specifying drop. Alternatively, you can use return to specify that packets matching a block rule will generate a TCP reset or an ICMP unreachable packet, depending on whether the triggering packet is TCP or UDP. This is similar to the REJECT target in Linux's Netfilter.

For example, to have PF drop packets silently by default, add a line like this to /etc/pf.conf:

```
set block-policy drop
```

In addition to setting the block-policy, you can collect other statistics, such as packet and byte counts, for an interface. To enable this for an interface, add a line similar to this to the configuration file:

```
set loginterface de0
```

Note that you can collect these statistics on only a single interface at a time. If you do not want to collect any statistics, you can replace the interface name with the none keyword.

To better utilize resources on busy networks, you can also modify the session-timeout values. Setting the timeout interval to a low value can help improve the performance of the firewall on high-traffic networks, but at the expense of dropping valid idle connections.

To set the session timeout (in seconds), put a line similar to this one in /etc/pf.conf:

```
set timeout interval 20
```

With this setting in place, any TCP connection that is idle for 20 seconds will automatically be reset.

PF can also optimize performance on low-end hardware by tuning its memory use regarding how many states can be stored at any one time or how many fragments may reside in memory for fragment reassembly. For example, to set the number of states to 20,000 and the number of entries used by the fragment reassembler to 15,000, you could put these lines in your pf.conf file:

```
set limit states 20000
set limit frags 15000
```

Alternatively, you could combine these entries into a single statement like this:

```
set limit { states 20000, frags 15000 }
```

Traffic Normalization Rules

The next section is for traffic normalization rules. Rules of this type ensure that packets passing through the firewall meet certain criteria regarding fragmentation, IP IDs, minimum TTLs, and other attributes of a TCP datagram. Rules in this section are all prefixed by the scrub keyword. In general, just putting scrub all is fine. However, if necessary, you can get quite detailed in specifying what you want normalized and how you want to normalize it. Since you can use PF's general filtering-rule syntax to determine what types of packets a scrub rule will match, you can normalize packets with a great deal of control.

One of the more interesting possibilities is to randomize all IP IDs in the packets leaving your network for the outside world. In doing this, you can make sure that passive operating-system-determination methods based on IP IDs will break when trying to figure out the operating system of a system protected by the firewall. Because such methods depend on analyzing how the host operating system increments the IP IDs in its outgoing packets, and your firewall ensures that the IP IDs in all the packets leaving your network are totally random, it will be pretty hard to match them against a known pattern for an operating system.

IP ID randomization also helps to prevent enumeration of machines in a network address translated (NAT) environment. Without random IP IDs, someone outside the network can perform a statistical analysis of the IP IDs being emitted by the NAT gateway in order to count the number of machines on the private network.

To enable random ID generation on an interface, put a line like this in */etc/pf.conf*:

```
scrub out on de0 all random-id
```

You can also use the scrub directive to reassemble fragmented packets before forwarding them to their destinations. This helps prevent specially fragmented packets (such as packets that overlap) from evading intrusion-detection systems that are sitting behind the firewall.

To enable fragment reassembly on all interfaces, simply put the following line in the configuration file:

```
scrub fragment reassemble
```

If you want to limit reassembly to just a single interface, change it to something like:

```
scrub in on de0 all fragment reassemble
```

This will enable fragment reassembly for the de0 interface.

Filtering Rules

The next two sections of the *pf.conf* file involve packet queuing and address translation, but since this hack focuses on packet filtering, we'll skip those. This brings us to the last section, which contains the actual packet-filtering rules. In general, the syntax for a filter rule can be defined by the following:

```
action direction [log] [quick] on int [af] [proto protocol] \
    from src_addr [port src_port] to dst_addr [port dst_port] \
    [tcp_flags] [state]
```

In PF, a rule can have only two actions: block and pass. As discussed previously, the block policy affects the behavior of the block action. However, you can modify the block action's behavior for specific rules by specifying block along with the action, as in block drop or block return. Additionally, you can use block return-icmp, which will return an ICMP unreachable message by default. You can also specify an ICMP type, in which case that type of ICMP message will be returned.

For most purposes, you'll want to start out with a default deny policy; that way, you can later add rules to allow the specific traffic that you want through the firewall.

To set up a default deny policy for all interfaces, put the following line in */etc/pf.conf*:

```
block all
```

Now you can add rules to allow traffic through the firewall. First, keep the loopback interface unfiltered by using this rule:

```
pass quick on lo0 all
```

Notice the use of the quick keyword. Normally, PF will continue through the rule list even if a rule has already allowed a packet to pass, in order to see whether a more specific rule that appears later in the configuration file will drop the packet. The use of the quick keyword modifies this behavior, causing PF to stop processing the packet at this rule if it matches the packet and to take the specified action. With careful use, this can greatly improve the performance of a ruleset.

To prevent external hosts from spoofing internal addresses, you can use the antispoof keyword:

```
antispoof quick for $INT_IF inet
```

Next, you'll want to block any packets that have a nonroutable RFC 1918 IP address from entering or leaving your external interface. Such packets, unless explicitly allowed later, would be caught by your default deny policy.

However, if you use a rule to specifically match these packets and use the quick keyword, as follows, you can increase performance:

```
block drop quick on $EXT_IF from any to <rfc1918>
```

If you want to allow traffic destined for a specific web server (say, 192.168.1. 20) into the network, use a rule like this:

```
pass in on $EXT_IF proto tcp from any to 192.168.1.20 port 80 \
    modulate state flags S/SA
```

This will allow packets destined to TCP port 80 at 192.168.1.20 only if they are establishing new connections (i.e., if the SYN flag is set), and will enter the connections into the state table. The modulate keyword ensures that a high-quality initial sequence number (ISN) is generated for the session, which is important if the operating system in use at either end of the connection uses a poor algorithm for generating its ISNs.

Similarly, if you want to pass traffic to and from a particular email server (say, IP address 192.168.1.21), use this rule:

```
pass in on $EXT_IF proto tcp from any to 192.168.1.21 \
    port { smtp, pop3, imap2, imaps } modulate state flags S/SA
```

Notice that you can specify multiple ports for a rule by separating them with commas and enclosing them in curly braces. You can also use service names, as defined in /etc/services, instead of specifying the services' port numbers.

To allow traffic to a specific DNS server (say, 192.168.1.18), add a rule like this:

```
pass in on $EXT_IF proto tcp from any to 192.168.1.18 port 53 \
    modulate state flags S/SA
```

This still leaves the firewall blocking UDP DNS traffic. To allow it through, add a rule like this:

```
pass in on $EXT_IF proto udp from any to 192.168.1.18 port 53 \
    keep state
```

Notice that even though this is a rule for UDP packets, you have still used the state keyword. In this case, PF will keep track of the connection using the source and destination IP address and port pairs. Also, since UDP datagrams do not contain sequence numbers, the modulate keyword is not applicable. Using keep state instead specifies stateful inspection when not modulating ISNs. In addition, since UDP datagrams do not contain flags, simply omit them.

Now you'll want to allow connections initiated within the network to pass through the firewall. To do this, you need to add the following rules to let the traffic into the internal interface of the firewall:

```
pass in on $INT_IF from $INT_IF:network to any
pass out on $INT_IF from any to $INT_IF:network
```

```
pass out on $EXT_IF proto tcp all modulate state flags S/SA
pass out on $EXT_IF proto { icmp, udp } all keep state
```

In the past few releases, the popular passive OS fingerprinting tool p0f has been integrated into PF. This enables PF to ascertain the operating systems running on hosts sending traffic to or through a system running PF. Consequently, you can create PF rules that are operating-system-specific. For instance, if you want to block traffic from any system that isn't running Linux, you can use something like this:

```
block in
pass in from any os "Linux"
```

But beware that OS fingerprinting is far from perfect. It's entirely possible for someone to modify the characteristics of her TCP/IP stack to mimic another operating system [Hack #65].

Once you're done editing *pf.conf*, you can enable PF by running the following commands:

```
# pfctl -e
# pfctl -f /etc/pf.conf
```

The first line enables PF, and the second line loads your configuration. If you want to make changes to your configuration, just run `pfctl -f /etc/pf.conf` again. To enable PF automatically at startup under OpenBSD, add the following line to */etc/rc.conf.local*:

```
pf=YES
```

FreeBSD is slightly different. You'll instead need to add the following line to */etc/rc.conf*:

```
pf_enable="YES"
```

The next time you reboot, PF should be enabled.

As you can see, OpenBSD has a very powerful and flexible firewalling system. There are too many features and possibilities to discuss here. For more information, look at the excellent PF documentation available online, or the *pf.conf* manpage.

HACK #46   Protect Your Computer with the Windows Firewall

Windows XP SP2 turns on the Windows Firewall by default, so you're automatically protected from incoming attacks. Here's how to configure the Windows Firewall for maximum protection and flexibility and use it to log potential attacks and send information about the intruders to your ISP.

The moment you connect to the Internet, you're in some danger of intrusion, especially if you have a broadband connection. PCs with broadband connections are tempting targets, because their high-speed connections are ideal springboards for attacking other networks or web sites.

Whenever you're connected, your system is among many constantly being scanned for weaknesses by crackers (malicious hackers) and wannabes (often called *script kiddies*) sending out automated probes looking for vulnerable PCs. In fact, these kinds of probes are so common and incessant, you can think of them as the background radiation of the Internet.

One of the best ways to protect yourself against these probes and more targeted attacks is to use a firewall. Firewall software sits between you and the Internet and acts as a gatekeeper of sorts, allowing only nonmalicious traffic through.

In this hack, we'll look at how to get the most out of the Windows Firewall, the firewall built into XP SP2, which is turned on by default when you install SP2.

> Before SP2, the firewall was called the Internet Connection Firewall (ICF). It was much the same as the Windows Firewall, with some notable differences in how the firewall and its features were accessed.

The Windows Firewall offers basic Internet security by stopping all unsolicited inbound traffic and connections to your PC and network, unless your PC or another PC on the network initially makes the request for the connection. However, it will not block outgoing requests and connections, so you can continue to use the Internet as you normally would for browsing the Web, getting email, using FTP, or similar services.

The Windows Firewall has one serious drawback: it won't protect you against Trojans, such as the Back Orifice Trojan. Trojans let other users take complete control of your PC and its resources. For example, someone could use your PC as a launchpad for attacking web sites, making it appear as though you were the culprit, or could copy all your files and find out personal information about you, such as your credit card numbers if you store them on your PC. The Windows Firewall won't stop Trojans because it blocks only incoming traffic, and Trojans work by making outbound connections from your PC.

> To stop Trojans, get a third-party firewall, such as CORE FORCE [Hack #48].

When you install XP SP2, you're automatically protected because it turns on the Windows Firewall. However, it is possible to turn off the firewall. To make sure it's turned on, click Security Center from the Control Panel. When the Security Center appears, there should be a green light next to the Firewall button and it should say ON, as shown in Figure 4-1.

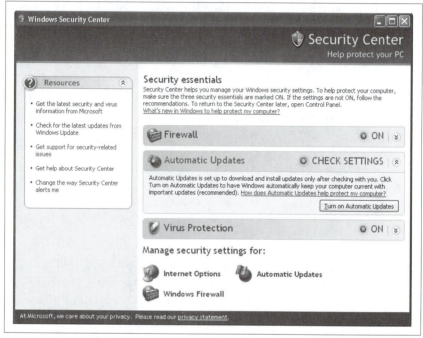

Figure 4-1. Making sure the Windows Firewall is turned on

If it's not on, click the Windows Firewall icon at the bottom of the screen, click ON, and then click OK.

Allow Programs to Bypass the Firewall

The Windows Firewall offers protection from inbound threats, but it can also cause problems. A variety of software needs to be able to accept inbound connections, and the firewall will initially prevent these programs from working. Instant messaging programs and FTP programs, for example, both need to be able to accept these kinds of connections, and the Windows Firewall blocks them.

Usually, but not always, the first time you run one of these programs, you'll get the warning from the Windows Firewall shown in Figure 4-2.

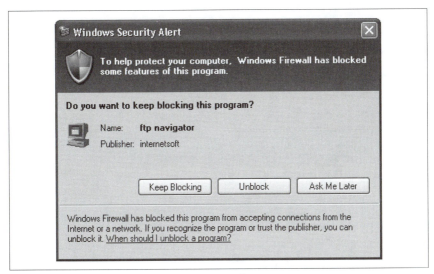

Figure 4-2. A warning from the Windows Firewall

The warning will show you the name of the program and the publisher and will ask if you want to keep blocking the program. If you'd like the Windows Firewall to let the program function, click Unblock. To keep blocking the program, click Keep Blocking. The Ask Me Later choice lets the program accept incoming connections for just this one time; after you exit, the next time you run the program, you'll get the same warning.

That's well and good, but the Windows Firewall won't always pop up this alert. So, you might find that some programs don't work with the firewall on, but you won't get a warning about them. Once you figure that out, you can manually tell the Windows Firewall to let those programs through by adding them to its exceptions list.

To do so, choose Control Panel → Security Center → Windows Firewall. Then click the Exceptions tab, shown in Figure 4-3.

> When you get a warning from the Windows Firewall and click Ask Me Later, the temporarily allowed program will be listed on the Exceptions tab, with no check next to it.

To add a program to the exceptions list, click Add Program to bring up the window shown in Figure 4-4.

This tab lists all the programs for which the firewall will accept inbound connections. If a program is listed here but doesn't have a check next to it, it means the firewall will block it. To tell the firewall to stop blocking inbound connections for the program, check the box next to it and click OK.

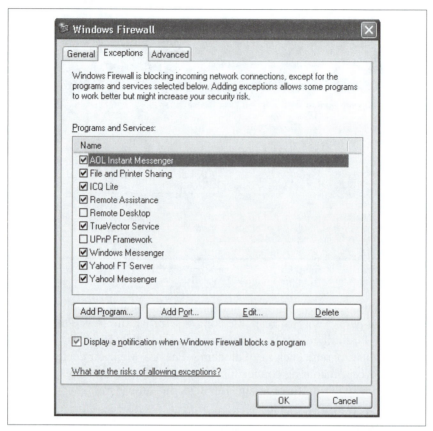

Figure 4-3. The Windows Firewall Exceptions tab

Choose a program from the list and click OK, and then click OK again to add it to your list. If the program you want to add isn't listed in the Add a Program dialog box, click the Browse button to find it and then add it.

There might be some programs for which you want to grant access to only certain people and not others. Maybe, for example, you want to allow an instant messaging program to work only with people on your own network. There's a way to do that.

First, add the program to the exceptions list. Then, highlight the program and choose Edit → Change Scope. The Change Scope dialog box appears, as shown in Figure 4-5.

Choose "My Network (subnet) only," click OK, and then click OK again, and the firewall will allow only inbound connections originating from your network. To allow inbound connections for the program for only specific IP addresses, choose "Custom list," type in the IP addresses you want to allow, and then click OK and OK again.

Figure 4-4. Choosing a program to add to your exceptions list

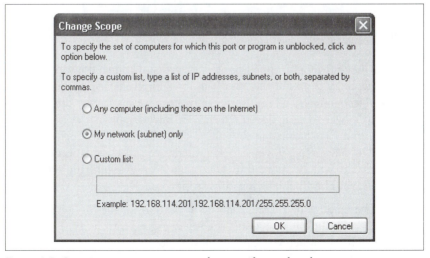

Figure 4-5. Granting access to your network to specific people only

Tracking Firewall Activity with a Windows Firewall Log

The Windows Firewall can do more than just protect you from intruders; it can also keep track of all intrusion attempts so that you know whether your PC has been targeted and what kinds of attacks the Windows Firewall has turned back. Then you can send that information to your ISP so they can track down the intruders.

First, create a Windows Firewall log. From the Security Center, choose Windows Firewall → Advanced, and click the Settings button in the Security Logging section. The dialog box shown in Figure 4-6 appears.

Figure 4-6. Creating a Windows Firewall log

Choose whether to log dropped packets, successful connections, or both. A *dropped packet* is a packet that the Windows Firewall has blocked. A *successful connection* refers to any connection you have made over the Internet, such as to a web site; it doesn't mean an intruder has successfully connected to your PC. Because of this, there's usually no reason for you to log successful connections. If you do log them, your log will become large quickly, and it will be more difficult to track only potentially dangerous activity. So, your best bet is to log only dropped packets.

After you've made your choices, choose a location for the log, set its maximum size, and click OK. I don't let my log get larger than 1 MB, but depending on how much you care about disk space and how much you plan to use the log, you might want yours to be larger or smaller.

The log will be created in a W3C Extended Log (*.log*) format that you can examine with Notepad or another text editor or by using a log analysis program such as the free AWStats (*http://awstats.sourceforge.net*). Figure 4-7 shows a log generated by the Windows Firewall, examined in Notepad.

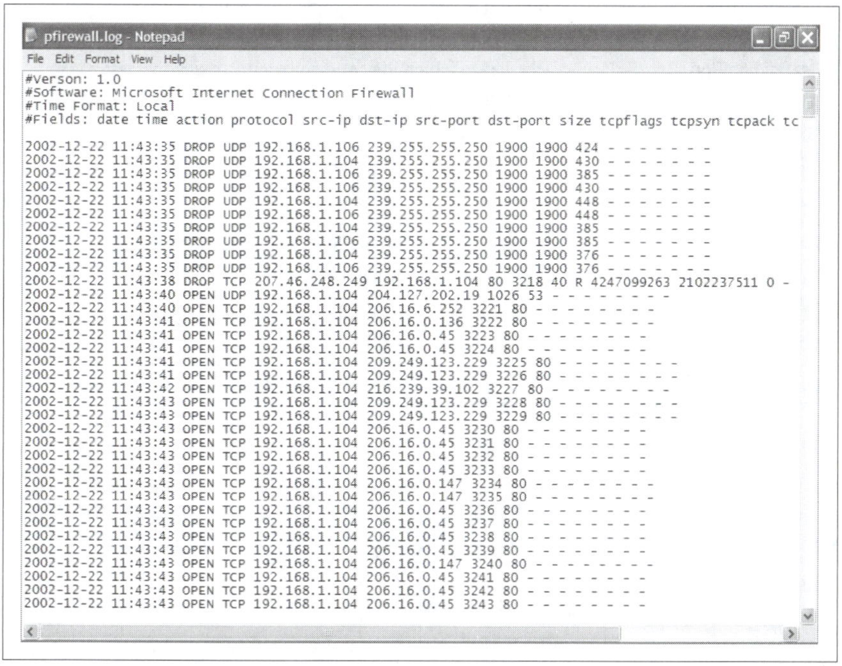

Figure 4-7. A log generated by the Windows Firewall

Each log entry has a total of up to 16 pieces of information associated with each event, but the most important columns for each entry are the first 8. (In a text editor, the names of the columns don't align over the data, but they will align in a log analyzer.)

Table 4-1 describes the most important columns.

Table 4-1. The columns in the Windows Firewall log

Name	Description
Date	Date of occurrence, in year-month-date format
Time	Time of occurrence, in hour:minute:second format
Action	The operation that was logged by the firewall, such as DROP for dropping a connection, OPEN for opening a connection, or CLOSE for closing a connection
Protocol	The protocol used, such as TCP, UDP, or ICMP
Source IP (src-ip)	The IP address of the computer that started the connection

Table 4-1. The columns in the Windows Firewall log (continued)

Name	Description
Destination IP (dst-ip)	The IP address of the computer to which the connection was attempted
Source Port (src-port)	The port number on the sending computer from which the connection was attempted
Destination Port (dst-port)	The port to which the sending computer was trying to make a connection
size	The packet size
tcpflags	Information about TCP control flags in TCP headers
tcpsyn	The TCP sequence of a packet
tcpack	The TCP acknowledgment number in the packet
tcpwin	The TCP window size of the packet
icmtype	Information about the ICMP messages
icmcode	Information about the ICMP messages
info	Information about an entry in the log

The source IP address is the source of the attack. If you notice the same source IP address continually cropping up, an intruder might be targeting you. It's also possible that the intruder is sending out automated probes to thousands of PCs across the Internet and your PC is not under direct attack. In either case, you can send the log information to your ISP and ask them to follow up by tracking down the source of the connection attempts. Either forward the entire log or cut and paste the relevant sections to a new file.

Problems with Email and the Windows Firewall

Depending on the email program you use and how it gets notification of new messages, the Windows Firewall could interfere with the way you retrieve your email. It won't stop you from getting your mail, but it could disable your email program's notification feature.

The Windows Firewall won't interfere with the normal notification feature of Outlook Express, because the initial request asking for notification of new email comes from Outlook Express, which is inside the firewall. When the server responds to the request, the firewall recognizes that the server is responding to the request from Outlook Express, so it lets the communication pass through.

However, if you use Outlook and connect to a Microsoft Exchange server using a remote procedure call (RPC) to send email notifications (which is usually the case with Exchange), you'll run into problems. Because the RPC initially comes from the server, not from Outlook, the firewall won't allow the notification to pass to you. In this case, you can still retrieve your email, but you'll have to check for new messages manually; you won't be able to get automatic notifications from the server. So, if you find that you stop getting new mail notifications after you install the Windows Firewall, it's not that coworkers, friends, and spammers are suddenly ignoring you; you'll just have to check for new mail manually.

Hacking the Hack

The Windows Firewall Exceptions tab is especially useful for anyone who uses file sharing on a home or corporate network but wants to turn it off when on a public network connection, such as a WiFi hotspot. When you get to a hotspot, before connecting, go to the Exceptions tab, uncheck the box next to File and Printer Sharing, and click OK. File sharing will be turned off. Then, when you get back to your home or business network, turn it back on again.

See Also

- For more information about the Windows Firewall, see Microsoft Knowledge Base Article 875357 (*http://support.microsoft.com/kb/875357*)

—Preston Gralla

HACK #47 Close Down Open Ports and Block Protocols

You don't need a firewall to protect your PC; you can manually close down ports and block certain protocols.

As noted in "Protect Your Computer with the Windows Firewall" **[Hack #46]**, firewalls can protect your PC and your network from intruders. But if you don't want to use a firewall and you still want protection, you can manually close down ports and block protocols.

Some of these ports and protocols are more dangerous than others. For example, if you leave open the port commonly used by telnet (port 23), someone could use that service to take control of your PC. Other risky ports include those used by the infamous Back Orifice Trojan, which also can give malicious users complete control of your PC. Back Orifice uses a variety of ports, including 31337 and 31338, among others. For a list of ports used by Trojans, go to *http://www.sans.org/resources/idfaq/oddports.php*.

In this hack, you'll need to know which ports you want to be open on your PC—such as port 80 for web browsing—and you'll close down all the others. For a complete list of well-known ports, go to *http://www.iana.org/assignments/port-numbers*.

To close down ports and protocols manually, right-click My Network Places and choose Properties to open the *Network Connections* folder. Right-click the connection for which you want to close ports and choose Properties. Highlight the Internet Protocol (TCP/IP) listing and choose Properties. On the General tab, click the Advanced button. Click the Options tab, highlight "TCP/IP filtering," and choose Properties. The TCP/IP Filtering dialog box appears. To block TCP ports, UDP ports, and IP protocols, choose the Permit Only option for each. Doing this will effectively block all TCP ports, UDP ports, and IP protocols.

You don't want to block all ports, though, so you have to add the ports you want to allow to pass. For example, you need to keep port 80 open if you want to browse the Web. Click Add to add the ports or protocols you will allow to be used, as shown in Figure 4-8. Keep adding as many ports and protocols as you want to be enabled, and click OK when you're done. You'll be able to use only the ports and protocols that are listed.

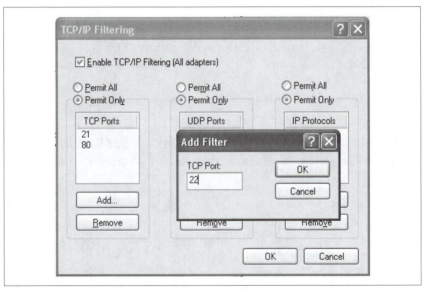

Figure 4-8. Blocking TCP ports, UDP ports, and IP protocols

Keep in mind that Internet applications and services use hundreds of TCP and UDP ports. If, for example, you enable only web access, you won't be able to use other Internet resources, such as FTP, email, file sharing, listening to streaming audio, viewing streaming video, and so on. So, use this hack only if you want your PC to use a very limited number of Internet services and applications.

—Preston Gralla

Replace the Windows Firewall

Block both incoming and outgoing traffic with CORE FORCE.

As of Windows XP SP2, Microsoft has done the world a favor by enabling the Windows Firewall [Hack #46] by default. However, the Windows Firewall can often give users a false sense of security, especially as the plagues of malware targeting Windows systems grow. While Windows XP's firewall is great at protecting systems from attacks against services, it does little to prevent keyloggers and other forms of malware from phoning home with your vital private information.

Where XP's firewall fails, CORE FORCE (*http://force.coresecurity.com*) from CORE Security excels. CORE FORCE includes a Windows port of Open-BSD's Packet Filter [Hack #45] in addition to a file and registry access monitor and an application binary integrity checker.

Installing CORE FORCE

Before you install CORE FORCE, exit any applications that need to maintain network connectivity in order to function properly, because the installation process might disrupt them. Then, install CORE FORCE by downloading the installer and launching it. Other than the previously noted caveat of losing network connectivity, the installation process is pretty normal; you select where to install the package files and it installs them.

As part of the process, CORE FORCE installs custom firewalling drivers into your network stack, so a dialog like the one shown in Figure 4-9 might alert you that hardware is being installed and ask if you want to stop the installation. This is a normal warning, so you can just click Continue Anyway. (You might be prompted multiple times; if so, just click the Continue Anyway button each time.)

The Configuration Wizard

After the installation has finished, you'll need to restart your computer. Once your system has finished booting up and you have logged in, you'll be presented with CORE FORCE's setup wizard, shown in Figure 4-10. This wizard helps you choose how restrictive you'd like the system to be and tell it about your network, DNS servers, and other servers that you access regularly, so that it can apply this information to its firewall rules.

After clicking Next, you'll be presented with a choice of which security level to use, Medium or High, as shown in Figure 4-11. For now, go ahead and select Medium. You can change this setting and make additional tweaks to your system's policy in CORE FORCE's configuration tool when the wizard's finished.

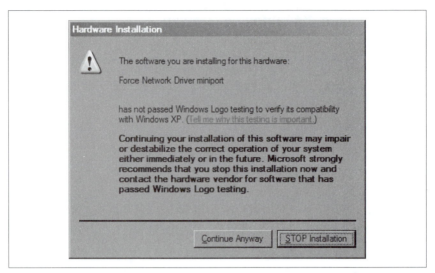

Figure 4-9. Window XP's hardware installation prompt

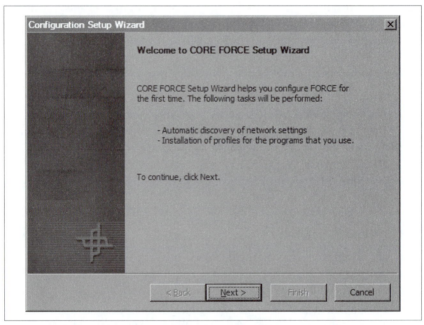

Figure 4-10. CORE FORCE's setup wizard

During the next step, the wizard prompts you to enter basic information about your network, as shown in Figure 4-12. This information includes the Classless Inter-Domain Routing (CIDR) address block your local network occupies, your broadcast address, and up to two name servers that you use.

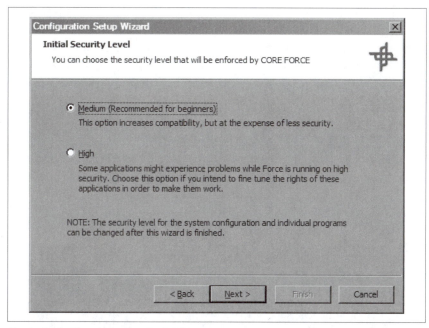

Figure 4-11. Choosing a security level

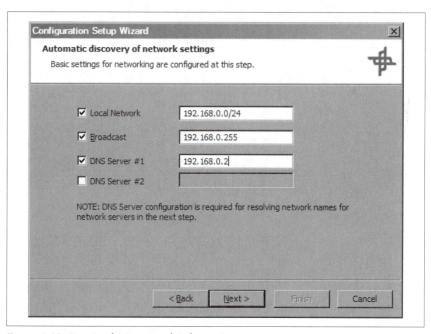

Figure 4-12. Entering basic network information

The next step (shown in Figure 4-13) prompts you for information about servers that you use, such as the hostnames of your incoming and outgoing mail servers, your news server and web proxy server (if you have them), and your domain controller.

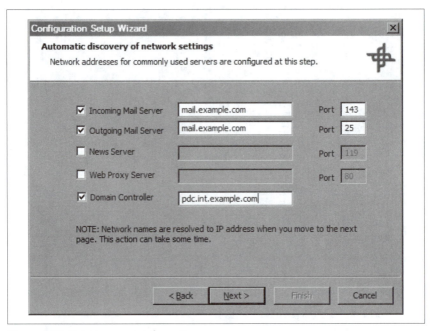

Figure 4-13. Entering server information

Items that require a port should have a default filled in for you, but you can change the port used if necessary. For instance, if you use IMAP or IMAP+SSL instead of POP3 for your incoming mail, change the port for your incoming mail server to either port 143 or 993, respectively.

After you've entered your server's information and clicked Next, the setup wizard scans your system for programs for which CORE FORCE has preconfigured profiles. For the most part, these preconfigured profiles limit their corresponding applications to performing only their core purposes. For instance, your email client should be able to connect to your incoming and outgoing mail servers only and, with the exception of saving attachments, it should write files only to certain well-known locations on your system. If someone attempts to exploit your mail client, this setting limits what the intruder can do.

When the setup wizard has finished looking for programs, you'll be presented with a dialog like the one shown in Figure 4-14.

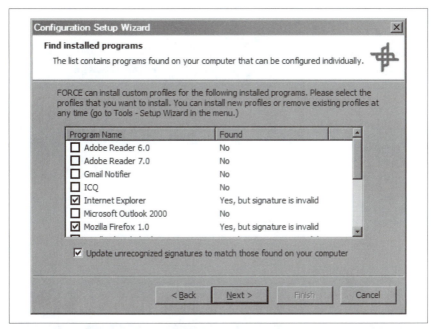

Figure 4-14. Selecting preconfigured application profiles

CORE FORCE adds a checkmark next to any program it locates. You might also see that some programs were found but that their signatures were invalid. Don't be alarmed about this. CORE FORCE maintains a database of valid program hashes for the applications for which it has preconfigured profiles, and it might display signatures as invalid simply because it does not have the signatures for the most recent versions of programs that are updated frequently (e.g., Internet Explorer and Firefox. You can update CORE FORCE's database to contain the signatures of what's currently on your system by checking the "Update unrecognized signatures..." box.

After you've finished selecting which profiles to install, click Next to import all of the profiles you have selected. Click Next again, then Finish, and you're done. CORE FORCE's configuration interface should appear, as shown in Figure 4-15.

Manual Configuration

CORE FORCE's configuration consists of a system-wide default security level and application-specific security levels. In turn, each security level consists of policies that have been assigned to it, such as "Cannot execute from temp," which define restrictions to be placed on the system or application. Things that can be defined for each policy include firewall rules, Registry access restrictions, and filesystem restrictions.

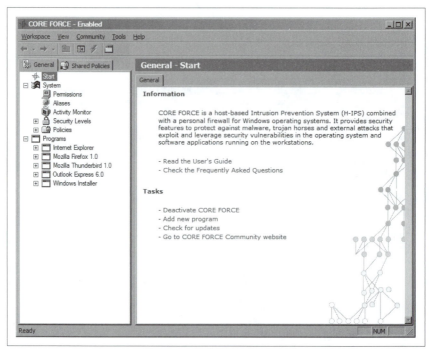

Figure 4-15. CORE FORCE's configuration interface

When going through the setup wizard, you selected a security level to use for the whole system. If you want to view exactly what policies a security level has, expand the Security Levels item in the tree view and then expand the security level that you want to examine. Figure 4-16 shows the policies comprising the Medium security level.

Look over the policies that your current security level enforces. If you decide that you want to change the security level for the entire system, right-click the System item in the tree view and choose Change Security Level. You should see a dialog like Figure 4-17. Use the slider to change the level.

If you want to make the current configuration more or less restrictive, you can modify it at either the system or application level by selecting the Permissions item in the tree view. For instance, Figure 4-18 shows the firewall permissions that are applied to any program that doesn't have its own settings defined.

To add a firewall rule, right-click within the pane displaying the firewall rules and choose New to insert a rule that allows any packet to pass through the firewall. You can then modify the rule by using the widgets located to the right of the rule list.

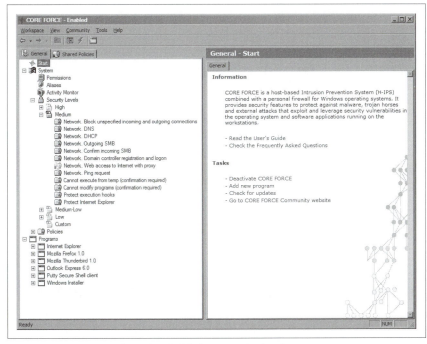

Figure 4-16. Viewing policies for the Medium security level

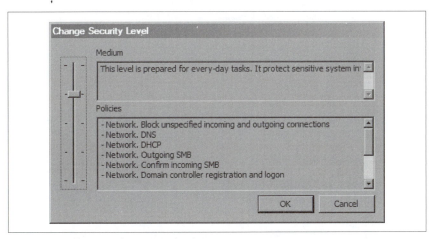

Figure 4-17. Changing the security level

One thing that CORE Security added when porting PF to Windows was a
new rule action: Ask. Choosing this action displays a dialog like Figure 4-19,
alerting you that an application is attempting to make a connection. From
the dialog, you can choose to either allow or deny the connection.

Replace the Windows Firewall

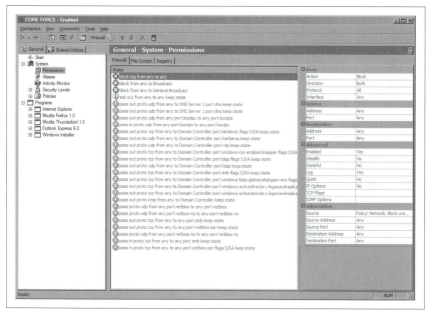

Figure 4-18. System firewall settings

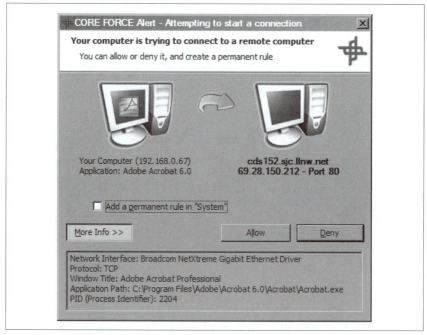

Figure 4-19. Allowing or denying a connection

This feature is especially useful for catching software phoning home, but you can also use it to spot an exploited program making network connections that it normally wouldn't.

As you can see, CORE FORCE is a powerful firewall and system-monitoring package. It provides a great deal of flexibility in terms of which system operations it can track and limit and is very configurable. Unfortunately, there's not enough space here to cover everything you can do with it, so be sure to take a look at CORE FORCE's excellent help file.

Create an Authenticated Gateway
Use PF to keep unauthorized users off the network.

Firewalling gateways have traditionally been used to block traffic from specific services or machines. Instead of watching IP addresses and port numbers, an *authenticated gateway* allows you to regulate traffic to or from machines based on a user's credentials. With an authenticated gateway, users have to log in and authenticate themselves to the gateway in order to gain access to the protected network. This can be useful in many situations, such as restricting Internet access or restricting a wireless segment to be used only by authorized users.

With the release of OpenBSD 3.1, you can implement this functionality via PF and the *authpf* shell. Using *authpf* also provides an audit trail by logging usernames and originating IP addresses, the time that each user authenticates with the gateway, and when users log off the network.

To set up authentication with *authpf*, you'll first need to create an account on the gateway for each user. Specify */usr/sbin/authpf* as the shell, and be sure to add authpf as a valid shell to */etc/shells*. When a user logs in through SSH, *authpf* will obtain the user's name and IP address through the environment.

After doing this, a template file containing NAT and filter rules is read in, and the username and IP address are applied to it. The resulting rules are then added to the running configuration. When the user logs out (i.e., types ^C), the rules that were created are unloaded from the current ruleset.

For user-specific rule templates, *authpf* looks in */etc/authpf/users/$USER/ authpf.rules*. Global rule templates are stored in */etc/authpf/authpf.rules*. Similarly, NAT entries are stored in *authpf.nat*, in either of these two directories. When a user-specific template is present for the user who has just authenticated, the template completely replaces the global rules, instead of just adding to them. When loading the templates, *authpf* will expand the $user_ip macro to the user's current IP address:

```
pass in quick on wi0 proto { tcp, udp } from $user_ip to any \
    keep state flags S/SA
```

This particular rule will pass in all traffic on the wireless interface from the newly authenticated user's IP address. This works particularly well with a default deny policy, where only the initial SSH connection to the gateway and DNS have been allowed from the authenticating IP address.

You could be much more restrictive and allow only HTTP-, DNS-, and email-related traffic through the gateway:

```
pass in quick on wi0 proto tcp from $user_ip to any \
    port { smtp, www, https, pop3, pop3s, imap, imaps } \
    keep state flags S/SA
pass in quick on wi0 proto udp from $user_ip to any port domain
```

After the template files have been created, you must then provide an entry point into *pf.conf* for the rules that *authpf* will create for evaluation by PF. These entry points are added to your *pf.conf* with the various anchor keywords:

```
nat-anchor authpf
rdr-anchor authpf
binat-anchor authpf
anchor authpf
```

Note that each anchor point needs to be added to the section to which it applies; you cannot just put them all at the end or beginning of your *pf.conf* file. Thus, the nat-anchor, rdr-anchor, and binat-anchor entries must go into the address translation section of *pf.conf*, while the anchor entry, which applies only to filtering rules, should be added to the filtering section.

When a user logs into the gateway, he should now be presented with a message like this:

```
Hello andrew, You are authenticated from host "192.168.0.61"
```

The user will also see the contents of */etc/authpf/authpf.message* if it exists and is readable.

If you examine */var/log/daemon*, you should also see log messages similar to these for when a user logs in and out:

```
Dec  3 22:36:31 zul authpf[15058]: allowing 192.168.0.61, \
    user andrew
Dec  3 22:47:21 zul authpf[15058]: removed  192.168.0.61, \
    user andrew- duration 650 seconds
```

Note that, since it is present in */etc/shells*, any user that has a local account is capable of changing his shell to *authpf*. If you want to ensure that a particular user cannot do this, you can create a file named after that user and put it in the */etc/authpf/banned* directory. The contents of this file will be displayed when the user logs into the gateway. Conversely, you can explicitly allow users by listing their usernames, one per line, in */etc/authpf/authpf.allow*. However, any bans that have been specified in */etc/authpf/banned* take precedence over entries in *authpf.allow*.

Since *authpf* relies on the SSH session to determine when the rules pertaining to a particular user are to be unloaded, care should be taken in configuring your SSH daemon to time out connections. Timeouts should happen fairly quickly, to revoke access as soon as possible once a connection has gone stale. This also helps prevent connections to systems outside the gateway from being held open by those conducting ARP spoof attacks.

You can set up OpenSSH to guard against this by adding these to lines to your *sshd_config*:

```
ClientAliveInterval 15
ClientAliveCountMax 3
```

This will ensure that the SSH daemon will send a request for a client response 15 seconds after it has received no data from the client. The `ClientAliveCountMax` option specifies that this can happen three times without a response before the client is disconnected. Thus, after a client has become unresponsive, it will disconnect after 45 seconds. These keepalive packets are sent automatically by the SSH client software and don't require any intervention on the part of the user.

authpf is powerful in its flexibility and integration with PF, OpenBSD's native firewalling system. It is easy to set up and has very little performance overhead, since it relies on SSH and the operating system to do authentication and manage sessions.

Keep Your Network Self-Contained

HACK #50
Use egress filtering to mitigate attacks and information leaks coming from your network.

By now you should be familiar with the concept of firewalling as it applies to blocking traffic coming into your network. But have you considered the benefits of filtering traffic that *leaves* your network? For instance, what would happen if someone compromised a host on your network and used it as a platform to attack other networks? What if a worm somehow made it onto your network and tried to infect hosts across the Internet? At the very least, you would probably receive some angry phone calls and emails.

Luckily, filtering your outbound traffic—otherwise known as *egress filtering*—can help to contain such malicious behavior. Egress filtering not only can protect others from attacks originating from your network, but also can be used to enforce network usage policies and make sure information doesn't leak out of your network onto the wider Internet. In many situations, egress filtering is just as important as filtering inbound traffic.

The general guideline when crafting egress-filtering rules is the same as when constructing any inbound-filtering rule: devices should be allowed to do only what they were meant to do. That is, a mail server should be allowed to serve and relay mail only, a web server should be allowed to serve web content only, a DNS server should service DNS requests only, and so on. By ensuring that this policy is implemented, you can better contain the threats mentioned earlier.

It might also be a good idea to force users to use internal services rather than Internet services wherever possible. For example, if you are using your own DNS servers, clients shouldn't be able to connect to external DNS servers to resolve hostnames. If clients are allowed to do this, you risk the chance that they will reveal intranet hostnames to outside parties when they attempt to resolve internal hostnames through an external DNS server.

This restriction can be accomplished in OpenBSD with a rule like this:

```
rdr on $INT_IF inet proto { tcp, udp } from $INT_IF:network to any port 53
-> $DNS_SERVER port 53
```

Of course, you'll need to set *INT_IF* to the interface facing your internal network and set *DNS_SERVER* to the IP address of your internal DNS server.

If you're using Netfilter [Hack #44], you'll have to use four rules to accomplish the same goal:

```
# iptables -t nat -A PREROUTING -p tcp -i $INT_IF --dport 53 -j DNAT \
--to-destination $DNS_SERVER:53
# iptables -t nat -A PREROUTING -p udp -i $INT_IF --dport 53 -j DNAT \
--to-destination $DNS_SERVER:53
# iptables -t nat -A POSTROUTING -p tcp -o $EXT_IF --sport 53 -j SNAT \
--to-source $SNAT_IP
# iptables -t nat -A POSTROUTING -p udp -o $EXT_IF --sport 53 -j SNAT \
--to-source $SNAT_IP
```

The first two rules specify that the destination address of any incoming packet destined for TCP or UDP port 53 should be rewritten to *DNS_SERVER*. However, this will cause any response to the rewritten packet to be sent to the host that initiated the connection. If the server to which the host originally intended to connect is not *DNS_SERVER*, the response from *DNS_SERVER* will be silently dropped.

The next two rules fix this by performing address translation on the source address of the packet before it is sent out. That sends *DNS_SERVER*'s response back to the host running Netfilter, and the host then translates the destination address back to the host that initiated the connection. You should set *SNAT_IP* to the IP address on the machine running Netfilter that is visible to *DNS_SERVER*.

Similarly, if you're running an internal mail server and want to monitor email that exits your enterprise, you'll need to prevent your users from sending email through external mail servers. In OpenBSD, can do this by using a similar rule to force all SMTP traffic to be redirected to your own SMTP server:

```
rdr on $INT_IF inet proto tcp from $INT_IF:network to any port 25 -> $SMTP_
HOST port 25
```

For Netfilter, the same result can be accomplished with these two rules:

```
# iptables -t nat -A PREROUTING -p tcp -i $INT_IF --dport 25 -j DNAT \
--to-destination $SMTP_HOST:25
# iptables -t nat -A POSTROUTING -p tcp -i $EXT_IF --sport 25 -j SNAT \
--to-source $SNAT_IP
```

Egress filtering can also prevent IP spoofing. By filtering on your external interface at the border of your network, you can verify that packets leaving your network have source addresses that match your address space. By filtering all other traffic, you can ensure that any IP spoofing attack performed from your network or routed through it will be dropped before the packets are able to leave.

Test Your Firewall

HACK #51

Find out if your firewall really works the way you think it should.

So, you've set up a firewall and done a few cursory tests to make sure it's working, but have you tested the firewall to be sure that it's blocking everything it's supposed to? You might not have done this because you think it will take too long or be too difficult. Luckily, there's *FTester* (*http://dev.inversepath.com/trac/ftester/*), a free tool for doing extensive firewall tests.

FTester consists of three Perl scripts. The *ftest* script is used for injecting custom packets as defined in the configuration file *ftest.conf*. If you are testing how the firewall behaves with ingress traffic, you should run this script on a machine outside of your firewalled network. If you want to test your firewall's behavior toward egress traffic, you will need to run *ftest* from a machine within your firewall's protected network.

One of the other scripts, *ftestd*, listens for the packets injected with *ftest* that
come through the firewall that you are testing. You should run this script on
a machine within your internal network if you are testing the firewall's
ingress behavior. If you are testing egress behavior, you'll need to run it on a
machine external to your network. Both of these scripts keep a log of what
they send or receive. After a test run, their respective logs can be compared
using the *freport* script, to quickly see what packets were able to get through
the firewall.

Before you can use FTester, you will need the Net::RawIP, Net::PcapUtils,
and NetPacket Perl modules. You will also need the Net::Pcap module if it is
not already installed, since the Net::PcapUtils module depends on it. If you
have the CPAN Perl module available, you can install these modules with
the following commands:

```
# perl -MCPAN -e "install Net::RawIP"
# perl -MCPAN -e "install Net::PcapUtils"
# perl -MCPAN -e "install NetPacket"
```

Once these modules are available on the systems you will be using to conduct your firewall test, you will need to create a configuration file to tell *ftest*
what packets it should generate.

Here's the general form for a TCP or UDP packet in *ftest.conf*, where *source
addr* and *source port* are the source IP address and port, and *dest addr* and
dest port are the destination IP address and port:

```
source addr:source port:dest addr:dest port:flags:proto:tos
```

Address ranges can be specified in the *low-high* format or by using CIDR
notation. You can also specify port ranges using the *low-high* format. The
flags field is where you specify the TCP flags that you want set for the
packet. Valid values for this field are S for SYN, A for ACK, P for PSH, U for URG, R
for RST, and F for FIN. The *proto* field specifies which protocol to use (either
TCP or UDP), and *tos* contains the number to set for the Type-of-Service (ToS)
field in the IP header. Sometimes, routers use the contents of this field to
make decisions about traffic prioritization. You can get more information on
the ToS field by reading RFC 791 (*http://www.ietf.org/rfc/rfc0791.txt*), which
defines the Internet Protocol.

You can define ICMP packets in a similar manner. Here's the general form
for one:

```
source addr::dest addr:::ICMP:type:code
```

As you can see, the main difference between the two forms is the omission
of port numbers and flags, which ICMP does not use. Instead, it uses types
and codes (hence the addition of the *type* and *code* fields). Currently, there

are over 40 ICMP types. The ones used by the *ping* utility, echo (type 8) and echo reply (type 0), or the type used by the traceroute command (type 30), might be familiar to you. ICMP codes are like subclassifications of ICMP types. Not all ICMP types have ICMP codes associated with them, although there are roughly the same number of ICMP codes as types. You can find out more about ICMP types and codes by reading the Internet Assigned Numbers Authority's assignments for them at *http://www.iana.org/assignments/icmp-parameters*.

Here's an *ftest.conf* that will check all of the privileged TCP ports on a machine with the IP address 10.1.1.1:

```
192.168.1.10:1025:10.1.1.1:1-1024:S:TCP:0
stop_signal=192.168.1.10:1025:10.1.1.1:22:S:TCP:0
```

stop_signal creates a payload for the packet that will tell *ftestd* that the testing is over. For quick tests, you can use the -c option and specify a packet to send using the syntax described previously. For instance, the following command sends a packet with the source IP address and port of 192.168.1.10:1025 to port 22 on 10.1.1.1.1:

```
# ./ftest -c 192.168.1.10:1025:10.1.1.1:22:S:TCP:0
```

Before starting *ftest*, you should start *ftestd*:

```
# ./ftestd -i eth0
```

Then, run *ftest*:

```
# ./ftest -f ftest.conf
```

This command creates a log file called *ftest.log* containing an entry for every packet *ftest* sent. When *ftestd* receives the signal to stop, it will exit. You can then find its log of what packets it received in *ftestd.log*.

Now, you can copy the logs to the same machine and run them through *freport*. If you used a configuration file like the one shown earlier and were allowing SSH, SMPTP, and HTTP traffic, you might get a report similar to this:

```
# ./freport ftest.log ftestd.log

Authorized packets:
-------------------

22 - 192.168.1.10:1025 > 10.1.1.1:22 S TCP 0
25 - 192.168.1.10:1025 > 10.1.1.1:25 S TCP 0
80 - 192.168.1.10:1025 > 10.1.1.1:80 S TCP 0

Modified packets (probably NAT):
--------------------------------
```

```
Filtered or dropped packets:
---------------------------

1 - 192.168.1.10:1025 > 10.1.1.1:1 S TCP 0
2 - 192.168.1.10:1025 > 10.1.1.1:2 S TCP 0
3 - 192.168.1.10:1025 > 10.1.1.1:3 S TCP 0
```

If you are using a stateful firewall and want to test this functionality, you can also specify packets that have flags other than SYN set. For instance, if the previous example had used ACK or some other flag instead of SYN, it would have been dropped by the firewall because only packets with the SYN flag set are used to initiate connections.

It's a good idea to run *ftest* each time you make changes to your firewall, or periodically just to make sure that your firewall works as you expect. While complex rulesets on your firewall can sometimes make it difficult to predict exactly how it will behave, *ftest* will tell you with good authority exactly what kinds of traffic are permitted.

HACK #52   MAC Filter with Netfilter

Keep unwanted machines off your network with MAC address whitelisting.

Media Access Control (MAC) address filtering is a well-known method for protecting wireless networks. This type of filtering works on the default deny principle: you specify the hosts that are allowed to connect, while leaving unknown ones behind. *MAC addresses* are unique 48-bit numbers that have been assigned to every Ethernet device that has ever been manufactured, including 802.11 devices, and are usually written as six 8-bit hexadecimal digits separated by colons.

In addition to Linux's native IP packet filtering system, Netfilter contains MAC address filtering functionality. While many of the wireless access points on the market today already support this, there are many older ones that do not. MAC filtering is also important if your access point is actually the Linux machine itself, using a wireless card. If you have a Linux-based firewall already set up, it's a trivial modification to enable it to filter at the MAC level. MAC address filtering with *iptables* is much like IP-based filtering and is just as easy to do.

The following example demonstrates how to allow a particular MAC address if your firewall policy is set to DROP [Hack #44]:

```
# iptables -A FORWARD -m state --state NEW \
-m mac --mac-source 00:DE:AD:BE:EF:00 -j ACCEPT
```

This command allows any traffic sent from the network interface with the address 00:DE:AD:BE:EF:00. Using rules like this along with a default deny policy enables you to create a whitelist of the MAC addresses that you want to allow through your gateway. To create a blacklist, you can employ a default accept policy and change the MAC address matching rule's target to DENY.

This is all pretty straightforward if you already know the MAC addresses for which you want to create rules, but what if you don't? If you have access to the system, you can find out the MAC address of an interface by using the ifconfig command:

```
$ ifconfig eth0
eth0      Link encap:Ethernet  HWaddr 00:0C:29:E2:2B:C1
          inet addr:192.168.0.41  Bcast:192.168.0.255  Mask:255.255.255.0
          UP BROADCAST RUNNING MULTICAST  MTU:1500  Metric:1
          RX packets:132893 errors:0 dropped:0 overruns:0 frame:0
          TX packets:17007 errors:0 dropped:0 overruns:0 carrier:0
          collisions:0 txqueuelen:100
          RX bytes:46050011 (43.9 Mb)  TX bytes:1601488 (1.5 Mb)
          Interrupt:10 Base address:0x10e0
```

Here you can see that the MAC address for this interface is 00:0C:29:E2:2B:C1. The output of ifconfig differs slightly on other operating systems, but much the same information is provided (this output is from a Linux system).

Finding the MAC address of a remote system is slightly more involved and can be done using the arp and ping commands. Pinging the remote system resolves its IP address to a MAC address, which can then be looked up using the arp command.

For example, to look up the MAC address that corresponds to the IP address 192.168.0.61, run the following commands:

```
$ ping -c 1 192.168.0.61
$ /sbin/arp 192.168.0.61 | awk '{print $3}'
```

Or use this very small and handy shell script:

```
#!/bin/sh
ping -c $1 >/dev/null && /sbin/arp $1 | awk '{print $3}' \
  | grep -v Hwaddress
```

When implementing MAC address filtering, be aware that it is not fool-proof. Under many circumstances, it is quite trivial to change the MAC address that an interface uses by simply instructing the driver to do so. It is also possible to send out link-layer frames with forged MAC addresses by using raw link-layer sockets. Thus, MAC address filtering should be considered only an additional (rather than a primary) network-protection mechanism. It's more like a "Keep Out" sign than a good deadbolt!

Block Tor

#53   Keep your users from bypassing egress filtering by blocking access to Tor.

Tor [Hack #37] is a great tool for protecting your privacy when using the Internet, but it can also provide a way for your users to circumvent security measures that you've put in place on your network, such as egress filtering [Hack #50] or proxies. Therefore, you might want a way to block your users from using it.

One simple way to do this is to block access to Tor's directory servers. When Tor starts up for the first time, it connects to one of these servers to get a list of all the possible nodes through which Tor can construct a virtual circuit. Logically, if you block access to all of these servers at the border, Tor will be unable to download the node list and won't be able to function.

If you look at *src/or/config.c* in the Tor source tree, you'll see a function called add_default_trusted_dirservers( ). This function contains the list of the directory servers:

```
const char *dirservers[] = {
    "moria1 v1 18.244.0.188:9031 "
      "FFCB 46DB 1339 DA84 674C 70D7 CB58 6434 C437 0441",
    "moria2 v1 18.244.0.114:80 "
      "719B E45D E224 B607 C537 07D0 E214 3E2D 423E 74CF",
    "tor26 v1 86.59.21.38:80 "
      "847B 1F85 0344 D787 6491 A548 92F9 0493 4E4E B85D",
    "lefkada 140.247.60.64:80 "
      "38D4 F5FC F7B1 0232 28B8 95EA 56ED E7D5 CCDC AF32",
    "dizum 194.109.206.212:80 "
      "7EA6 EAD6 FD83 083C 538F 4403 8BBF A077 587D D755",
    NULL
};
```

This list of servers can change, so be sure to check new releases of Tor to see if any have been added.

All you have to do is block them at your border firewall. For instance, you could use the following rules in PF:

```
table <tor_dirservers> { 18.244.0.188, 18.244.0.114, 86.59.21.38, 140.247.
60.64, 194.109.206.212 }
block from any to <tor_dirservers>
```

However, it will still be possible for someone who's already obtained a copy of the Tor node list to use Tor. To combat this situation, you can download the list manually from one of the directory servers, then individually block each Tor node, like so:

```
$ links -source http://18.244.0.114:80/ | egrep '^router '
router moria2 18.244.0.114 443 0 80
router anselcomputers 24.170.55.120 9001 0 0
router sic4gh 84.172.97.158 443 0 0
router Sivusto9022 80.222.75.74 9001 0 9030
router vader 149.9.0.21 9001 0 9030
router duglha 82.227.178.224 9001 0 9002
router nycbug 64.90.179.108 443 0 80
router BlueNeedle 12.222.100.156 6571 0 0
router 1984jhb 84.58.246.2 43567 0 0
router Pastis 82.67.175.80 9001 0 9030
...
```

The first item after the router keyword is the router's nickname, the next field is its IP address, and the remaining fields are the ports on which that particular router is listening for Tor connections. Here's a quick little Perl script to transform this into a more easily readable form:

```perl
#!/usr/bin/perl

while (<>) {

  if (/^router\ /) {
    @router_stmt = split( );
    for($i = 3; $i < $#router_stmt; $i++) {
      if ($router_stmt[$i] != 0) {
        print "$router_stmt[2]:$router_stmt[$i]\n";
      }
    }
  }
}
```

Here is what the output looks like when the script is executed:

```
$ links -source http://18.244.0.114:80/ | ~/src/tor_routers.pl
18.244.0.114:443
24.170.55.120:9001
84.172.97.158:443
80.222.75.74:9001
149.9.0.21:9001
82.227.178.224:9001
64.90.179.108:443
12.222.100.156:6571
84.58.246.2:43567
154.35.254.172:9001
...
```

This script can easily be modified to output firewall rules for whatever firewall you're using, be it Netfilter [Hack #44], PF [Hack #45], or something else. You'll also want to update the rules periodically to cover new nodes that have joined the Tor network.

## CHAPTER FIVE

Encrypting and Securing Services
Hacks 54–61

A network is only as secure as the weakest host connected to it. Therefore, it follows that a host is only as secure as the weakest service that it's running. After all, the only way into a system from the network (barring esoteric kernel-level network stack vulnerabilities) is through the services that it offers. Because of this, a large part of network security involves ensuring that your services are configured securely. This entails configuring services to provide only the functionality that's required of them to accomplish the tasks they need to perform. Additionally, you should give services access to only the bare minimum of system resources needed.

That's just part of the solution, though. If a network service operates in clear-text, all of your work spent locking it down can be for nothing. In most cases, all an attacker has to do to gain access to such a service is use a packet sniffer to capture the login details of a user authenticating with the service.

This chapter shows how to deploy IMAP, POP3, and SMTP servers that are protected with encryption, in order to prevent your users from accidentally disclosing their login credentials and keep their data safe from prying eyes. You'll also learn how to securely deploy DNS services and MySQL. In addition, you'll learn how to deploy Apache with SSL support and how to keep your users' CGI scripts from accessing files that they normally wouldn't be able to access.

HACK #54 Encrypt IMAP and POP with SSL

Keep your email safe from prying eyes while also protecting your POP and IMAP passwords.

Having your email available on an IMAP server is invaluable when you need to access it from multiple locations. Unlike POP, IMAP stores all your email and any folders you create on the server, so you can access all of your messages from whatever email client you decide to use. You can even set up a web-based email client so that you can access your messages from literally any machine with an Internet connection and a web browser. However, you'll almost certainly need to cross untrusted networks along the way. How do you protect your email and your account password from others with undesirable intentions? You use encryption, of course!

If you already have an IMAP or POP daemon installed that does not have the ability to use SSL natively, you can use stunnel [Hack #100] to wrap the service in an SSL tunnel. If you're starting from scratch, though, you have the luxury of choosing a daemon that has SSL support compiled directly into the binary.

One daemon that supports SSL out of the box is Dovecot (*http://www.dovecot.org*). Dovecot includes support for both IMAP and POP3 and has the added benefit that it was designed and written with security in mind from the very beginning. In pursuit of that goal, it makes use of best-of-breed secure coding practices as well as privilege separation and chroot( )-ing. Additionally, Dovecot is very flexible and supports a number of authentication methods, as well as both mbox and MailDir mailbox formats.

To compile and install Dovecot, download the compressed tar archive and run the following commands:

```
$ tar xfz dovecot-1.0.beta5.tar.gz
$ cd dovecot-1.0.beta5
$ ./configure && make
```

This will build Dovecot with facilities to support most commonly used authentication mechanisms. If you want to use LDAP or an SQL database for authentication, you can build a copy that supports those mechanisms as well. Run ./configure --help to see the full range of options.

Once you've compiled Dovecot, become root and run make install.

Next, to create self-signed certificates, run the following command:

```
$ openssl req -new -x509 -nodes -out /etc/ssl/certs/dovecot.pem -keyout \
/etc/ssl/private/dovecot.pem -days 3650
```

Alternatively, you can sign the certificates with your own Certificate Authority (CA) [Hack #69].

All that's left to do now is to create a *dovecot.conf* file. To do this, find the *dovecot-example.conf* file, which should be located in */usr/local/etc* (or wherever you told *configure* to install it), and copy it to *dovecot.conf*. Creating your own custom configuration is a fairly easy process, because the example configuration is replete with comments and displays the default values for each configuration variable.

Of particular interest is the protocols variable. By default this variable is set to support unencrypted IMAP and IMAP+SSL:

```
protocols = imap imaps
```

However, if you want to support POP3 or POP3+SSL, you can add pop3 and/or pop3s to the list of values. If you want to disable unencrypted IMAP, remove the imap value.

If you placed your SSL certificate and key in a location other than the one mentioned in the previous example, you'll need to tell Dovecot where to find them. To do this, modify the ssl_cert_file and ssl_key_file variables. For example, to use */usr/local/ssl/certs/myhostname.crt* and */usr/local/ssl/private/myhostname.key*, make the following changes:

```
ssl_cert_file = /usr/local/ssl/certs/myhostname.crt
ssl_key_file = /usr/local/ssl/private/myhostname.key
```

Now that you've done that, you'll need to create a user account called *dovecot* for the *imap-login* process to run under. This allows the *imap-login* process, which is responsible for handling client connections before they have been authenticated, to operate with the least amount of privileges possible.

One other thing to be aware of is that, if you are using mbox mailboxes, you'll need to set the mail_extra_groups variable to the group owner of your mail spool directory. For instance, if the group owner of */var/mail* is *mail*, use the following:

```
mail_extra_groups = mail
```

Setting this enables Dovecot to create locks when it is accessing a user's mail spool file.

Now that you've finished configuring Dovecot, you can launch the daemon by running */usr/local/sbin/dovecot*. You should then see log entries like these:

```
Apr 10 19:27:29 freebsd5-vm1 dovecot: Dovecot v1.0.beta5 starting up
Apr 10 19:27:29 freebsd5-vm1 dovecot: Generating Diffie-Hellman parameters
for the first time. This may take a while..
Apr 10 19:27:58 freebsd5-vm1 dovecot: ssl-build-param: SSL parameters
regeneration completed
```

That's the final task for the server end of things. All you need to do now is configure your email clients to connect to the secure version of the service that they were using. Usually, there will be a Use Encryption, Use SSL, or some other similarly named checkbox in the incoming mail settings for your client. Just check the box and reconnect, and you should be using SSL. Be sure your client trusts your CA certificate, though, or you will be nagged with annoying (but important!) trust warnings.

Use TLS-Enabled SMTP with Sendmail

#55 Protect your users' in-transit email from eavesdroppers.

If you have set up encrypted POP and IMAP services [Hack #54], your users' incoming email is protected from others once it reaches your servers, but what about their outgoing email? You can protect outgoing email quickly and easily by setting up your mail server to use Transport Layer Security (TLS) encryption. Virtually all modern email clients support TLS; enable it by simply checking a box in the email account preferences.

If you're using Sendmail, you can check to see if it has compiled-in TLS support by running this command:

```
$ sendmail -bt -d0.1
```

This prints out the options with which your *sendmail* binary was compiled. If you see a line that says STARTTLS, all you need to do is supply some additional configuration information to get TLS support working. If you don't see this line, you'll need to recompile *sendmail*.

Before recompiling *sendmail*, go into the directory containing *sendmail*'s source code and add the following lines to the *devtools/Site/site.config.m4* file:

```
APPENDDEF(`conf_sendmail_ENVDEF', `-DSTARTTLS')
APPENDDEF(`conf_sendmail_LIBS', `-lssl -lcrypto')
```

If this file doesn't exist, simply create it. The build process will automatically include the file. The first line in the previous example compiles TLS support into the *sendmail* binary, and the second line links the binary with *libssl.so* and *libcrypto.so*.

After adding these lines, you can recompile and reinstall *sendmail* by running this command:

```
# ./Build -c && ./Build install
```

You'll need to create a certificate/key pair [Hack #69] to use with *Sendmail* and then reconfigure Sendmail to use the certificate and key that you created. You can do this by editing the file from which your *sendmail.cf* file is generated, which is usually */etc/mail/sendmail.mc*. Once you've located the file, add lines similar to the following, to point to your Certificate Authority's certificate as well as the certificate and key you generated earlier:

```
define(`confCACERT_PATH', `/etc/mail/certs')
define(`confCACERT', `/etc/mail/certs/cacert.pem')
define(`confSERVER_CERT', `/etc/mail/certs/cert.pem')
define(`confSERVER_KEY', `/etc/mail/certs/key.pem')
define(`confCLIENT_CERT', `/etc/mail/certs/cert.pem')
define(`confCLIENT_KEY', `/etc/mail/certs/key.pem')
```

The first line tells *sendmail* where your Certificate Authority is located, and the second one tells it where to find the CA certificate itself. The next two lines tell *sendmail* which certificate and key to use when it is acting as a server (i.e., accepting mail from a mail user agent or another mail server). The last two lines tell *sendmail* which certificate and key to use when it is acting as a client (i.e., relaying mail to another mail server).

Usually, you can then rebuild your *sendmail.cf* by typing make sendmail.cf while inside the */etc/mail* directory. Now, kill *sendmail* and then restart it.

After you've restarted *sendmail*, you can check whether TLS is set up correctly by connecting to it:

```
# telnet localhost smtp
Trying 127.0.0.1...
Connected to localhost.
Escape character is '^]'.
220 mail.example.com ESMTP Sendmail 8.12.9/8.12.9; Sun, 11 Jan 2004 12:07:43
-0800 (PST)ehlo localhost
250-mail.example.com Hello IDENT:6l4ZhaGP3Qczqknqm/KdTFGsrBe2SCYC@localhost
[127.0.0.1], pleased to meet you
250-ENHANCEDSTATUSCODES
250-PIPELINING
250-EXPN
250-VERB
250-8BITMIME
250-SIZE
250-DSN
250-ETRN
250-AUTH DIGEST-MD5 CRAM-MD5
250-STARTTLS
250-DELIVERBY
250 HELP
QUIT
221 2.0.0 mail.example.com closing connection
Connection closed by foreign host.
```

When *sendmail* relays mail to another TLS-enabled mail server, your mail will be encrypted. Now, all you need to do is configure your mail client to use TLS when connecting to your mail server, and your users' email will be protected all the way to the message transfer agent (MTA).

While there isn't enough room in this hack to cover every MTA available, nearly all support some variant of TLS. If you are running Exim (*http://www.exim.org*) or Courier (*http://www.courier-mta.org*), you can build TLS support straight out of the box. Postfix (*http://www.postfix.org*) has TLS support and is designed to be used in conjunction with Cyrus-SASL (see the HOWTO at *http://postfix.state-of-mind.de/patrick.koetter/smtpauth/*). Qmail [Hack #56] also has a patch that adds TLS support. With TLS support in virtually all MTAs and email clients, there is no longer any good reason to send email "in the clear."

Use TLS-Enabled SMTP with Qmail

HACK #56

Protect your users' in-transit email from eavesdroppers the Qmail way.

If you want to protect your users' email with strong encryption, you might be wary of using a package with a less-than-illustrious security track record, such as Sendmail [Hack #55]. Another option is to use Qmail (*http://cr.yp.to/ qmail.html*).

Setting up Qmail to support TLS can seem daunting at first, because there is no "official" patch for doing so; all enhancements to Qmail are like this. This hack uses a patch that integrates SMTP AUTH and TLS, so that you can also require that your users authenticate with your SMTP server before it will allow them to relay mail through it.

First, download the patch (*http://shupp.org/smtp-auth-tls/*), change to the directory containing the Qmail source code, and apply the patch:

```
# cd /usr/local/src/netqmail-1.05/netqmail-1.05
# patch -p0 < ../../netqmail-1.05-tls-smtpauth-20060105.patch
```

Then, check to see if the patch applied cleanly:

```
# find . -name \*.rej
```

After you've verified that the patch was applied correctly, stop Qmail by running the following commands:

```
# svc -d /service/qmail-smtpd /service/qmail-smtpd/log
# svc -d /service/qmail-send /service/qmail-send/log
```

Now, run make setup check to reinstall it. If you need to generate x.509 certificates, you can run make -f Makefile-cert cert. This will prompt you for information to create a certificate/key pair that will be used to encrypt traffic between your Qmail server and other SMTP servers, as well as between it and your users' mail clients.

Once the certificate and key have been generated, they'll be placed in */var/ qmail/control/servercert.pem* (with a symbolic link to */var/qmail/control/ clientcert.pem*). Of course, you could just skip this step and make a symbolic link to those locations from a certificate/key pair that you've already created [Hack #69]. Once you've gotten your certificates squared away, run make tmprsadh to generate the Diffie-Hellman key exchange parameters.

Now, you're ready to restart Qmail:

```
# svc -u /service/qmail-send /service/qmail-send/log
# svc -u /service/qmail-smtpd /service/qmail-smtpd/log
```

If you telnet to port 25 of your server and issue an EHLO command, you should now see that the server supports STARTTLS and SMTP AUTH:

```
$ telnet mail.example.com 25
Trying 192.168.0.2...
Connected to mail.example.com.
Escape character is '^]'.
220 mail.example.com ESMTP
EHLO
250-freebsd5-vm1.nnc
250-STARTTLS
250-PIPELINING
250-8BITMIME
250-SIZE 0
250 AUTH LOGIN PLAIN CRAM-MD5
```

You're almost done. All you need is a way to let Qmail check your users' passwords for it to authenticate them. This is done with the *checkpassword* program (*http://cr.yp.to/checkpwd.html*). If you're using Qmail as a POP3 server, you probably already have it installed properly, so you're done. If you don't, download and unpack the source tarball for *checkpassword*, change to the directory that was extracted (e.g., *checkpassword-0.90*), and run make setup check as root.

After it's installed, you'll need to make *checkpassword* SUID, so it can verify user passwords:

```
# chmod 4711 /bin/checkpassword
```

You're now set on the server side. Your users can enjoy encrypted email between their clients and your server. In addition, you can allow your users to send email from wherever they are, since you don't have to restrict relaying based on hostnames any longer.

However, keep in mind that email will be encrypted only between the clients, your server, and any destination servers that support TLS. If a recipient's server doesn't support TLS, the message will be sent in the clear at some point. For true end-to-end encryption, you can use GnuPG [Hacks #42 and #43].

HACK #57 Install Apache with SSL and suEXEC

Help secure your web applications with mod_ssl and suEXEC.

Web server security is a very important issue these days, especially since people are always finding new and creative ways to put the Web to use. If you're using any sort of web application that needs to handle authentication or provides some sort of restricted information, you should seriously consider installing a web server with SSL capabilities. Without SSL, any authentication information your users send to the web server is sent over the network in the clear, and anyone with a sniffer can view any information that clients can access. If you are already using Apache 2.x, you can easily rebuild it to add SSL capabilities. If you're using Apache 1.x, you can do this with mod_ssl (*http://www.modssl.org*).

In addition, if your web server serves up dynamic content for multiple users, you might want to enable Apache's suEXEC functionality. suEXEC allows your web server to execute server-side scripts as the user that owns them, rather than as the account under which the web server is running. Otherwise, any user could create a script and run code as the account under which the web server is running. This is a bad thing, particularly on a multiuser web server. If you don't review the scripts that your users write before allowing them to be run, they could very well write code that allows them to access other users' data or other sensitive information, such as database accounts and passwords.

Apache 1.x

To compile Apache with mod_ssl, download the appropriate mod_ssl source distribution for the version of Apache that you'll be using.

 If you don't want to add mod_ssl to an existing Apache source tree, you will also need to download and unpack the Apache source.

After you've done that, unpack the mod_ssl distribution and go into the directory that it creates. Then, run a command like this:

```
$ ./configure \
--with-apache=../apache_1.3.36 \
--with-ssl=SYSTEM \
--prefix=/usr/local/apache \
--enable-module=most \
--enable-module=mmap_static \
--enable-module=so \
--enable-shared=ssl \
--disable-rule=SSL_COMPAT \
--server-uid=www \
--server-gid=www \
--enable-suexec \
--suexec-caller=www \
--suexec-uidmin=500 \
--suexec-gidmin=500
```

This both patches the Apache source tree with extensions provided with mod_ssl and configures Apache for the build process.

You will probably need to change a number of options in order to build Apache. The directory specified in the --with-apache switch should point to the directory that contains the Apache source code for the version you are building. In addition, if you want to use a version of OpenSSL that has not been installed yet, specify the location of its build tree with the --with-ssl switch.

If you elect to do that, you should configure and build OpenSSL in the specified directory before attempting to build Apache and mod_ssl. The --server-uid and --server-gid switches specify the user and group under which the web server will run. Apache defaults to the *nobody* account. However, many programs that can be configured to drop their privileges also default to the *nobody* account; if you end up accepting these defaults with every program, the *nobody* account can become quite privileged. So, it is recommended that you create a separate account for every program that provides this option.

The remaining options enable and configure Apache's suEXEC. To provide the suEXEC functionality, Apache uses a SUID wrapper program to execute users' scripts. This wrapper program makes several checks before it allows a program to execute. One thing that the wrapper checks is the UID of the process that invoked it. If it is not the account that was specified with the --suexec-caller option, execution of the user's script will abort. Since the web server will call the suEXEC wrapper, set this option to the same value as --server-uid.

Additionally, since most privileged accounts and groups on a system usually all have a UID and GID beneath a certain value, the suEXEC wrapper will check to see if the UID or GID of the process invoking it is below this threshold. For this to work, you must specify the appropriate value for your system. In this example, Apache and mod_ssl are being built on a Red Hat system, which starts regular user accounts and groups at UID and GID 500. In addition to these checks, suEXEC performs a multitude of other checks, such as ensuring that the script is writable only by the owner, that the owner is not root, and that the script is not SUID or SGID.

After the *configure* script completes, change to the directory that contains the Apache source code and run make and make install. You can run make certificates if you would like to generate an SSL certificate to test out your installation. You can also run make certificate TYPE=custom to generate a certificate signing request to be signed by either a commercial Certificate Authority or your own CA [Hack #69].

After installing Apache, you can start it by running this command:

```
# /usr/local/apache/bin/apachectl startssl
```

If you want to start out by testing it without SSL, run this:

```
# /usr/local/apache/bin/apacectl start
```

You can then run this command to verify that suEXEC support is enabled:

```
# grep suexec /usr/local/apache/logs/error_log
[Thu Jan  1 16:48:17 2004] [notice] suEXEC mechanism enabled (wrapper:
/usr/local/apache/bin/suexec)
```

Now, add a `Directory` entry to enable CGI scripts for user directories:

```
<Directory /home/*/public_html>
    AllowOverride FileInfo AuthConfig Limit
    Options MultiViews Indexes SymLinksIfOwnerMatch Includes ExecCGI
    <Limit GET POST OPTIONS PROPFIND>
        Order allow,deny
        Allow from all
    </Limit>
    <LimitExcept GET POST OPTIONS PROPFIND>
        Order deny,allow
        Deny from all
    </LimitExcept>
</Directory>
```

In addition, add this line to enable CGI scripts outside of the *ScriptAlias* directories:

```
AddHandler cgi-script .cgi
```

After you've done that, you can restart Apache by running this command:

```
# /usr/local/apache/bin/apachectl restart
```

Now, test out suEXEC with a simple script that runs the `id` command, which will print out information about the user under which the script is executed:

```
#!/bin/sh

echo -e "Content-Type: text/plain\r\n\r\n"
/usr/bin/id
```

Put this script in a directory such as *usr/local/apache/cgi-bin*, name it *suexec-test.cgi*, and make it executable. Now, enter the URL for the script (e.g., *http://webserver/cgi-bin/suexec-test.cgi*) into your favorite web browser. You should see something like this:

```
uid=80(www) gid=80(www) groups=80(www)
```

As you can see, it is being executed under the same UID as the web server.

Now, copy the script into a user's *public_html* directory:

```
$ mkdir public_html && chmod 711 ~/ ~/public_html
$ cp /usr/local/apache/cgi-bin/suexec-test.cgi ~/public_html
```

After you've done that, enter the URL for the script (e.g., *http://webserver/ ~user/suexec-test.cgi*) in your web browser. You should see something similar to this:

```
uid=500(andrew) gid=500(andrew) groups=500(andrew)
```

In addition to handling scripts in users' private HTML directories, suEXEC can execute scripts as another user within a virtual host. However, to enable this, you will need to create all of your virtual host's directories beneath the web server's document root (e.g., */usr/local/apache/htdocs*). When doing this, you can configure what user and group the script will execute as by using the User and Group configuration directives within the VirtualHost statement:

```
<VirtualHost>
    User myuser
    Group mygroup
    DocumentRoot /usr/local/apache/htdocs/mysite
    ...
</VirtualHost>
```

Apache 2.x

Setting up Apache 2.x isn't very different from setting up Apache 1.x. The main difference is that SSL functionality is already included and just needs to be enabled. The options used to enable suEXEC are also slightly different:

```
$ ./configure \
--with-ssl=SYSTEM \
--prefix=/usr/local/apache2 \
--enable-module=most \
--enable-module=mmap_static \
--enable-module=so \
--enable-ssl  \
--enable-suexec \
--with-suexec-caller=daemon \
--with-suexec-uidmin=500 \
--with-suexec-gidmin=500
```

One thing that you'll notice is absent is the ability to specify the user and group under which the server executes. Apache 2 defaults to the *daemon* user and group, which you can change later by modifying the User and Group lines in the configuration file, *httpd.conf*. If you use the --prefix option the way it's shown in this example, *httpd.conf* will be in */usr/local/apache2/conf*. When you change these lines you'll also need to rebuild the daemon and tell the *configure* script the new user with the --with-suexec-caller option.

After the *configure* script completes, build and install the daemon by running make and then changing to root and running make install. Once that has finished, you'll need to edit the configuration file to set up SSL. Do this by uncommenting the line that includes the SSL-specific configuration options:

```
#Include conf/extra/httpd-ssl.conf
```

Now, you need to tell Apache where to find your certificate and key by editing the file specified in the Include entry. By default, it looks for *server.crt* and *server.key* in the same directory as *httpd.conf*:

```
SSLCertificateFile /usr/local/apache2/conf/server.crt
SSLCertificateKeyFile /usr/local/apache2/conf/server.key
```

Once you have your certificate and key configured, start Apache by using apachectl:

```
# /usr/local/apache2/bin/apachectl start
```

The difference between Apache 1.x and 2.x here is that apachectl no longer differentiates between SSL and non-SSL configurations, so the startssl argument isn't accepted anymore. Aside from these differences, you can follow the same steps used for Apache 1.x.

Unfortunately, suEXEC is incompatible with mod_perl and mod_php, because the modules run within the Apache process itself instead of in a separate program. Since the Apache process is running as a nonroot user, it cannot change the UID under which the scripts execute. suEXEC works by having Apache call a special SUID wrapper (e.g., */usr/local/apache/bin/suexec*) that can only be invoked by Apache processes.

If you care to make the security/performance trade-off by using suEXEC but still need to run Perl scripts, you can do so through the standard CGI interface. You can also run PHP programs through the CGI interface, but you'll have to create a php binary and specify it as the interpreter in all the PHP scripts you wish to execute through suEXEC. Alternatively, you can execute your scripts through mod_perl or mod_php by locating them outside the directories where suEXEC will work.

HACK #58 Secure BIND

Lock down your BIND setup to help contain potential security problems.

Due to BIND's not-so-illustrious track record with regard to security, if you want to use it you'll probably want to spend some time hardening your setup. One way to make running BIND a little safer is to run it inside a sandboxed environment [Hack #10]. This is easy to do with recent versions of BIND, since it natively supports running as a nonprivileged user within a chroot( ) jail. All you need to do is set up the directory you're going to have it chroot( ) to and change the command you're using to start *named* to reflect this.

To begin, create a user and group to run *named* as (e.g., *named*). To prepare the sandboxed environment, you'll need to create the appropriate directory structure. You can create the directories for such an environment within */named_chroot* by running the following commands:

```
# mkdir /named_chroot
# cd /named_chroot
# mkdir -p dev etc/namedb/slave var/run
```

Next, you'll need to copy your *named.conf* file and *namedb* directory to the sandboxed environment:

```
# cp /etc/named.conf /named_chroot/etc
# cp -a /var/namedb/* /named_chroot/etc/namedb
```

These commands assume you store your zone files in */var/namedb*.

If you're setting up BIND as a secondary DNS server, you will need to make the */named_chroot/etc/namedb/slave* directory writable so that *named* can update the records it contains when it performs a domain transfer from the master DNS node:

```
# chown -R named:named /named_chroot/etc/namedb/slave
```

In addition, *named* will need to write its process ID (PID) file to */named_chroot/var/run*, so you'll have to make this directory writable by the *named* user as well:

```
# chown named:named /named_chroot/var/run
```

Now, create the device files that *named* will need to access after it has called chroot( ):

```
# cd /named_chroot/dev
# ls -la /dev/null /dev/random
crw-rw-rw-   1 root      root      1,   3 Jan 30  2003 /dev/null
crw-r--r--   1 root      root      1,   8 Jan 30  2003 /dev/random
# mknod null c 1 3
# mknod random c 1 8
# chmod 666 null random
```

You'll also need to copy your time zone file from */etc/localtime* to */named_chroot/etc/localtime*. Additionally, *named* usually uses */dev/log* to communicate its log messages to *syslogd*. Since this doesn't exist inside the sandboxed environment, you will need to tell *syslogd* to create a socket that the chroot( )-ed named process can write to. You can do this by modifying your *syslogd* startup command and adding -a /named_chroot/dev/log to it. Usually, you can do this by modifying an existing file in */etc*.

For instance, under Fedora, edit */etc/sysconfig/syslogd* and modify the SYSLOGD_OPTIONS line to read:

```
SYSLOGD_OPTIONS="-m 0 -a /named_chroot/dev/log"
```

Or, if you're running FreeBSD, modify the `syslogd_flags` line in */etc/rc.conf*:

```
syslogd_flags="-s -a /named_chroot/dev/log"
```

After you restart *syslogd*, you should see a log socket in */named_chroot/dev*.

Now, to start *named*, all you need to do is run this command:

```
# named -u named -t /named_chroot
```

Other tricks for increasing the security of your BIND installation include limiting zone transfers to your slave DNS servers and altering the response to BIND version queries. Restricting zone transfers ensures that random attackers will not be able to request a list of all the hostnames for the zones hosted by your name servers. You can globally restrict zone transfers to certain hosts by putting an `allow-transfer` section within the `options` section in your *named.conf*.

For instance, if you want to restrict transfers on all zones hosted by your DNS server to only 192.168.1.20 and 192.168.1.21, you can use an `allow-transfer` section like this:

```
allow-transfer {
    192.168.1.20;
    192.168.1.21;
};
```

If you don't want to limit zone transfers globally and instead want to specify the allowed hosts on a zone-by-zone basis, you can put the `allow-transfer` section inside the zone section.

Before an attacker attempts to exploit a BIND vulnerability, she will often scan for vulnerable versions of BIND by connecting to name servers and performing a version query. Since you should never need to perform a version query on your own name server, you can modify the reply BIND sends to the requester. To do this, add a `version` statement to the `options` section in your *named.conf*:

```
version "SuperHappy DNS v1.5";
```

This statement doesn't really provide extra security, but if you don't want to advertise what software and version you're running to the entire world, you don't have to.

Also, if you're running a publicly facing name server that is used to serve zones, you'll want to disable recursion. Otherwise, your server could be used in a denial of service (DoS) attack. To disable recursion, you'll need to add a `recursion` statement to the `options` section of *named.conf*:

```
recursion no;
```

You should allow recursion only on servers where you have a reasonable level of trust in the clients that can query it, such as an internal name server on your network.

See Also

- The section "Securing BIND" in *Building Secure Servers with Linux*, by Michael D. Bauer (O'Reilly)

HACK #59 Set Up a Minimal and Secure DNS Server

Use Djbdns, a more secure alternative to BIND, to serve your DNS records.

For many years BIND has been the workhorse of the Internet, serving up DNS records. But with that history comes a long track record of security vulnerabilities. While the rate at which vulnerabilities are being discovered has decreased over the years (it's gotten "more secure"), you might want to err on the side of caution and use a different software package that doesn't have such a colorful history. One such package is Djbdns (*http://cr.yp.to/djbdns. html*), written by Daniel J. Bernstein, for which no security vulnerabilities have been disclosed to date.

One of the things that makes Djbdns so secure is its architecture. BIND uses one big monolithic program to perform all DNS-related duties. On the other hand, Djbdns uses many separate specialized programs to serve authoritative zones, do recursive queries, perform zone transfers, and carry out logging, amongst other things. Each of these subprograms is smaller and easier to audit for vulnerabilities.

This hack focuses primarily on the *tinydns* program, which Djbdns uses to serve authoritative DNS zones.

Installing daemontools

Before you can get Djbdns up and running, you'll first need to install *daemontools* (*http://cr.yp.to/daemontools.html*), another package used to manage server processes on Unix systems. Download the tarball from *http:// cr.yp.to/daemontools/daemontools-0.76.tar.gz* and create a */package* directory:

```
# mkdir /package
# chmod 1755 /package
```

Then, change into */package* and unpack the tarball. You might be wondering why we're using this */package* directory. The reason is because *daemontools*'s installation process makes symbolic links from the binaries that were compiled during the build process to other locations within the system's filesystems. So, you need a good permanent place to keep the source tree; any directory that satisfies that requirement will do.

Once the source code has been unpacked into *package*, change the directory to *admin/daemontools-0.76* and run the installation script:

```
# cd admin/daemontools-0.76
# package/install
```

You might encounter an error like this:

```
/usr/bin/ld: errno: TLS definition in /lib/libc.so.6 section .tbss
mismatches non-TLS reference in envdir.o
/lib/libc.so.6: could not read symbols: Bad value
collect2: ld returned 1 exit status
make: *** [envdir] Error 1
Copying commands into ./command...
cp: cannot stat `compile/svscan': No such file or directory
```

If you do, download the patch available at *http://www.qmailrocks.org/downloads/patches/daemontools-0.76.errno.patch* and apply it:

```
# cd /package/admin/daemontools-0.76/src
# patch < <path to patch file>
```

Now, run package/install again.

If the system uses a SysV init process (i.e., if an */etc/inittab* file and an */etc/rc.d* directory are used), an entry for *daemontools* will be added to */etc/ininttab*. This will cause *daemontools* to automatically start now and with each system boot. Otherwise, the install process will add a line to */etc/rc.local* to start it at boot time. Instead of rebooting to start *daemontools*, locate this line and run it manually:

```
# csh -cf '/command/svscanboot &'
```

Now it's time to install Djbdns.

Installing Djbdns

Once you've installed *daemontools*, download and unpack the Djbns tarball (available at *http://cr.yp.to/djbdns/djbdns-1.05.tar.gz*) and change to the directory that is created (e.g., *djbdns-1.05*). On Linux systems, run the following before starting the build:

```
$ echo gcc -O2 -include /usr/include/errno.h > conf-cc
```

Build Djbdns by simply running make. After compilation finishes, run make setup check to install it. You'll need to create two user accounts under which to run *tinydns* and its logging process:

```
# adduser _tinydns
# adduser _dnslog
```

Now, set up *tinydns* to use these accounts and tell *daemontools* to start it (replace *192.168.0.40* with your system's IP address):

```
# tinydns-conf _tinydns _dnslog /etc/tinydns 192.168.0.40
# ln -s /etc/tinydns /service
```

After a few seconds, *daemontools* will start *tinydns*, and you should see it and its logger process:

```
# ps -aux | egrep '_tinydns|_dnslog'
_tinydns 49485  0.0  0.2  1328   552  p1  I   12:53AM  0:00.12 /usr/local/
bin/tinydns
_dnslog  49486  0.0  0.2  1208   480  p1  I   12:53AM  0:00.07 multilog t
./main
```

Now it's time to add some DNS records.

Adding Records

Setting up an authoritative zone with Djbdns is much less complex than doing so with BIND. In fact, it's surprisingly easy. Simply put authoritative DNS records into a plain-text file and then compile them into a binary database format that *tinydns* can read.

Now, you'll need to create some records. Some programs for adding records are included, but you'll probably want to add NS and MX records by hand, because the included tools enforce a certain DNS- and mail-server-naming scheme that you might not want to use.

First, create NS and SOA records for the domain and an A record for your name server:

```
# cd /service/tinydns/root
# echo ".example.com:192.168.0.40:ns1.example.com" > data
# echo ".0.168.192.in-addr.arpa:192.168.0.40:ns1.example.com" >> data
```

The first character of each entry signifies the record type. A dot (.) causes *tinydns* to create an NS record for *example.com* pointing to *ns1.example. com*, an A record for *ns1.example.com*, and an SOA record for *example.com*. The second entry delegates the reverse zone for 192.168.0.0/24 to the name server. After adding these entries, run make to create the database that *tinydns* reads its data from, *data.cdb*. Remember to do this after every change you make to *data*.

Now, take a look at the records that were created:

```
# dig -t any example.com @192.168.0.40

; <<>> DiG 9.3.1 <<>> -t any example.com @192.168.0.40
; (1 server found)
;; global options:  printcmd
;; Got answer:
```

```
;; ->>HEADER<<- opcode: QUERY, status: NOERROR, id: 18791
;; flags: qr aa rd; QUERY: 1, ANSWER: 2, AUTHORITY: 0, ADDITIONAL: 1

;; QUESTION SECTION:
;example.com.                     IN      ANY

;; ANSWER SECTION:
example.com.             2560    IN      SOA     ns1.example.com. hostmaster.
example.com. 1151133345 16384 2048 1048576 2560
example.com.             259200  IN      NS      ns1.example.com.

;; ADDITIONAL SECTION:
ns1.example.com.         259200  IN      A       192.168.0.40

;; Query time: 6 msec
;; SERVER: 192.168.0.40#53(192.168.0.40)
;; WHEN: Sat Jun 24 01:15:48 2006
;; MSG SIZE  rcvd: 110
```

Try adding an MX record. This time, use the *add-mx* helper program:

```
# ./add-mx example.com 192.168.0.42
This will create the following entry in the data file:
@example.com:192.168.0.42:a::86400
```

This results in an A record and an MX entry pointing to *a.mx.example.com*. This is an example of the helper programs enforcing their own naming scheme. Change the entry to look like the following to create an A and MX record for *mail.example.com* instead:

```
@example.com:192.168.0.42:mail.example.com:10:86400
```

The helper programs aren't good for everything, but they are good for adding generic hosts. To add a host, use the appropriately named *add-host* program:

```
# ./add-host caligula.example.com 192.168.0.41
```

This creates an = entry, which causes *tinydns* to serve up an A record for *caligula.example.com* and its corresponding reverse DNS PTR record:

```
=caligula.example.com:192.168.0.41:86400
```

To add additional A (but not PTR) records for a host, use the add-alias command. Entries created with this command start with a +:

```
# ./add-alias www.example.com 192.168.0.41
# cat data
.example.com:192.168.0.40:ns1.example.com
.0.168.192.in-addr.arpa:192.168.0.40:ns1.example.com
@example.com:192.168.0.42:mail.example.com:10:86400
=caligula.example.com:192.168.0.41:86400
+www.example.com:192.168.0.41:86400
```

The types of entries discussed here should satisfy most situations. However, there are several other types, including a generic type that allows you to specify entries that generate any type of DNS record. For more information on these, consult *http://cr.yp.to/djbdns/tinydns-data.html*.

Secure MySQL
#60
Take some basic steps to harden your MySQL installation.

MySQL (*http://www.mysql.com*), one of the most popular open source database systems available today, is often used in conjunction with both the Apache web server and the PHP scripting language to drive dynamic content on the Web. However, MySQL is a complex piece of software and, given the fact that it often has to interact both locally and remotely with a broad range of other programs, special care should be taken to secure it as much as possible.

Some steps you can take include running MySQL in a chroot( )-ed environment [Hack #10], running it as a nonroot user, and disabling MySQL's ability to load data from local files. Luckily, none of these are as hard to do as they might sound. To start, let's look at how to chroot( ) MySQL.

First, create a user and group for MySQL to run as and download the MySQL source distribution. After you've done that, unpack the source and go into the directory that it creates. Run this command to build MySQL and set up its directory structure for chroot( )-ing:

```
$ ./configure --prefix=/mysql --with-mysqld-ldflags=-all-static && make
```

This configures MySQL to be installed in */mysql* and statically links the *mysqld* binary; this makes setting up the chroot( ) environment much easier, since you won't need to copy any additional libraries to the environment.

After the compilation finishes, become root and run these commands to install MySQL:

```
# make install DESTDIR=/mysql_chroot && ln -s /mysql_chroot/mysql /mysql
# scripts/mysql_install_db
```

The first command installs MySQL, but instead of placing the files in */mysql*, it places them in */mysql_chroot/mysql*. It also creates a symbolic link from that directory to */mysql*, which makes administering MySQL much easier after installation.

The second command creates MySQL's default databases. If you hadn't created the symbolic link prior to running this command, the *mysql_install_db* script would have failed, because it expects to find MySQL installed beneath */mysql*. Many other scripts and programs will expect the same, so creating the symbolic link will make your life easier.

Next, you need to set up the correct directory permissions so that MySQL will be able to function properly:

```
# chown -R root:mysql /mysql
# chown -R mysql /mysql/var
```

Now, try running MySQL:

```
# /mysql/bin/mysqld_safe&
Starting mysqld daemon with databases from /mysql/var
# ps -aux | grep mysql | grep -v grep
root     10137 0.6  0.5  4156   744 pts/2   S    23:01  0:00 /bin/sh /
mysql/bin/
mysqld_safe
mysql    10150 7.0  9.3 46224 11756 pts/2   S    23:01  0:00 [mysqld]
mysql    10151 0.0  9.3 46224 11756 pts/2   S    23:01  0:00 [mysqld]
mysql    10152 0.0  9.3 46224 11756 pts/2   S    23:01  0:00 [mysqld]
mysql    10153 0.0  9.3 46224 11756 pts/2   S    23:01  0:00 [mysqld]
mysql    10154 0.0  9.3 46224 11756 pts/2   S    23:01  0:00 [mysqld]
mysql    10155 0.3  9.3 46224 11756 pts/2   S    23:01  0:00 [mysqld]
mysql    10156 0.0  9.3 46224 11756 pts/2   S    23:01  0:00 [mysqld]
mysql    10157 0.0  9.3 46224 11756 pts/2   S    23:01  0:00 [mysqld]
mysql    10158 0.0  9.3 46224 11756 pts/2   S    23:01  0:00 [mysqld]
mysql    10159 0.0  9.3 46224 11756 pts/2   S    23:01  0:00 [mysqld]
# /mysql/bin/mysqladmin shutdown
040103 23:02:45  mysqld ended

[1]+  Done                    /mysql/bin/mysqld_safe
```

Now that you know MySQL is working outside of its chroot( ) environment, you can create the additional files and directories it will need to work inside the chroot( ) environment:

```
# mkdir /mysql_chroot/tmp /mysql_chroot/dev
# chmod 1777 /mysql_chroot/tmp
# ls -l /dev/null
crw-rw-rw-    1 root     root       1,  3 Jan 30 2003 /dev/null
# mknod /mysql_chroot/dev/null c 1 3
```

Now, try running mysqld in the chroot( )-ed environment:

```
# /usr/sbin/chroot /mysql_chroot /mysql/libexec/mysqld -u 100
```

In this example, the UID of the user you want mysqld to run as is specified with the -u option. This should correspond to the UID of the user created earlier.

To ease management, you might want to modify the *mysqld_safe* shell script to chroot( ) *mysqld* for you. You can accomplish this by finding the lines where *mysqld* is called and modifying them to use the *chroot* program.

Open up */mysql/bin/mysqld_safe* and locate the block of lines that looks like this:

```
if test -z "$args"
  then
```

```
        $NOHUP_NICENESS $ledir/$MYSQLD $defaults \
        --basedir=$MY_BASEDIR_VERSION \
        --datadir=$DATADIR $USER_OPTION \
        --pid-file=$pid_file --skip-locking >> $err_log 2>&1
    else
      eval "$NOHUP_NICENESS $ledir/$MYSQLD $defaults \
      --basedir=$MY_BASEDIR_VERSION \
      --datadir=$DATADIR $USER_OPTION \
      --pid-file=$pid_file --skip-locking $args >> $err_log 2>&1"
    fi
```

Change them to look like this:

```
    if test -z "$args"
      then
        $NOHUP_NICENESS /usr/sbin/chroot /mysql_chroot \
        $ledir/$MYSQLD $defaults \
        --basedir=$MY_BASEDIR_VERSION \
        --datadir=$DATADIR $USER_OPTION \
        --pid-file=$pid_file  --skip-locking >> $err_log 2>&1
      else
        eval "$NOHUP_NICENESS /usr/sbin/chroot /mysql_chroot \
        $ledir/$MYSQLD $defaults \
        --basedir=$MY_BASEDIR_VERSION \
        --datadir=$DATADIR $USER_OPTION \
        --pid-file=$pid_file --skip-locking $args >> $err_log 2>&1"
      fi
```

Now, you can start MySQL by using the *mysqld_safe* wrapper script, like this:

```
# /mysql/bin/mysqld_safe --user=100
```

You might also want to create a separate *my.conf* file for the MySQL utilities and server. For instance, in */etc/my.cnf*, you could specify socket = /mysql_chroot/tmp/mysql.sock in the [client] section so that you don't have to specify the socket manually every time you run a MySQL-related program.

You'll also probably want to disable MySQL's ability to load data from local files. To do this, you can add set-variable=local-infile=0 to the [mysqld] section of your */mysql_chroot/etc/my.cnf*. This disables MySQL's LOAD DATA LOCAL INFILE command. Alternatively, you can disable it from the command line by using the --local-infile=0 option.

Share Files Securely in Unix
Use SFS to help secure your remote filesystems.

If you are using Unix systems and sharing files on your network, you are most likely using the Network File System (NFS). However, NFS has many security problems, not only with individual implementations, but also in the design of the protocol itself. For instance, if a user can spoof an IP address and mount an NFS share that is only meant for a certain computer, that user will essentially have root access to all the files on that share. In addition, NFS employs secret file handles that are used with each file request. Since NFS does not encrypt its traffic, it's easy for attackers to guess these file handles. If they guess correctly, they effectively gain total root access to the remote filesystem.

The Self-certifying File System (SFS), available at *http://www.fs.net*, fixes all of these problems by employing a drastically different design philosophy. NFS was created with the notion that you can (and should) trust your network. SFS has been designed from the beginning with the idea that no network should ever be trusted until it can definitively prove its identity.

To accomplish this level of security, SFS makes use of public keys on both the client and server ends. It uses these keys to verify the identity of servers and clients, and it also provides access control on the server side. One particularly nice side effect of such strong encryption is that SFS provides a much finer-grained level of access control than NFS. With NFS, you are limited to specifying which hosts can or cannot connect to a given exported filesystem. In order to access an SFS server, a user must create a key pair and then authorize the key by logging into the SFS server and registering the key manually.

Building SFS can take up quite a lot of disk space. Before you attempt it, make sure you have at least 550 MB of space available on the filesystem on which you'll be compiling SFS. You will also need to make sure that you have the GNU Multiple Precision (GMP) math library (*http://www.swox.com/gmp/*) installed.

Before you begin to build SFS, you also need to create a user and group for SFS's daemons. By default, these are both called *sfs*. If you want to use a different user or group, you can do this by passing options to the *configure* script.

Once your system is ready, check out the most recent version of the SFS code (hit Enter at the password prompt):

```
$ cvs -d :pserver:sfscvs@cvs.fs.net:/cvs login
Logging in to :pserver:sfscvs@cvs.fs.net:2401/cvs
CVS password:
```

```
$ cvs -z5 -d :pserver:sfscvs@cvs.fs.net:/cvs co -P sfs1
```

Then, change to the *sfs1* directory and build SFS by running this command:

```
$ sh ./setup && ./configure && make
```

Once that process is finished, become root and type `make install`.

If you want to use a user and group other than *sfs*, you can specify these
with the --with-sfsuser and --with-sfsgroup options:

```
$ ./configure --with-sfsuser=nobody --with-sfsgroup=nobody
```

Building SFS can take quite a bit of time, so you might want to take the
opportunity to enjoy a cup of coffee, a snack, or maybe even a full meal,
depending on the speed of your machine and the amount of memory it has.

After SFS has finished building and you have installed it, you can test it out
by connecting to the SFS project's public server. To do this, start the SFS client daemon, *sfscd*, and then change to the directory under which the SFS
server will be mounted:

```
# sfscd
# cd /sfs/@sfs.fs.net,uzwadtctbjb3dg596waiyru8cx5kb4an
# ls
CONGRATULATIONS  cvs  pi0  reddy  sfswww
# cat CONGRATULATIONS
You have set up a working SFS client.
#
```

sfscd automatically creates the */sfs* directory and the directory for the SFS
server.

> SFS relies on the operating system's *portmap* daemon and
> NFS mounter; you'll need to have those running before run-
> ning the client.

To set up an SFS server, first log into your server and generate a public and
private key pair:

```
# mkdir /etc/sfs
# sfskey gen -P /etc/sfs/sfs_host_key
```

sfskey will ask you to bang on the keys for a little while in order to gather
entropy for the random number generator.

Now, you will need to create a configuration file for *sfssd*, the SFS server
daemon. Create a file in */etc/sfs* called *sfsrwsd_config*, which is where you'll
configure the filesystem namespace that SFS will export to other hosts.

If you want to export the */home* filesystem, create a configuration file like
this:

```
Export /var/sfs/root /
Export /home /home
```

Then, create the */var/sfs/root* and */var/sfs/home* directories. After that, create
NFS exports so that the */home* filesystem can be mounted under */var/sfs/
root/home*. These are then re-exported by *sfssd*. The NFS exports need to
allow mounting only from *localhost*.

Here's what */etc/exports* looks like for exporting */home*:

```
/var/sfs/root    localhost(rw)
/home        localhost(rw)
```

This *exports* file is for Linux. If you are running the SFS server on another
operating system (such as Solaris or OpenBSD), consult your operating system's *mountd* manpage for the proper way to add these shares.

Now, start your operating system's NFS server. Once NFS has started, you
can start *sfssd*. After attempting to connect to the *sfssd* server, you should
see some messages like these in your logs:

```
Jun 10 10:14:47 colossus : sfssd: version 0.8pre, pid 30880
Jun 10 10:14:47 colossus : rexd: version 0.8pre, pid 30882
Jun 10 10:14:47 colossus : sfsrwsd: version 0.8pre, pid 30884
Jun 10 10:14:47 colossus : rexd: serving @colossus.
nnc,kkvt3kzmqry5gy4s3es97yu9gip2f967
Jun 10 10:14:47 colossus : rexd: spawning /usr/local/lib/sfs-0.8pre/ptyd
Jun 10 10:14:47 colossus : sfsauthd: version 0.8pre, pid 30883
Jun 10 10:14:47 colossus : sfssd: listening on TCP port 4
Jun 10 10:14:47 colossus : sfsauthd: dbcache_refresh_delay = 0
Jun 10 10:14:47 colossus : sfsauthd: Disabling authentication server cache
refresh...
Jun 10 10:14:47 colossus rpc.mountd: authenticated mount request from
localhost.localdomain:956 for /var/sfs/root (/var/sfs/root)
Jun 10 10:14:47 colossus : sfsauthd: serving @colossus.
nnc,kkvt3kzmqry5gy4s3es97yu9gip2f967
Jun 10 10:14:47 colossus rpc.mountd: authenticated mount request from
localhost.localdomain:956 for /home (/home)
Jun 10 10:14:47 colossus : sfsrwsd: serving /sfs/@colossus.
nnc,kkvt3kzmqry5gy4s3es97yu9gip2f967
```

The last log entry shows the path that users can use to mount your filesystem. Before mounting any filesystems on your server, users will have to create a key pair and register it with your server. They can do this by logging
into your server and running the sfskey command:

```
$ sfskey register
sfskey: /home/andrew/.sfs/random_seed: No such file or directory
sfskey: creating directory /home/andrew/.sfs
sfskey: creating directory /home/andrew/.sfs/authkeys
/var/sfs/sockets/agent.sock: No such file or directory
sfskey: sfscd not running, limiting sources of entropy
Creating new key: andrew@colossus.nnc#1 (Rabin)
        Key Label: andrew@colossus.nnc#1
Enter passphrase:
        Again:

sfskey needs secret bits with which to seed the random number generator.
Please type some random or unguessable text until you hear a beep:
DONE
```

```
UNIX password:
colossus.nnc: New SRP key: andrew@colossus.nnc/1024
wrote key: /home/andrew/.sfs/authkeys/andrew@colossus.nnc#1
```

Alternatively, if you already have an existing key pair on another server, you can type sfskey *user@otherserver* instead. This command retrieves the key from the remote machine and registers it with the server you are currently logged into.

Now that you have registered a key with the server, you can log into the SFS server from another machine. This is also done with the *sfskey* program:

```
$ sfskey login andrew@colossus.nnc
Passphrase for andrew@colossus.nnc/1024:
SFS Login as andrew@colossus.nnc
```

Now, try to access the remote server:

```
$ cd /sfs/@colossus.nnc,fd82m36uwxj6m3q8tawp56ztgsvu7g77
$ ls
home
```

As you can see, SFS is a powerful tool for sharing files across a network, and even across the Internet. Not only does it provide security, but it also provides a unique and universal method for referencing a remote host and its exported filesystems. You can even put your home directory on an SFS server, simply by linking the universal pathname of the exported filesystem */home*.

Network Security

Hacks 62–75

As we come to rely more and more on massively interconnected networks, the stability and security of those networks becomes more vital than ever. The world of business has adopted information technology to help streamline processes, increase productivity, and cut costs. As such, a company's IT infrastructure is often a core asset, and many businesses would cease to function if disaster (whether natural or digital) were to significantly disrupt their network operations. At the same time, the widespread adoption of the Internet as a global communications medium has also brought computer networks out of the business and academic world and into our personal lives. That largest of networks is now used not only for information and entertainment, but also as a means to keep in touch with friends, family, and loved ones.

Although this book as a whole is meant to address network security, the information it contains extends into many other areas. After all, a network is simply a means to connect machines and services so that they can communicate. This chapter, however, deals primarily with the security and integrity of the network itself. In this chapter, you'll learn how to detect and prevent certain types of spoofing attacks that can be used to compromise the core integrity of a TCP/IP Ethernet network at its lowest level. You'll also see how to protect against brute-force attacks against SSH, how to keep track of vulnerabilities, and how to scan for viruses on Unix servers.

Although it is not always a direct security threat, network reconnaissance is often a precursor to an attack. In this chapter, you'll learn how to fool those who are trying to gather information about the hosts on your network, as well as ways to detect eavesdroppers who are monitoring your network for juicy bits of information.

Detect ARP Spoofing

#62   Find out if there's a "man in the middle" impersonating your server.

One of the biggest threats to a computer network is a rogue system pretending to be a trusted host. Once someone has successfully impersonated another host, he can do a number of nefarious things. For example, he can intercept and log traffic destined for the real host, or lie in wait for clients to connect and begin sending the rogue host confidential information.

Spoofing a host has especially severe consequences in IP networks, because it opens many other avenues of attack. One technique for spoofing a host on an IP network is Address Resolution Protocol (ARP) spoofing. *ARP spoofing* is limited only to local segments and works by exploiting the way IP addresses are translated to hardware Ethernet addresses.

When an IP datagram is sent from one host to another on the same physical segment, the IP address of the destination host must be translated into a MAC address. This is the hardware address of the Ethernet card that is physically connected to the network. To accomplish this, the Address Resolution Protocol is used.

When a host needs to know another host's Ethernet address, it sends out a broadcast frame that looks like this:

```
01:20:14.833350 arp who-has 192.168.0.66 tell 192.168.0.62
```

This is called an *ARP request*. Since this is sent to the broadcast address, all Ethernet devices on the local segment should see the request. The machine that matches the request then responds by sending an *ARP reply* like the following:

```
01:20:14.833421 arp reply 192.168.0.66 is-at 0:0:d1:1f:3f:f1
```

Since the ARP request already contained the MAC address of the sender in the Ethernet frame, the receiver can send this response without making yet another ARP request.

ARP's biggest weakness is that it is a *stateless protocol*. This means that it does not track responses to the requests that are sent out and therefore will accept responses without having sent a request. Someone who wanted to receive traffic destined for another host could send forged ARP responses matching any chosen IP address to that host's MAC address. The machines that receive these spoofed ARP responses can't distinguish them from legitimate ARP responses and will begin sending packets to the attacker's MAC address.

Another side effect of ARP being stateless is that a system's ARP tables usually use only the results of the last response. In order for someone to continue to spoof an IP address, it is necessary to flood the host with ARP responses that overwrite legitimate ARP responses from the original host. This particular kind of attack is commonly known as *ARP cache poisoning*.

Several tools—such as Ettercap (*http://ettercap.sourceforge.net*) and Dsniff (*http://www.monkey.org/~dugsong/dsniff/*)—employ techniques like this to both sniff on switched networks and perform "man-in-the-middle" attacks. This technique can, of course, be used between any two hosts on a switched segment, including the local default gateway. To intercept traffic bidirectionally between hosts A and B, the attacking host C will poison host A's ARP cache, making it think that host B's IP address matches host C's MAC address. C will then poison B's cache, to make it think A's IP address corresponds to C's MAC address.

Luckily, there are methods to detect just this kind of behavior, whether you're using a shared or switched Ethernet segment. One program that can help accomplish this is Arpwatch (*ftp://ftp.ee.lbl.gov/arpwatch.tar.gz*), which works by monitoring an interface in promiscuous mode and recording MAC/IP address pairings over a period of time. When it sees anomalous behavior, such as a change to one of the MAC/IP address pairs that it has learned, it will send an alert to *syslog*. This can be very effective in a shared network using a hub, since a single machine can monitor all ARP traffic. However, due to the unicast nature of ARP responses, this program will not work as well on a switched network.

To achieve the same level of detection coverage in a switched environment, Arpwatch should be installed on as many machines as possible. After all, you can't know with 100% certainty what hosts an attacker will decide to target. If you're lucky enough to own one, many high-end switches allow you to designate a *monitor port* that can see the traffic on all other ports. If you have such a switch, you can install a server on that port for network monitoring, and simply run Arpwatch on it.

After downloading Arpwatch, you can compile and install it in the usual manner:

```
# ./configure && make && make install
```

When running Arpwatch on a machine with multiple interfaces, you'll probably want to specify the interface on the command line by using the -i option:

```
# arpwatch -i iface
```

As Arpwatch begins to learn the MAC/IP address pairings on your network, you'll see log entries similar to this:

```
Nov  1 00:39:08 zul arpwatch: new station 192.168.0.65 0:50:ba:85:85:ca
```

When a MAC/IP address pair changes, you should see something like this:

```
Nov  1 01:03:23 zul arpwatch: changed ethernet address 192.168.0.65 0:e0:81:
3:d8:8e
(0:50:ba:85:85:ca)
Nov  1 01:03:23 zul arpwatch: flip flop 192.168.0.65 0:50:ba:85:85:ca (0:e0:
81:3:d8:8e)
Nov  1 01:03:25 zul arpwatch: flip flop 192.168.0.65 0:e0:81:3:d8:8e (0:50:
ba:85:85:ca)
```

In this case, the initial entry is from the first fraudulent ARP response that was received, and the subsequent two are from a race condition between the fraudulent and authentic responses.

To make it easier to deal with multiple Arpwatch installs in a switched environment, you can send the log messages to a central *syslogd* [Hack #79], aggregating all the output into one place. However, because your machines can be manipulated by the same attacks that Arpwatch is looking for, it would be wise to use static ARP table entries [Hack #63] on your *syslog* server, as well as all the hosts running Arpwatch.

H A C K
#63

Create a Static ARP Table

Use static ARP table entries to combat spoofing and other nefarious activities.

As discussed in "Detect ARP Spoofing" [Hack #62], a lot of bad things can happen if someone successfully poisons the ARP table of a machine on your network. The previous hack discussed how to monitor for this behavior, but how do you prevent the effects of someone attempting to poison an ARP table?

One way to prevent the ill effects of this behavior is to create static ARP table entries for all of the devices on your local network segment. When this is done, the kernel will ignore all ARP responses for the specific IP address used in the entry and use the specified MAC address instead.

You can create static entries with the arp command, which allows you to directly manipulate the kernel's ARP table entries. To add a single static ARP table entry, run this command:

```
# arp -s ipaddr macaddr
```

For example, if you know that the MAC address that corresponds to 192.168.0.65 is 00:50:BA:85:85:CA, you could add a static ARP entry for it like this:

```
# arp -s 192.168.0.65 00:50:ba:85:85:ca
```

For more than a few entries, this can be a time-consuming process. And for it to be fully effective, you must add an entry for each device on your network on every host that allows you to create static ARP table entries.

Luckily, most versions of the arp command can take a file as input and use it to create static ARP table entries. Under Linux, this is done with the -f command-line switch. So, all you need to do is generate a file containing the MAC and IP address pairings, which you can then copy to all the hosts on your network.

To make this easier, you can use this quick-and-dirty Perl script:

```perl
#!/usr/bin/perl
#
# gen_ethers.pl <from ip> <to ip>
#

my ($start_1, $start_2, $start_3, $start_4) = split(/\./, $ARGV[0], 4);
my ($end_1, $end_2, $end_3, $end_4) = split(/\./, $ARGV[1], 4);
my $ARP_CMD="/sbin/arp -n";

for(my $oct_1 = $start_1; $oct_1 <= $end_1 && $oct_1 <= 255; $oct_1++ ){
  for(my $oct_2 = $start_2; $oct_2 <= $end_2 && $oct_2 <= 255; $oct_2++){
    for(my $oct_3 = $start_3; $oct_3 <= $end_3 && $oct_3 <= 255; $oct_3++){
      for(my $oct_4 = $start_4; $oct_4 <= $end_4 && $oct_4 < 255; $oct_4++){
      system("ping -c 1 -W 1 $oct_1.$oct_2.$oct_3.$oct_4 > /dev/null 2>&1");
          my $ether_addr = `$ARP_CMD $oct_1.$oct_2.$oct_3.$oct_4 | egrep
'HWaddress|
(incomplete)' | awk '{print \$3}'`;
      chomp($ether_addr);
      if(length($ether_addr) == 17){
        print("$ether_addr\t$oct_1.$oct_2.$oct_3.$oct_4\n");
      }
       }
      }
    }
  }
}
```

This script will take a range of IP addresses and attempt to ping each one once. This will cause each active IP address to appear in the machine's ARP table. After an IP address is pinged, the script will then look for that IP address in the ARP table and print out the MAC/IP address pair in a format suitable for putting into a file to load with the arp command. (This script was written with Linux in mind, but it should work on other Unix-like operating systems as well.)

For example, if you want to generate a file for all the IP addresses ranging from 192.168.1.1 to 192.168.1.255 and store the results in /etc/ethers, run the script like this:

```
# ./gen_ethers 192.168.1.1 192.168.1.255 > /etc/ethers
```

When you run arp with the -f switch, it will automatically use the */etc/ethers* file to create the static entries. However, you can specify any file you prefer. For example, to use */root/arp_entries* instead, run this:

```
# arp -f /root/arp_entries
```

This script isn't perfect, but it can save a lot of time when creating static ARP table entries for the hosts on your network. Once you've generated the file with the MAC/IP address pairings, you can copy it to the other hosts and add an arp command to the system startup scripts, to automatically load them at boot time.

The main downside to using this method is that all the devices on your network need to be powered on when the script runs; otherwise, they will be missing from the list. In addition, if the machines on your network change frequently, you'll have to regenerate and distribute the file often, which may be more trouble than it's worth. However, this method can protect devices that never change their IP or MAC addresses from ARP poisoning attacks.

Protect Against SSH Brute-Force Attacks

HACK #64

Thwart automated attacks against your Internet-facing servers.

If you remotely administer a server across the Internet, you might notice large numbers of failed login attempts from time to time. These often have the telltale sign of coming from a single IP address for an account that is not meant for interactive logins but is commonly found on Unix systems.

For example:

```
Jun 24 22:15:52 oceana sshd[11632]: Failed password for www from 218.22.3.51
port 39766 ssh2
Jun 24 22:16:24 oceana sshd[11678]: Failed password for news from 218.22.3.
51 port 40394 ssh2
Jun 24 22:16:33 oceana sshd[11687]: Failed password for games from 218.22.3.
51 port 40563 ssh2
Jun 24 22:17:22 oceana sshd[11747]: Failed password for cvs from 218.22.3.51
port 41462 ssh2
```

Often, these are brute-force attacks coming from compromised computers in foreign countries, which usually makes contacting those responsible for the network block or domain and asking them to put a stop to the attacks an exercise in futility. Theoretically, you should be safe from them, as long as your users use adequately strong passwords and the attacks don't persist for long enough to try a significant number of possible passwords. However, such attacks can make it more difficult to spot other attacks that might pose a more significant risk to your systems. Because of this, you'll want to put a stop to them quickly.

Changing the Port

Some methods for doing this are more effective than others. For instance, the most simple thing to do is to tell the SSH daemon to listen on a nonstandard port. For example, to have *sshd* listen on port 2200 instead of 22, you could put the following line in your *sshd_config* file (replacing the existing Port entry):

```
Port 2200
```

This might stop an attacker who's just looking for SSH daemons on their standard port, but it only requires a port scan to discover that you're running the service on a nonstandard port. Also, this measure will cost your users the convenience of not having to specify the port to connect to when logging in via SSH. Nevertheless, it should significantly decrease the number of failed login attempts you see in your logs.

Disabling Password Authentication

Another method is to disable password authentication. This will mean that users can only successfully connect when they have configured public-key authentication by generating a public/private key pair and copying the public key to *~/.ssh/authorized_keys* on the server. Adding the following line to your *sshd_config* disables authentication via passwords:

```
PasswordAuthentication no
```

However, this will require that your users carry their private keys with them on portable media if they wish to be able to log in when traveling.

Firewalling the SSH Daemon

The next method is to firewall your SSH daemon. Here there are three approaches you can take.

Limiting connections to your sshd. The most restrictive approach is to allow connections to your *sshd* only from a specific list of IP addresses (i.e., a *whitelist*).

For instance, you could use something similar to the following PF rules:

```
table <ssh_allow> { 10.0.0.47, 10.0.0.98, 10.0.0.27 }
block from any to any port 22
pass from <ssh_allow> to any port 22
```

However, this is obviously of limited use if your users need to be able to connect to their accounts when traveling.

Parsing logs and blocking an IP. The next approach is to parse your logs for failed login attempts and automatically block a given IP address once it has reached a threshold. If you go this route, make sure to whitelist any IP addresses that you connect from regularly, to avoid being inadvertently locked out if you mistype your password too many times.

Rate-limiting SYN packets. The last approach is to rate-limit SYN packets going to the port on which your SSH daemon is listening. The effect of this should be unnoticed by legitimate users, but it will delay an attacker that is making many repeated connections because it allows only a certain number of undelayed connections. For instance, PF lets you specify a rate for any stateful rule. This one limits the connection rate to port 22 to three per minute:

```
pass inet proto tcp from any to any port 22 \
keep state (max-src-conn-rate 3 / 60)
```

This will most likely cause the attacker to give up, because of the inordinate amount of time that will be needed to successfully brute-force an account.

Fool Remote Operating System Detection Software
#65   Evade remote OS detection attempts by disguising your TCP/IP stack.

One method to thwart operating-system-detection attempts is to modify the behavior of your system's TCP/IP stack and make it emulate the behavior of another operating system. This might sound difficult, but it can be done fairly easily in Linux by patching your kernel with code available from the IP Personality project (*http://ippersonality.sourceforge.net*). This code extends the kernel's built-in firewalling system, Netfilter [Hack #44], as well as its user-space component, the iptables command.

> This currently works for 2.4.x kernels only. However, this kernel version is still in widespread use.

To set up IP Personality, download the package that corresponds to your kernel. If you can't find the correct one, visit the SourceForge patches page for the project (*http://sourceforge.net/tracker/?group_id=7557&atid=307557*), which usually has more recent kernel patches available.

To patch your kernel, unpack the IP Personality source distribution and go to the directory containing your kernel source. Then run the patch command:

```
# cd /usr/src/linux
# patch -p1 < \ ../ippersonality-20020819-2.4.19/patches/ippersonality-
20020819-linux-2.4.19.diff
```

If you are using a patch downloaded from the patches page, just substitute your patch command. To verify that the patch has been applied correctly, run this command:

```
# find ./ -name \*.rej
```

If the patch was applied correctly, this command should not find any files.

Now that the kernel is patched, you will need to configure the kernel for IP Personality support. As mentioned in "Lock Down Your Kernel with grsecurity" [Hack #13], running make xconfig, make menuconfig, or even make config while you are in the kernel source's directory will allow you to configure your kernel. Regardless of the method you choose, the menu options will remain the same.

First, be sure that "Prompt for development and/or incomplete code/drivers" is enabled under "Code maturity level options." Under "Networking Options," find and enable the option for Netfilter Configuration.

Figure 6-1 shows the list displayed by make xconfig. Find the option labeled IP Personality Support, and either select y to statically compile it into your kernel or select m to create a dynamically loaded module.

After you have configured support for IP Personality, save your configuration. Now, compile the kernel and modules and install them by running the following commands:

```
# make dep && make clean
# make bzImage && make modules
# cp arch/i386/boot/bzImage /boot/vmlinuz
# make modules_install
```

Reboot with your new kernel. In addition to patching your kernel, you'll also need to patch the user-space portion of Netfilter, the iptables command. Go to the Netfilter web site (http://www.netfilter.org) and download the version specified by the patch that came with your IP Personality package. For instance, the iptables patch included in *ippersonality-20020819-2.4.19.tar.gz* is for Netfilter Version 1.2.2.

After downloading the proper version and unpacking it, you will need to patch it with the patch included in the IP Personality package. Then, build and install it in the normal way:

```
# tar xfj iptables-1.2.2.tar.bz2
# cd iptables-1.2.2
# patch -p1 < \../ippersonality-20020819-2.4.19/patches/ippersonality-
20020427-iptables-\1.2.2.diff
patching file pers/Makefile
patching file pers/example.conf
patching file pers/libipt_PERS.c
patching file pers/pers.h
```

```
patching file pers/pers.l
patching file pers/pers.y
patching file pers/pers_asm.c
patching file pers/perscc.c
# make KERNEL_DIR=/usr/src/linux && make install
```

This will install the modified iptables command, its supporting libraries, and the manpage under the */usr/local* hierarchy. If you would like to change the default installation directories, you can edit the makefile and change the values of the BINDIR, LIBDIR, MANDIR, and INCDIR macros. Be sure to set KERNEL_DIR to the directory containing the kernel sources you built earlier.

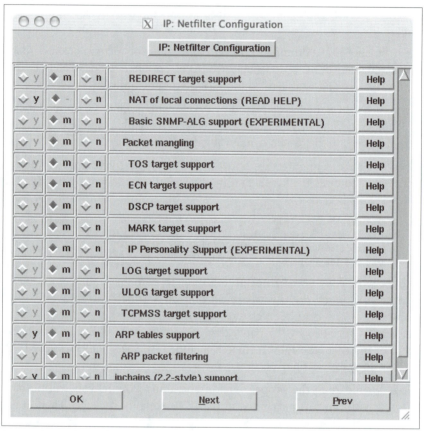

Figure 6-1. Enabling IP Personality support

If you are using Red Hat Linux, you can replace the iptables command that is installed by changing the macros to these values:

```
LIBDIR:=/lib
BINDIR:=/sbin
MANDIR:=/usr/share/man
```

```
INCDIR:=/usr/include
```

In addition to running make install, you might want to create a directory for the operating system personality configuration files. These files are located in the /samples directory within the IP Personality distribution. For example, you could create a directory called /etc/personalities and copy them there.

Before setting up IP Personality, try running Nmap (http://www.insecure.org/nmap/) against the machine to see which operating system it detects:

```
# nmap -O colossus
```

```
Starting nmap 3.48 ( http://www.insecure.org/nmap/ ) at 2003-12-12 18:36 MST
Interesting ports on colossus (192.168.0.64):
(The 1651 ports scanned but not shown below are in state: closed)
PORT    STATE SERVICE
22/tcp  open  ssh
25/tcp  open  smtp
111/tcp open  rpcbind
139/tcp open  netbios-ssn
505/tcp open  mailbox-lm
631/tcp open  ipp
Device type: general purpose
Running: Linux 2.4.X|2.5.X
OS details: Linux Kernel 2.4.0 - 2.5.20
Uptime 3.095 days (since Tue Dec 9 16:19:55 2003)

Nmap run completed -- 1 IP address (1 host up) scanned in 7.375 seconds
```

If your machine has an IP address of 192.168.0.64 and you want it to pretend that it's running Mac OS 9, you can run iptables commands like these:

```
# iptables -t mangle -A PREROUTING -d 192.168.0.64 -j PERS \
--tweak dst --local --conf /etc/personalities/macos9.conf
# iptables -t mangle -A OUTPUT -s 192.168.0.64 -j PERS \
--tweak src --local --conf /etc/personalities/macos9.conf
```

Now, run Nmap again:

```
# nmap -O colossus
```

```
Starting nmap 3.48 ( http://www.insecure.org/nmap/ ) at 2003-12-12 18:47 MST
Interesting ports on colossus (192.168.0.64):
(The 1651 ports scanned but not shown below are in state: closed)
PORT    STATE SERVICE
22/tcp  open  ssh
25/tcp  open  smtp
111/tcp open  rpcbind
139/tcp open  netbios-ssn
505/tcp open  mailbox-lm
631/tcp open  ipp
Device type: general purpose
```

```
Running: Apple Mac OS 9.X
OS details: Apple Mac OS 9 - 9.1
Uptime 3.095 days (since Tue Dec 9 16:19:55 2003)

Nmap run completed -- 1 IP address (1 host up) scanned in 5.274 seconds
```

You can, of course, emulate other operating systems that aren't provided with the IP Personality package. All you need is a copy of Nmap's operating system fingerprints file, *nmap-os-fingerprints*. You can then construct your own IP Personality configuration file for any operating system Nmap knows about.

HACK #66   Keep an Inventory of Your Network

Use Nmap to keep track of the devices and services on your network.

As introduced in "Fool Remote Operating System Detection Software" [Hack #65], Nmap (*http://www.insecure.org/nmap/*) is a free tool that can be used to conduct various sorts of scans on networks. Normally, when people think of Nmap, they assume it's used to conduct some sort of nefarious network reconnaissance in preparation for an attack. But as with all powerful tools, Nmap can be used for far more than breaking into networks.

For example, it allows you to conduct simple TCP connect scans without needing root privileges:

```
$ nmap rigel

Starting nmap 3.48 ( http://www.insecure.org/nmap/ ) at 2003-12-15 17:42 MST
Interesting ports on rigel (192.168.0.61):
(The 1595 ports scanned but not shown below are in state: filtered)
PORT       STATE  SERVICE
7/tcp      open   echo
9/tcp      open   discard
13/tcp     open   daytime
19/tcp     open   chargen
21/tcp     open   ftp
22/tcp     open   ssh
23/tcp     open   telnet
25/tcp     open   smtp
37/tcp     open   time
79/tcp     open   finger
111/tcp    open   rpcbind
512/tcp    open   exec
513/tcp    open   login
514/tcp    open   shell
587/tcp    open   submission
4045/tcp   open   lockd
7100/tcp   open   font-service
32771/tcp  open   sometimes-rpc5
32772/tcp  open   sometimes-rpc7
```

```
32773/tcp open   sometimes-rpc9
32774/tcp open   sometimes-rpc11
32775/tcp open   sometimes-rpc13
32776/tcp open   sometimes-rpc15
32777/tcp open   sometimes-rpc17

Nmap run completed -- 1 IP address (1 host up) scanned in 75.992 seconds
```

This is tremendously useful for checking on the state of your own machines. You could probably guess that this scan was performed on a Solaris machine, and one that needs to have some services disabled at that.

Nmap can also scan ranges of IP addresses, indicated by either specifying the range or using CIDR notation, as follows:

```
$ nmap 192.168.0.1-254
$ nmap 192.168.0.0/24
```

Nmap can provide much more information if you run it as root. When run as root, it can use special packets to determine the operating system of the remote machine by using the -O flag. Additionally, you can do half-open TCP scanning by using the -sS flag. When doing a half-open scan, Nmap sends a SYN packet to the remote host and waits to receive the ACK from it; if it receives an ACK, it knows that the port is open. This is different from a normal three-way TCP handshake, where the client sends a SYN packet and then sends an ACK back to the server once it has received the initial server ACK. Attackers typically use this option to avoid having their scans logged on the remote machine.

Try it out for yourself:

```
# nmap -sS -O rigel

Starting nmap V. 3.00 ( www.insecure.org/nmap/ )
Interesting ports on rigel.nnc (192.168.0.61):
(The 1578 ports scanned but not shown below are in state: filtered)
Port      State      Service
7/tcp     open       echo
9/tcp     open       discard
13/tcp    open       daytime
19/tcp    open       chargen
21/tcp    open       ftp
22/tcp    open       ssh
23/tcp    open       telnet
25/tcp    open       smtp
37/tcp    open       time
79/tcp    open       finger
111/tcp   open       sunrpc
512/tcp   open       exec
513/tcp   open       login
514/tcp   open       shell
587/tcp   open       submission
```

```
7100/tcp   open          font-service
32771/tcp  open          sometimes-rpc5
32772/tcp  open          sometimes-rpc7
32773/tcp  open          sometimes-rpc9
32774/tcp  open          sometimes-rpc11
32775/tcp  open          sometimes-rpc13
32776/tcp  open          sometimes-rpc15
32777/tcp  open          sometimes-rpc17
Remote operating system guess: Solaris 9 Beta through Release on SPARC
Uptime 44.051 days (since Sat Nov  1 16:41:50 2003)

Nmap run completed -- 1 IP address (1 host up) scanned in 166 seconds
```

With OS detection enabled, Nmap has confirmed that the operating system is Solaris, but now you also know that it's probably Version 9 running on a SPARC processor.

One powerful feature you can use to help keep track of your network is Nmap's XML output capabilities, activated with the -oX command-line switch:

```
# nmap -sS -O -oX scandata.xml rigel
```

This is especially useful when scanning a range of IP addresses or your whole network, because you can put all the information gathered from the scan into a single XML file that can be parsed and inserted into a database. Here's what an XML entry for an open port looks like:

```
<port protocol="tcp" portid="22">
<state state="open" />
<service name="ssh" method="table" conf="3"  />
</port>
```

This is especially powerful when combined with the Nmap::Parser Perl module (*http://npx.sourceforge.net*), which allows you to read Nmap's XML output. When paired with Perl's DBI for database access, you have the makings of a tool that can easily generate a database of network devices. Parsing an Nmap XML file is as easy as this:

```
use Nmap::Parser;
my $np = new Nmap::Parser;
my $file_xml = "an_nmap_xml_file.xml"
$np->parsefile($file_xml);
```

Then, all you need to do is call the parser object's accessor methods to get at the data.

Nmap is a powerful tool. By using its XML output capabilities, a little bit of scripting, and a database, you can create an even more powerful tool that can monitor your network for unauthorized services and machines.

Scan Your Network for Vulnerabilities

#67 Use Nessus to quickly and easily scan your network for services that are vulnerable to attack.

As a network administrator, you need to know not only which hosts are on your network and what services they are running, but also if those services are vulnerable to exploits. While a port scanner can show you what machines and ports are reachable on your network, a security scanner such as Nessus (*http://www.nessus.org*) can tell you if those machines are vulnerable to known exploits.

Unlike a regular port scanner, a *security scanner* first locates listening services and then connects to those services and attempts to execute exploits against them. It then records whether the exploits were successful and continues scanning until all available services have been tested. The key benefit here is that you'll know at a glance how your systems perform against known exploits, and thus whether they truly are vulnerable to attack.

With the release of Version 3, Nessus has become a closed-source project. Because of this, the current release and future versions are available only as packages, instead of as source code. However, the old Version 2.8.8 is still available in source form. If you want to use Nessus 2.x, read on. Otherwise, skip to the "Nessus 3.x" section.

Nessus 2.x

If you want to use Version 2.8.8, download the *nessus-installer-2.2.8.sh* script from the Nessus download page (*http://www.nessus.org/download/index.php*) and execute it. You will be asked where you want to install Nessus (the default is */usr/local*) and prompted for your root password. The script will then create a temporary SUID shell that is accessible only through your user account. This might sound alarming at first, but it tells you the filename for the shell, so you can verify that it is indeed accessible only to you and make sure that it is deleted when the installation is complete.

After the installation has finished, you'll need to create a Nessus user (not the same thing as a Unix account). Since Nessus uses a client/server model, you'll also need to generate a certificate so that all communications can be encrypted.

To create a new Nessus user, run `nessus-adduser`. You'll be prompted for a name and a password. To create a certificate, you can run `nessus-mkcert`, or, if you have your own Certificate Authority (CA) [Hack #69], you can use that to create a certificate for Nessus to use. If you do use your own CA, you'll need to edit *nessus.conf* to tell it where to look for the CA certificate and the certificate and key that you generated.

The configuration file usually lives in */etc* or */usr/local/etc*. To tell Nessus the location of its certificates, add lines similar to the following:

```
cert_file=/etc/ssl/nessus.key
key_file=/etc/ssl/nessus.crt
ca_file=/etc/ssl/ca.crt
```

If you generated a certificate/key pair and used a password, you can specify that password here as well:

```
pem_password=mypassword
```

After you've done that, you can start the Nessus daemon. This is the business end of Nessus and is what actually performs the scans against the hosts on your network.

To start it, run this command:

```
# /usr/local/sbin/nessusd -D
```

Now, you can start the Nessus client and connect to the server. Several Nessus clients are available, including a command-line interface, an X11 application, and a Windows client. The figures in this hack show the X11 interface.

Start the client by simply typing nessus. You should see a window like the one shown in Figure 6-2.

Fill in the information for the user that you created and click the Log In button. You'll be presented with a dialog that allows you to verify the information contained in the server's certificate.

To select which types of vulnerabilities to scan for, click on the Plugins tab to display the screen shown in Figure 6-3.

In the top pane, you can enable or disable types of scans, and in the bottom pane, you can disable individual vulnerability checks that belong to the category selected in the top pane.

> Scans listed in the bottom pane that have an exclamation icon next to them will potentially crash the server against which they're run. If you want to enable all scans except for these, you can click the "Enable all but dangerous plugins" button. If you're running Nessus on a noncritical machine, you can probably leave these scans on, but you have been warned!

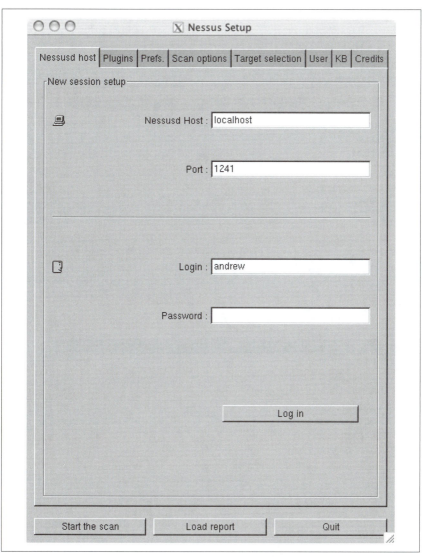

Figure 6-2. Nessus 2.x client setup

You'll probably want to disable several types of scans, unless you need to scan a machine or group of machines that run a wide variety of services; otherwise, you'll waste time having Nessus scan for services that you aren't running. For instance, if you want to scan a Solaris system, you might disable CGI abuses, CISCO, Windows, Peer-To-Peer File Sharing, Backdoors, Firewalls, Windows User Management, and Netware plug-ins.

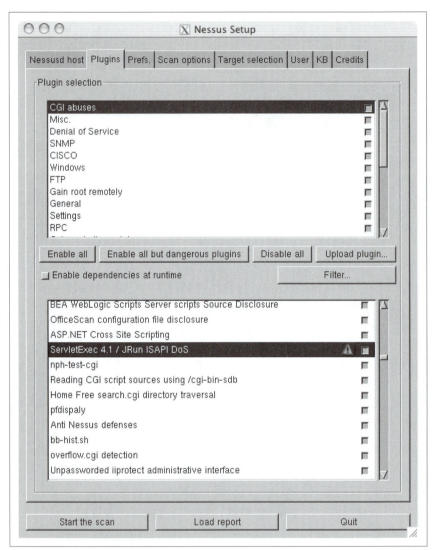

Figure 6-3. Nessus 2.x plug-in selection

To enable Nessus to more thoroughly test your services, you can supply it with login information for various services. This way, it can actually log into the services that it is testing and have access just like any normal user. You can tell Nessus about the accounts to use with the Prefs tab, shown in Figure 6-4.

In addition, you can tell Nessus to attempt brute-force logins to the services it is scanning. This can be a good test not only of the services themselves, but also of your intrusion detection system (IDS) [Hack #106] and log-monitoring infrastructure.

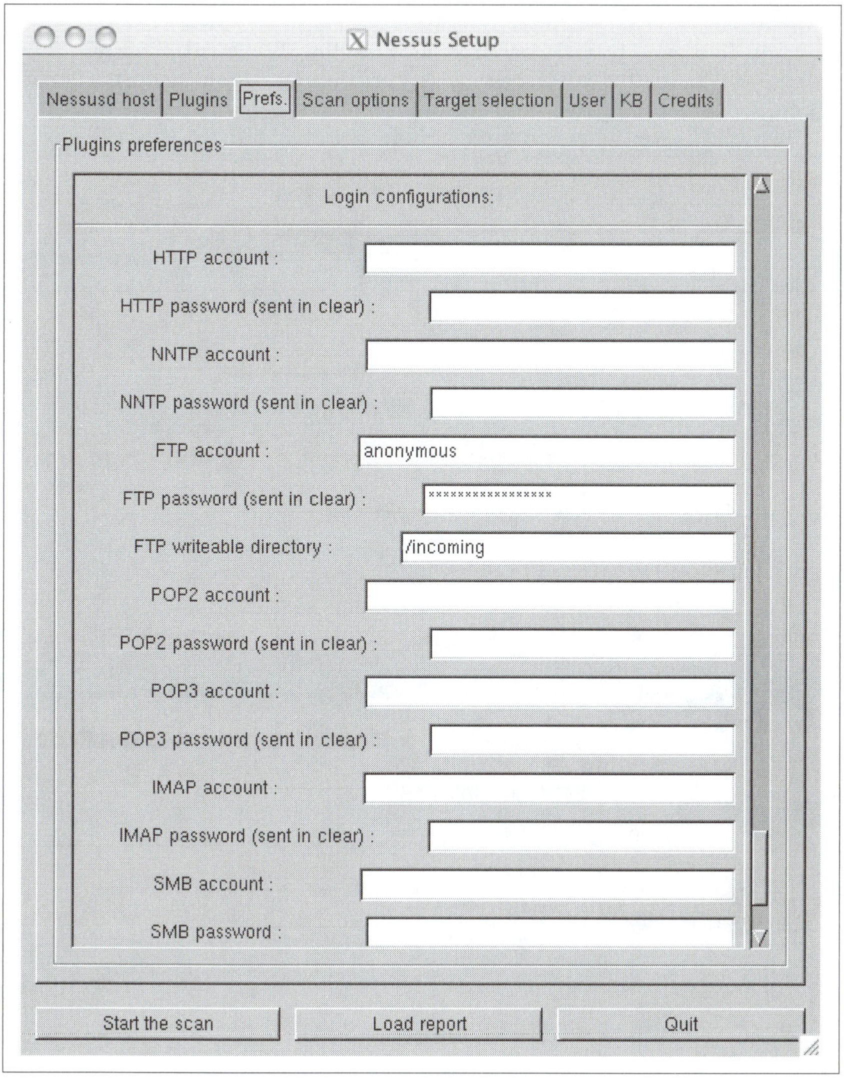

Figure 6-4. Nessus 2.x's Prefs tab

The "Scan options" tab lets you configure how Nessus conducts its port scans. You can leave most of these settings at their default values, unless you are also checking to see whether Nessus can evade detection by the hosts that you are scanning. For instance, Nessus is configured by default to perform full TCP connect scans and to ping the remote host that it is scanning. You can change this behavior by going to the "Scan options" tab, enabling "SYN scans" instead of "TCP connect," and disabling the ping. To specify which hosts you want to scan, use the "Target selection" tab.

After you've made your selections, try scanning a host by clicking "Start the scan" at the bottom of the window. You should now see a window similar to Figure 6-5. In this case, Nessus is performing a scan against a Solaris machine.

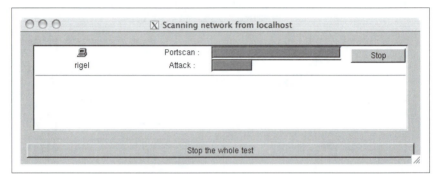

Figure 6-5. Performing a vulnerability scan in Nessus 2.x

Figure 6-6 shows the results of the scan.

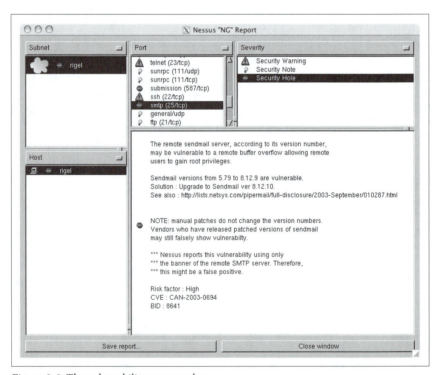

Figure 6-6. The vulnerability scan results

If you scanned multiple subnets, you can select those in the Subnet pane. Any hosts that are in the selected subnet will then appear in the Host pane. Similarly, when you select a host, the list of open ports on it will appear in the Port pane. You can select these to view the warnings, notes, and possible security holes that were found for the selected port.

You can view the information that Nessus provides for these by clicking on them in the Severity pane. Don't be too alarmed by most of Nessus's security notes and warnings; they are designed mainly to let you know what services you are running and to tell you if those services present potential vulnerabilities. Security holes are far more serious and should be investigated.

To save the report that you are viewing, click the "Save report" button. Nessus will let you save reports in a variety of formats. If you want to view the report in Nessus again at a later date, use Nessus's own report format (NBE). To view reports in this format, click the "Load report" button in the main Nessus client window. Additionally, you can save reports in XML, HTML, ASCII, and even LaTeX format.

Nessus 3.x

As mentioned at the beginning of this hack, Nessus 3.0 and later are available only in package form for Linux, FreeBSD, Solaris, and Windows. Download the package appropriate for your system and install it. In order to do this, you'll have to provide some personal information. You'll also receive a registration code that can be used to download the latest Nessus plug-ins.

Nessus will install certificates as part of the installation process, so you no longer need to run `nessus-mkcert`. You can also choose to install your own certificates using the same method used for Nessus 2.x.

Once you've installed the package, you'll need to create a user in the Nessus system (unless you're using Windows) by running `nessus-adduser`, which will prompt you for a name and a password. Next, download the plug-ins. Run `nessus-fetch`, specifying your registration code:

```
# nessus-fetch --register XXXX-XXXX-XXXX-XXXX-XXXX
Your activation code has been registered properly - thank you.
Now fetching the newest plugin set from plugins.nessus.org...

Your Nessus installation is now up-to-date.
If auto_update is set to 'yes' in nessusd.conf, Nessus will
update the plugins by itself.
```

As mentioned in the output, putting auto_update=yes in your *nessusd.conf* file instructs Nessus to automatically update its plug-ins, but it should already be set up to update its plug-ins every 24 hours.

Another key difference between Nessus 2.x and 3.x is that the latter doesn't come with a GUI client (the exception to this is the Windows package). For that, you'll need to go back to the Nessus site, download the NessusClient package, and install it.

After you've installed the NessusClient package, you can launch it by simply typing NessusClient. Then, open the File menu and click Connect. You should be presented with a dialog like the one shown in Figure 6-7, where you can choose what server to connect to and specify your username and password.

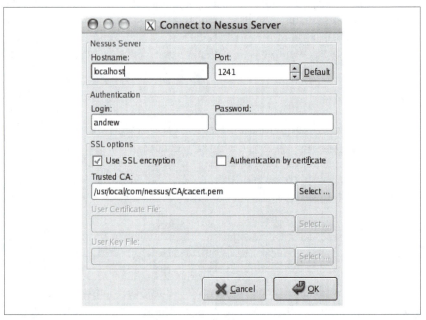

Figure 6-7. Logging in with NessusClient

After you've connected to the Nessus server, you can configure the global settings that will serve as a basis for all of the scans that you conduct. If you want to limit the ports that are scanned on each host, whether to do TCP connect( ) scanning or SYN scanning, or any other general scanning engine parameters, click the General icon in the Options tab, as shown in Figure 6-8.

Enable or disable plug-ins by clicking the Plugins icon. As shown in Figure 6-9, Nessus 3 organizes the plug-ins into a categorized tree view, unlike previous versions.

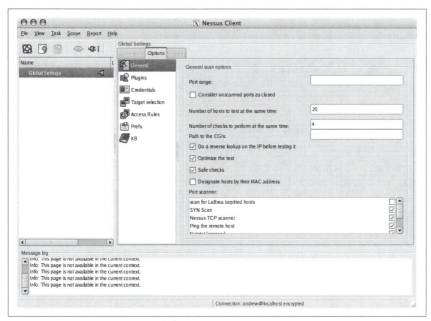

Figure 6-8. Configuring general settings

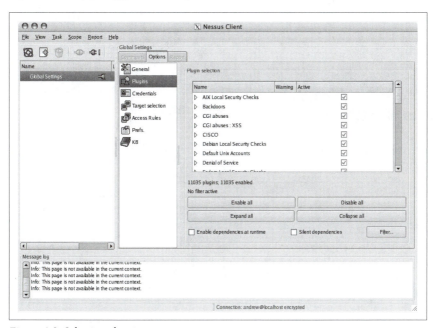

Figure 6-9. Selecting plug-ins

You can disable whole categories of plug-ins by unchecking them. Likewise, you can disable an individual plug-in by using the checkbox next to it.

> As in previous versions of Nessus, plug-ins with an exclamation icon next to them are likely to disrupt service on the device they're scanning.

After you're done configuring Nessus's global settings, the easiest way to start scanning your network is to use the Scan Assistant, which is accessible under the File menu. This is where the new Nessus client departs greatly from the 2.x version. NessusClient uses the concept of tasks and scopes. A *task* is something like "Scan the local subnet" or "Scan a single host." When a task is being performed, it has a *scope* that defines what systems are scanned in order to complete the task. The Scan Assistant prompts you to create a task and then to define a scope. Once that's been done, you can execute the scan.

After the scan has completed, you'll see the task and scope that the Scan Assistant created in the left pane of NessusClient. Here, you can also view reports of the current and past scans, as shown in Figure 6-10, in just the same way as in previous versions of Nessus.

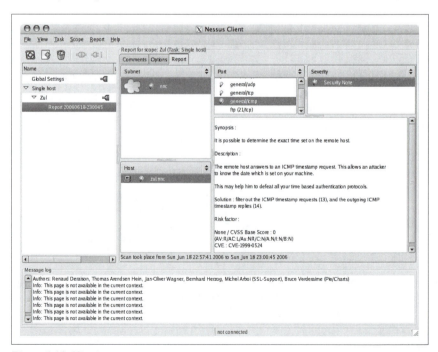

Figure 6-10. Viewing reports

If you want to perform the scan again, simply open the Scope menu and click Execute. You can also modify the scan settings for an individual scope by selecting it and then changing any settings, just as you would for the Global Settings.

While Nmap [Hack #66] is probably the champion of network reconnaissance, Nessus goes even further to demonstrate whether your own services are vulnerable to known attacks. Of course, new exploits surface all the time, so it's important to keep your Nessus plug-ins up-to-date. Using Nessus, you can protect your own services by attempting to break into them before the bad boys do.

HACK #68 Keep Server Clocks Synchronized

Make log analysis easier by keeping the time on your systems in sync.

Correlating events that have occurred on multiple servers can be a chore if there are discrepancies between the machines' clocks. Keeping the clocks on your systems synchronized can save valuable time when analyzing router, firewall, and host logs after a compromise, or when debugging everyday networking issues. Luckily, doing this isn't hard, with a little help from the Network Time Protocol (NTP).

NTP is a peer-to-peer protocol designed to provide subsecond precision and accuracy between host clocks. To get it going, all you need is the NTP distribution (*http://www.ntp.org/downloads.html*), which contains a daemon for performing clock synchronization, plus other supporting tools. Though NTP might not be installed on your system, it usually comes with the various Linux distributions, FreeBSD, and OpenBSD as an optional package or port, so poke around your installation media or the ports tree if it's not already installed. If it isn't available with your OS of choice, you can still download and compile it yourself.

Configuring *ntpd* as a client is a fairly simple process, but first you'll need to find out whether you have a local time server, either on your network or at your ISP. If you don't, you'll have to locate an NTP server that will let you query from it. You'll want to find servers that are as geographically close to you as possible. Don't worry, though; a list of all the publicly accessible time servers is available at *http://www.eecis.udel.edu/~mills/ntp/servers.html*.

One new term you will encounter when looking for a server is *stratum* (e.g., stratum 1 or stratum 2). This refers to the hierarchy of the server within the public NTP infrastructure. A stratum 1 server will usually have a direct time-sync source, such as a GPS or atomic clock signal that provides updates to the daemon running on that machine. Stratum 2 servers obtain their time sync from stratum 1 servers. Using stratum 2 servers helps to reduce the load on stratum 1 servers, and they're accurate enough for this hack's purposes.

With this in mind, let's look for some NTP servers that we can use (using more than one is generally a good idea, in case one fails). I live in Colorado, so after following the link to the stratum 2 server list (*http://www.eecis.udel. edu/~mills/ntp/clock2a.html*), I found two entries:

```
# US CO ntp1.linuxmedialabs.com
Location: Linux Media Labs LLC, Colorado Springs, CO
Service Area: US
Synchronization: NTP Secondary (stratum 2), i686/Linux
Access Policy: open access
Contact: ntp@linuxmedialabs.com
Note: ntp1 is an alias and the IP address may change, please use DNS

# US CO ntp1.tummy.com
Location: tummy.com, ltd., Fort Collins, CO
Service Area: US
Synchronization: NTP Secondary (stratum 2), i686/Linux
Access Policy: open access.
Contact: ntp@tummy.com
Note: ntp1 is an alias and the IP address may change, please use DNS.
```

Because they're both listed as open access, I can just add them to my */etc/ ntp.conf*:

```
server ntp1.linuxmedialabs.com
server ntp1.tummy.com
```

Alternatively, you can simplify your configuration by using `pool.ntp.org`, which is a round-robin DNS scheme to resolve to multiple time servers. You'll find these servers on the published lists of NTP servers, but they have also elected to become a part of the pool. For instance:

```
server 0.pool.ntp.org
server 1.pool.ntp.org
server 2.pool.ntp.org
```

The following zones resolve to a pool of NTP servers that are located within a given geographical region: `asia.pool.ntp.org`, `europe.pool.ntp.org`, `north-america.pool.ntp.org`, `oceania.pool.ntp.org`, and `south-america.pool.ntp. org`. Using these will cut down on Internet traffic and latency.

There are also zones that resolve to NTP servers in specific countries (e.g., `us.pool.ntp.org`); you can get a complete list of them at *http://ntp.isc.org/ bin/view/Servers/NTPPoolServers*.

In addition, *ntpd* can automatically correct for the specific clock frequency drift of your machine. It does this by learning the average drift over time as it receives sync messages. Just add a line like this to your *ntp.conf* file to enable this feature:

```
driftfile /etc/ntp.drift
```

Of course, if you're keeping all of your *ntpd* configuration files in */etc/ntp*, you'll want to use a directory similar to */etc/ntp/ntp.drift* instead.

That's it. Simply add *ntpd* to your startup scripts, start it up, and you're ready to go.

Create Your Own Certificate Authority
Sign your own certificates to use in securing your network.

SSL certificates are usually thought of as being used for secure communications over the HTTP protocol. However, they are also useful in providing both a means for authentication and a means for initiating key exchange for a myriad of other services where encryption is desired, such as POP and IMAP **[Hack #54]**, SMTP **[Hack #55]**, IPsec **[Hack #93]**, and, of course, SSL tunnels **[Hack #100]**. To make the best use of SSL, you will need to properly manage your own certificates.

If an SSL client needs to verify the authenticity of an SSL server, the cert used by the server needs to be signed by a Certificate Authority (CA) that is already trusted by the client. Well-known CAs (such as Thawte and Veri-Sign) exist to serve as authoritative, trusted third parties for authentication. They are in the business of signing SSL certificates that are used on sites dealing with sensitive information (such as account numbers or passwords).

If a trusted authority has signed a site's SSL certificate, presumably it is possible to verify the identity of a server supplying that cert's credentials. However, for anything other than e-commerce applications, a self-signed certificate is usually sufficient for gaining all of the security advantages that SSL provides. Of course, an authority that the client recognizes must sign even a self-signed cert.

OpenSSL, a free SSL implementation, is perfectly capable of generating everything you need to run your own Certificate Authority. The *CA.pl* utility makes the process very simple.

In these examples, you'll need to type anything in boldface, and enter passwords wherever appropriate (they don't echo to the screen).

Creating the CA

To establish your new Certificate Authority, first change to the */misc* directory under wherever OpenSSL is installed (*/System/Library/OpenSSL* on Mac OS X; */usr/ssl* or */usr/local/ssl* on most Linux systems). Then, use these commands:

```
$./CA.pl -newca
CA certificate filename (or enter to create)

Making CA certificate ...
Generating a 1024 bit RSA private key
..........++++++
....................++++++
writing new private key to './demoCA/private/cakey.pem'
Enter PEM pass phrase:
Verifying - Enter PEM pass phrase:
-----
You are about to be asked to enter information that will be incorporated
into your certificate request.
What you are about to enter is what is called a Distinguished Name or a DN.
There are quite a few fields but you can leave some blank
For some fields there will be a default value,
If you enter '.', the field will be left blank.
-----
Country Name (2 letter code) []:US
State or Province Name (full name) []:Colorado
Locality Name (eg, city) []:Denver
Organization Name (eg, company) []:NonExistant Enterprises
Organizational Unit Name (eg, section) []:IT Services
Common Name (eg, fully qualified host name) []:ca.nonexistantdomain.com
Email Address []:certadmin@nonexistantdomain.com
```

Note that you don't necessarily need root permissions, but you will need write permissions on the current directory.

Congratulations! You're the proud owner of your very own Certificate Authority. Take a look around:

```
$ ls -l demoCA/
total 16
-rw-r--r--  1 andrew  andrew  1399  3 Dec 19:52 cacert.pem
drwxr-xr-x  2 andrew  andrew    68  3 Dec 19:49 certs
drwxr-xr-x  2 andrew  andrew    68  3 Dec 19:49 crl
-rw-r--r--  1 andrew  andrew     0  3 Dec 19:49 index.txt
drwxr-xr-x  2 andrew  andrew    68  3 Dec 19:49 newcerts
drwxr-xr-x  3 andrew  andrew   102  3 Dec 19:49 private
-rw-r--r--  1 andrew  andrew     3  3 Dec 19:49 serial
```

The public key for your new CA is contained in *cacert.pem*, and the private key is in *private/cakey.pem*. You can now use this private key to sign other SSL certs.

By default, *CA.pl* creates keys that are good for only one year. To change this behavior, edit *CA.pl* and change the line that reads:

```
$DAYS="-days 365";
```

Alternatively, you can forego *CA.pl* altogether and generate the public and private keys manually with a command like this:

```
$ openssl req -new -x509 -keyout cakey.pem -out cakey.pem -days 3650
```

This creates a key pair that is good for the next 10 years (to change that period, use a different argument to the -days switch). Additionally, you should change the private key's permissions to 600, to ensure that it is protected from being read by anyone.

Signing Certificates

So far, you've only created the Certificate Authority. To actually create keys that you can use with your services, you need to create a certificate-signing request and a key. Again, this can be done easily with *CA.pl*. First, create a certificate-signing request:

```
$ ./CA.pl -newreq-nodes
Generating a 1024 bit RSA private key
...++++++
..........................................++++++
writing new private key to 'newreq.pem'
-----
You are about to be asked to enter information that will be incorporated
into your certificate request.
What you are about to enter is what is called a Distinguished Name or a DN.
There are quite a few fields but you can leave some blank
For some fields there will be a default value,
If you enter '.', the field will be left blank.
-----
Country Name (2 letter code) [AU]:US
State or Province Name (full name) [Some-State]:Colorado
Locality Name (eg, city) []:Denver
Organization Name (eg, company) [Internet Widgits Pty Ltd]:NonExistant
Enterprises
Organizational Unit Name (eg, section) []:IT Services
Common Name (eg, YOUR name) []:mail.nonexistantdomain.com
Email Address []:postmaster@nonexistantdomain.com

Please enter the following 'extra' attributes
to be sent with your certificate request
A challenge password []:
An optional company name []:NonExistant Enterprises
Request (and private key) is in newreq.pem
```

If you want to encrypt the private key, you can use the -newreq switch in place of -newreq-nodes. However, if you encrypt the private key, you will have to enter the password for it each time the service that uses it is started.

If you decide not to use an encrypted private key, be extremely cautious with your private key, as anyone who can obtain a copy of it can impersonate your server.

Now, to actually sign the request and generate the signed certificate, issue this command:

```
$ ./CA.pl -sign
Using configuration from /System/Library/OpenSSL/openssl.cnf
Enter pass phrase for ./demoCA/private/cakey.pem:
Check that the request matches the signature
Signature ok
Certificate Details:
        Serial Number: 1 (0x1)
        Validity
          Not Before: Dec  3 09:05:08 2003 GMT
          Not After : Dec  3 09:05:08 2004 GMT
        Subject:
            countryName              = US
            stateOrProvinceName      = Colorado
            localityName             = Denver
            organizationName         = NonExistant Enterprises
            organizationalUnitName   = IT Services
            commonName               = mail.nonexistantdomain.com
            emailAddress             = postmaster@nonexistantdomain.com
        X509v3 extensions:
            X509v3 Basic Constraints:
            CA:FALSE
            Netscape Comment:
            OpenSSL Generated Certificate
            X509v3 Subject Key Identifier:
            94:0F:E9:F5:22:40:2C:71:D0:A7:5C:65:02:3E:BC:D8:DB:10:BD:88
            X509v3 Authority Key Identifier:
            keyid:7E:AF:2D:A4:39:37:F5:36:AE:71:2E:09:0E:49:23:70:61:28:5F:
4A
            DirName:/C=US/ST=Colorado/L=Denver/O=NonExistant Enterprises/
OU=IT Services/
CN=Certificate Administration/emailAddress=certadmin@nonexistantdomain.com
            serial:00

Certificate is to be certified until Dec  7 09:05:08 2004 GMT (365 days)
Sign the certificate? [y/n]:y


1 out of 1 certificate requests certified, commit? [y/n]:y
Write out database with 1 new entries
Data Base Updated
Signed certificate is in newcert.pem
```

Now you can set up keys in this manner for each server that needs to provide an SSL-encrypted service. It is easier to do this if you designate a single workstation to maintain the CA and all the files associated with it. Don't forget to distribute your CA cert [Hack #70] to programs that need to trust it.

Distribute Your CA to Clients

#70   Be sure all of your clients trust your new Certificate Authority.

Once you have created a Certificate Authority (CA) [Hack #69], any program that trusts your CA will trust any certificates that are signed by your CA. To establish this trust, you need to distribute your CA's certificate to each program that needs to trust it. This could include email programs, IP security (IPsec) installations, or web browsers.

Because SSL uses public-key cryptography, there is no need to keep the certificate a secret. You can simply install it on a web server and download it to your clients over plain old HTTP. While the instructions for installing a CA cert are different for every program, this hack will show you a quick and easy way to install your CA on web browsers.

Browsers accept two possible formats for new CA certs: *pem* and *der*. You can generate a *der* from your existing *pem* with a single openssl command:

```
$ openssl x509 -in demoCA/cacert.pem -outform DER -out cacert.der
```

Then add the following line to the *conf/mime.types* file in your Apache installation:

```
application/x-x509-ca-cert      der pem crt
```

Restart Apache for the change to take effect. You should now be able to place both the *cacert.der* and *demoCA/cacert.pem* files anywhere on your web server and have clients install the new cert by simply clicking on either link.

Early versions of Netscape expected the *pem* format, but recent versions accept either. Internet Explorer is just the opposite (early IE accepted only the *der* format, but recent versions take both). Other browsers generally accept either format.

When downloading the new Certificate Authority, your browser will ask if you'd like to continue. Accept the certificate, and that's all there is to it. Now, SSL certs that are signed by your CA will be accepted without warning the user.

Keep in mind that Certificate Authorities aren't to be taken lightly. If you accept a new CA in your browser, you had better trust it completely; a mischievous CA manager could sign all sorts of certs that you should never trust, but your browser would never complain (since you claimed to trust the CA when you imported it). Be very careful about whom you extend your trust to when using SSL-enabled browsers. It's worth looking around in the CA cache that ships with your browser to see exactly who you trust by default. For example, did you know that AOL/Time Warner has its own

CA? How about GTE? Or Visa? CA certs for all of these entities (and many others) ship with Netscape 7.0 for Linux, and they are all trusted authorities for web sites, email, and application add-ons by default. Keep this in mind when browsing to SSL-enabled sites: if any of the default authorities have signed online content, your browser will trust it without requiring operator acknowledgment.

If you value your browser's security (and, by extension, the security of your client machine), make it a point to review your trusted CA relationships.

—Rob Flickenger

HACK #71 Back Up and Restore a Certificate Authority with Certificate Services

Backing up your local Certificate Authority is essential, because it forms the foundation for public-key cryptography for your organization.

If you're thinking of using IPsec in an enterprise environment to encrypt virtual private network (VPN) communications for your remote users, or if you're considering securing email communications in your enterprise by encrypting messages and signing them digitally, chances are you've thought of deploying your own local Certificate Authority by using the Certificate Services component of Windows 2000 and Windows Server 2003.

The advantage of doing this using Certificate Services, instead of letting a public third-party organization issue and manage your CA, is that it costs nothing; you can issue, manage, renew, and revoke digital certificates for users throughout your enterprise for free. However, the hidden cost of this approach is that you need to know what you're doing. What if something goes wrong with the server that functions as your root CA? Proper backups are the key, but knowing how to restore in different situations is even more important.

At the heart of your certificate system is the *root CA*, which authorizes and validates all digital certificates issued by your enterprise. A small or mid-sized company will typically have only one CA, which functions as the root CA and issues certificates for all users and systems on the network. A large enterprise might find that this single-CA solution doesn't scale well enough and instead might choose to deploy a hierarchy of CAs, with a single root CA at the top and one or more subordinate CAs underneath.

In a CA hierarchy, the job of the root CA is simpler: to issue certificates for subordinate CAs, which then issue other certificates directly to users. In either case, the key to holding the whole situation together is your root CA. If it goes missing or becomes corrupt, all the certificates issued by the hierarchy become invalid, because they can't be validated back to the root. So, protecting your root CA is protecting the heart of your network's whole system of encrypted communication and certificate-based authentication.

Backing Up a CA

The simplest way to back up your root CA is the most straightforward: simply use the Backup utility (System Tools → Accessories) and select the option to back up the System State of the machine. This will back up everything on the machine that is critical for restoring it, in case a disaster occurs and your root CA server is toast. Then, if you ever need to rebuild your server and restore the System State information from tape, your new server will become the root CA for your enterprise, and all the certificates that were previously issued by your old machine will still be valid.

To be safe, Microsoft generally recommends that you restore your root CA on a machine with a hardware setup that is identical to your old machine. But the critical issue here is that the disk layout must be similar to the layout of the old machine, especially if you stored your certificate database and log files in a nonstandard location (by default, they are located in the *%SystemRoot%\system32\CertLog* folder, but you can change this location when you install Certificate Services).

You also have to make sure your new server has the same name as the old machine, as the name of a CA can't be changed after Certificate Services is installed. Because the name of the machine is included within the root CA's own certificate, changing its name would cause the whole certification-validation process to fail (for a similar reason, you can't change the domain membership of a CA either).

However, System State backups are useful only for recovering from a complete failure of your server, and other things might go wrong with your root CA, such as corruption of the certificate database or certificate log files, some unknown problem that prevents Certificate Services from starting and requires you to reinstall this service, or the need to move your root CA to a different machine on your network (something you might not have considered).

To prepare for the eventuality of recovering a still-functioning but corrupted root CA or moving the root CA role to another server, you need to perform a different kind of backup, one that backs up only what's essential for the machine to function in that role. Fortunately, Microsoft has made this easy by providing a Certification Authority Backup Wizard. Let's see how this wizard works and what it does.

The Certification Authority Backup Wizard

The Certification Authority Backup Wizard facilitates backing up key data found on your root CA, including the server's own digital certificate (called a *CA certificate*), its private key (used for generating digital signatures and decrypting encrypted information), the database and associated log files containing certificates previously issued by the server, and the queue of pending certificate requests waiting to be processed by the machine. This information is sufficient to restore your root CA if it becomes corrupted and Certificate Services stops working. As you'll soon see, however, there's one additional piece of information you need to restore this data to a different machine.

To start the Certification Authority Backup Wizard, open the Certification Authority console under Administrative Tools. Then, right-click on the node that represents your root CA (or the subordinate CA you want to back up in a distributed enterprise scenario) and select All Tasks → Backup CA to start the wizard. The main screen of the wizard offers several choices, as shown in Figure 6-11.

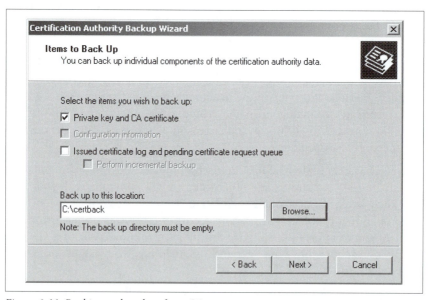

Figure 6-11. Backing up key data for a CA

The first time you back up your CA using this method, be sure to at least select the option to back up the private key and CA certificate for your CA. This will ensure that you can at least restore your CA in the event of an emergency. However, if you do only this, you will still have to reissue certificates to users. Therefore, in addition to backing up the private key and CA certificate, it's a good idea to also include in your backup the issued certificate log and pending certificate request queue for your server (the "Certificate database and certificate database log" option), which contain information about all certificates already issued by your CA and any pending requests from clients. When you choose this option in the Certification Authority Backup Wizard screen (shown in Figure 6-11), you also have the option to perform an incremental backup of your CA, which makes a backup of only those changes to the certificate database made since your last full backup.

This is trickier than it looks, so let's look deeper at the results of the backup process. If you choose only the first option, to back up the private key and CA certificate, and specify a folder such as *C:\certback* as the target for your backup, the result of the backup will be a file named *CA_Name.p12*, where *CA_Name* is the name you specified for your CA when you installed Certificate Services on the machine (the *.p12* file extension means the file uses standard PKCS #12 cryptographic syntax). Since you are required to specify a password later in the wizard, this backup file is itself secured by being password-protected. Best practice here is to choose a complex, difficult password to protect your backup, but make sure you don't forget the password; otherwise, you won't be able to restore your root CA later.

If you choose the other option, to back up the issued certificate log and pending certificate request queue, a subfolder named *Database* will be created in your *certback* folder. Inside this *Database* folder, copies of the certificate database files and certificate database log files for your CA will be created. The log files are basically transaction files that record changes made and pending to the database.

Now, let's say you backed up everything—private key, CA certificate, certificate log, and queue—on Monday, but on Thursday you processed a lot of certificate requests from users and now you need to update the backup. There are two ways you can do this. First, you can simply back up everything again to a new (empty) folder and then discard your old backup—nice and simple.

The other way (the way recommended by Microsoft) is to make an incremental backup of your certificate log and queue. Now, if you try to save your incremental backup in the *certback* folder, you'll get an error saying that you can make backups only to an empty folder. In this case, you might then create a subfolder under *certback*—perhaps a folder such as *certback\ 17Nov03*, which indicates the date you made your incremental backup— and then back up to this folder instead of *certback*.

The result will be the creation of another folder named *DataBase*, this one located at *certback\17Nov03\DataBase*. Within this folder, you'll find transaction logs but no database. Then, the following week, you can perform an incremental backup to a new folder named *certback\24Nov03*, and so on.

Now, should you ever need to restore your CA from backup, you'll have to restore the full backup first, followed by all your incremental backups, in order. That's a lot of work. See why you might want to just perform a full backup every time instead?

By the way, if you're wondering about the grayed-out "Configuration information" option in Figure 6-11, that option is used only for backing up a standalone CA (i.e., a CA installed on a standalone server in a workgroup environment). If you're working in an Active Directory environment (which is more likely), the configuration information for your CA is stored in Active Directory and therefore doesn't need to be backed up separately like this. The nice thing in Windows Server 2003 is that this option is not even visible in the wizard when you're backing up an enterprise CA (i.e., a CA installed on a domain controller or member server in an Active Directory environment).

Restoring a CA to a Working Server

If your root CA becomes corrupt or Certificate Services fails to start but your server is otherwise working fine, you can use your previously created backup to restore the private key, root CA, certificate database, and transaction logs to their most recent working state. Just start the Certification Authority console in Administrative Tools, right-click on the root CA node, and select Restore CA to open the Certification Authority Restore Wizard, which is basically a mirror image of the Backup Wizard.

If Certificate Services is running, it will be stopped temporarily to continue the restore. Select which components you want to restore, browse to locate the *.p12* backup file created earlier, and enter your password to begin the restore process. Once the restore is finished, Certificate Services will restart and you should have a working CA again for your organization.

What if it still doesn't work? In that case, you might have a corrupt metabase. Internet Information Services (IIS) is a supporting component for the CA web enrollment portion of Certificate Services, and if the IIS metabase becomes corrupt, your CA won't be able to process CA enrollment requests. The solution, once you've restored the CA, is to restore the metabase as well. Once the metabase has been restored, you should be able to load the Certificate Services web pages and process certificate requests again.

If your root CA still doesn't work, your only solution might be to rebuild the machine from scratch and restore System State from tape backup media. This is usually a time-consuming process, but if your server is running Windows Server 2003 you might be able to speed it up by using that platform's new Automated System Recovery feature.

Restoring a CA to a Different Server

While root CAs are intended to last decades for large organizations, the actual hardware platforms they run on become obsolete in time spans much shorter than the projected lifetime of the CA. As a result, you might someday find yourself wanting to move the role of root CA from an old machine to a more powerful new one. Once you've deployed a public-key infrastructure (PKI) within your organization and started issuing certificates to users for encrypted messaging and secure communications, users become dependent on the transparency of the whole process from their own point of view. The last thing you want to do is build a nice, functional PKI system for your network and have to tear it all down someday and build another, all because you have to change which server hosts the role of root CA.

Leaving aside the problem of upgrading the operating system itself (who knows what version of Windows we'll be running 10 years from now?), here we'll look at how to move the root CA role from one server to another, a process usually called "upgrading" your CA.

First, make a full backup of the private key, CA certificate, certificate database, and transaction logs by using the wizard-based method described earlier in this hack. The result of the backup process is a password-protected file named *CA_Name.p12* that contains the root CA's own certificate and private key, plus a *Database* folder that contains the database files and transaction logs.

Next, back up the following Registry key on your old root CA:

```
HKLM\SYSTEM\CurrentControlSet\Services\CertSvc\Configuration\CA_Name
```

This key contains critical information about how Certificate Services is configured on your machine, and you will need this key to move your CA role to a different machine. Make sure you also make a note of the location where the certificate database and log files are located on your server. By default, they are both in the *%SystemRoot%\system32\CertLog* folder, but you might have placed them on a separate drive for increased performance when you installed Certificate Services on your old machine.

Next, you need to prepare your new server to host the role of root CA for your organization. Take the server off the network and rename it with the same name as the old root CA. This step is essential, because the name of the server is included in all certificates issued by the CA. In order for previously issued certificates to be validated, the new root CA must have the same name as the old one. While Windows Server 2003 now supports a process that lets you rename your domains and domain controllers, it's obviously simplest if you use a member server for your root CA, because member servers are easier to rename than domain controllers. Copy the *CA_Name.p12* file and *Database* folder from your old machine to a temporary folder somewhere on your new machine, and have the Registry key exported from the old machine ready to import as well.

Now, begin installing Certificate Services on your machine by using Add/Remove Windows Components (Control Panel → Add/Remove Programs). When prompted to specify which kind of CA you want to install (enterprise or standalone, root or subordinate), select "Advanced options" (Windows Server 2003 replaces "Advanced options" with "Use custom settings to generate the key pair and CA certificate instead," but everything else is similar) and click Next to display the Public and Private Key Pair screen of the Windows Components Wizard, shown in Figure 6-12.

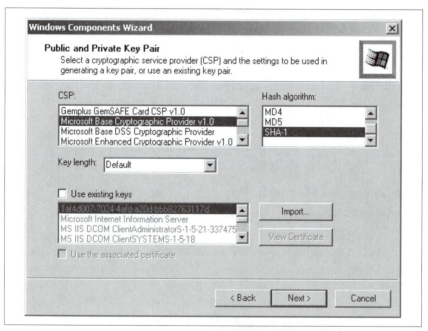

Figure 6-12. Importing backed-up information from your old root CA

Click the Import button, browse to locate the *CA_Name.p12* backup file on your server, and enter the password you specified when you backed up your old CA. Complete the remaining steps of the wizard, being sure to specify the same path for the certificate database and log files that you were using on your old CA. Then, restore your database and log files from backup, as discussed earlier in this hack. Finally, restore the Registry key you backed up on the old CA to your new CA.

Restart Certificate Services, and you should now have a working root CA running on new hardware that will last you...five years? Three years? Who knows, the way hardware platforms are advancing these days! In any event, be sure to test your new root CA thoroughly in all its aspects (e.g., processing certificate requests, validating certificates, and renewing and revoking certificates) before finally decommissioning your old root CA.

Decommissioning the Old CA

If you want to use your old server for some other purpose on your network (as opposed to discarding it in the big blue bin behind your building), you still have to do two things. First, you have to remove Certificate Services from it. But before you do this, you need to remove the CA certificate and private key themselves, because you don't want them kicking around on some old machine on your network.

To remove these cryptographic items, open a command prompt and type `certutil -shutdown` to stop Certificate Services on the machine. Then, type `certutil -key` to display a list of all cryptographic keys installed on the machine. Contained within this list should be a key named for the CA itself (*CA_Name*), which you can remove from the server by typing `certutil -delkey` *CA_Name* (enclose *CA_Name* in quotes if it contains spaces). Now you can use Add/Remove Programs in the Control Panel to uninstall Certificate Services, allowing you to use your old machine for some other purpose on your network.

But don't forget this second step: rename your server so it won't conflict with the new root CA on your network!

—Mitch Tulloch

Detect Ethernet Sniffers Remotely
HACK #72

Detect potential spies on your network without having to trust compromised machines.

Ethernet sniffers are one of the most powerful tools in your network security arsenal. However, in the wrong hands, they can be one of the biggest threats to the security of your network. Once a system has been compromised, whether by an insider or a malicious intruder, the attacker will most likely begin sniffing the local network. This network reconnaissance will help the "spy" to find his next target, or simply to collect juicy bits of information (such as usernames and passwords, emails, or other sensitive data).

Sniffing Shared Mediums

Not too long ago, it was commonly thought that only shared-medium Ethernet networks were vulnerable to being sniffed. These networks employed a central hub, which rebroadcast every transmitted packet to each port on the hub. In this configuration, every node on the local network segment receives every frame sent by any network node. Each node's network interface then performs a quick check to see if it is the node for which the frame is destined. If it is not the destination host, the frame is discarded. If it is, the frame is passed up through the operating system's protocol stack and is eventually processed by an application.

Because of this, sniffing traffic meant for other systems on the network was trivial. Since all the traffic reached each system, one needed only to disable the check that the network interface performs to grant a system access to traffic meant for others. This is usually referred to as putting the network interface into *promiscuous mode*, which usually can be done only by a privileged user.

Sniffing in Switched Environments

Eventually, switched Ethernet networks began to replace shared-medium networks. Thus, the main facilitator of sniffing was removed. Unlike hubs, Ethernet switches send traffic only to the device for which it is destined. To do this, an Ethernet switch learns which network device's MAC address corresponds to what port on the switch as traffic passes through the switch. When the switch sees an Ethernet frame with a certain destination MAC address, it looks up which port on the switch corresponds to it and forwards the frame to only that port. In doing this, the switch effectively creates a virtual dedicated connection from the sending station to the receiving station every time an Ethernet frame is transmitted on the network. Thus, only the machine that the frame was originally intended for is able to see it. This would be fine, but certain aspects of the Ethernet specification and TCP/IP can cause problems.

One problem is that switches can memorize only a limited number of MAC addresses. The maximum number will often be several orders of magnitude higher than the number of ports that the switch has, which allows switches to be connected to each other hierarchically. In order to do this efficiently, however, each switch must memorize the MAC addresses available on the switches to which it is connected.

For example, suppose you have a 24-port switch (switch A) with 23 machines plugged into it and the 24th port occupied by another switch. This other switch (switch B) has 48 ports, with the 47 other ports being occupied by machines. In this situation, switch A will learn the MAC addresses of the 47 systems on switch B and associate it with its 24th port, and switch B will learn the MAC addresses of the 23 systems connected directly to switch A and associate it with its own 48th port.

Even though the average switch can memorize upwards of several thousand MAC addresses, it is still possible to overflow a switch's MAC address table by generating large amounts of traffic with fake MAC addresses. This tactic is desirable for a malicious user because many switches will revert to behaving like hubs once their MAC address tables have been filled. Once this happens, the network is no different from a shared-medium segment using a hub. A malicious user can then sniff the network by simply putting her network interface into promiscuous mode.

Luckily, this approach is fairly invasive; in order for it to work, the network will need to be flooded with bogus traffic, which is something that can be detected passively with a tool such as Arpwatch [Hack #62]. A flood of bogus MAC and IP address pairings will cause Arpwatch to likewise flood your system logs. As long as you're good about monitoring your logs, this attack should be fairly easy to spot. As mentioned in "Detect ARP Spoofing" [Hack #62], Arpwatch is also capable of detecting ARP table poisoning. That makes it an effective tool for detecting the two most common types of ARP attacks that are usually precursors to data logging: ARP flooding and targeted ARP poisoning.

Another way to monitor switched networks is to simply change the MAC address of the Ethernet card in the system that is going to be used for sniffing. In Linux and many other Unix and Unix-like operating systems, this can be done with the `ifconfig` command:

```
# /sbin/ifconfig eth1
eth1      Link encap:Ethernet  HWaddr 00:E0:81:03:D8:8F
          BROADCAST MULTICAST  MTU:1500  Metric:1
          RX packets:0 errors:0 dropped:0 overruns:0 frame:0
          TX packets:0 errors:0 dropped:0 overruns:0 carrier:0
          collisions:0 txqueuelen:100
          RX bytes:0 (0.0 b)  TX bytes:0 (0.0 b)
          Interrupt:11 Base address:0x1c80

# /sbin/ifconfig eth0 hw ether 00:DE:AD:BE:EF:00
# /sbin/ifconfig eth1
eth1      Link encap:Ethernet  HWaddr 00:DE:AD:BE:EF:00
          BROADCAST MULTICAST  MTU:1500  Metric:1
          RX packets:0 errors:0 dropped:0 overruns:0 frame:0
```

```
TX packets:0 errors:0 dropped:0 overruns:0 carrier:0
collisions:0 txqueuelen:100
RX bytes:0 (0.0 b)  TX bytes:0 (0.0 b)
Interrupt:11 Base address:0x1c80
```

The purpose of doing this is to trick the switch into forwarding the traffic to two different nodes on the segment. This is sometimes a hit-or-miss deal, since different switches will behave differently when there are duplicate MAC addresses in use on the same network. The switch might forward traffic to both ports, distribute the traffic unpredictably between them, stop passing traffic altogether, or raise an error.

All of these methods can be detected and stopped with more expensive managed switches, which allow you to specify what MAC addresses are allowed on each individual port. This feature is sometimes called *port security*.

However, even if attackers choose not to employ these methods, they can still gather quite a bit of information by just putting the network interface into promiscuous mode. For example, broadcast traffic such as DHCP and ARP requests will still be sent to every port on the switch.

Installing SniffDet

One tool that can help to detect promiscuous interfaces on both switched and unswitched networks is SniffDet (*http://sniffdet.sourceforge.net*). For a tool that really serves only a single purpose, SniffDet is fairly versatile, and it can detect sniffers in several ways. The main difference between SniffDet and a tool like Arpwatch is that SniffDet actively scans for sniffers. That is, if you suspect that a machine might be running a sniffer, you can simply run SniffDet and point it at that machine to determine whether its network device is in promiscuous mode.

To build and install SniffDet, you will first have to obtain the *libnet* packet injection library (*http://www.packetfactory.net/projects/libnet/*). Make sure to download the latest 1.0.x version; the 1.1 versions of *libnet* are incompatible with programs written for the 1.0.x versions.

To compile *libnet*, unpack the source distribution and go into the directory that it creates. Then run this command:

```
$ ./configure && make
```

After it has finished compiling, become root and type make install.

Building SniffDet is a similar affair. As with *libnet*, you will need to unpack the source distribution and change to the directory that it creates. Then, to build and install it, do the same thing you did for *libnet*. You'll also want to download two patches: one that fixes several compilation issues and one that fixes a bug that limits the functionality of SniffDet (the latter has been submitted to the authors of SniffDet but has not been integrated into a new release at the time of this writing). Both patches can be obtained from *http:// snort-wireless.org/other/patches/sniffdet-0.9*.

Before compiling SniffDet, apply the patches using commands such as these:

```
$ tar xfz sniffdet-0.9.tar.gz
$ cd sniffdet-0.9
$ patch -p1 < sniffdet-get_mac.patch
$ patch -p1 < sniffdet-compile_fixes.patch
```

Testing with ARP Queries

SniffDet has several methods for determining whether a target machine is running a sniffer. However, only two of the methods that it employs—the ARP and DNS tests—will work with repeatable and predictable results.

The ARP test relies on how the sniffing system's protocol stack deals with ARP queries while in promiscuous mode. To run this test, SniffDet sends out an ARP query to the target machine. This request has fake source and destination MAC addresses but uses the correct IP address of the machine being checked. If the target machine is in promiscuous mode, the ARP query with the fake MAC address will be passed up the protocol stack, and the target machine will send a reply. If the machine is not in promiscuous mode, this ARP query will be quietly discarded. This method is effective on both switched and unswitched networks.

The ARP test works because of the way in which network adapters implement multicast addressing. IP multicast groups have associated MAC addresses. In order to receive multicast data, a network interface will set itself to not filter out data sent to the MAC address corresponding to the multicast group to which it belongs, as well as to the broadcast address and the interface's normal address. One interesting side effect of the way this is implemented is that when a network interface is in promiscuous mode it will respond to any frame with the group bit set in the destination address, even if the address does not correspond to a multicast group to which the host belongs. This same bit will also cause the frame to be broadcast by the switch. So, one only needs to send an ARP request with a destination address like FF:00:00:00:00:00 instead of the normal broadcast address, FF: FF:FF:FF:FF:FF, to detect if the machine is in promiscuous mode.

One interesting thing to note is that different operating systems will respond to MAC addresses with the group bit set in different ways. For instance, Linux and many other Unix-like operating systems will respond to the address mentioned earlier when in promiscuous mode, but Windows systems will not. On the other hand, both Unix-like and Windows systems will respond when FF:FF:FF:FF:FF:FE is used as the destination address. However, because of a bug in SniffDet's MAC address parsing code, you won't be able to use FF:FF:FF:FF:FF:FE as a destination address unless you apply the previously mentioned patch.

Let's look at a *sniffdet* scan against *sirius* (192.168.0.2) from *colossus* (192. 168.0.64), two machines that are on the same switched network.

Here are the results of running *sniffdet* against *sirius*:

```
colossus # sniffdet -i eth0 -t arp sirius
----------------------------------------------------------------
Sniffdet Report
Generated on: Wed Dec 31 03:49:28 2003
----------------------------------------------------------------
Tests Results for target sirius
----------------------------------------------------------------
Test: ARP Test (single host)
      Check if target replies a bogus ARP request (with wrong MAC)
Validation: OK
Started on: Wed Dec 31 03:49:08 2003
Finished on: Wed Dec 31 03:49:28 2003
Bytes Sent: 252
Bytes Received: 0
Packets Sent: 6
Packets Received: 0
----------------------------------------------------------------
RESULT: NEGATIVE
----------------------------------------------------------------


----------------------------------------------------------------
Number of valid tests: #1
Number of tests with positive result: #0
----------------------------------------------------------------
```

Now start a sniffer on *sirius* and run the scan again:

```
sirius # tcpdump -i le0 arp
tcpdump: listening on le0
06:58:00.458836 arp who-has sirius.nnc tell colossus.nnc
06:58:00.458952 arp reply sirius.nnc is-at 8:0:20:81:a4:a3
06:58:00.466601 arp who-has sirius.nnc (ff:0:0:0:0:0) tell colossus.nnc
06:58:00.466928 arp reply sirius.nnc is-at 8:0:20:81:a4:a3
```

Here are the results of the scan:

```
----------------------------------------------------------------
Sniffdet Report
Generated on: Wed Dec 31 06:58:01 2003
----------------------------------------------------------------
Tests Results for target sirius
----------------------------------------------------------------
Test: ARP Test (single host)
      Check if target replies a bogus ARP request (with wrong MAC)
```

```
Validation: OK
Started on: Wed Dec 31 06:58:00 2003
Finished on: Wed Dec 31 06:58:01 2003
Bytes Sent: 84
Bytes Received: 60
Packets Sent: 2
Packets Received: 1
------------------------------------------------------------
RESULT: POSITIVE
------------------------------------------------------------


------------------------------------------------------------
Number of valid tests: #1
Number of tests with positive result: #1
------------------------------------------------------------
```

The DNS test also works very well, particularly on shared-medium networks such as hubs or wireless LANs. However, it does rely on name resolution being enabled in the sniffer. When performing DNS tests, *sniffdet* will send bogus packets that contain IP addresses that are not in use on the local network segment. If name resolution is enabled, the sniffer will attempt to do a reverse lookup in order to determine the hostname that corresponds to the IP addresses. Since these addresses are not in use, *sniffdet* will determine that the target machine is in promiscuous mode when it sees the DNS queries.

A DNS test is performed just like an ARP test, but using -t dns instead of -t arp.

HACK #73 Help Track Attackers

Contribute firewall logs to DShield to build a better picture of dangers on the Internet.

The Internet can be a scary place, and given its sheer size it's a probability that at any moment numerous attacks are being carried out against networks and hosts across the globe. But what does this mean for you and your network? Wouldn't it be nice to know what the most commonly attacked services are? One project that seeks to gather this information is DShield (*http://www.dshield.org*), a project sponsored by the SANS Institute (*http://www.sans.org*) that seeks to be a distributed IDS for the Internet.

DShield accomplishes its mission by allowing users across the globe to submit their firewall logs to be processed and correlated. This enables the project to determine what ports are attacked the most and where those attacks originate, and to inform the Internet community at large of these facts. In addition, it can let you know if your systems have been used to attack other systems that are participating in the project (though, hopefully, you already know if your system is being misused).

DShield includes a web interface (*http://www.dshield.org/report.php*) that you can use to manually upload log files, though it supports only a few formats: Linux *ipchains* and *iptables*, ZoneAlarm, SonicWall, and Raptor. If you want to submit your logs automatically, there are many more options to choose from (see *http://www.dshield.org/howto.php*). There are too many different types of logs that can be submitted to DShield to completely do justice to them all here, so we'll focus on how to submit logs from a Linux *iptables* firewall.

First, you'll need to decide if you want to register with DShield. Although registration isn't required to submit logs, it is encouraged. One extra thing that registration allows is participation in DShield's FightBack initiative, through which DShield submits reports to ISPs where attacks originate. By registering and electing to participate in FightBack, you allow DShield to use your logs for this purpose.

To submit logs for an *iptables* firewall, download the appropriate client (*http://www.dshield.org/clients/framework/iptables.tar.gz*). Then, create a user to run the client under (e.g., _dshield). When doing that, make sure to create a valid home directory for the user; this is a good place to put the log submission script and its accompanying configuration files.

After you've created the account, unpack the tarball and copy the submission script into the user's *bin* directory (e.g., ~_dshield/bin):

```
# cd /tmp
# tar xvfz iptables.tar.gz && cd iptables
# cp iptables.pl ~_dshield/bin
```

Then, copy the *dshield.cnf* and *.lst* files into */etc*:

```
# cp dshield.cnf *.lst /etc
```

Edit the configuration file, *dshield.cnf*, changing the from and userid lines to the email address you registered with and the ID that you received afterwards. If you didn't register, you can leave these alone. You can also change the cc and bcc lines to send yourself copies of the submissions. If your firewall logs are stored in a file other than */var/log/messages*, you'll need to change the log line as well.

If you are using */var/log/messages*, you'll have log entries for things other than your firewall. These other entries are ignored via the line_filter variable in the configuration file, which lets you specify a regular expression to match the lines pertaining to the firewall. For most situations, the default should be fine. If you want to filter out some of the matching lines, set a regular expression for line_exclude.

To protect the information that's leaving your network, you can also exclude entries by their source or destination IP address and port number. To exclude source and destination IP addresses, add individual IP addresses or CIDR ranges on separate lines to *dshield-source-exclude.lst* and *dshield-target-exclude.lst*, respectively. The *dshield-source-exclude.lst* file already excludes RFC 1918 private IP addresses. To exclude source and destination ports, add single ports or ranges (e.g., 21-25) to *dshield-source-port-exclude.lst* and *dshield-target-port-exclude.lst*, respectively.

Additionally, to prevent your network's vulnerabilities from being revealed to a third party, you'll probably want to set the obfus variable to Y. This will cause the submission script to substitute 10 for the first octet of the target IP addresses in your logs in order to obfuscate them. However, this will prevent the logs from being used in FightBack.

After you've finished editing the configuration file, add an entry to the DShield user's crontab to run it periodically (once a day works well). For instance, this entry will cause it to run each day at 11:59 P.M.:

```
23 59 * * * cd /home/dshield/bin; \
./iptables.pl > /home/dshield/bin/iptables_debug.txt
```

There are a few other options that can be configured, but this hack has covered the major ones. The *dshield.cnf* file is fully commented, so it's pretty easy to figure out what to do. If you want to check up on the statistics that have been generated, go to *http://www.dshield.org/reports.php*.

HACK #74 Scan for Viruses on Your Unix Servers

Use ClamAV to identify infected files under Unix.

Traditionally, antivirus concerns have been an afterthought in the Unix world. After all, Unix machines don't have the history of being attacked by malware that Windows PCs (and Macs, to a lesser extent) have enjoyed. However, with the widespread use of heterogeneous systems, it makes sense to take a look at Unix antivirus approaches in a new light. While your Unix servers might not themselves be targeted or affected by viruses, attackers may try to use them for propagating malware to PCs on your network.

One software package that lets you scan for viruses under Unix is ClamAV (*http://www.clamav.net*). ClamAV is especially useful on Samba servers and on mail servers, where it can scan email attachments for virus payloads and block them before they hit a user's inbox. And best of all, it's free!

Installing ClamAV

To get started with ClamAV, you'll first need to create a user and group to run it under (e.g., _clamav). Then, download the source tarball, unpack it, change to the directory that it creates, and run ./configure. If you want to use ClamAV to scan email, you can add the --enable-milter option, which builds *clamav-milter* for you to tie in with Sendmail.

Once the *configure* script finishes executing, run the usual make command, and then run make install as root. You'll then need to update ClamAV's virus signature database by editing */usr/local/etc/freshclam.conf*.

Locate the following two lines:

```
# Comment or remove the line below.
Example
```

Simply comment out the Example line and run freshclam. The last line it outputs should look similar to the following, confirming that the signatures have been updated:

```
Database updated (60082 signatures) from database.clamav.net
(IP: 199.239.233.95)
```

Now, you can test ClamAV by running the standalone command-line scanner *clamscan*. The ClamAV source tree contains some files that ClamAV will recognize as malware, so try scanning it:

```
# clamscan -r -l scan.txt .
./FAQ: OK
./etc/Makefile.am: OK
./etc/Makefile.in: OK
./etc/clamd.conf: OK
./etc/freshclam.conf: OK
./etc/Makefile: OK
./BUGS: OK
./NEWS: OK
./TODO: Empty file
./docs/man/sigtool.1: OK
./docs/man/clamscan.1: OK
./docs/man/clamdscan.1: OK
./docs/man/freshclam.1: OK
./docs/man/freshclam.conf.5.in: OK
./docs/man/clamd.conf.5: OK
...
./test/clam.cab: ClamAV-Test-File FOUND
./test/clam.exe: ClamAV-Test-File FOUND
./test/clam.rar: ClamAV-Test-File FOUND
./test/clam.zip: ClamAV-Test-File FOUND
./test/clam.exe.bz2: ClamAV-Test-File FOUND
```

```
----------- SCAN SUMMARY -----------
Known viruses: 60082
Engine version: 0.88.2
Scanned directories: 45
Scanned files: 757
Infected files: 5
Data scanned: 13.19 MB
Time: 33.362 sec (0 m 33 s)
```

Now, take a look at *scan.txt*:

```
# cat scan.txt

----------------------------------------
Scan started: Sun Jun 25 21:43:00 2006

./test/clam.cab: ClamAV-Test-File FOUND
./test/clam.exe: ClamAV-Test-File FOUND
./test/clam.rar: ClamAV-Test-File FOUND
./test/clam.zip: ClamAV-Test-File FOUND
./test/clam.exe.bz2: ClamAV-Test-File FOUND

-- summary --
Known viruses: 60082
Engine version: 0.88.2
Scanned directories: 45
Scanned files: 757
Infected files: 5
Data scanned: 13.19 MB
Time: 33.362 sec (0 m 33 s)
```

As you can see, both the *clamscan* output and the contents of *scan.txt* show the same five infected files. However, *scan.txt* only shows the infected files and a summary of the scan, whereas the status of every scanned file is shown in the *clamscan* output.

Configuring clamd

To get the ClamAV daemon (*clamd*) working, you'll first need to remove or comment out the Example line from */usr/local/etc/clamd.conf*, just as you did with the *freshclam.conf* file. Then you'll need to tell *clamd* to run as the user you created earlier, using the User option. Add a line like this:

```
User _clamav
```

There are many other configuration options you can change here, and the configuration file is fully documented with comments to make choosing the right options easy. One notable configuration option is LogSyslog, which causes *clamd* to log any viruses that are detected via *syslog*.

To enable logging via *syslog*, simply locate the option and uncomment it. By default, *clamd* uses the *local6* facility, but you can change this with the LogFacility option. Take a look at the *syslog* manpage to find other *syslog* facilities that you can use.

Once you're done editing the configuration file, start *clamd*; just typing clamd should work. If you enabled logging via *syslog*, you should see something like the following in your logs:

```
Jun 25 22:29:12 mail clamd[15819]: Daemon started.
Jun 25 22:29:12 mail clamd[15819]: clamd daemon 0.88.2 (OS: freebsd5.4,
ARCH: i386, CPU: i386)
Jun 25 22:29:12 mail clamd[15819]: Log file size limited to 1048576 bytes.
Jun 25 22:29:12 mail clamd[15819]: Reading databases from /usr/local/share/
clamav
Jun 25 22:29:16 mail clamd[15819]: Protecting against 60082 viruses.
Jun 25 22:29:16 mail clamd[15828]: Unix socket file /tmp/clamd
Jun 25 22:29:16 mail clamd[15828]: Setting connection queue length to 15
Jun 25 22:29:16 mail clamd[15828]: Archive: Archived file size limit set to
10485760 bytes.
Jun 25 22:29:16 mail clamd[15828]: Archive: Recursion level limit set to 8.
Jun 25 22:29:16 mail clamd[15828]: Archive: Files limit set to 1000.
Jun 25 22:29:16 mail clamd[15828]: Archive: Compression ratio limit set to
250.
Jun 25 22:29:16 mail clamd[15828]: Archive support enabled.
Jun 25 22:29:16 mail clamd[15828]: Archive: RAR support disabled.
Jun 25 22:29:16 mail clamd[15828]: Portable Executable support enabled.
Jun 25 22:29:16 mail clamd[15828]: Mail files support enabled.
Jun 25 22:29:16 mail clamd[15828]: OLE2 support enabled.
Jun 25 22:29:16 mail clamd[15828]: HTML support enabled.
Jun 25 22:29:16 mail clamd[15828]: Self checking every 1800 seconds.
```

Now, try running the same AV scan with *clamdscan*:

```
# /usr/local/bin/clamdscan -l scan.txt .
/usr/home/andrew/clamav-0.88.2/./test/clam.cab: ClamAV-Test-File FOUND
/usr/home/andrew/clamav-0.88.2/./test/clam.exe: ClamAV-Test-File FOUND
/usr/home/andrew/clamav-0.88.2/./test/clam.zip: ClamAV-Test-File FOUND
/usr/home/andrew/clamav-0.88.2/./test/clam.exe.bz2: ClamAV-Test-File FOUND

----------- SCAN SUMMARY -----------
Infected files: 4
Time: 32.749 sec (0 m 32 s)
```

Check your logs. You should see the same results reflected there:

```
Jun 25 22:29:31 freebsd5-vm1 clamd[15828]: /usr/home/andrew/clamav-0.88.2/./
test/clam.cab: ClamAV-Test-File FOUND
Jun 25 22:29:31 freebsd5-vm1 clamd[15828]: /usr/home/andrew/clamav-0.88.2/./
test/clam.exe: ClamAV-Test-File FOUND
Jun 25 22:29:31 freebsd5-vm1 clamd[15828]: /usr/home/andrew/clamav-0.88.2/./
test/clam.zip: ClamAV-Test-File FOUND
Jun 25 22:29:31 freebsd5-vm1 clamd[15828]: /usr/home/andrew/clamav-0.88.2/./
test/clam.exe.bz2: ClamAV-Test-File FOUND
```

Finally, if you want to have Sendmail use ClamAV to scan mail, you'll need to create a directory to hold the Unix sockets through which Sendmail, *clamd*, and *clamav-milter* will communicate:

```
# mkdir /var/run/clamav
# chown _clamav:_clamav /var/run/clamav
```

Then, add the following line to */usr/local/etc/clamd.conf*:

```
LocalSocket /var/run/clamav/clamd.sock
```

You'll need to tell Sendmail to use *clamav-milter* to filter messages through it. Add the following to the end of your *sendmail.mc* file:

```
INPUT_MAIL_FILTER(`clmilter',`S=local:/var/run/clamav/clmilter.sock, F=, \
T=S:4m;R:4m')
define(`confINPUT_MAIL_FILTERS', `clmilter')
```

After you've done that, rebuild your *sendmail.cf* and start *clamav-milter*:

```
# /usr/local/sbin/clamav-milter -lo /var/run/clamav/clmilter.sock --external
```

Now, restart Sendmail. You can quickly test your new AV scanning setup by trying to send the test files included with the ClamAV distribution as attachments. You should see something similar to this in your logs:

```
Jun 26 00:08:03 freebsd5-vm1 sm-mta[27946]: k5Q6831tO27946: Milter add:
header: X-Virus-Scanned: ClamAV version 0.88.2, clamav-milter version 0.88.2
on freebsd5-vm1.nnc
Jun 26 00:08:03 freebsd5-vm1 sm-mta[27946]: k5Q6831tO27946: Milter add:
header: X-Virus-Status: Not Scanned
Jun 26 00:08:03 freebsd5-vm1 sm-mta[27946]: k5Q6831tO27946: Milter: data,
reject=451 4.3.2 Please try again later
```

The client sending the message will be blocked from doing so.

These are just a few of the possibilities for using ClamAV. For another interesting use, take a look at "Scan Network Traffic for Viruses" **[Hack #118]**, which shows how to integrate ClamAV with Snort.

HACK #75 Track Vulnerabilities

Keep abreast of the latest vulnerabilities that affect your network.

One of the key steps toward keeping any network secure is making sure all of the systems and devices connected to it are patched against the latest vulnerabilities that have been discovered. After all, if you spend all of your time implementing some "gee whiz" security architecture but are compromised due to unpatched vulnerabilities, you've been wasting your time.

Keeping track of all of the latest vulnerabilities that affect your systems and the patches and workarounds for them can be quite time-consuming, especially in highly heterogeneous environments. The most devastating vulnerabilities might make it to commonly read computer news sites, but most are rarely reported on. It's possible that the vendor of a program in which a security hole is discovered will notify you if you have a support contract, but where does that leave you if you don't have such a contract, or if you use open source software? This hack provides a few resources that can be of help for not only open source projects, but commercial products as well.

Mailing Lists

Mailing lists are some of easiest-to-use resources available. Many vendors and open source projects report security advisories and patch notifications to BugTraq (*http://www.securityfocus.com/archive/1/description*) and the Full-Disclosure (*http://lists.grok.org.uk/full-disclosure-charter.html*) mailing lists.

At BugTraq, vendors publicly announce vulnerabilities that have been reported to them by security researchers or have been discovered internally. Vulnerabilities posted there usually have patches or workarounds available at the time of announcement as well, since the vendors themselves are often the ones disclosing them.

On the other hand, Full-Disclosure often includes vulnerabilities posted by independent researchers who haven't been able to get the vendors to cooperate with them in fixing the flaws they've found.

Many open source projects also offer mailing lists to announce security issues. Check the project pages for your favorite open source software packages to see if they have security-related lists, and subscribe to them.

Finally, the United States Computer Emergency Response Team (US CERT) offers several security-related mailing lists (*https://forms.us-cert.gov/maillists/*). However, usually only the most wide-reaching vulnerabilities are posted there.

RSS Feeds

In addition to mailing lists, many resources that track vulnerabilities provide RSS feeds. SecurityFocus (*http://www.securityfocus.com*), the site that hosts the BugTraq list, also offers an RSS feed (*http://www.securityfocus.com/rss/vulnerabilities.xml*) that features selected postings from the list, and Secunia offers an RSS feed (*http://secunia.com/information_partner/anonymous/o.rss*) that distills information from various sources into a consistent format.

Another great resource is the Open Source Vulnerability Database (*http://www.osvdb.org*), which offers an RSS feed of the most recent vulnerabilities added to the database (*http://www.osvdb.org/backend/rss.php?n=10*).

However, since the OSVDB seeks to catalog historical vulnerabilities as well as the most current ones, vulnerabilities that are several years old will often show up in the feed.

If you're interested in wireless-network-specific vulnerabilities, you can subscribe to the Wireless Vulnerabilities and Exploits project's RSS feed (*http://www.wirelessve.org/entries/rss2/*). As the name suggests, this site seeks to catalog wireless device- and application-specific vulnerabilities along with the tools used to exploit them. There is often overlap with other vulnerability databases, but the site also focuses on vulnerabilities that affect the various wireless protocols themselves.

Cassandra

Subscribing to all of the available resources might seem like drinking from a fire hose of information. One tool that can help stem the flood is Cassandra (*https://cassandra.cerias.purdue.edu*), from Purdue University's CERIAS project (*http://www.cerias.purdue.edu*).

The beauty of Cassandra is that it monitors Secunia's database as well as the National Vulnerability Database (*http://nvd.nist.gov*), which also offers an RSS feed (*http://nvd.nist.gov/download.cfm#RSS*), and figures out what new vulnerabilities were added each day. You can register an account with Cassandra and input what vendors and products you're interested in, and Cassandra will email you when any relevant vulnerabilities are reported.

Summary

Whatever information sources you decide to use, it's of the utmost importance that you keep your systems and any devices attached to your network up-to-date and free of known vulnerabilities. Failing to do so only makes it easier for attackers to compromise your enterprise. After all, if they determine a certain software package or device is on your network, all they have to do is look up what vulnerabilities have been published for it and attempt to exploit them.

## CHAPTER SEVEN

Wireless Security
Hacks 76–78

Wireless networks have been plagued with many well-publicized issues since they became popular at the end of the 1990s. Because of such problems and the risks they pose, some people might argue that they shouldn't be used at all. But due to their ease of use and convenience, it's clear that wireless networks are here to stay, so you'd better do everything you can to make them as secure as possible.

Because of the many problems that have afflicted Wired Equivalent Privacy (WEP), anyone seeking to implement a secure wireless network should realize that it's not a good solution. And, while the pre-shared key (PSK) varieties of WiFi Protected Access (WPA) and WPA2 offer better security than WEP, they still have their problems. As you'll see in this chapter, the best solution is to use WPA or WPA2 with 802.1X to provide fine-grained authentication for your wireless network. You'll also see how to unleash the potential of your commodity wireless router or access point (AP) by replacing its firmware with a compact Linux distribution.

For more community-minded users who want to share their wireless networks, this chapter also covers the use of captive portals. By using a captive portal, you can provide open wireless access to nearby users but still maintain some control over who can access your network.

HACK #76 Turn Your Commodity Wireless Routers into a Sophisticated Security Platform

Upgrade your SOHO wireless router into a sophisticated network device with OpenWRT.

As network device manufacturers have moved to cut costs and increase profits, many have sought to utilize open source technologies wherever they can. This has created a pool of hackable (in the good sense) devices that can easily be modified by tweaking their open source components. One such line of devices is Linksys's WRT54G line of low-end wireless routers. These devices have proven so popular with the open source community that many alternate firmware distributions have been created for them. In fact, when Linksys recently made changes to the latest revisions of the WRT54G that prevented it from running Linux, they created a new model for fans of the earlier versions, the WRT54GL, that continued to use Linux for its firmware.

One of the more flexible firmware distributions available is OpenWRT (*http: //openwrt.org*). The beauty of OpenWRT as opposed to other alternative firmwares is that it's a bare-bones minimal system with a large set of pre-compiled packages from which you can pick and choose, installing what-ever suits your needs. For instance, you can easily use OpenWRT to monitor wireless network traffic with the same tools you'd use with a Linux-based laptop. OpenWRT also supports a significant number of other routers avail-able from Linksys and other vendors that have been built on a common hardware platform.

> Before you begin installing OpenWRT, be sure to check the rather lengthy list of supported models (*http://wiki.openwrt. org/TableOfHardware*). Because so many models are sup-ported, this hack covers only the most common: the Linksys WRT54G. Supported models should have links to installa-tion notes specific to them.

For the WRT54G, begin by downloading the firmware image, *openwrt-wrt54g-jffs2.bin*, from *http://downloads.openwrt.org/whiterussian/newest/bin*. Then, log into your router's web administration interface and go to the Administration section. After it loads, click the Firmware Upgrade link and you'll be presented with a page that allows you to upload a firmware image with which the router will reflash itself. Select the firmware image that you downloaded and click the Upgrade button. You should see a page like the one shown in Figure 7-1.

Once the router has been reflashed with the OpenWRT image, you should see a page letting you know that the upgrade was successful. The router will also automatically reboot once the upgrade has completed. After it has rebooted, you should be able to telnet to the IP address that you had the router configured to use before you installed OpenWRT, using a command like the following:

```
$ telnet 192.168.0.4
Trying 192.168.0.4...
Connected to 192.168.0.4.
```

```
Escape character is '^]'.
=== IMPORTANT ============================
Use 'passwd' to set your login password
this will disable telnet and enable SSH
-----------------------------------------


BusyBox v1.00 (2006.03.27-00:00+0000) Built-in shell (ash)
Enter 'help' for a list of built-in commands.


  _____       _____     __ __
 |       |.-----.-----.-----.| | | | |.-----.| |_
 |   -   ||  _  |  -__|     ||  |  |  |  ||   __||   _|
 |_____||   __|_____|__|__||_____||__|  |____|
          |__| W I R E L E S S   F R E E D O M
WHITE RUSSIAN (RC5) -------------------------------
 * 2 oz Vodka   Mix the Vodka and Kahlua together
 * 1 oz Kahlua  over ice, then float the cream or
 * 1/2oz cream  milk on the top.
---------------------------------------------------
root@openwrt:/#
```

Figure 7-1. Upgrading the WRT54G's firmware

When you log in, you should see a banner like the one shown in the previous output. The banner tells you two things. If you set a password for the root account, the telnet daemon will be disabled and the SSH daemon will be enabled, so that you can connect to your router securely. The banner also tells you how to make a White Russian, which is the code name for this particular version of firmware (White Russian RC5).

Now, type reboot to reboot the router and unpack the JFFS2 filesystem. After it has finished booting, log in again. Then set a password for the root account by running passwd, and reboot the router yet again.

You should now be able to log in via SSH:

```
$ ssh root@192.168.0.4
The authenticity of host '192.168.0.4 (192.168.0.4)' can't be established.
RSA key fingerprint is 26:ed:7b:ae:7f:0d:aa:63:e8:f4:c1:6c:b3:09:8b:10.
Are you sure you want to continue connecting (yes/no)? yes
Warning: Permanently added '192.168.0.4' (RSA) to the list of known hosts.
root@192.168.0.4's password:
sh: /usr/X11R6/bin/xauth: not found


BusyBox v1.00 (2006.03.27-00:00+0000) Built-in shell (ash)
Enter 'help' for a list of built-in commands.
```

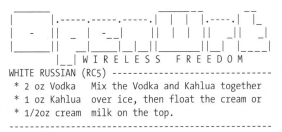

```
                             |__| W I R E L E S S   F R E E D O M
WHITE RUSSIAN (RC5) ------------------------------------
 * 2 oz Vodka   Mix the Vodka and Kahlua together
 * 1 oz Kahlua  over ice, then float the cream or
 * 1/2oz cream  milk on the top.
 ------------------------------------------------------
root@openwrt:~#
```

Now you'll need to set a DNS server for OpenWRT to use when resolving DNS names. You might think this is as straightforward as just editing */etc/resolv.conf*, but this file is created dynamically at boot according to the contents of the NVRAM. Therefore, you'll need to set the lan_dns NVRAM variable. You'll also need to set the default gateway (lan_gateway):

```
# nvram set lan_dns=192.168.0.2
# nvram set lan_gateway=192.168.0.1
# nvram commit
# reboot
```

Now, log in again and run ipkg update:

```
# ipkg update
Downloading http://downloads.openwrt.org/whiterussian/packages/Packages
Updated list of available packages in /usr/lib/ipkg/lists/whiterussian
Downloading http://downloads.openwrt.org/whiterussian/packages/non-free/
Packages
Updated list of available packages in /usr/lib/ipkg/lists/non-free
Successfully terminated.
```

This command contacts the OpenWRT package repositories and updates the list of packages that are available for installation. After it's finished updating, you can run ipkg list to see all of the packages. If you want to see the ones that are actually installed, run ipkg list_installed instead. To install a package, simply run ipkg install *<package name>*.

Out of the box, most of your wireless settings should carry over from the standard Linksys firmware to OpenWRT. However, if you're using WPA-PSK or 802.1X instead of WEP (please do, because WEP is horribly insecure), you'll need to install the *nas* package. After you've done that and rebooted, you should see the *nas* binary running:

```
# ps -aux | grep nas
  431 root       480 S   /usr/sbin/nas -P /var/run/nas.lan.pid -l br0 -H
34954 -i eth2 -A -m 132 -k XXXXXXXXXXXXXXX
```

You should now be able to connect to your router without reconfiguring any of your wireless clients.

In the case shown in this example, WPA-PSK is being used and the Xs correspond to the password, which is now set via the wl0_wpa_psk NVRAM variable. For more information on what NVRAM variables you can use for configuring your router, take a look at *http://wiki.openwrt.org/OpenWrtDocs/Configuration*.

As you've seen, there are many more packages available for OpenWRT. For instance, you can easily install TcpDump or Kismet through *ipkg*. The possibilities are nearly limitless. For just two examples, you can set up a RADIUS server to authenticate your wireless users [Hack #77] or turn your router into a captive portal [Hack #78].

HACK #77 Use Fine-Grained Authentication for Your Wireless Network

Use RADIUS and 802.1X to offer per-user authentication for your 802.11 networks.

One of the big downsides of using WPA-PSK or WEP (which you shouldn't be using) to control access to a wireless network is that they require all valid users to know the key to the network. Not only does this make changing the key more difficult, but it also forces you to change it if you ever need to deny access to a single user. Enter 802.1X, a port-based authentication protocol originally developed for use on Ethernet LANs to control access to physical ports on a switch.

802.1X came into play with wireless LANs when work began on the 802.11i standard, which adds significant security features to 802.11-based networks. However, IEEE standards often take a long time to ratify (they're designed by committee), so the WiFi Alliance, an industry trade group, adopted some portions of the standard under the WiFi Protected Access (WPA) moniker. Once 802.11i was ratified, the designation of WPA2 became used to denote full compliance with the standard. For this reason, you'll often see the combined use of 802.1X and 802.11 referred to as WPA Enterprise or WPA2 Enterprise.

To do its job, 802.1X makes use of a Remote Access Dial-In User Service (RADIUS) server to provide authentication, authorization, and accounting. Other components in an 802.1X-controlled network include the authenticator and the supplicant. The *authenticator* is the device that provides access to the network's resources (e.g., a switch or AP). When a device is connected to the network, the authenticator detects it and asks it to identify itself. The *supplicant* is a piece of software on the connecting device that responds. The authenticator then acts as an intermediary between the supplicant and the authentication server until access is granted. This process is governed by the Extensible Authentication Protocol (EAP), which, as the name suggests, allows 802.1X to support many different authentication mechanisms.

Of the many available authentication mechanisms, two are widely supported by Windows, Mac OS X, and Linux: EAP/TLS and Protected EAP (PEAP). EAP/TLS makes use of your PKI infrastructure and the TLS protocol to provide authentication. That is, you need to have a Certificate Authority set up and you must generate certificate/key pairs for your authentication server and all of your clients. Many network administrators might see this as a considerable amount of work. On the other hand, PEAP requires a certificate/key pair for the server only. This hack shows how to set up 802.1X to use PEAP for authentication.

Deploying the RADIUS Server

The first thing to do is to set up a RADIUS server. One excellent (and free) server is FreeRADIUS (*http://www.freeradius.org*). Begin by downloading the FreeRADIUS tarball from the site's download page (*http://www.freeradius. org/getting.html*); then unpack it and change into the directory that it creates. Build it by running ./configure && make. After it finishes, become root and run make install.

Now, you'll need to create a user and group for it to run under (something like _radiusd). After you've done that, edit FreeRADIUS's configuration file, *radiusd.conf*. If you didn't specify an alternate installation prefix when running *configure*, it should be in */usr/local/etc/raddb*.

You'll need to tell it the user and group that you just created. Search for user = nobody to find a good location in the file to do this. Then, add a couple of lines similar to these:

```
user = _radiusd
group = _radiusd
```

Now, edit the *eap.conf* file in the same directory and locate the following line in the eap section:

```
default_eap_type = md5
```

Change it to read:

```
default_eap_type = peap
```

If you don't already have a Certificate Authority, create one now **[Hack #69]** and generate a certificate/key pair for the authentication server. You should also distribute your CA's certificate to your clients **[Hack #70]** so that they can verify that the authentication server is legitimate when they connect to your wireless network.

Once you've done this, uncomment the tls section and set all of the certificate variables to point to your server's certificate, key, and CA certificate files.

Also uncomment the following lines:

```
dh_file = ${raddbdir}/certs/dh
random_file = ${raddbdir}/certs/random
```

Now, uncomment the peap section and then uncomment the following line:

```
#    default_eap_type = mschapv2
```

You're almost done configuring the RADIUS server. The only thing left is to allow the authenticator to access it. Do this by editing *clients.conf* and adding an entry similar to this:

```
client 192.168.0.5 {
        secret = authpass
        shortname = openwrt-ap
}
```

where *secret* is a password that the authenticator will use to access the server and *shortname* is a short descriptive name for the device. Of course, the password you use for *secret* should be a much longer, higher-quality one than the example shown here.

To add users to the RADIUS server, edit the *users* file and add entries like this:

```
andrew User-Password == "wlanpass"
```

After you've done that, you need to change the owner of *radiusd*'s *log* and *run* directories to the user that you created:

```
# chown _radiusd /usr/local/var/log/radius
# chown _radiusd /usr/local/var/run/radiusd
```

Then, you can start *radiusd*:

```
# /usr/local/sbin/radiusd
```

Configuring Your AP

If your AP supports 802.1X, there should be a WPA Enterprise, WPA2 Enterprise, or 802.1X setting in the section of the device's configuration interface where you tell it whether you want to use WEP, WPA-PSK, or no authentication at all. Once you change it to use 802.1X, you'll need to tell your AP the IP address of your RADIUS server and the password to use when talking to it.

If you're using OpenWRT [Hack #76], it's a little more complicated and involves setting NVRAM variables. Still, it's not very difficult.

First, log into your AP using SSH and enter commands similar to these:

```
# nvram set wl0_akm="wpa wpa2"
# nvram set wl0_crypto="aes+tkip"
# nvram set wl0_radius_key="authpass"
# nvram set wl0_radius_ipaddr=192.168.0.43
# nvram get wl0_radius_port=1812
# nvram commit
```

When running the preceding commands, be sure to substitute the IP address of your RADIUS server for the value of *wl0_radius_ipaddr*. Also, replace *authpass* with the password you set when configuring FreeRADIUS.

These commands allow your AP to support both WPA and WPA2. However, if you want to allow only WPA, you can substitute different values for wl0_akm and wl0_crypto:

```
# nvram set wl0_akm="wpa"
# nvram set wl0_crypto="tkip"
```

For WPA2, use these:

```
# nvram set wl0_akm="wpa2"
# nvram set wl0_crypto="aes"
```

If you don't have the *nas* package installed, you should install it now:

```
# ipkg install nas
```

This is the piece of software that will talk to the supplicants and to your authentication server.

After you've ensured that the *nas* package is installed and have set the NVRAM variables, reboot your AP. You should now be able to access your wireless network by setting your client to use 802.1X with PEAP and then entering any of the usernames and passwords that you entered in the *users* file.

Now, you can have the benefits of a well-protected wireless network without the overhead of distributing keys to each of your users.

For deployments with a large number of users, the simple *users* text file might become unwieldy. Fortunately, FreeRADIUS is flexible in being able to interface with many different authentication mechanisms, from Unix accounts to SQL databases and LDAP servers. If you need to interface with any of those kinds of systems, be sure to check out FreeRADIUS's documentation.

Deploy a Captive Portal

Use WiFiDog to loosely control access to your wireless network.

Having a secure wireless network is important not only for the protection of your network infrastructure, but also to ensure against being liable for attacks on other networks perpetrated through your own by malicious wireless users. This is easy if you're using strong authentication mechanisms, but what if you want to share your wireless network with guests and neighbors?

One way to do this is to employ a *captive portal*, which allows you to keep tabs on who's using your wireless network without anything like a WEP key or password to authenticate with it. Instead, users who try to access the Internet through your network are redirected to a web page where they can register for an account that is linked to an email address. Once they register and receive their confirmation emails, users can activate their accounts.

One incredibly flexible portal is WiFiDog (*http://wifidog.org*), which consists of a central authentication server and a gateway component that can be deployed on an AP running OpenWRT [Hack #76].

The Authentication Server

Before you begin, make sure you have set up a PostgreSQL (*http://www. postgresql.org*) database server. This doesn't need to be on the same machine as your web server, but it can be. You'll need PHP 5.x (*http://www.php.net*) installed on your web server as well.

After you've met these two conditions, you can install the authentication server. Begin by checking out the source code from the project's Subversion repository:

```
$ svn checkout https://dev.wifidog.org/svn/trunk/wifidog-auth
```

Once the checkout has finished, change into the directory that it created and move the contents of the *wifidog* directory along with the *sql* directory to an area on your web server capable of executing PHP scripts.

After you've done that, browse to the URL corresponding to where you put the files. You should see a page similar to Figure 7-2.

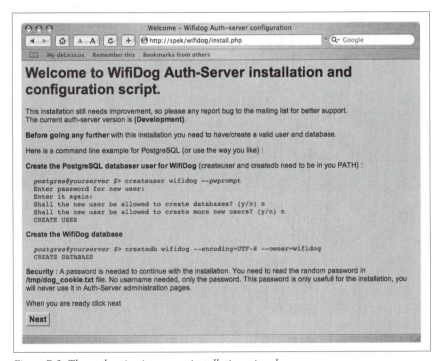

Figure 7-2. The authentication server installation wizard

Follow the instructions on the page to create the PostgreSQL database. After you've created the database and a user to access it, click Next. In order to proceed, you'll need to enter the password found in */tmp/dog_cookie.txt* on your web server. After the next page has loaded, you should see something similar to Figure 7-3.

Install any prerequisites with ERROR listed next to them, and refresh the page. The missing prerequisites should now have OK next to them.

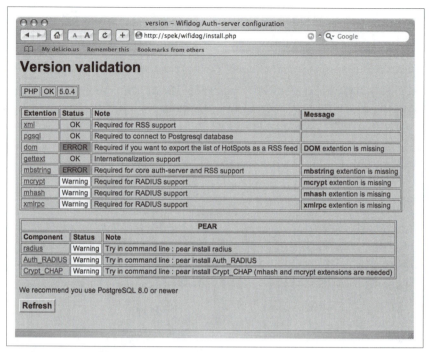

Figure 7-3. Status of prerequisite software packages

You might need to restart your web server for the changes to take effect.

The rest of the installation process is pretty straightforward. The wizard will make sure directory permissions are correct, allow you to automatically install optional software packages, and configure access to the database that you created. In addition, you'll be prompted to create an administrator account.

Once you've completed all the steps in the installation wizard, you can browse to the authentication server's home page, shown in Figure 7-4.

Here, you can log in with your administrator account and configure every aspect of your portals. But first, let's set up the gateway component.

Installing the Gateway

Installing the gateway component is incredibly easy, thanks to the availability of prebuilt packages for OpenWRT. Log into your OpenWRT-based AP,

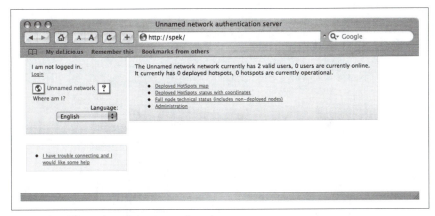

Figure 7-4. The authentication server's main page

download the WiFiDog gateway package from *http://www.ilesansfil.org/dist/
wifidog/bin/openwrt/*, and *run the following commands:*

```
# cd /tmp
# wget http://www.ilesansfil.org/dist/wifidog/bin/openwrt/whiterussian-rc3/
wifidog_1.1.3_beta2-1_mipsel.ipk
```

Then, install it:

```
# ipkg install wifidog_1.1.3_beta2-1_mipsel.ipk
```

This command also downloads any missing packages that WiFiDog depends
on. Make sure you also have the *libgcc* package installed:

```
# ipkg list_installed | grep gcc
libgcc - 3.4.4-8 - GCC support library
```

If you don't get any output from the previous command, you can install the
libgcc package by running ipkg install libgcc.

Now, edit */etc/wifidog.conf*, following the instructions in the file. At the very
minimum, you'll need to tell it where to find the authentication server
you've set up. You can do this with an AuthServer statement, like so:

```
AuthServer {
  Hostname spek.nnc
  Path /
}
```

Once you've finished editing the configuration file, reboot your AP. After it
finishes booting, associate a wireless client with it and try to browse to a
web site. You should be automatically redirected to a page that looks like
Figure 7-5, your authentication server's login page.

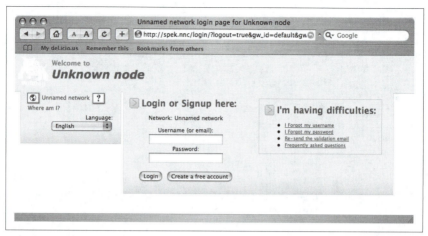

Figure 7-5. The login page

If you log in with your administrator account, you'll be given access to the Internet and the rest of the network. You can also create a regular user account by clicking the Create Free Account button. If you decide to do this, you'll see a page like Figure 7-6.

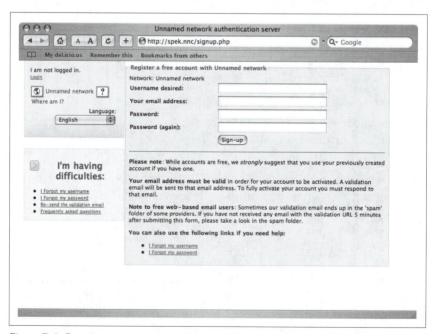

Figure 7-6. Creating a user account

Once you've filled in and submitted the form, you'll be given access for a short period of time, so that you can check your email for the validation message. When you check your email, you should receive a message that looks similar to this:

```
Hello,
Please follow the link below to validate your account.
http://spek.nnc/validate.php?user_
id=b1ffadf3826c1a6ad1fdb494f212a419&token=949baa02b3b3921bc4bd949c6f963400

Thank you,
The Team.
```

Go to the URL in the email, and the account will be given access without a time limit.

Nearly every aspect of WiFiDog is configurable. Be sure to log into the authentication server with your administrator account and take a look at all of the options available to you. The user interface is friendly and easy to use.

## CHAPTER EIGHT

Logging
Hacks 79–86

Keeping logs is an important aspect of maintaining the security of your network, because logs can assist in everything from alerting you to an impending attack to debugging network problems. After an incident has occurred, good logs can help you track down how the attacker got in, fix the security hole, and figure out which machines were affected. In addition, logs can help with tracing the attack back to its source, so you can identify or take legal action against the intruder. In short, log files are worth their weight in gold (just pretend that bits and bytes weigh a lot). As such, they should be given at least as much protection as any other information that's stored on your servers—even the patent schematics for your perpetual motion machine.

This chapter deals mostly with various ways to set up remote logging, whether you're setting up a simple central *syslogd* for your servers to log to, setting up your Windows machines to log events to your *syslog* server, or using *syslog-ng* to collect logs from remote sites through an encrypted TCP connection. Using these methods, you can ensure that your logs are sitting safely on a dedicated server that's running minimal services, to decrease the chance that the logs will be compromised.

Once you have all your logs collected in a central place, what can you do with them? This chapter also covers ways to summarize your logs into reports that are easy to read and understand, so you can quickly spot the most pertinent information. If that's not fast enough for you, you'll also learn how to set up real-time alerts that will notify you as soon as a critical event occurs. In some circumstances, responding immediately to an event—rather than waiting around for it to end up in a report that you read the next morning—can save hours of effort.

Finally, you'll see how to set up a host intrusion detection system (IDS) that goes the extra mile so that you don't have to; it will monitor your logs, correlate events, and respond to them automatically.

HACK #79 Run a Central Syslog Server

Keep your logs safe from attackers by storing them remotely.

How do you find out when or if an intruder has gained entry into one of your systems? By checking your logs, of course. But what if the intruder modified the logs? In this situation, centralized logging definitely saves the day. After all, if a machine is compromised but the log evidence isn't kept on that machine, it's going to be much more difficult for the attacker to cover his tracks. In addition to providing an extra level of protection, it's much easier to monitor the logs for a whole network of machines when they're all in one place.

To set up a central *syslog* server quickly, just start your *syslogd* with the switch that causes it to listen for messages from remote machines on a UDP port.

Under Linux, do this by specifying the -r command-line option:

```
# /usr/sbin/syslogd -m 0 -r
```

Under FreeBSD, run *syslogd* without the -s command-line option:

```
# /usr/sbin/syslogd
```

The -s option causes FreeBSD's *syslogd* to not listen for remote connections. FreeBSD's *syslogd* also allows you to restrict the hosts from which it will receive messages. To set these restrictions, use the -a option, which has the following forms:

```
ipaddr/mask[:service]
domain[:service]
*domain[:service]
```

The first form allows you to specify a single IP address or group of IP addresses by using the appropriate netmask. The *service* option allows you to specify a source UDP port. If nothing is specified, it defaults to port 514, which is the default for the *syslog* service. The next two forms allow you to restrict access to a specific domain name, as determined by a reverse lookup of the IP address of the connecting host. The difference between the second and third forms is the use of the * wildcard character, which specifies that all machines ending in *domain* may connect.

Moving on, OpenBSD uses the -u option to listen for remote connections:

```
# /usr/sbin/syslogd -a /var/empty/dev/log -u
```

whereas Solaris's *syslogd* uses -T:

```
# /usr/sbin/syslogd -T
```

Now, let's set up the clients. If you want to forward all logging traffic from a machine to your central log host, simply put the following in your */etc/syslog.conf* file:

```
*.*            @loghost
```

You can either make this the only line in the configuration file, in which case messages will be logged only to the remote host, or add it to what is already there, in which case logs will be stored both locally and remotely for safe-keeping.

One drawback to remote logging is that the stock *syslogd* for most operating systems fails to provide any measure of authentication or access control with regard to who may write to a central log host. Firewalls can provide some protection, keeping out everyone but those who are most determined to undermine your logging infrastructure; however, intruders who have already gained access to your local network can easily spoof their network connections and bypass any firewall rules that you set up. If you've determined that this is a concern for your network, set up remote logging using public-key authentication and SSL-encrypted connections **[Hack #84]**.

HACK #80   Steer Syslog

Make syslog work harder, and spend less time looking through huge log files.

The default *syslog* installation on many distributions doesn't do a very good job of filtering classes of information into separate files. If you see a jumble of messages from Sendmail, *sudo*, BIND, and other system services in */var/log/messages*, you should probably review your */etc/syslog.conf* file.

Syslog can filter on a number of facilities and priorities, including auth, auth-priv, cron, daemon, kern, lpr, mail, news, syslog, user, uucp, and local0 through local7. In addition, each facility can have one of eight priorities: debug, info, notice, warning, err, crit, alert, and emerg.

Note that most applications decide for themselves what facility and priority to log at (although the best apps let you choose), so they might not be logged as you expect. Here's a sample */etc/syslog.conf* that attempts to shuffle around what gets logged where:

```
auth.warning            /var/log/auth
mail.err                /var/log/maillog
kern.*                  /var/log/kernel
cron.crit               /var/log/cron
*.err;mail.none         /var/log/syslog
```

```
*.info;auth.none;mail.none            /var/log/messages

#*.=debug                             /var/log/debug

local0.info                           /var/log/cluster
local1.err                            /var/log/spamerica
```

All of the lines in this example log the specified priority (or higher) to the respective file. The special priority none tells *syslog* not to bother logging the specified facility at all. The local0 through local7 facilities are supplied for use with your own programs, however you see fit. For example, the */var/log/spamerica* file fills with *local1.err* (or higher) messages that are generated by our spam processing job. It's nice to have those messages separate from the standard mail delivery log (which is in */var/log/maillog*).

The commented *.=debug line is useful when debugging daemonized services. It tells *syslog* to specifically log only debug priority messages of any facility, and it generally shouldn't be running (unless you don't mind filling your disks with debug logs).

Another approach is to log debug information to a FIFO. This way, debug logs take up no space, but they will disappear unless a process is watching the FIFO. To log to a FIFO, first create it in the filesystem:

```
# mkfifo -m 0664 /var/log/debug
```

Then, uncomment the debug line in *syslog.conf* and amend it to include a |, like this:

```
*.=debug         |/var/log/debug
```

Now, debug information will be constantly logged to the FIFO and can be viewed with a command like less -f /var/log/debug.

A FIFO is also handy if you want a process to constantly watch all system messages and perhaps notify you via email about any critical messages. Try making a FIFO called */var/log/monitor* and adding a rule like this to your *syslog.conf*:

```
*.*              |/var/log/monitor
```

Now, every message (at every priority) is passed to the */var/log/monitor* FIFO, and any process watching it can react accordingly, all without taking up any disk space.

If you notice a bunch of lines like the following in */var/log/messages*, you might be wondering why they're there:

```
Dec 29 18:33:35 catlin -- MARK --
Dec 29 18:53:35 catlin -- MARK --
Dec 29 19:13:35 catlin -- MARK --
Dec 29 19:33:35 catlin -- MARK --
```

```
Dec 29 19:53:35 catlin -- MARK --
Dec 29 20:13:35 catlin -- MARK --
Dec 29 20:33:35 catlin -- MARK --
Dec 29 20:53:35 catlin -- MARK --
Dec 29 21:13:35 catlin -- MARK --
```

These are generated by the mark functionality of *syslog*, as a way of "touching base" with the system, so that you can (theoretically) tell if *syslog* has unexpectedly died. This generally only serves to fill up your log files, and unless you are having problems with *syslog*, you probably don't need it. To turn this function off, pass the -m 0 switch to *syslogd* (after first killing any running *syslogd* processes), like this:

```
# killall syslogd; /usr/sbin/syslogd -m 0
```

If all of this fiddling about with facilities and priorities strikes you as arcane Unix-speak, you're not alone. These examples are provided for systems that include the default (and venerable) *syslogd*. If you have the opportunity to install a new *syslogd*, you will likely want to look into *syslog-ng*. This new implementation of *syslogd* allows much more flexible filtering and offers a slew of new features. "Aggregate Logs from Remote Sites" **[Hack #84]** takes a look at some of what is possible with *syslog-ng*.

—*Rob Flickenger*

Integrate Windows into Your Syslog Infrastructure
Keep track of all of your Windows hosts the Unix way.

Keeping tabs on all the Event Logs for all your Windows hosts can be hard enough, but it's even more difficult if your propensities predispose you to Unix. After all, Unix systems keep their logs in plain-text files that are easily searchable with common shell commands. This is a world apart from the binary logs that Windows keeps in its Event Log.

Wouldn't it be nice if you could have your Windows machines work more like Unix machines? Fortunately, you're not the first one to think that. *NTsyslog* (*http://ntsyslog.sourceforge.net*) is a freely available service written for Windows 2000 and XP that allows you to log to a remote *syslogd*. For Windows 2003 Server, you can use *EventLog to Syslog* (*https://engineering. purdue.edu/ECN/Resources/Documents/UNIX/evtsys/*).

Using NTsyslog

To set up NTsyslog, just download and unpack the ZIP file available at *http:// sourceforge.net/projects/ntsyslog/*, and then run the setup program (e.g., *SetupNTSyslog-1.13.exe*).

To verify that it was installed, open up the Administrative Tools Control Panel applet and double-click the Services icon. Then, scroll around and look for the NTsyslog service. You should see something similar to Figure 8-1.

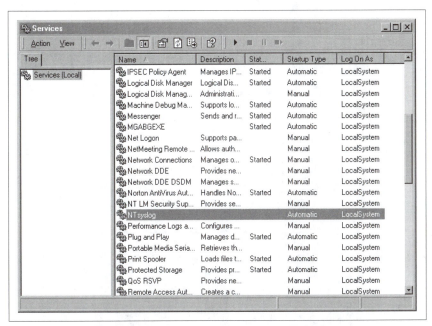

Figure 8-1. The Services Control Panel applet with the NTsyslog service shown

By default, NTsyslog installs itself to run under the Local System account, which has complete access to the resources of the local host. This is obviously not the optimal configuration, since the NTsyslog service needs access to the Event Log and nothing else. You can change the default by double-clicking the NTsyslog line in the Services Control Panel applet, as shown in Figure 8-1, which brings up the Properties dialog for the service.

However, before you do this, you might want to create an account specifically for the NTsyslog service that has only the necessary privileges for NTsyslog to run properly. To do this, go back to the Administrative Tools window and double-click the Computer Management icon. After clicking the Local Users and Groups icon, you should see something similar to Figure 8-2.

Right-click the *Users* folder and click New User to bring up a dialog where you can enter the information for the new user. Enter information similar to that shown in Figure 8-3, and make sure you pick a strong password.

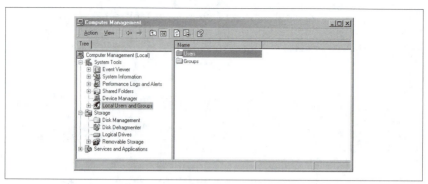

Figure 8-2. The Computer Management Control Panel applet with the Users folder shown

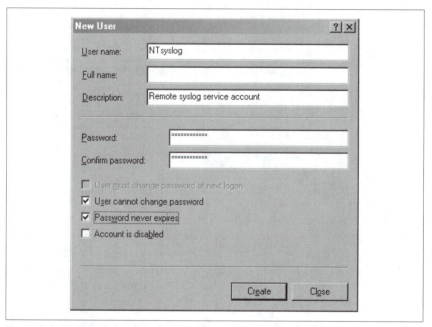

Figure 8-3. Creating a new user for NTsyslog

Now, you need to give your new user the rights it needs to do its job. Double-click the Local Security Policy icon in the Administrative Tools window. Choose the *Local Policies* folder in the left pane of the Local Security Settings window, and then double-click the *User Rights Assignment* folder in the right pane of the window. You should now see something similar to Figure 8-4.

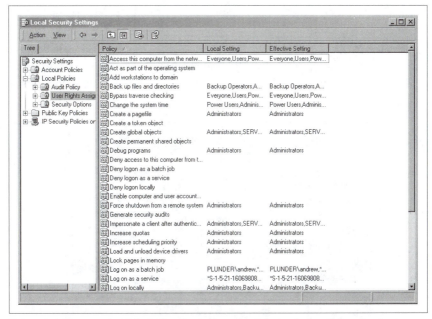

Figure 8-4. Viewing the User Rights Assignments settings in the Local Security Settings Control Panel applet

The access right you're looking for is "Manage auditing and security log." Double-click it in the Policy list to bring up a dialog like the one shown in Figure 8-5.

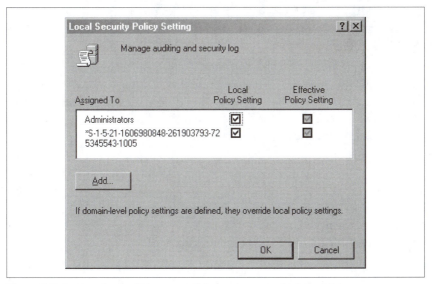

Figure 8-5. Settings for the "Manage auditing and security log" user right

Click the Add button, select the name of the user from the list, and then click OK.

You now have the account and have given it the proper access rights, so go back to the Services window and double-click the NTsyslog service to bring up its Properties dialog. Click the Log On tab to bring up the dialog shown in Figure 8-6.

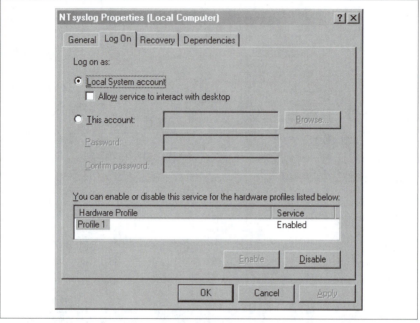

Figure 8-6. The Log On tab for the NTsyslog service Properties dialog

Click the "This account" radio button to enable the Browse... button. Now, click the Browse... button and locate and select the account that you created. Then click the OK button. You should now see the account name in the text box to the right of the "This account" radio button. Enter the password you set for the account and confirm it.

After you click the Apply button, a new dialog will confirm that the Log On As A Service right has been granted to the account. Click the OK button, and then go to the General tab in the Properties dialog. To start the service as the new user that you created, click the Start button. If you get an error dialog, you will need to change the ACL for the *ntsyslog.exe* file and add Read and Execute permissions for the new account.

Now, you'll use the included configuration program to configure the settings particular to NTsyslog. You can use this to set up a primary and secondary *syslogd* to send messages to, as well as to specify the types of Event Log events to send and their mappings to *syslog* facilities and severities. You can also start and stop the NTsyslog service from this screen. To use the configuration program, run *NTSyslogCtrl.exe*. You should see a window like the one shown in Figure 8-7.

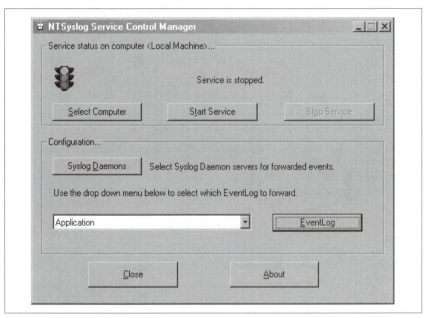

Figure 8-7. The NTsyslog configuration program

To start the service, click the Start Service button; to stop the service, click the Stop Service button. Clicking the Syslog Daemons button brings up the dialog shown in Figure 8-8.

Again, this is pretty straightforward. Just put in the host you want to log to, and, if you have a secondary *syslog* host, put that in the appropriate field.

The most difficult part of the configuration is setting up the mappings of the Event Log entry types to the *syslog* facilities and severity levels, but even this is fairly easy. In the drop-down list (shown in Figure 8-7), you can select between the Application, Security, and System Event Logs. To configure one, simply select it and click the EventLog button. If you select the Security log and click the EventLog button, you should see something similar to Figure 8-9.

To enable the forwarding of a particular type of event, click the checkbox next to it. Using the drop-down listboxes, you can also configure the facility and severity mappings for each type. Since this is the Security log, you

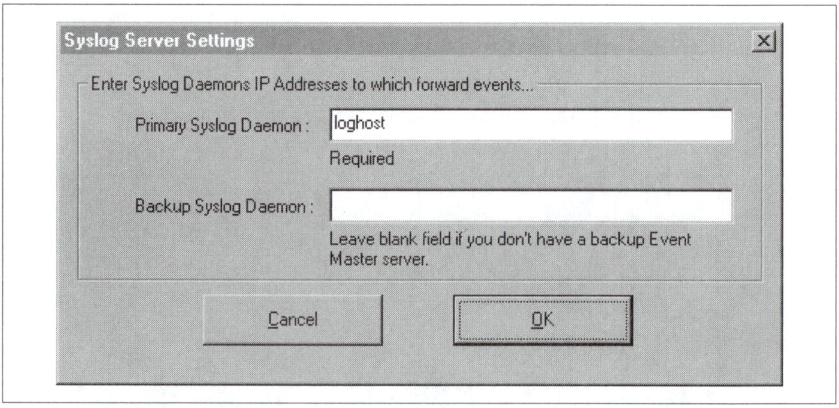

Figure 8-8. Specifying a primary and backup syslog server

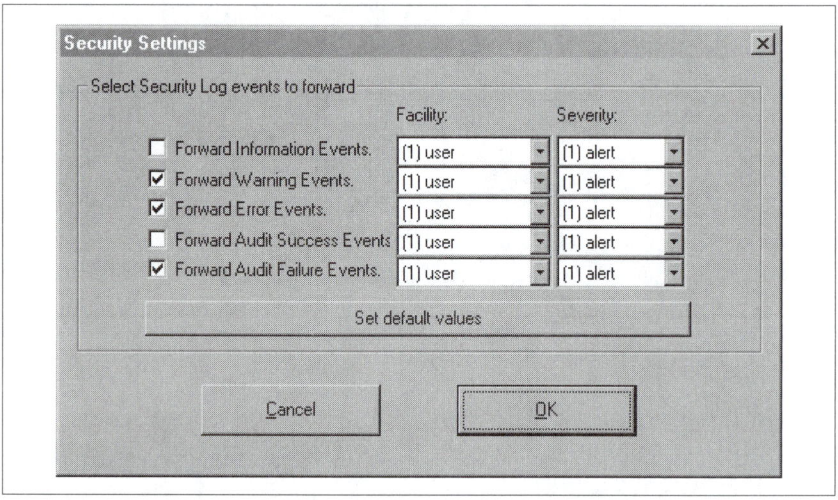

Figure 8-9. Mapping Security Event Log entries to syslog facilities and severities

should probably pick one of the security/auth *syslog* facilities. For the severity, choose something that sounds similar to the Event Log type. For example, I selected (4)security/auth1 and (6)information for the Information type for the Security Event Log.

Alternatively, you can select a facility and severity that are not used on any of your Unix servers, and have your *syslogd* log all Windows events to a common file separate from your Unix logs. Or, if you're using *syslog-ng* [Hack #84], you can use any facility you like and filter out your Windows hosts by IP address.

When you're finished, try logging in and out a few times using an incorrect password so that you can see that everything is working.

If it is, you should see login failure messages similar to this:

```
Oct 29 17:19:04 plunder security[failure] 529 NT AUTHORITY\\SYSTEM  Logon
Failure:
Reason:Unknown user name or bad password  User Name:andrew  Domain:PLUNDER
Logon Type:2
Logon Process:User32   Authentication Package:Negotiate  Workstation Name:
PLUNDER
```

Using Eventlog to Syslog

If you're using Windows 2003, NTsyslog might appear to work, but in fact it will repeatedly send the same log messages to your *syslog* server. If that's the case, you can use Eventlog to Syslog to fill in for NTsyslog. Setting up Eventlog to Syslog involves downloading the prebuilt executables from its project page, extracting them from their ZIP file, and then copying *evtsys.dll* and *evtsys.exe* to your *%systemroot%\system32* directory (e.g., *C:\ WINDOWS\system32*). Then, open a command prompt and run a command similar to the following:

```
C:\> WINDOWS\system32\evtsys -i -h 192.168.0.43
```

Replace the IP address with the IP address of your *syslog* server. While you have the command prompt window open, you can then start the service by running net start evtsys. As it starts, you should see entries similar to these on your *syslog* server:

```
May  6 20:01:37 192.168.0.204 Eventlog to Syslog Service Started: Version 3.
4.1
May  6 20:01:43 192.168.0.204 Service Control Manager: Administrator: The
Eventlog to Syslog service was successfully sent a start control.
May  6 20:01:43 192.168.0.204 Service Control Manager: N/A: The Eventlog to
Syslog service entered the running state.
```

As with NTsyslog, you can create an account that has access only to the Event Logs and have Eventlog to Syslog run with its privileges. Unfortunately, unlike NTsyslog, Eventlog to Syslog won't allow you to specify what log facilities and levels to use.

Now that you have your Windows logs going to a Unix log host, you can use the wealth of flexible Unix log-monitoring tools to keep tabs on all your Windows systems.

Summarize Your Logs Automatically

HACK #82

Wade through that haystack of logs to find the proverbial needle.

If you're logging almost every piece of information you can from all services and hosts on your network, no doubt you're drowning in a sea of information. One way to keep abreast of the real issues affecting your systems is by summarizing your logs. This is easy with the *logwatch* tool (*http://www. logwatch.org*).

logwatch analyzes your system logs over a given period of time and automatically generates reports, and it can easily be run from *cron* so that it can email you the results. *logwatch* is available with most Red Hat Linux distributions. You can also download RPM packages from the project's web site if you are using another RPM-based Linux distribution.

To compile logwatch from source, download the source code package. Since it is a script, there is no need to compile anything. Thus, installing it is as simple as copying the *logwatch* script to a directory.

You can install it by running these commands:

```
# tar xfz logwatch-5.0.tar.gz
# cd logwatch-5.0
# mkdir /etc/log.d
# cp -R conf lib scripts /etc/log.d
```

You can also install the manual page and, for added convenience, create a link from the *logwatch.pl* script to */usr/sbin/logwatch*:

```
# cp logwatch.8 /usr/share/man/man8
# (cd /usr/sbin && \
ln -s ../../etc/log.d/scripts/logwatch.pl logwatch)
```

Running the following command will give you a taste of the summaries logwatch creates:

```
# logwatch --print | less
################### LogWatch 4.3.1 (01/13/03) ###################
        Processing Initiated: Sat Dec 27 21:12:26 2003
        Date Range Processed: yesterday
    Detail Level of Output: 0
        Logfiles for Host: colossus
 ###############################################################

 -------------------- SSHD Begin -----------------------

Users logging in through sshd:
    andrew logged in from kryten.nnc (192.168.0.60) using password: 2 Time(s)

 -------------------- SSHD End -------------------------

 ###################### LogWatch End ######################
```

If you have an */etc/cron.daily* directory, you can simply make a symbolic link from the *logwatch.pl* script to */etc/cron.daily/logwatch.pl*, and the script will run daily. Alternatively, you can create an entry in root's crontab, in which case you can also modify logwatch's behavior by passing it command-line switches. For instance, you can change the email address that logwatch sends reports to by using the --mailto command-line option. They are sent to the local root account by default, which is probably not what you want.

logwatch supports most standard log files without any additional configuration, but you can easily add support for any other type of log file. To do this, you first need to create a log file group configuration for the new file type in */etc/log.d/conf/logfiles*. This file just needs to contain an entry pointing *logwatch* to the log file for the service and another entry specifying a globbing pattern for any archived log files for that service.

For example, if you have a service called *myservice*, you can create */etc/log.d/ conf/logfiles/myservice.conf* with these contents:

```
LogFile = /var/log/myservice
Archive = /var/log/myservice.*
```

Next, you need to create a service definition file. This should be called */etc/ log.d/conf/services/myservice.conf* and should contain the following line:

```
LogFile = myservice
```

Finally, since *logwatch* is merely a framework for generating log file summaries, you'll also need to create a script in */etc/log.d/scripts/services* called *myservice*. When *logwatch* executes, it will strip all time entries from the logs and pass the rest of the log entry through standard input to the *myservice* script. Therefore, you must write your script to read from standard input, parse out the pertinent information, and then print it to standard output.

This hack just scratches the surface of how to get *logwatch* running on your system. There is a great deal of information in the HOWTO-Make-Filter, which is included with the *logwatch* distribution.

H A C K **Monitor Your Logs Automatically**
#83 Use swatch to alert you to possible problems as they happen.

Automatically generated log file summaries are fine for keeping abreast of what's happening with your systems and networks, but if you want to know about events as they happen, you'll need to look elsewhere. One tool that can help keep you informed in real time is *swatch* (*http://swatch.sourceforge.net*), the "Simple WATCHer."

swatch is a highly configurable log file monitor that can watch a file for user-defined triggers and dispatch alerts in a variety of ways. It consists of a Perl program, a configuration file, and a library of actions to take when it sees a trigger in the file it is monitoring.

Installing swatch

To install *swatch*, download the package, unpack it, and go into the directory that it creates. Then, run these commands:

```
# perl Makefile.PL
# make && make install
```

Before *swatch* will build, you'll need to install the Date::Calc, Date::Parse, and Time::HiRes Perl CPAN modules. If they're not already installed, running perl Makefile.PL will produce the following error message:

```
Warning: prerequisite Date::Calc 0 not found.
Warning: prerequisite Date::Parse 0 not found.
Warning: prerequisite Time::HiRes 1.12 not found.
Writing Makefile for swatch
```

If you already have Perl's CPAN modules installed, simply run these commands:

```
# perl -MCPAN -e "install Date::Calc"
# perl -MCPAN -e "install Date::Parse"
# perl -MCPAN -e "Time::HiRes"
```

By default, *swatch* looks for its configuration in a file called *.swatchrc* in the current user's home directory. This file contains regular expressions to watch for in the file that you are monitoring with *swatch*. If you want to use a different configuration file, tell *swatch* by using the -c command-line switch.

For instance, to use */etc/swatch/messages.conf* to monitor */var/log/messages*, invoke *swatch* like this:

```
# swatch -c /etc/swatch/messages.conf -t /var/log/messages
```

Configuration Syntax

Here's the general format for entries in the configuration file:

```
watchfor /<regex>/
<action1>
[action2]
[action3]
...
```

Alternatively, you can ignore specific log messages that match a regular expression by using the ignore keyword:

```
ignore /<regex>/
```

You can also specify multiple regular expressions by separating them with the pipe (|) character.

swatch is very configurable in terms of the actions it can take when a string matches a regular expression. Some useful actions that you can specify in your *.swatchrc* file are echo, write, exec, mail, pipe, and throttle.

The echo action simply prints the matching line to the console; additionally, you can specify what text mode it will use. Thus, lines can be printed to the console as bold, underlined, blinking, inverted, or colored text.

For instance, if you want to print a matching line in red, blinking text, use the following action:

```
echo blink,red
```

The write action is similar to the echo action, except it does not support text modes. It can, however, write the matching line to any specified user's TTY:

```
write user:user2:...
```

The exec action allows you to execute any command:

```
exec <command>
```

You can use the $0 or $* variables to pass the entire matching line to the command that you execute, or use $1 to pass the first field in the line, $2 for the second, and so on. So, if you want to pass only the second and third fields from the matching line to the command *mycommand*, use an action like this:

```
exec "mycommand $2 $3"
```

In addition to the exec action, *swatch* can execute external commands with the pipe action. The only difference is that instead of passing arguments to the command, *swatch* will execute the command and pipe the matching line to it. To use this action, just put the pipe keyword followed by the command you want to use.

Alternatively, to increase performance, you can use the keep_open option to keep the pipe to the program open until *swatch* exits or needs to perform a different pipe action:

```
pipe mycommand,keep_open
```

The mail action is especially useful if you have an email-enabled or text-messaging-capable cell phone or pager. When using the mail action, you can list as many recipient addresses as you like, in addition to specifying a subject line. *swatch* will send the line that matched the regular expression to these addresses with the subject you set.

Here is the general form of the `mail` action:

```
mail addresses=address:address2:...,subject=mysubject
```

When using the `mail` action, be sure to escape the @ characters in the email addresses (i.e., @ becomes \@). Escape any spaces in the subject of the email as well.

One problem with executing commands or sending emails whenever a specific string occurs in a log message is that sometimes the same log message might be generated over and over again rapidly. Clearly, if this were to happen, you wouldn't want to get paged or emailed 100 times within a 10-minute period. To alleviate this problem, *swatch* provides the `throttle` action. This action lets you suppress a specific message or any message that matches a particular regular expression for a specified amount of time.

The general form of the `throttle` action is:

```
throttle h:m:s
```

The `throttle` action will throttle based on the contents of the message by default. If you would like to throttle the actions based on the regular expression that caused the match, you can add `,use=regex` to the end of your `throttle` statement.

swatch is an incredibly useful tool, but it can take some work to create a good *.swatchrc* file. The best way to figure out what to look for is to examine your log files for behavior that you want to monitor closely.

HACK #84   Aggregate Logs from Remote Sites

Integrate collocated and other remote systems or networks into your central syslog infrastructure.

Monitoring the logs of a remote site or even a collocated server can often be overlooked when faced with the task of monitoring activity on your local network. You could use the traditional *syslog* facilities to send logging information from the remote network or systems, but since the *syslog* daemon uses UDP for sending to remote systems, this is not an ideal solution. UDP provides no reliability in its communications, so you risk losing logging information. In addition, the traditional *syslog* daemon has no means to encrypt the traffic that it sends, so your logs might be viewable by anyone with access to the intermediary networks between you and your remote hosts or networks.

Compiling syslog-ng

To get around these issues, you'll have to look beyond the *syslog* daemon that comes with your operating system and find a replacement. One such replacement *syslog* daemon is *syslog-ng* (*http://www.balabit.com/products/syslog_ng/*). *syslog-ng* is not only a fully functional replacement for the traditional *syslog* daemon, but it also adds flexible message filtering capabilities, as well as support for logging to remote systems over TCP (in addition to support for the traditional UDP protocol). With the addition of TCP support, you can also employ *stunnel* or *ssh* to securely send the logs across untrusted networks.

You can build *syslog-ng* by running commands like these:

```
$ tar xfz syslog-ng-1.6.11.tar.gz
$ cd syslog-ng-1.6.11
$ ./configure
$ make
```

If you want to compile in TCP wrappers support, add the `--enable-tcp-wrapper` flag to the *configure* script. After *syslog-ng* is finished compiling, become root and run `make install`. This will install the *syslog-ng* binary and manpages. To configure the daemon, create the */usr/local/etc/syslog-ng* directory and then create a *syslog-ng.conf* file to put in it. To start, you can use one of the sample configuration files in the *doc* directory of the *syslog-ng* distribution.

Configuring syslog-ng

There are five types of configuration file entries for *syslog-ng*, each of which begins with a specific keyword:

options

> The `options` entry allows you to tweak the behavior of the daemon, such as how often the daemon will sync (write) the logs to the disk, whether the daemon will create directories automatically, and hostname expansion behavior.

source

> `source` entries tell *syslog-ng* where to collect log entries. Sources can include Unix sockets, TCP or UDP sockets, files, or pipes.

destination

> `destination` entries allow you to specify possible places for *syslog-ng* to send logs to. You can specify files, pipes, Unix sockets, TCP or UDP sockets, TTYs, or programs.

filter

> Sources and destinations are then combined with filters, which let you select *syslog* facilities and log levels, using the `filter` keyword.

log

> Finally, these are all used together in a `log` entry to define precisely where the information is logged.

Thus, you can arbitrarily specify any source, select what *syslog* facilities and levels you want from it, and then route it to any destination. This is what makes *syslog-ng* an incredibly powerful and flexible tool.

Translating Your syslog.conf

To set up *syslog-ng* on the remote end so that it can replace *syslogd* on the system and send traffic to a remote *syslog-ng*, you'll first need to translate your *syslog.conf* to equivalent source, destination, and log entries.

Here's the *syslog.conf* for a FreeBSD system:

```
*.err;kern.debug;auth.notice;mail.crit          /dev/console
*.notice;kern.debug;lpr.info;mail.crit;news.err /var/log/messages
security.*                                      /var/log/security
auth.info;authpriv.info                         /var/log/auth.log
mail.info                                       /var/log/maillog
lpr.info                                        /var/log/lpd-errs
cron.*                                          /var/log/cron
*.emerg                                         *
```

First, you'll need to configure a source. Under FreeBSD, */dev/log* is a link to */var/run/log*. The following source entry tells *syslog-ng* to read entries from this file:

```
source src { unix-dgram("/var/run/log"); internal(); };
```

Linux users specify unix-stream and */dev/log*, like this:

```
source src { unix-stream("/dev/log"); internal() };
```

The internal() entry is for messages generated by *syslog-ng* itself. Notice that you can include multiple sources in a source entry. Next, include destination entries for each of the actual log files:

```
destination console { file("/dev/console"); };
destination messages { file("/var/log/messages"); };
destination security { file("/var/log/security"); };
destination authlog { file("/var/log/auth.log"); };
destination maillog { file("/var/log/maillog"); };
destination lpd-errs { file("/var/log/lpd-errs"); };
destination cron { file("/var/log/cron"); };
destination slip { file("/var/log/slip.log"); };
destination ppp { file("/var/log/ppp.log"); };
destination allusers { usertty("*"); };
```

In addition to these destinations, you'll also want to specify one for remote logging to another *syslog-ng* process. This can be done with a line similar to this:

```
destination loghost { tcp("192.168.0.2" port(5140)); };
```

The port number can be any available TCP port.

Defining the filters is straightforward. You can simply create one for each *syslog* facility and log level, or you can create them according to those used in your *syslog.conf*. If you do the latter, you will only have to specify one filter in each log statement, but it will still take some work to create your filters.

Here are some example filters for the *syslog* facilities:

```
filter f_auth { facility(auth); };
filter f_authpriv { facility(authpriv); };
filter f_console { facility(console); };
filter f_cron { facility(cron); };
filter f_daemon { facility(daemon); };
filter f_ftp { facility(ftp); };
filter f_kern { facility(kern); };
filter f_lpr { facility(lpr); };
filter f_mail { facility(mail); };
filter f_news { facility(news); };
filter f_security { facility(security); };
filter f_user { facility(user); };
filter f_uucp { facility(uucp); };
```

and some examples for the log levels:

```
filter f_emerg { level(emerg); };
filter f_alert { level(alert..emerg); };
filter f_crit { level(crit..emerg); };
filter f_err { level(err..emerg); };
filter f_warning { level(warning..emerg); };
filter f_notice { level(notice..emerg); };
filter f_info { level(info..emerg); };
filter f_debug { level(debug..emerg); };
```

Now, you can combine the sources with the proper filters and destinations within the log entries:

```
# *.err;kern.debug;auth.notice;mail.crit              /dev/console
log { source(src); filter(f_err); destination(console); };
log { source(src); filter(f_kern); filter(f_debug); destination(console); };
log { source(src); filter(f_auth); filter(f_notice); destination(console);
};
log { source(src); filter(f_mail); filter(f_crit); destination(console); };

# *.notice;kern.debug;lpr.info;mail.crit;news.err       /var/log/messages
log { source(src); filter(f_notice); destination(messages); };
```

```
log { source(src); filter(f_kern); filter(f_debug); destination(messages);
};
log { source(src); filter(f_lpr); filter(f_info); destination(messages); };
log { source(src); filter(f_mail); filter(f_crit); destination(messages); };
log { source(src); filter(f_news); filter(f_err); destination(messages); };

# security.*                                     /var/log/security
log { source(src); filter(f_security); destination(security); };

# auth.info;authpriv.info                    /var/log/auth.log
log { source(src); filter(f_auth); filter(f_info); destination(authlog); };
log { source(src); filter(f_authpriv); filter(f_info); destination(authlog);
};

# mail.info                                   /var/log/maillog
log { source(src); filter(f_mail); filter(f_info); destination(maillog); };

# lpr.info                                    /var/log/lpd-errs
log { source(src); filter(f_lpr); filter(f_info); destination(lpd-errs); };

# cron.*                                      /var/log/cron
log { source(src); filter(f_cron); destination(cron); };

# *.emerg                                              *
log { source(src); filter(f_emerg); destination(allusers); };
```

You can set up the machine that will be receiving the logs in much the same way as if you were replacing the currently used *syslogd*.

To configure *syslog-ng* to receive messages from a remote host, you must specify a source entry for that machine:

```
source r_src { tcp(ip("192.168.0.2") port(5140)); };
```

Alternatively, you can dump all the logs from the remote machine(s) into the same destinations that you use for your local log entries. This is not really recommended, because it can be a nightmare to manage, but you can do it by including multiple source drivers in the source entry that you use for your local logs:

```
source src {
    unix-dgram("/var/run/log");
    tcp(ip("192.168.0.2") port(5140));
    internal();
};
```

Now, logs gathered from remote hosts will appear in any of the destinations that were combined with this source.

If you would like all logs from remote hosts to go into a separate file named for each host in */var/log*, you could use a destination entry like this:

```
destination r_all { file("/var/log/$HOST"); };
```

syslog-ng will expand the $HOST macro to the hostname of the system send-ing it logs and create a file named after it in */var/log*. This would be an appropriate log entry to use in this case:

```
log { source(r_src); destination(r_all); };
```

However, an even better method is to recreate all of the remote *syslog-ng* log files on your central log server. For instance, a destination for a remote machine's messages file would look like this:

```
destination fbsd_messages { file("/var/log/$HOST/messages"); };
```

Notice here that the $HOST macro is used in place of a directory name. If you are using a destination entry like this, be sure to create the directory before-hand, or use the create_dirs( ) option:

```
options { create_dirs(yes); };
```

syslog-ng's macros are a powerful feature. For instance, if you want to sepa-rate logs by hostname and day, you can use a destination like this:

```
destination fbsd_messages {
    file("/var/log/$HOST/$YEAR.$MONTH.$DAY/messages");
};
```

You can combine the remote source with the appropriate destinations for the logs coming in from the network, just as you did when configuring *syslog-ng* for local logging; just specify the remote source with the proper destination and filters.

Another neat thing you can do with *syslog-ng* is collect logs from a number of remote hosts and then send all of those to yet another *syslog-ng* daemon. You can do this by combining a remote source and a remote destination with a log entry:

```
log { source(r_src); destination(loghost); };
```

Since *syslog-ng* is now using TCP ports, you can use any encrypting tunnel you like to secure the traffic between your *syslog-ng* daemons. You can use SSH port forwarding **[Hack #96]** or *stunnel* **[Hack #100]** to create an encrypted channel between each of your servers. By limiting connections on the listen-ing port to include only localhost (using firewall rules, as in "Firewall with Netfilter" **[Hack #44]** or "Firewall with OpenBSD's PacketFilter" **[Hack #45]**), you can eliminate the possibility of bogus log entries or denial-of-service attacks.

Server logs provide some of the most critical information that a system administrator needs to do her job. Using new tools and strong encryption, you can keep your valuable log data safe from prying eyes.

Log User Activity with Process Accounting

#85   Keep a detailed audit trail of what's being done on your systems.

Process accounting allows you to keep detailed logs of every command a user runs, including CPU time and memory used. From a security standpoint, this means the system administrator can gather information about what user ran which command and at what time. This information is useful not only in assessing a break-in or local root compromise, but also for spotting attempted malicious behavior by legitimate users.

> Remember that intrusions don't always come from the outside.

To enable process accounting, run these commands:

```
# mkdir /var/account
# touch /var/account/pacct && chmod 660 /var/account/pacct
# /sbin/accton /var/account/pacct
```

Alternatively, if you are running Red Hat or SuSE Linux and have the process accounting package installed, you can run a startup script to enable process accounting. On Red Hat, try this:

```
# chkconfig psacct on
# /sbin/service psacct start
```

On SuSE, use these commands:

```
# chkconfig acct on
# /sbin/service acct start
```

The process accounting package provides several programs to make use of the data being logged. The *ac* program analyzes total connect time for users on the system. Running it without any arguments prints out the number of hours logged by the current user:

```
[andrew@colossus andrew]$ ac
        total       106.23
```

If you want to display connect time for all users who have logged onto the system, use the -p switch:

```
# ac -p
        root                                0.07
        andrew                              106.05
        total       106.12
```

The `lastcomm` command lets you search the accounting logs by username, command name, or terminal:

```
# lastcomm andrew
ls                       andrew    ??        0.01 secs Mon Dec 15 05:58
```

```
rpmq                 andrew    ??        0.08 secs Mon Dec 15 05:58
sh                   andrew    ??        0.03 secs Mon Dec 15 05:44
gunzip               andrew    ??        0.00 secs Mon Dec 15 05:44

# lastcomm bash
bash            F    andrew    ??        0.00 secs Mon Dec 15 06:44
bash            F    root      stdout    0.01 secs Mon Dec 15 05:20
bash            F    root      stdout    0.00 secs Mon Dec 15 05:20
bash            F    andrew    ??        0.00 secs Mon Dec 15 05:19
```

To summarize the accounting information, you can use the sa command. By default, it lists all the commands found in the accounting logs and prints the number of times that each one has been executed:

```
# sa
    14     0.04re    0.03cp    0avio    1297k  troff
     7     0.03re    0.03cp    0avio     422k  lastcomm
     2    63.90re    0.01cp    0avio     983k  info
    14    34.02re    0.01cp    0avio     959k  less
    14     0.03re    0.01cp    0avio    1132k  grotty
    44     0.02re    0.01cp    0avio     432k  gunzip
```

You can also use the -u flag to output per-user statistics:

```
# sa -u
root       0.01 cpu     344k mem    0 io which
root       0.00 cpu    1094k mem    0 io bash
root       0.07 cpu    1434k mem    0 io rpmq
andrew     0.02 cpu     342k mem    0 io id
andrew     0.00 cpu     526k mem    0 io bash
andrew     0.01 cpu     526k mem    0 io bash
andrew     0.03 cpu     378k mem    0 io grep
andrew     0.01 cpu     354k mem    0 io id
andrew     0.01 cpu     526k mem    0 io bash
andrew     0.00 cpu     340k mem    0 io hostname
```

Peruse the output of these commands every so often to look for suspicious activity, such as increases in CPU usage or commands that are known to be used for mischief.

HACK #86 Centrally Monitor the Security Posture of Your Servers

Use OSSEC HIDS to monitor logs and the filesystem integrity of your servers and to correlate events.

Securing a server doesn't end with locking it down. Servers need to be monitored constantly. While network intrusion detection systems are invaluable for alerting you to possible attacks against any number of systems on your network, they should really only be thought of as early warning systems. Ultimately, you'll need to monitor each of your systems in greater detail.

This involves keeping an eye on many different pieces of information for each system, watching multitudes of different log files for evidence of attacks, and inspecting important binaries for signs of tampering.

While you can use a variety of tools to aggregate logs from multiple systems [Hack #79], automatically alert on certain strings [Hack #83], and check for modified files [Hack #122] and rootkits [Hack #124], these tools lack integration and, in the end, become just more things that need to be monitored.

Thankfully, one tool can perform all of these tasks and more: OSSEC HIDS (*http://www.ossec.net*). This leads to a sort of synergy that is not achievable with the separate monitoring systems without additional integration work. For instance, OSSEC can correlate events across different log files to trigger specialized alerts. You can also deploy OSSEC in a client/server architecture and easily scale it to monitor additional servers as you add them to your infrastructure. And OSSEC is available for both Windows and Unix systems, which enables you to monitor the integrity of all your systems with a single tool.

Installation

Getting started with OSSEC is easy. To install it, download the tarball from the OSSEC HIDS web site and unpack it. Then, change into the directory that was created (e.g., *ossec-hids-0.8*) and run the *install.sh* script. After being asking which language to use for the installation, you'll see a prompt like this:

```
1- What kind of installation do you want (server, agent, local or help)?
```

If you want to install OSSEC on only a single machine, choose local. Of course, if you want to set up an OSSEC client or a server, choose either agent or server, respectively.

After you've chosen the type of installation to perform, the script will ask you where to install it and where to send email alerts. At this point, you can choose whether to install the system integrity checking and rootkit detection components and whether to enable active responses. This feature allows you to react to events automatically as they happen, so you can prevent intrusions from succeeding.

If you chose to do a local installation, all you need to do is configure OSSEC. But before we look at how to do that, let's look at how to do a client/server installation.

First, you'll need to perform a server installation on a machine. Then, you'll need to perform an agent install on one or more hosts. When selecting an agent install, you'll get this additional prompt:

```
3.1- What's the IP Address of the OSSEC HIDS server?:
```

Type the IP address of the machine on which you performed the server installation. The rest of the prompts will be the same. The process that listens for agents, `ossec-remoted`, uses UDP port 1514, so make sure that your firewall rules will let traffic from the agents reach it.

Adding Agents

After you've installed an agent, go to the system where you've installed the server and add the agent:

```
# /var/ossec/bin/manage_agents

****************************************
* OSSEC HIDS v0.8 Agent manager.       *
* The following options are available: *
****************************************
   (A)dd an agent (A).
   (E)xtract key for an agent (E).
   (L)ist already added agents (L).
   (R)emove an agent (R).
   (Q)uit.
Choose your actions: A,E,L,R or Q: a

- Adding a new agent (use '\q' to return to main menu).
  Please provide the following:
   * A name for the new agent: spek
   * The IP Address for the new agent: 192.168.0.62
   * An ID for the new agent[001]:
Agent information:
   ID:001
   Name:spek
   IP Address:192.168.0.62

Confirm adding it?(y/n): y
Added.
```

You'll then need to extract the key that was generated for the agent and import it into the agent itself, so that it can talk to the server. Do this by running manage_agents again and typing e at the prompt:

```
...
Choose your actions: A,E,L,R or Q: e

Available agents:
   ID: 001, Name: spek, IP: 192.168.0.62
Provide the ID of the agent to extract the key (or '\q' to quit): 1
Agent key information for '001' is:
MDAxIHNwZWsgMTkyLjE2OC4wLjYyIDhhNzVmNGY1ZjBmNTIzNzI5NzAzMTRjMTFmNGVlOWZhZDEz
Y2QxZWY1ODQyZDEyMmFjYjYjM2YzVmY2JmYTg5OGM=

** Press ENTER to return main menu.
```

Now, go to the agent and do the following:

```
# /var/ossec/bin/manage_agents
```

```
****************************************
* OSSEC HIDS v0.8 Agent manager.      *
* The following options are available: *
****************************************
   (I)mport key for the server (I).
   (Q)uit.
Choose your actions: I or Q: i

* Provide the Key generated from the server.
* The best approach is to cut and paste it.
*** OBS: Do not include spaces or new lines.

Paste it here (or '\q' to quit):
MDAxIHNwZWsgMTkyLjE2OC4wLjYyIDhhNzVmNGY1ZjBmNTIzNzI5NzAzMTRjMTFmNGVlOWZ
hZDEzY2QxZWY1ODQyZDEyMmFjYjM2YzVmY2JmYTg5OGM=

Agent information:
   ID:001
   Name:spek
   IP Address:192.168.0.62

Confirm adding it?(y/n): y
Added.
** Press ENTER to return main menu.
```

Then start the server:

```
# /var/ossec/bin/ossec-control start
Starting OSSEC HIDS v0.8 (by Daniel B. Cid)...
Started ossec-maild...
Started ossec-execd...
Started ossec-analysisd...
Started ossec-logcollector...
Started ossec-remoted...
Started ossec-syscheckd...
Completed.
```

Finally, start the agents:

```
# /var/ossec/bin/ossec-control start
Starting OSSEC HIDS v0.8 (by Daniel B. Cid)...
Started ossec-execd...
Started ossec-agentd...
Started ossec-logcollector...
Started ossec-syscheckd...
Completed.
```

Unfortunately, the server will not provide any indication that the client can
or has connected to it until an alert is generated, so you'll want to test it out

by attempting to generate an alert. For instance, if you're running an SSH daemon on the agent system, you could try to SSH to the root account (hopefully, you have root logins disabled, so this will be innocuous). If you chose the default installation location for the server, you should be able to find the alerts in */var/ossec/logs/alerts*. Alerts are organized into directories by year and month with separate files for each day (e.g., *2006/Jun/ossec-alerts-01.log*).

Check the proper alerts file, and you should see something similar to this:

```
** Alert 1149663466.1082:
2006 Jun 01 00:57:46 (spek) 192.168.0.62->/var/log/messages
Rule: 401 (level 5) -> 'User authentication failure.'
Src IP: (none)
User: (none)
sshd(pam_unix)[7917]: authentication failure; logname= uid=0 euid=0 tty=ssh
ruser= rhost=kryten.nnc  user=root

** Alert 1149663468.1362:
2006 Jun 01 00:57:48 (spek) 192.168.0.62->/var/log/secure
Rule: 1516 (level 5) -> 'SSHD authentication failed.'
Src IP: 192.168.0.60
User: root
sshd[7917]: Failed password for root from 192.168.0.60 port 64206 ssh2

** Alert 1149663480.1604: mail
2006 Jun 01 00:58:00 (spek) 192.168.0.62->/var/log/messages
Rule: 402 (level 10) -> 'User missed the password more than one time'
Src IP: (none)
User: (none)
sshd(pam_unix)[7917]: 2 more authentication failures; logname= uid=0 euid=0
tty=ssh ruser= rhost=kryten.nnc  user=root
```

You should also receive these alerts at the email address you specified on the server during the installation process.

Installing a Windows Agent

The Windows version of OSSEC supports only the agent installation, which you can set up by simply downloading the installer and launching it. When it starts, it will ask you where to install the files and then execute the *manage_agents* program. Here, you can import the key that you've generated for it the same way you did for the Unix version of the agent. After you've entered the key and exited the agent management program, the installer will present you with the OSSEC configuration file *ossec.conf*, which is stored in the directory into which you chose to install the agent.

Unfortunately, the Windows installer isn't as automated as the Unix *install* script is, so you'll have to enter the IP address of your OSSEC server manually. Locate the line that looks like this:

```
<server-ip>a.b.c.d</server-ip>
```

and replace a.b.c.d with the IP address of your server. After the installation has completed, go to the Services Control Panel applet, locate the OSSEC HIDS service, and start it. While you're at it, you'll probably want to also set it to start automatically at system boot.

Now you can test it out with an approach similar to the one previously used to test out the Unix agent. If you have account login auditing enabled for the system, you can attempt to log into an account with an incorrect password, which should create something like this in the current log file on your OSSEC server:

```
** Alert 1149742916.124085:
2006 Jun 02 23:01:56 (blackbird) 192.168.0.67->WinEvtLog
Rule: 8005 (level 4) -> 'Windows audit failure event.'
Src IP: (none)
User: SYSTEM
WinEvtLog: Security: AUDIT_FAILURE(680): Security: SYSTEM: NT AUTHORITY:
BLACKBIRD: Logon attempt by: MICROSOFT_AUTHENTICATION_PACKAGE_V1_0    Logon
account:  andrew    Source Workstation: BLACKBIRD    Error Code: 0xC000006A
```

Configuration

OSSEC's default configuration file is formatted in XML and located at */var/ossec/etc/ossec.conf* (on Windows, this file will be in the directory into which you chose to install OSSEC). Sections of particular interest for servers are the <syscheck>, <localfile>, <alerts>, and <global> sections. The <syscheck> section defines what files and directories OSSEC should check for signs of tampering. The <frequency> tag specifies how often to perform the check:

```
<frequency>7200</frequency>
```

7200 seconds (every two hours) is the default. If you're running services that are highly taxing on your disk subsystem, you might want to increase this value, because checksumming files can be quite I/O intensive.

Specify which directories to check with the <directories> tag. The default is to perform all checks on the files in each of the directories enclosed within the tag in a comma-delimited list. This means that OSSEC will compare each file's MD5 checksum to previous values, as well as its size, owner, group, and permissions. The default configuration file checks in the following directories:

```
<directories check_all="yes">/etc,/usr/bin,/usr/sbin</directories>
<directories check_all="yes">/bin,/sbin</directories>
```

Turn individual checks on or off by replacing the check_all attribute with any combination of check_sum, check_size, check_owner, check_group, or check_perm and setting them to either yes or no. If you want to ignore a particular file or directory, enclose it in <ignore> tags:

```
<ignore>/etc/mtab</ignore>
```

Moving on, <localfile> sections are used to specify log files to monitor. Within them, you can use the <location> tag to specify the full path to the log file. Specify the format of the file with the <log_format> tag. Valid values for the format are syslog, snort-full, snort-fast, squid, or apache. Additionally, Windows users will find the iis and eventlog formats to be of particular interest, because they allow OSSEC to parse your IIS and Event Logs.

When an alert is triggered, OSSEC associates a severity level with it (from 1 to 16). You can use the <alerts> section to set the threshold at which to log an alert or generate an email. Here are the defaults for these settings:

```
<alerts>
    <log_alert_level>1</log_alert_level>
    <email_alert_level>7</email_alert_level>
</alerts>
```

Finally, use the <globals> section to define miscellaneous options that affect OSSEC as a whole. For instance, you can modify the email settings that the install script configured for you in this section.

This is also where you can use the <white_list> tag to specify the hosts that should never be blocked with active responses. For instance, to make sure that 10.0.0.123 is never blocked, add a line like this to the <globals> section:

```
<white_list>10.0.0.123</white_list>
```

Now, let's look at how to configure active responses.

Active Responses

Active responses can vary from blocking hosts via firewalls to automatically disabling user accounts. This is a powerful feature, but take special care when using it. An active response might cause you to inadvertently DoS yourself or provide easy means for an attacker to do so. That's why OSSEC provides a white-listing feature, to make sure dynamically added firewall rules don't lock out trusted hosts.

Active responses in OSSEC work by tying a command to an alert level and any number of rule IDs. The active response is triggered when an alert for one of the rules you've specified is generated and its level meets or exceeds the one specified.

When setting up an active response, you must first define the command to run and its parameters. Within a `<command>` block, define a name for the command that will be executed when the command is associated with one or more rules in an `<active-response>` block.

Here's an example from OSSEC's default configuration file. The following command locks out a user account that is associated with an alert:

```
<command>
    <name>disable-account</name>
    <executable>disable-account.sh</executable>
    <expect>user</expect>
    <timeout_allowed>yes</timeout_allowed>
</command>
```

You can later reference this `<command>` block in an `<active-response>` block, like this:

```
<active-response>
    <command>disable-account</command>
    <location>local</location>
    <level>10</level>
    <rules_id>402</rules_id>
    <timeout>900</timeout>
</active-response>
```

This response will cause any accounts that trigger the 'User missed the password more than one time' alert shown earlier to be locked out for 15 minutes. One thing to note in this example is the `<location>` tag. This tag lets you specify where you'd like the response to be triggered. Using `local` will cause the response to be triggered on the machine that generated the alert, whereas `analysis-server` will cause it to be triggered on the server. Alternatively, you can use `all` or `defined-agent` to cause the response to be triggered on all of the systems or a specific agent, respectively. In the latter case you'll also need to use the `<agent_id>` tag to specify the agent on which to trigger the response.

When a response is triggered, an entry will appear in */var/ossec/active-response/ossec-hids-responses.log*. For instance, when the response shown above is triggered, something similar to this will appear:

```
Thu Jun  2 04:01:31 MDT 2006 ../active-response/bin/disable-account.sh add
andrew
```

As you can see, OSSEC's active response feature can be very powerful. You can even write your own active response scripts, which gives you a literally unlimited number of possibilities in automatically reacting to attacks. This and many other features of OSSEC can be replicated by combining other tools. However, OSSEC provides them in an integrated manner and saves you the time spent gluing them together with your favorite scripting language—time that you can spend dealing with actual security issues.

See Also

- The OSSEC HIDS Usage Manual (*http://www.ossec.net/en/manual.html*)

## CHAPTER NINE

Monitoring and Trending
Hacks 87–91

While the importance of reliable system logs can't be overestimated, logs tell only part of the story of what is happening on your network. When something out of the ordinary happens, the event is duly logged to the appropriate file, where it waits for a human to notice and take the appropriate action. But logs are valuable only if someone actually reads them. When log files simply add to the deluge of information that most network administrators must wade through each day, they might be put aside and go unread for days or weeks. This situation is made worse when the log files are clogged with irrelevant information. For example, a cry for help from an overburdened mail server can easily be lost if it is surrounded by innocuous entries about failed spam attempts. All too often, logs are used as a resource to figure out what happened when systems fail, rather than as a guide to what is happening now.

Another important aspect of log entries is that they only provide a "spot check" of your system at a particular moment. Without a history of what normal performance looks like, it can be difficult to tell the difference between ordinary network traffic, a denial-of-service (DoS) attack, and a visitation from Slashdot readers. While you can easily build a report on how many times the */var* partition filled up, how can you track what normal usage looks like over time? Is the mail spool clogged due to one inconsiderate user, or is it part of an attack by an adversary? Or is it simply a general trend that is the result of trying to serve too many users on too small a disk?

This chapter describes a number of methods for tracking the availability of services and resources over time. Rather than having to watch system logs manually, it is usually far better to have the systems notify you when there is a problem—and *only* when there is a problem. This chapter also contains a number of suggestions about how to recognize trends in your network traffic by monitoring flows and plotting the results on graphs. Sure, you might know what your average outbound Internet traffic looks like, but how much of that traffic is made up of HTTP versus SMTP requests? You may know roughly how much traffic each server on your network generates, but what if you want to break the traffic down by protocol? The hacks in this chapter will show you how.

Monitor Availability

Use Nagios to keep tabs on your network.

Remote exploits can often crash the service that is being broken into or cause its CPU use to skyrocket, so it's essential to monitor the services that are running on your network. Just looking for an open port (using a tool such as Nmap [Hack #66]) isn't enough. The machine may be able to respond to a TCP connect request, but the service may be unable to respond (or worse, could have been replaced by a different program entirely!). One tool that can help you verify your services at a glance is *Nagios* (*http://www. nagios.org*).

Nagios is a network-monitoring application that monitors not only the services running on the hosts on your network, but also the resources on each host, such as CPU usage, disk space, memory usage, running processes, log files, and much more. In the advent of a problem, it can notify you via email, a pager, or any other method that you define, and you can check the status of your network at a glace by using its web GUI. Nagios is also easily extensible through its plug-in API.

Installing Nagios

To install Nagios, download the source distribution from the Nagios web site. Then, unpack the source distribution and go into the directory it creates:

```
$ tar xfz nagios-1.1.tar.gz
$ cd nagios-1.1
```

Create a user and group for Nagios to run as (e.g., *nagios*), and then run the *configure* script:

```
$ ./configure --with-nagios-user=nagios --with-nagios-grp=nagios
```

This installs Nagios in */usr/local/nagios*. As usual, you can modify this behavior by using the --prefix switch. After the *configure* script finishes, compile Nagios by running make all. Then, become root and run make install to install it. You can optionally install Nagios's initialization scripts by running make install-init.

If you look in the */usr/local/nagios* directory at this point, you will see four directories. The *bin* directory contains *nagios*, which is the core of the package. This application does the actual monitoring. The *sbin* directory contains the CGI scripts that will be used in the web-based interface. Inside the *share* directory, you'll find the HTML files and documentation. Finally, the *var* directory is where Nagios stores its information once it starts running.

Before you can use Nagios, you will need to run the following command:

```
$ make install-config
```

This command creates an *etc* directory populated with a sample copy of each configuration file required by Nagios. We'll look at how to configure those files shortly.

The Nagios installation is now complete. However, it is not very useful in its current state, because it lacks the actual monitoring applications. These applications, which check whether a particular monitored service is functioning properly, are called *plug-ins*. Nagios comes with a default set of plug-ins, but they must be downloaded and installed separately.

Installing Plug-ins

Download the latest Nagios *Plugins* package and decompress it. You will need to run the provided *configure* script to prepare the package for compilation on your system. You will find that the plug-ins are installed in a fashion similar to the actual Nagios program.

To compile the plug-ins, run these commands:

```
$ ./configure --prefix=/usr/local/nagios \
--with-nagios-user=nagios --with-nagios-group=nagios
$ make all
```

You might get notifications about missing programs or Perl modules while the script is running. These are mostly fine, unless you specifically need the mentioned applications to monitor a service.

After compilation is finished, become root and run make install to install the plug-ins. The plug-ins will be installed in the *libexec* directory of your Nagios base directory (e.g., */usr/local/nagios/libexec*).

There are a few options that all Nagios plug-ins should implement, making them suitable for use by Nagios. Each plug-in provides a --help option that displays information about the plug-in and how it works. This feature is helpful when you're trying to monitor a new service using a plug-in you haven't used before.

For instance, to learn how the check_ssh plug-in works, run the following command:

```
$ /usr/local/nagios/libexec/check_ssh
check_ssh (nagios-plugins 1.4.3) 1.27
Copyright (c) 1999 Remi Paulmier <remi@sinfomic.fr>
Copyright (c) 2000-2004 Nagios Plugin Development Team
        <nagiosplug-devel@lists.sourceforge.net>

Try to connect to an SSH server at specified server and port

Usage: check_ssh [-46] [-t <timeout>] [-r <remote version>] [-p <port>]
<host>

Options:
 -h, --help
    Print detailed help screen
 -V, --version
    Print version information
 -H, --hostname=ADDRESS
    Host name, IP Address, or unix socket (must be an absolute path)
 -p, --port=INTEGER
    Port number (default: 22)
 -4, --use-ipv4
    Use IPv4 connection
 -6, --use-ipv6
    Use IPv6 connection
 -t, --timeout=INTEGER
    Seconds before connection times out (default: 10)
 -r, --remote-version=STRING
    Warn if string doesn't match expected server version (ex: OpenSSH_3.9p1)
 -v, --verbose
    Show details for command-line debugging (Nagios may truncate output)

Send email to nagios-users@lists.sourceforge.net if you have questions
regarding use of this software. To submit patches or suggest improvements,
send email to nagiosplug-devel@lists.sourceforge.net
```

Now that both Nagios and the plug-ins are installed, you're almost ready to begin monitoring servers. However, Nagios will not even start before it's configured properly.

Configuring Nagios

Configuring Nagios can be an arduous task, but the sample configuration files provide a good starting point:

```
$ cd /usr/local/nagios/etc
$ ls -1
bigger.cfg-sample
cgi.cfg-sample
checkcommands.cfg-sample
```

```
minimal.cfg-sample
misccommands.cfg-sample
nagios.cfg-sample
resource.cfg-sample
```

Since these are sample files, the Nagios authors added a *.cfg-sample* suffix to each file. First, you'll need to copy or rename each one to end in *.cfg*, so that the software can use them properly.

> If you don't change the file extensions, Nagios will not be able to find the configuration files.

You can either rename each file manually or use the following command to take care of them all at once:

```
# for i in *.cfg-sample; do mv $i `basename $i .cfg-sample`.cfg; done;
```

To get Nagios running, you must modify all but a few of the sample configuration files. First, there is the main configuration file, *nagios.cfg*. You can pretty much leave everything as is here; the Nagios installation process will make sure the file paths used in the configuration file are correct. There's one option, however, that you might want to change: check_external_ commands, which is set to 0 by default. If you would like to run commands directly through the web interface, set this to 1. Depending on your network environment, this may or may not be an acceptable security risk, because enabling this option permits the execution of scripts from the web interface. Other options you need to set in *cgi.cfg* configure which usernames are allowed to run external commands.

Configuring Nagios to monitor your servers is not as difficult as it looks. To help you, you can use the verbose mode of the Nagios binary by running this command:

```
# /usr/local/nagios/bin/nagios -v /usr/local/nagios/etc/nagios.cfg
```

This goes through the configuration files and reports any errors. Start fixing the errors one by one, running the command again to find the next error.

Adding hosts to monitor. You'll first need to add your host definition and configure some options for that host. You can add as many hosts as you like, but here we will stick with one for the sake of simplicity.

Here are the contents of *hosts.cfg*:

```
# Generic host definition template
define host{
# The name of this host template - referenced in other host definitions,
# used for template recursion/resolution
name                        generic-host
```

```
# Host notifications are enabled
notifications_enabled            1
# Host event handler is enabled
event_handler_enabled            1
# Flap detection is enabled
flap_detection_enabled           1
# Process performance data
process_perf_data                1
# Retain status information across program restarts
retain_status_information        1
# Retain non-status information across program restarts
retain_nonstatus_information     1
# DONT REGISTER THIS DEFINITION - ITS NOT A REAL HOST,
# JUST A TEMPLATE!
register                         0
contact_groups                   flcd-admins
}

# Host Definition
define host{
# Name of host template to use
use                     generic-host
host_name               freelinuxcd.org
alias                   Free Linux CD Project Server
address                 www.freelinuxcd.org
check_command           check-host-alive
max_check_attempts      10
notification_interval   120
notification_period     24x7
notification_options    d,u,r
}
```

Be sure to remove the lines beginning with # when creating your *hosts.cfg*; otherwise, you'll receive errors.

The first host defined is not a real host but a template from which other host definitions are derived. This mechanism is used in other configuration files as well and makes configuration based on a predefined set of defaults a breeze.

With this setup, we are monitoring only one host, *www.freelinuxcd.org*, to see if it is alive. The host_name parameter is important because other configuration files will refer to this server by this name.

Once you've finished editing *hosts.cfg*, uncomment the line that includes it in *nagios.cfg*:

```
#cfg_file=/usr/local/nagios/etc/hosts.cfg
```

Creating host groups. Now that you have a host to monitor, it needs to be added to a hostgroup, so that the application knows which contact group to send notifications to. Here's what *hostgroups.cfg* looks like:

```
define hostgroup{
  hostgroup_name  flcd-servers
  alias           The Free Linux CD Project Servers
  contact_groups  flcd-admins
  members         freelinuxcd.org
}
```

This defines a new hostgroup and associates the flcd-admins contact_group with it. As with *hosts.cfg*, you'll need to edit *nagios.cfg* and uncomment the following line to include your *hostgroups.cfg*:

```
#cfg_file=/usr/local/nagios/etc/hostgroups.cfg
```

Creating contacts and contact groups. Now, you'll need to define the flcd-admins contact group in *contactgroups.cfg*:

```
define contactgroup{
  contactgroup_name    flcd-admins
  alias                FreeLinuxCD.org Admins
  members              oktay, verty
}
```

Here, the flcd-admins contact_group is defined with two members, *oktay* and *verty*. This configuration ensures that both users will be notified when something goes wrong with a server that flcd-admins is responsible for. The next step is to set the contact information and notification preferences for these users.

Here are the definitions for those two members in *contacts.cfg*:

```
define contact{
  contact_name                  oktay
  alias                         Oktay Altunergil
  service_notification_period   24x7
  host_notification_period      24x7
  service_notification_options  w,u,c,r
  host_notification_options     d,u,r
  service_notification_commands notify-by-email,notify-by-epager
  host_notification_commands    host-notify-by-email,host-notify-by-epager
  email                         oktay@freelinuxcd.org
  pager                         dummypagenagios-admin@localhost.localdomain
}

define contact{
  contact_name                  verty
  alias                         David 'Verty' Ky
  service_notification_period   24x7
  host_notification_period      24x7
```

```
service_notification_options     w,u,c,r
host_notification_options        d,u,r
service_notification_commands    notify-by-email,notify-by-epager
host_notification_commands       host-notify-by-email
email                            verty@flcd.org
}
```

In addition to providing contact details for a particular user, the contact_
name in the *contacts.cfg* file is also used by the CGI scripts (i.e., the web interface) to determine whether a particular user is allowed to access a particular
resource.

Configuring services to monitor. Now that your hosts and contacts are configured, you can start to configure monitoring for individual services on your
server.

This is done in *services.cfg* (remove the comments when creating yours):

```
# Generic service definition template
define service{
# The 'name' of this service template, referenced in other service
definitions
 name    generic-service
 # Active service checks are enabled
 active_checks_enabled  1
 # Passive service checks are enabled/accepted
 passive_checks_enabled  1
 # Active service checks should be parallelized
 # (disabling this can lead to major performance problems)
 parallelize_check  1
 # We should obsess over this service (if necessary)
 obsess_over_service  1
 # Default is to NOT check service 'freshness'
 check_freshness    0
 # Service notifications are enabled
 notifications_enabled  1
 # Service event handler is enabled
 event_handler_enabled  1
 # Flap detection is enabled
 flap_detection_enabled  1
 # Process performance data
 process_perf_data  1
 # Retain status information across program restarts
 retain_status_information 1
 # Retain non-status information across program restarts
 retain_nonstatus_information 1
 # DONT REGISTER THIS DEFINITION - ITS NOT A REAL SERVICE, JUST A TEMPLATE!
 register   0
 }

# Service definition
define service{
```

```
# Name of service template to use
use     generic-service
host_name    freelinuxcd.org
service_description  HTTP
is_volatile   0
check_period    24x7
max_check_attempts  3
normal_check_interval  5
retry_check_interval  1
contact_groups   flcd-admins
notification_interval  120
notification_period  24x7
notification_options  w,u,c,r
check_command    check_http
}

# Service definition
define service{
# Name of service template to use
use     generic-service
host_name    freelinuxcd.org
service_description  PING
is_volatile   0
check_period    24x7
max_check_attempts  3
normal_check_interval  5
retry_check_interval  1
contact_groups   flcd-admins
notification_interval  120
notification_period  24x7
notification_options  c,r
check_command    check_ping!100.0,20%!500.0,60%
}
```

This setup configures monitoring for two services. The first service definition, which has been called HTTP, monitors whether the web server is up and notifies you if there's a problem. The second definition monitors the ping statistics from the server and notifies you if the response time or packet loss becomes too high. The commands used are check_http and check_ping, which were installed into the *libexec* directory during the plug-in installation. Please take your time to familiarize yourself with all the other available plug-ins and configure them similarly to the previous example definitions.

Defining time periods. Now, you'll need to define the time periods that you've been using in the notification_period directives by creating a *timeperiods.cfg* file. The previous examples use a time period. Here's a definition for it that can be put in your *timeperiods.cfg*:

```
define timeperiod{
        timeperiod_name       24x7
        alias                 24x7
```

```
sunday                  00:00-24:00
monday                  00:00-24:00
tuesday                 00:00-24:00
wednesday               00:00-24:00
thursday                00:00-24:00
friday                  00:00-24:00
saturday                00:00-24:00
}
```

Now, all you need to do is to include each of these files within your main *nagios.conf* by using the `cfg_file` directive. The sample *nagios.cfg* contains a directive to load all of the configuration files mentioned here, but they're commented out by default. Locate the entries and uncomment them.

Once you're happy with your configuration, run Nagios with the -v switch one last time to make sure everything checks out. Then, run it as a daemon by using the -d switch:

```
# /usr/local/nagios/bin/nagios -d /usr/local/nagios/etc/nagios.cfg
```

After you've gotten Nagios up and running, point your favorite web server to Nagios's *sbin* directory (it contains CGI scripts) and restart it. That's all there is to it. Give Nagios a couple of minutes to generate some data, and then point your browser to the machine and look at the pretty service warning lights.

HACK #88 Graph Trends

Use RRDtool to easily generate graphs for just about anything.

You might be familiar with graphing bandwidth usage with tools such as MRTG. From a security standpoint, graphing bandwidth usage is useful because it can help you spot anomalous behavior. Having a history of typical bandwidth usage gives you a baseline to judge activity. This can make it easier to determine if somebody is performing a DoS attack on your site, or if a machine on your network is acting as a Warez depot.

RRDtool (*http://people.ee.ethz.ch/~oetiker/webtools/rrdtool/*) provides functionality similar to MRTG, but it is much more flexible. RRDtool is basically a tool for storing data in a general-purpose database that will never grow in size. RRD stands for *round-robin database*, which is a special type of database that maintains a fixed number of entries: the oldest entry is constantly being replaced by the newest data. RRDtool also has the ability to generate graphs of the data contained in this database.

The most common use of RRDtool is to make pretty bandwidth graphs, which is easily done with RRDtool and *snmpget*, a utility that queries devices managed with SNMP. First, you'll need to create a round-robin database by running a command similar to this one:

```
$ rrdtool create zul.rrd --start N \DS:de0_in:COUNTER:600:U:U \DS:de0_out:
COUNTER:600:U:U \RRA:AVERAGE:0.5:1:600 \RRA:AVERAGE:0.5:6:700 \RRA:AVERAGE:
0.5:24:775 \RRA:AVERAGE:0.5:288:797 \RRA:MAX:0.5:1:600 \RRA:MAX:0.5:6:700 \
RRA:MAX:0.5:24:775 \RRA:MAX:0.5:288:797
```

This command creates a database containing entries for two separate counters: de0_in and de0_out. These entries store samples of interface statistics collected every five minutes from an SNMP daemon on a router. In addition, the database contains several fields for automatically maintaining running averages.

You can populate the database by running a command like this:

```
$ rrdtool update zul.rrd N:\`snmpget -Oqv zul public interfaces.ifTable.
ifEntry.ifInOctets.4`:\`snmpget -Oqv zul public interfaces.ifTable.ifEntry.
ifOutOctets.4`
```

This command queries the input and output statistics for the *de0* interface on a computer named *zul*. To schedule it to run every five minutes, you can make a crontab entry similar to the following:

```
0-55/5 * * * * rrdtool update /home/andrew/rrdbs/zul.rrd N:`snmpget -Oqv zul
public
interfaces.ifTable.ifEntry.ifInOctets.4`:`snmpget -Oqv zul public
interfaces.ifTable.ifEntry.ifOutOctets.4`
```

However, you can use whatever methods you want to collect the data. To generate hourly graphs of the data, you can run a command like this:

```
$ rrdtool graph zul_de0-hourly.png -t "Hourly Bandwidth" --start -3600 \
DEF:inoctets=zul.rrd:de0_in:AVERAGE \
DEF:outoctets=zul.rrd:de0_out:AVERAGE \
AREA:inoctets#00FF00:"de0 In" \
LINE1:outoctets#0000FF:"de0 Out"
```

This command creates an image like the one shown in Figure 9-1.

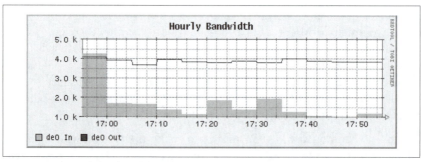

Figure 9-1. A graph generated by RRDtool

The -3600 in the command tells rrdtool that you want to graph the data collected over the last hour (there are 3,600 seconds in an hour). Likewise, if you want to create a graph over the course of a day, use -86400.

But that's just the beginning. After collecting multiple data sources, you can combine them all into a single graph that gives you a great deal of information at a glance. Figure 9-2 shows the relative outbound usage of several servers simultaneously, with the total average for all servers just below it. While this figure is in grayscale, the actual graph uses a different color for each server, making it easy to tell at a glance which one is hogging all of the bandwidth.

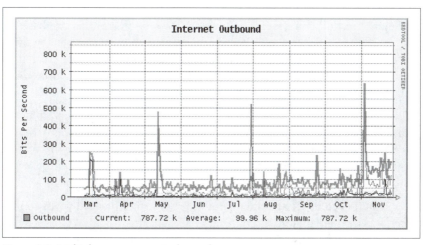

Figure 9-2. Multiple servers on a single graph

As you can see, RRDtool is a flexible tool. All you need to do is tell it how much data you want to store and then set up some method to collect the data at a regular interval. Then, you can easily generate a graph of the data whenever you want it.

HACK
#89 Get Real-Time Network Stats

See who's doing what on your network over time with ntop.

If you're looking for real-time network statistics, check out the terrific *ntop* tool (*http://www.ntop.org*), a full-featured protocol analyzer with a web frontend, complete with SSL and graphing support. *ntop* isn't exactly lightweight (the precise amount of resources required depends on the size of your network and the volume of network traffic), but it can give you a very nice picture of who's talking to whom on your network.

ntop needs to run initially as root, to throw your interfaces into promiscuous mode and start capturing packets, but it then releases its privileges to a user that you specify. If you decide to run *ntop* for long periods of time, you'll probably be happiest running it on a dedicated monitoring box (with few other services running on it, for security and performance reasons).

Here's a quick reference on how to get *ntop* up and running. First, create an *ntop* user and group:

```
# groupadd ntop
# useradd -c "ntop user" -d /usr/local/etc/ntop -s /bin/true -g ntop ntop
```

Then, unpack and build *ntop* per the instructions in *docs/BUILD-NTOP.txt*. After *ntop* has finished compiling, install it by running make install as root. During the installation process, a directory for *ntop* to store its databases in will be created. If you didn't use the --prefix option when running *configure*, this directory should be */usr/local/var/ntop*. It will be created as root during the install, so you'll need to change its owner to the user you'll be running *ntop* as in order for *ntop* to be able to write to it.

ntop will also copy a self-signed certificate to */usr/local/etc/ntop/ntop-cert. pem* as part of the install process, so that you can securely access its web interface. Note that the default SSL key will not be built with the correct hostname for your server, so you'll probably want to generate your own SSL certificate and key pair [Hack #69].

Now, you'll need to set an administrative password to be used when configuring *ntop* through its web interface:

```
# ntop -A -u ntop
Fri May 5 22:03:27 2006  NOTE: Interface merge enabled by default
Fri May 5 22:03:27 2006  Initializing gdbm databases


ntop startup - waiting for user response!


Please enter the password for the admin user:
Please enter the password again:
Fri May 5 22:03:31 2006  Admin user password has been set
```

Finally, run *ntop* as a daemon, and start the SSL server on your favorite port (4242, for example):

```
# ntop -u ntop -W4242 -d
```

By default, *ntop* also runs a standard HTTP server on port 3000. You should seriously consider locking down access to these ports, either at your firewall or by using command-line iptables rules [Hack #44].

Let *ntop* run for a while, and then connect to *https://your.server.here:4242/*.
You can find out all sorts of details about what traffic has been seen on your
network, as shown in Figure 9-3.

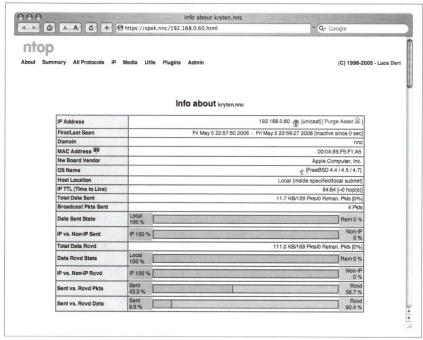

Figure 9-3. Displaying a host's statistics in ntop's web interface

While tools like *tcpdump* and Ethereal give you detailed, interactive analyses
of network traffic, *ntop* delivers a wealth of statistical information in a very
slick and easy-to-use web interface. When properly installed and locked
down, it will likely become a favorite tool in your network analysis tool
chest.

—Rob Flickenger

HACK #90 Collect Statistics with Firewall Rules

Make your firewall ruleset do the work for you when you want to collect
statistics.

If you want to start collecting statistics on your network traffic but dread
setting up SNMP, you don't have to worry. You can use the firewalling code
in your operating system to collect statistics for you.

For instance, if you are using Linux, you can use `iptables` commands similar to the following to keep track of bandwidth consumed by a particular machine that passes traffic through your firewall:

```
# iptables -N KRYTEN && iptables -A KRYTEN -j ACCEPT
# iptables -N KRYTEN_IN && iptables -A KRYTEN_IN -j KRYTEN
# iptables -N KRYTEN_OUT && iptables -A KRYTEN_OUT -j KRYTEN
# iptables -A FORWARD -s 192.168.0.60 -j KRYTEN_OUT
# iptables -A FORWARD -d 192.168.0.60 -j KRYTEN_IN
```

This approach leverages the packet and byte counters associated with each iptables rule to provide input and output bandwidth statistics for traffic forwarded through the firewall. It works by first defining a chain named KRYTEN, which is named after the host on which the statistics will be collected. This chain contains an unconditional accept rule and will be used to quickly add up the total bandwidth that *kryten* consumes.

To compute the downstream bandwidth *kryten* is using, another chain called KRYTEN_IN is created. Likewise, to compute the outbound bandwidth *kryten* is using, a chain called KRYTEN_OUT is created. Each of these chains contains only one rule, which unconditionally jumps to the KRYTEN chain. This enables the outbound bandwidth to be added to the inbound bandwidth being consumed. Finally, rules are added to the FORWARD chain that direct each packet to the correct chain, depending on whether it's coming from or going to *kryten*.

After applying these rules, you can view the total bandwidth (inbound and outbound) consumed by *kryten* by running a command like this:

```
# iptables -vx -L KRYTEN
Chain kryten (2 references)
 pkts    bytes target   prot opt in   out   source    destination
 442    46340 ACCEPT    all  --  any  any   anywhere  anywhere
```

You can easily parse out the bytes field, and thereby generate graphs with RRDtool [Hack #88], by using a command like this:

```
# iptables -vx -L KRYTEN | egrep -v 'Chain|pkts' | awk '{print $2}'
```

To get the amount of inbound or outbound bandwidth consumed, just replace KRYTEN with KRYTEN_IN or KRYTEN_OUT, respectively. Of course, you don't have to limit your statistic collection criteria to just per-computer bandwidth usage. You can collect statistics on anything that you can create an iptables rule for, including specific ports, MAC addresses, or just about anything else that passes through your gateway.

You can also do something similar for systems using OpenBSD's PacketFilter [Hack #45]. For every rule, PF keeps track of how many times it has been evaluated, how many packets have triggered the rule, how many bytes were in those packets, and how many states were created (in the case of stateful rules). The problem is getting at the data. You can view the rule statistics by running pfctl -s rules -vv, but the data is not in an easily parseable form:

```
@3 pass inet from 192.168.0.60 to any
  [ Evaluations: 125      Packets: 60      Bytes: 4976      States: 0
]
  [ Inserted: uid 0 pid 15815 ]
@4 pass inet from any to 192.168.0.60
  [ Evaluations: 128      Packets: 65      Bytes: 7748      States: 0
]
  [ Inserted: uid 0 pid 15815 ]
```

However, you can add the label keyword to the end of each rule, so that they read like this:

```
pass inet from 192.168.0.60 to any label "KRYTEN_OUT"
pass inet from any to 192.168.0.60 label "KRYTEN_IN"
```

Then, you can get the statistics on the rules by running pfctl -s labels:

```
KRYTEN_OUT 175 77 6660 77 6660 0 0
KRYTEN_IN 176 93 11668 0 0 93 11668
```

Not only are the statistics easier to parse, but you also get more of them. The numbers above, from left to right, represent the number of evaluations, total packets, total bytes, outgoing packets, total outgoing bytes, incoming packets, and total incoming bytes.

Just as with iptables, you can collect statistics on anything for which you can create a rule.

HACK #91 Sniff the Ether Remotely

Monitor your networks remotely with rpcapd.

If you've ever tried to monitor network traffic from another segment using a graphical protocol analyzer such as Ethereal (*http://www.ethereal.com*), you know how time-consuming it can be. First, you have to capture the data. Then you have to get it onto the workstation on which you're running the analyzer, and then you have to load the file into the analyzer itself. This creates a real problem because it increases the time between performing an experiment and seeing the results, which makes diagnosing and fixing network problems take much longer than it should.

One tool that solves this problem is *rpcapd*, a program included with WinPcap (*http://winpcap.polito.it*). *rpcapd* is a daemon that monitors network interfaces in promiscuous mode and sends the data that it collects back to a sniffer running on a remote machine. You can run *rpcapd* either from the command line or as a service.

To start *rpcapd*, you will probably want to use the -n flag, which tells the daemon to use null authentication. Using this option, you will be able to monitor the data stream that *rpcapd* produces with any program that uses the WinPcap capture interface. Otherwise, you'll have to add special code to the program you are using to allow it to authenticate itself with *rpcapd*. Since the -n option allows anyone to connect to the daemon, you'll also want to use the -l option, which allows you to specify a comma-separated list of hosts that can connect.

So, to run *rpcapd* from the command line, use a command similar to this:

```
C:\Program Files\WinPcap>rpcapd -l obsidian -n
Press CTRL + C to stop the server...
```

When run as a service, *rpcapd* uses the *rpcapd.ini* file for its configuration information. This file resides in the same directory as the executable and is easily created by running *rpcapd* with the -s switch, which instructs *rpcapd* to save its configuration to the file you specify.

To create a file called *rpcapd.ini*, run a command like this:

```
C:\Program Files\WinPcap>rpcapd -l obsidian -n -s rpcapd.ini
Press CTRL + C to stop the server...
```

Now, press Ctrl-C to see what the file contains:

```
C:\Program Files\WinPcap>type rpcapd.ini
# Configuration file help.

# Hosts which are allowed to connect to this server (passive mode)
# Format: PassiveClient = <name or address>

PassiveClient = obsidian

# Hosts to which this server is trying to connect to (active mode)
# Format: ActiveClient = <name or address>, <port | DEFAULT>

# Permit NULL authentication: YES or NOT

NullAuthPermit = YES
```

To start the service, you can either use the Services Control Panel applet or use the net command from the command line:

```
C:\Program Files\WinPcap>net start rpcapd

The Remote Packet Capture Protocol v.0 (experimental) service was started
successfully.
```

Now, to connect to the daemon, you will need to find out the name that WinPcap uses to refer to the network device you want to monitor. To do this, you can use either WinDump, a command-line packet sniffer for

Windows, or Ethereal. WinDump is available from the same web site as WinPcap.

To get the device name with WinDump, simply run it with the -D flag:

```
C:\Program Files\WinPcap>windump -D
1.\Device\NPF_{EE07A5AE-4D19-4118-97CE-3BF656CD718F} (NDIS 5.0 driver)
```

You can use Ethereal to obtain the device name by starting up Ethereal, going to the Capture menu, and clicking Start. After you do that, a dialog containing a list of the available adapters on the system will open, as shown in Figure 9-4. The device names in the list are those that you will later specify when connecting to *rpcapd* from a remote system.

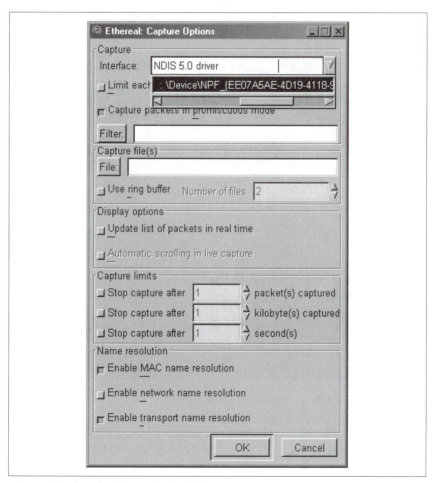

Figure 9-4. Ethereal Capture Options dialog

When you connect to a remote machine with your favorite sniffer, simply put the device name for the interface you want to monitor prefixed by rpcap and the hostname, like this:

```
rpcap://plunder/\Device\NPF_{EE07A5AE-4D19-4118-97CE-3BF656CD718F}
```

Figure 9-5 shows an example of using a remote capture source with Ethereal.

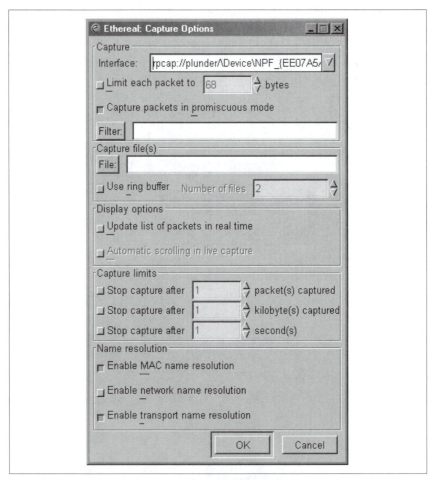

Figure 9-5. Using a remote capture source with Ethereal

If you've set up everything correctly, you should see traffic streaming from the remote end into your sniffer, just as if it were being captured from a local interface.

Secure Tunnels
Hacks 92–105

Untrusted computer networks (such as the Internet and public wireless networks) can be pretty hostile environments, but they can be tamed to some degree. This chapter primarily deals with how to set up secure, encrypted communications over networks that you don't completely trust. Some of the hacks focus mainly on providing a secure and encrypted transport mechanism, while others discuss how to create a virtual private network (VPN). As you'll see here, by leveraging encryption and some encapsulation tricks you can build more trustworthy networks on top of an untrusted network, even if the latter is full of miscreants trying to spy on or otherwise manipulate your data.

By reading this chapter, you'll learn how to set up IPsec-based encrypted links on several operating systems, how to create virtual network interfaces that can be tunneled through an encrypted connection, and how to forward TCP connections over an encrypted channel. In addition, you'll learn how to set up a cross-platform VPN solution.

The beauty of most of these hacks is that after reading them, you can mix and match transport-layer encryption solutions with whatever virtual-network-oriented approach best meets your needs. In this way, you can safely build vast, powerful private networks leveraging the public Internet as infrastructure. You can use these techniques for anything from securely connecting two remote offices to building a completely routed private network enterprise on top of the Internet.

HACK #92 Set Up IPsec Under Linux

Secure your traffic in Linux with Openswan.

The most popular way of configuring IPsec connections under Linux is by using the *Openswan* (*http://www.openswan.org*) package. *Openswan* is made

up of two components: *pluto* and, optionally, *KerneL IP Security* (KLIPS). As
of Version 2.6, the Linux kernel includes support for IPsec, but KLIPS can
be used instead for some additional features. *pluto* is the user-land daemon
that controls Internet Key Exchange (IKE) negotiation.

To get started, download the latest source for the Openswan tools from the
project's web site and unpack the source tree. Then, change to the directory
that was extracted and build it:

```
$ tar xfz openswan-2.4.6rc3.tar.gz
$ cd openswan-2.4.6rc3
$ make programs
```

After it finishes compiling, become root and run make install.

If you want to try out Openswan's opportunistic encryption support [Hack
#95], use KLIPS instead of native IPsec support in the kernel. To do this,
download the appropriate patch from the Openswan download page. Apply
the patch to your kernel source with the following commands:

```
# cd /usr/src/kernels/linux-2.6.14.6
# zcat /tmp/openswan-2.4.6rc3.kernel-2.6-klips.patch.gz | patch -p1
```

If you configured your kernel source prior to applying the patch, you can
quickly and easily enable KLIPS by running make oldconfig. Here are the
options that you need enabled:

```
Openswan IPsec (KLIPS26) (KLIPS) [N/m/y/?] (NEW) m
    *
    * KLIPS options
    *
    Encapsulating Security Payload - ESP ("VPN") (KLIPS_ESP) [Y/n/?] (NEW)
    Authentication Header - AH (KLIPS_AH) [N/y/?] (NEW) y
    HMAC-MD5 authentication algorithm (KLIPS_AUTH_HMAC_MD5) [Y/n/?] (NEW)
    HMAC-SHA1 authentication algorithm (KLIPS_AUTH_HMAC_SHA1) [Y/n/?] (NEW)
    CryptoAPI algorithm interface (KLIPS_ENC_CRYPTOAPI) [N/y/?] (NEW)
    3DES encryption algorithm (KLIPS_ENC_3DES) [Y/n/?] (NEW)
    AES encryption algorithm (KLIPS_ENC_AES) [Y/n/?] (NEW)
    IP compression (KLIPS_IPCOMP) [Y/n/?] (NEW)
    IPsec debugging (KLIPS_DEBUG) [Y/n/?] (NEW)
```

This output shows KLIPS set up to be compiled as a module; however, you
can link it into the kernel statically if you prefer.

If you patched your kernel for KLIPS, rebuild it and reboot with it. When
you next boot up, the *ipsec* service will automatically start. If you chose to
use the kernel's built-in IPsec support, you can go ahead and start it now:

```
# /etc/init.d/ipsec start
ipsec_setup: Starting Openswan IPsec 2.4.6rc3...
ipsec_setup: insmod /lib/modules/2.6.16-1.2115_FC4/kernel/net/key/af_key.ko
ipsec_setup: insmod /lib/modules/2.6.16-1.2115_FC4/kernel/net/ipv4/ah4.ko
ipsec_setup: insmod /lib/modules/2.6.16-1.2115_FC4/kernel/net/ipv4/esp4.ko
```

```
ipsec_setup: insmod /lib/modules/2.6.16-1.2115_FC4/kernel/net/ipv4/ipcomp.ko
ipsec_setup: insmod /lib/modules/2.6.16-1.2115_FC4/kernel/net/ipv4/xfrm4_
tunnel.ko
ipsec_setup: insmod /lib/modules/2.6.16-1.2115_FC4/kernel/crypto/des.ko
ipsec_setup: insmod /lib/modules/2.6.16-1.2115_FC4/kernel/crypto/aes.ko
```

Now, verify that your system settings are configured correctly to use IPsec:

```
# /usr/local/sbin/ipsec verify
Checking your system to see if IPsec got installed and started correctly:
Version check and ipsec on-path                             [OK]
Linux Openswan U2.4.6rc3/K2.6.16-1.2115_FC4 (netkey)
Checking for IPsec support in kernel                        [OK]
NETKEY detected, testing for disabled ICMP send_redirects   [FAILED]

    Please disable /proc/sys/net/ipv4/conf/*/send_redirects
    or NETKEY will cause the sending of bogus ICMP redirects!

NETKEY detected, testing for disabled ICMP accept_redirects [FAILED]

    Please disable /proc/sys/net/ipv4/conf/*/accept_redirects
    or NETKEY will accept bogus ICMP redirects!

Checking for RSA private key (/etc/ipsec.secrets)           [OK]
Checking that pluto is running                              [OK]
Two or more interfaces found, checking IP forwarding        [FAILED]
Checking for 'ip' command                                   [OK]
Checking for 'iptables' command                             [OK]
Opportunistic Encryption Support                            [DISABLED]
```

Be sure to investigate any item that shows up as FAILED. The previous example shows that you'll need to disable sending and accepting ICMP redirects and enable IP forwarding. To disable ICMP redirects, run the following commands:

```
# for f in /proc/sys/net/ipv4/conf/*/accept_redirects; do echo 0 > $f; done
# for f in /proc/sys/net/ipv4/conf/*/send_redirects; do echo 0 > $f; done
```

To disable IP forwarding, run this:

```
# echo 1 > /proc/sys/net/ipv4/ip_forward
```

Now, verify the settings again to make sure that everything shows up as OK:

```
# /usr/local/sbin/ipsec verify
Checking your system to see if IPsec got installed and started correctly:
Version check and ipsec on-path                             [OK]
Linux Openswan U2.4.6rc3/K2.6.16-1.2115_FC4 (netkey)
Checking for IPsec support in kernel                        [OK]
NETKEY detected, testing for disabled ICMP send_redirects   [OK]
NETKEY detected, testing for disabled ICMP accept_redirects [OK]
Checking for RSA private key (/etc/ipsec.secrets)           [OK]
Checking that pluto is running                              [OK]
Two or more interfaces found, checking IP forwarding        [OK]
Checking NAT and MASQUERADEing                              [N/A]
```

```
Checking for 'ip' command                           [OK]
Checking for 'iptables' command                     [OK]
Opportunistic Encryption Support                    [DISABLED]
```

Now, you can get on with the task of configuring Openswan. *Openswan's* configuration is controlled by two configuration files: */etc/ipsec.conf* and */etc/ipsec.secrets*. The *ipsec.conf* file breaks a VPN connection into right and left segments. This is merely a logical division. The segment on the left can be either the internal or the external network; this allows the same configuration file to be used for both ends of a VPN network-to-network tunnel.

Now, start with a simple *ipsec.conf* to test out Openswan. Adding an entry like this creates an encrypted tunnel between two hosts:

```
conn host-to-host
    left=192.168.0.64
    leftid=@colossus.nnc
    #leftnexthop=%defaultroute
    right=192.168.0.62
    rightid=@spek.nnc
    #rightnexthop=%defaultroute
    auto=add
```

This will work if the hosts are both on the same network. If they're not, you can uncomment the `leftnexthop` and `rightnexthop` entries. For authentication purposes, this connection uses RSA signatures, which are obtained by running `/usr/local/sbin/ipsec showhostkey` on both hosts.

Log into the host that you specified for `left`, run the following command, and then paste the output into your configuration file:

```
# /usr/local/sbin/ipsec showhostkey --left
        # RSA 2192 bits   colossus.nnc    Thu Jul 13 20:48:58 2006
        leftrsasigkey=0sAQNpOndA2SO5aQnEmxqlM5c3JerA9cMwGBOwPE9PshVFBgY44
Ml8Lw7usdMzZTMNaSeXu3+8ofK7aXWqBGVXWpIEw2EAFlGcbg1mrEoAVpLwbpM7ZmZPr6ClOA
dFyTFxFK4k52y7O2h6xsdSoeTWabs2vkzPLDR8QqvlzIzPkDHE+MQG4q/F+fVUkn/TNeGL7ax
xfVkepqTHI1nwbNsLdPXdWGKL9c28ho8TTSgmVMgr9jVLYMNwWjN/BgKMF5J/glALr6kjy19u
NEpPFpcq9dOonjTMOts1xyfjObst2+IMufX21ePuCRDkWuYsfcTMlo7o7Cu+alWOAP4mZHz8Z
e8PzRm9h3oGrUMmwCoLWzMeruud
```

Now, get the key to paste in for the `right` host by logging into it and running the same command, this time replacing `--left` with `--right`.

Copy the configuration file to both hosts and restart the *ipsec* service on both systems:

```
# /etc/init.d/ipsec restart
ipsec_setup: Stopping Openswan IPsec...
ipsec_setup: Starting Openswan IPsec 2.4.6rc3...
ipsec_setup: insmod /lib/modules/2.6.16-1.2115_FC4/kernel/net/key/af_key.ko
ipsec_setup: insmod /lib/modules/2.6.16-1.2115_FC4/kernel/net/ipv4/xfrm4_
tunnel.ko
```

Then, create the IPsec connection by running the following command on one of the hosts:

```
# /usr/local/sbin/ipsec auto --up host-to-host
104 "host-to-host" #6: STATE_MAIN_I1: initiate
003 "host-to-host" #6: received Vendor ID payload [Openswan (this version)
2.4.6rc3  X.509-1.5.4 PLUTO_SENDS_VENDORID PLUTO_USES_KEYRR]
003 "host-to-host" #6: received Vendor ID payload [Dead Peer Detection]
003 "host-to-host" #6: received Vendor ID payload [RFC 3947] method set
to=110
106 "host-to-host" #6: STATE_MAIN_I2: sent MI2, expecting MR2
003 "host-to-host" #6: NAT-Traversal: Result using 3: no NAT detected
108 "host-to-host" #6: STATE_MAIN_I3: sent MI3, expecting MR3
004 "host-to-host" #6: STATE_MAIN_I4: ISAKMP SA established {auth=OAKLEY_
RSA_SIG cipher=oakley_3des_cbc_192 prf=oakley_md5 group=modp1536}
117 "host-to-host" #7: STATE_QUICK_I1: initiate
004 "host-to-host" #7: STATE_QUICK_I2: sent QI2, IPsec SA established {ESP=>
0x070009a9 <0xca6c0796 xfrm=AES_0-HMAC_SHA1 NATD=none DPD=none}
```

If you want to test out your connection, ping one of the hosts in the tunnel from the other one:

```
$ ping spek.nnc
PING spek.nnc (192.168.0.62) 56(84) bytes of data.
64 bytes from spek.nnc (192.168.0.62): icmp_seq=0 ttl=64 time=3.56 ms
64 bytes from spek.nnc (192.168.0.62): icmp_seq=1 ttl=64 time=0.975 ms
64 bytes from spek.nnc (192.168.0.62): icmp_seq=2 ttl=64 time=1.73 ms
64 bytes from spek.nnc (192.168.0.62): icmp_seq=3 ttl=64 time=2.29 ms
...
```

Now, start *tcpdump* on the other host:

```
# /usr/sbin/tcpdump -n -i eth0
tcpdump: verbose output suppressed, use -v or -vv for full protocol decode
listening on eth0, link-type EN10MB (Ethernet), capture size 96 bytes
23:57:35.280722 IP 192.168.0.43 > 192.168.0.62: ESP(spi=0x070009a9,seq=0x18)
23:57:35.280893 IP 192.168.0.43 > 192.168.0.62: icmp 64: echo request seq 19
23:57:35.280963 IP 192.168.0.62 > 192.168.0.43: ESP(spi=0xca6c0796,seq=0x18)
23:57:36.267451 IP 192.168.0.43 > 192.168.0.62: ESP(spi=0x070009a9,seq=0x19)
23:57:36.267451 IP 192.168.0.43 > 192.168.0.62: icmp 64: echo request seq 20
23:57:36.269713 IP 192.168.0.62 > 192.168.0.43: ESP(spi=0xca6c0796,seq=0x19)
```

Notice the ESP packets in the output. The contents of these packets are encrypted using IPsec's Encapsulated Security Payload. Don't worry about the ICMP echo (ping) packets that you see, though. They show up because the kernel's IPsec stack uses the same interface for encrypted and decrypted packets, rather than using a virtual interface for the decrypted packets. If you're able to sniff the packets from a third host, you'll see only the ESP ones.

Congratulations! All traffic between the two hosts you configured will now be seamlessly encrypted. However, Openswan has many possible configurations, such as network-to-network and host-to-network tunnels, as well as seamless opportunistic encryption [Hack #95]. For more information, check out the *ipsec.conf* manual page (man ipsec.conf), as well as the examples in the */etc/ipsec.d/examples* directory and in the *doc/examples* file distributed with the Openswan source code.

Set Up IPsec Under FreeBSD

#93   Use FreeBSD's built-in IPsec support to secure your traffic.

Using IPsec with IKE under FreeBSD requires enabling IPsec in the kernel and installing a user-land program, *racoon*, to handle the IKE negotiations.

Make sure that your kernel has been compiled with the following options:

```
options         IPSEC            #IP security
options         IPSEC_ESP        #IP security (crypto; define w/IPSEC)
options         IPSEC_DEBUG      #debug for IP security
```

If it hasn't, you'll need to define them and then rebuild and install the kernel. After you've done that, reboot to verify that it works.

You can install *racoon* by using the network section of the ports tree or by downloading it from *ftp://ftp.kame.net/pub/kame/misc/*. Install *raccoon* per the instructions provided with the distribution.

On the client, you should first configure *racoon* by modifying this example *racoon.conf* file to suit your needs:

```
path include "/usr/local/etc/racoon" ;
path pre_shared_key "/usr/local/etc/racoon/psk.txt" ;
remote anonymous
{
        exchange_mode aggressive,main;
        my_identifier user_fqdn "user1@domain.com";
        lifetime time 1 hour;
        initial_contact on;

        proposal {
                encryption_algorithm 3des;
                hash_algorithm sha1;
                authentication_method pre_shared_key ;
                dh_group 2 ;
        }
}
sainfo anonymous
{
        pfs_group 1;
        lifetime time 30 min;
        encryption_algorithm 3des ;
        authentication_algorithm hmac_sha1;
        compression_algorithm deflate ;
}
```

In your firewall configuration, be sure you allow IKE connections to your machine (UDP port 500). You must configure *racoon* to start at boot time.

Client Configuration

The */usr/local/etc/racoon/psk.txt* file contains your credentials. This file must be readable by root only. If the permissions are not set correctly, *racoon* will not function. For a shared-secret IPsec connection, the file contains your identification (in this case, your email address) and the secret, in this format:

```
user1@domain.com    supersecret
```

Now, set up the security policy, using the *setkey* utility to add entries to the kernel Security Policy Database (SPD). Create a *client.spd* file for *setkey* to load, with entries like the following:

```
spdadd 192.168.0.104/32 0.0.0.0/0 any -P out ipsec \
  esp/tunnel/192.168.0.104-192.168.0.1/require ;
spdadd 0.0.0.0/0 192.168.0.104/32 any -P in ipsec \
  esp/tunnel/192.168.0.1-192.168.0.104/require ;
```

For this setup, the station IP is 192.168.0.104 and the gateway is 192.168.0. 1. The first entry creates a security policy that sends all traffic to the VPN endpoint. The second entry creates a security policy that allows all traffic back from the VPN endpoint.

 In this configuration, the client is unable to talk to any hosts on the local subnet, except for the VPN gateway. In a wireless network where the client is a prime target for attack, this is probably a good thing for your workstation.

Load the SPD by running the following command:

```
# setkey -f client.spd
```

The gateway *racoon.conf* is the same as the file for the client side. This allows any client to connect. The *psk.txt* file must contain the identifications and shared secrets of all clients who can connect:

```
user1@domain.com    supersecret
user2@domain.com    evenmoresecret
user3@domain.com    notsosecret
```

Gateway Configuration

Again, make sure *psk.txt* is readable by root only. Start *racoon* and make sure there are no errors. Finally, set up a *gateway.spd* file that creates an SPD for each client. The following example assumes your clients are at 192.168.0.10[4-6]:

```
spdadd 0.0.0.0/0 192.168.0.104/32 any -P out ipsec \
  esp/tunnel/192.168.0.1-192.168.0.104/require ;
spdadd 192.168.0.104/32 0.0.0.0/0 any -P in ipsec \
  esp/tunnel/192.168.0.104-192.168.0.1/require ;
spdadd 0.0.0.0/0 192.168.0.105/32 any -P in ipsec \
  esp/tunnel/192.168.0.1-192.168.0.105/require ;
spdadd 192.168.0.105/32 0.0.0.0/0 any -P out \
  ipsec esp/tunnel/192.168.0.105-192.168.0.1/require ;
spdadd 0.0.0.0/0 192.168.0.106/32 any -P in ipsec \
  esp/tunnel/192.168.0.1-192.168.0.106/require ;
spdadd 192.168.0.106/32 0.0.0.0/0 any -P out ipsec \
  esp/tunnel/192.168.0.106-192.168.0.1/require ;
```

Load the SPD by issuing setkey -f gateway.spd. Verify the SPD entries using the spddump command in *setkey*. At this point, you should be able to ping a client from the gateway. It might take a packet or two for the VPN negotiation to complete, but the connection should be solid after that. If you are unable to ping, examine your *syslog* output for errors and warnings.

Using x.509 Certificates

You can use x.509 certificates to perform authentication instead of a pre-shared key, but if you're going to do this, you'll first need to set up a Certificate Authority (CA) [Hack #69]. After you've done that, modify your *racoon.conf* file to look like this:

```
path certificate "/etc/ssl";
remote anonymous
{
        exchange_mode main;
        lifetime time 1 hour;
        certificate_type x509 "cletus.crt" "cletus.key";
        verify_cert on;
        my_identifier asn1dn;
        peers_identifier asn1dn;

        proposal {
                encryption_algorithm 3des;
                hash_algorithm sha1;
                authentication_method rsasig;
                dh_group 2;
        }
}
sainfo anonymous
{
        pfs_group 1;
        lifetime time 30 min;
        encryption_algorithm 3des ;
```

```
                 authentication_algorithm hmac_sha1;
                 compression_algorithm deflate ;
    }
```

With this configuration, *racoon* expects to find the x.509 certificates in */etc/ssl*, so copy your certificate/key pair (*cletus.crt* and *cletus.key*) to the location you decide to use. On your other systems, modify the configuration file accordingly, replacing the certificate and key filenames with the proper ones for each system.

Copy your CA's certificate to your certificate directory. This will be used to verify that your CA has signed the certificates on each system. If it has, they'll be allowed to connect.

You'll notice that the CA certificate isn't specified anywhere in the configuration file. This is because *racoon* looks for it in a filename named after a hash of it. To enable *racoon* to find the CA cert, run a command similar to this:

```
# ln -s CA.crt `openssl x509 -noout -hash < CA.crt`.0
```

> The previous command assumes that you've copied your CA
> certificate to */etc/ssl* and named it *CA.crt*.

Restart *racoon* by running /usr/local/etc/rc.d/racoon restart. Now, you can test it by having the hosts ping each other. Then, run tcpdump on one of your systems. You should begin to see ESP packets:

```
# tcpdump -n
tcpdump: verbose output suppressed, use -v or -vv for full protocol decode
listening on lnc0, link-type EN10MB (Ethernet), capture size 96 bytes
03:35:57.481254 IP 192.168.0.40 > 192.168.0.41: ESP(spi=0x05d628a3,seq=0xd)
03:35:57.483451 IP 192.168.0.41 > 192.168.0.40: ESP(spi=0x0c53fadb,seq=0xd)
03:35:58.490287 IP 192.168.0.40 > 192.168.0.41: ESP(spi=0x05d628a3,seq=0xe)
03:35:58.491160 IP 192.168.0.41 > 192.168.0.40: ESP(spi=0x0c53fadb,seq=0xe)
03:35:59.500509 IP 192.168.0.40 > 192.168.0.41: ESP(spi=0x05d628a3,seq=0xf)
03:35:59.501289 IP 192.168.0.41 > 192.168.0.40: ESP(spi=0x0c53fadb,seq=0xf)
```

These are the ping packets in encrypted form.

Set Up IPsec in OpenBSD
HACK #94
Use IPsec the OpenBSD way.

Setting up IPsec in OpenBSD is fairly easy, because it's compiled into the kernel that ships with each release and is enabled by default. All that is left to do is to create the appropriate */etc/isakmpd/isakmpd.conf* and */etc/isakmpd/isakmpd.policy* files and start *isakmpd* (the IPsec key-management daemon).

This might sound daunting, but OpenBSD's outstanding documentation and example configuration files make it easier than you might think.

Password Authentication

First, to set a password to use for the IPsec connection, you'll need to put these lines in your */etc/isakmpd/isakmpd.policy*:

```
KeyNote-Version: 2
Authorizer: "POLICY"
Licensees: "passphrase:squeamishossifrage"
Conditions: app_domain == "IPsec policy" &&
            esp_present == "yes" &&
            esp_enc_alg == "aes" &&
            esp_auth_alg == "hmac-sha" -> "true";
```

Now, edit your */etc/isakmpd/isakmpd.conf* file to contain the following lines:

```
[General]
Listen-on=              10.1.0.11
Shared-SADB=            Defined
Policy-File=            /etc/isakmpd/isakmpd.policy

[Phase 1]
10.1.0.11=              ISAKMP-peer-west
10.1.0.12=              ISAKMP-peer-east
Default=                ISAKMP-peer-east-aggressive

[Phase 2]
Connections=            IPsec-west-east

[ISAKMP-peer-east]
Phase=                  1
Local-address=          10.1.0.11
Address=                10.1.0.12
Configuration=          Default-main-mode
Authentication=         squeamishossifrage

[ISAKMP-peer-west]
Phase=                  1
Local-address=          10.1.0.12
Address=                10.1.0.11
Configuration=          Default-main-mode
Authentication=         squeamishossifrage


[ISAKMP-peer-east-aggressive]
Phase=                  1
Local-address=          10.1.0.11
Address=                10.1.0.12
Configuration=          Default-aggressive-mode
Authentication=         squeamishossifrage
```

```
[ISAKMP-peer-west-aggressive]
Phase=                  1
Local-address=          10.1.0.12
Address=                10.1.0.11
Configuration=          Default-aggressive-mode
Authentication=         squeamishossifrage

[IPsec-east-west]
Phase=                  2
ISAKMP-peer=            ISAKMP-peer-west
Configuration=          Default-quick-mode
Local-ID=               Host-east
Remote-ID=              Host-west

[IPsec-west-east]
Phase=                  2
ISAKMP-peer=            ISAKMP-peer-east
Configuration=          Default-quick-mode
Local-ID=               Host-west
Remote-ID=              Host-east

[Host-west]
ID-type=                IPV4_ADDR
Address=                10.1.0.11

[Host-east]
ID-type=                IPV4_ADDR
Address=                10.1.0.12

[Default-main-mode]
EXCHANGE_TYPE=          ID_PROT
Transforms=             3DES-SHA

[Default-aggressive-mode]
EXCHANGE_TYPE=          AGGRESSIVE
Transforms=             3DES-SHA-RSA

[Default-quick-mode]
DOI=                    IPSEC
EXCHANGE_TYPE=          QUICK_MODE
Suites=                 QM-ESP-AES-SHA-PFS-SUITE
```

The same configuration file can be used on both endpoints of the tunnel, with only a few changes. First, the example configuration shown above is for use on a machine with an IP address of 10.1.0.11. You can modify it to work on the other endpoint (10.1.0.12) by changing the IP address specified in Listen-on:

```
Listen-on=              10.1.0.12
```

Then, change the Default line to this:

```
Default=                ISAKMP-peer-west-aggressive
```

Finally, change the Connections line:

```
Connections=            IPsec-east-west
```

After you've edited the configuration files, you can start *isakmpd* by running this command:

```
# /sbin/isakmpd
```

Then, use one host in your tunnel to ping the other host. While doing this, start *tcpdump* on one of the systems. You should see some ESP packets:

```
# tcpdump -n
tcpdump: listening on pcn0, link-type EN10MB
21:19:38.920316 esp 10.1.0.11 > 10.1.0.12 spi 0xB9C862E7 seq 1 len 132
21:19:38.921420 esp 10.1.0.12 > 10.1.0.11 spi 0xBC4069F4 seq 1 len 132
21:19:39.926389 esp 10.1.0.11 > 10.1.0.12 spi 0xB9C862E7 seq 2 len 132
21:19:39.927216 esp 10.1.0.12 > 10.1.0.11 spi 0xBC4069F4 seq 2 len 132
21:19:40.940115 esp 10.1.0.11 > 10.1.0.12 spi 0xB9C862E7 seq 3 len 132
21:19:40.940711 esp 10.1.0.12 > 10.1.0.11 spi 0xBC4069F4 seq 3 len 132
```

If you want to see the decrypted packet contents, you can use *tcpdump* to monitor the *enc0* interface:

```
# tcpdump -n -i enc0
tcpdump: WARNING: enc0: no IPv4 address assigned
tcpdump: listening on enc0, link-type ENC
21:21:53.281316 (authentic,confidential): SPI 0xb9c862e7: 10.1.0.11 > 10.1.
0.12: icmp: echo request (encap)
21:21:53.281480 (authentic,confidential): SPI 0xbc4069f4: 10.1.0.12 > 10.1.
0.11: icmp: echo reply (encap)
21:21:54.240855 (authentic,confidential): SPI 0xb9c862e7: 10.1.0.11 > 10.1.
0.12: icmp: echo request (encap)
21:21:54.241059 (authentic,confidential): SPI 0xbc4069f4: 10.1.0.12 > 10.1.
0.11: icmp: echo reply (encap)
```

Certificate Authentication

The configuration shown in the previous section allows anyone to connect with the password *squeamishossifrage*, but what if you want to use x.509 certificates for authentication? You'll first need to set up a Certificate Authority (CA) [Hack #69], if you don't already have one. Once you've done that, you'll need to make sure that each of your certificates has a subjectAltName, so that *isakmpd* can identify what certificate to use for a connection.

If you're using a version of OpenBSD prior to 3.8, you can do this easily with the *certpatch* tool. Otherwise, you'll need to regenerate the certificates for each endpoint from their certificate signing requests.

Using *certpatch* is easy; you supply the certificate to modify, the IP address or fully qualified domain name (FQDN), and the CA's key required to sign the modified certificate. If you want to patch a certificate to include an IP address in the subjectAltName field, use certpatch like this:

```
$ certpatch -i 10.1.0.11 -k CA.key 10.1.0.11.crt 10.1.0.11.crt
Reading ssleay created certificate 10.1.0.11.crt and modify it
Enter PEM pass phrase:
Creating Signature: PKEY_TYPE = RSA: X509_sign: 128 OKAY
Writing new certificate to 10.1.0.11.crt
```

If you want to use the FQDN, run something like this:

```
$ certpatch -t fqdn -i puffy -k CA.key puffy.crt puffy.crt
Reading ssleay created certificate asdf.crt and modify it
Enter PEM pass phrase:
Creating Signature: PKEY_TYPE = RSA: X509_sign: 128 OKAY
Writing new certificate to puffy.crt
```

To add the subjectAltName field when signing a certificate, add -extfile /etc/ssl/x509v3.cnf -extensions x509v3_IPAddr to the openssl command you use to sign your certificates. If you want to use an FQDN rather than an IP address, replace x509v3_IPAddr with x509v3_FQDN. If your CA resides on a non-OpenBSD system, you'll need to copy /etc/ssl/x509v3.cnf to it from an OpenBSD system.

Once you're done adding the subjectAltName field, copy your CA's certificate to /etc/isakmpd/ca. Then, copy your certificates to /etc/isakmpd/certs on their corresponding host. Likewise, you'll need to copy your keys to /etc/isakmpd/private/local.key.

After you've gotten the certificate business out of the way, it's time to modify your *isakmpd.conf* and *isakmpd.policy* files. First, remove all of the Authenticate lines in the *isakmpd.conf* file. Then, locate the Transforms line in the Default-main-mode section and change it to read 3DES-SHA-RSA_SIG. This is what tells *isakmpd* to use the x.509 certificates for authentication.

To tell *isakmpd* to allow only systems that are using certificates signed by your CA to connect, you need to modify your *isakmpd.policy* and tell it the distinguished name (DN) of your CA certificate:

```
$ openssl x509 -subject -noout -in ca/CA.crt
subject= /C=GB/ST=Berkshire/L=Newbury/O=My Company Ltd/CN=CA Root
```

Then, replace the Licensees line in your *isakmpd.policy*:

```
KeyNote-Version: 2
Comment: This policy accepts ESP SAs from hosts with certs signed by our CA
Authorizer: "POLICY"
Licensees: "DN: /C=GB/ST=Berkshire/L=Newbury/O=My Company Ltd/CN=CA Root"
Conditions: app_domain == "IPsec policy" &&
            esp_present == "yes" &&
            esp_enc_alg != "null" -> "true";
```

Finally, to have *isakmpd* start up with each system boot, edit your */etc/rc. conf.local* file (or create one if it doesn't exist) and put the following line in it:

```
isakmpd_flags=""
```

That should do it. As usual, check your system logs if your tunnel has trouble connecting.

H A C K Encrypt Traffic Automatically with Openswan
#95
Use Openswan and DNS TXT records to automatically create encrypted connections between machines.

One particularly cool feature supported by Openswan [Hack #92] is *opportunistic encryption* with other hosts running Openswan. This allows Openswan to transparently encrypt traffic between all hosts that also support opportunistic encryption. For this to work, each host must have a public key generated to use with Openswan. This key can then be stored in a DNS TXT record for that host. When a host that is set up for opportunistic encryption wants to initiate an encrypted connection with another host, it looks up the host's public key through DNS and uses it to initiate the connection.

 Before you get started, if you're using a 2.6.x Linux kernel, make sure that you've installed Openswan with KLIPS [Hack #92] rather than Linux's native IPsec support. The native support in the kernel doesn't work properly with opportunistic encryption.

You'll need to generate a key for each host with which you want to use this feature. Usually, Openswan creates a key for you when you install it. You can check if you have one by running the following command:

```
# /usr/local/sbin/ipsec showhostkey --left
```

If you see the following output, you'll need to create one:

```
ipsec showhostkey: no default key in "/etc/ipsec.secrets"
```

You can do that by running this command:

```
# /usr/local/sbin/ipsec newhostkey --output - >> /etc/ipsec.secrets
```

Next, you'll need to generate a TXT record to put into your DNS zone, using a command like the following:

```
# /usr/local/sbin/ipsec showhostkey --txt @colossus.nnc
; RSA 2192 bits   colossus   Mon Jul 13    03:02:07 2004
        IN     TXT    "X-IPsec-Server(10)=@colossus.nnc" "
AQOR7rM7ZMBXu2ej/1vtzhNnMayZO1jwVHUyAIubTKpd/
```

```
PyTMogJBAdbb3IOxzGLaxadPGfiqPN2AQn76zLIsYFMJnoMbBTDY/2xK1X/
pWFRUUIHzJUqCBIijVWEMLNrIhdZbei1s5/
MgYIPaX2OUL+yAdxV4RUU3JJQhV7adVzQqEmdaNUnCjZOvZG6m4zv6dGROrVEZmJFP54v6WhckYf
qSkQu3zkctfFgzJ/rMTB6Y38yObyBg2HuWZMtWI"
"8VrTQqi7IGGHK+mWk+wSoXer3iFD7JxRTzPOxLk6ihAJMibtKna3j7QP9ZHGOnm7NZ/
L5M9VpK+Rfe+evUUMUTfAtSdlpus2BIeXGWcPfz6rw3O5H9"
```

Add this record to your zone (be sure to add the hostname to the beginning of the record) and reload it . By default, opportunistic encryption support is disabled. To enable it, open */etc/ipsec.conf* and comment out the following line:

```
include /etc/ipsec.d/examples/no_oe.conf
```

Save the file, and then restart the *ipsec* service by running /etc/init.d/ipsec restart.

Verify that DNS is working correctly by running this command:

```
# /usr/local/sbin/ipsec verify
Checking your system to see if IPsec got installed and started correctly
Version check and ipsec on-path                       [OK]
Checking for KLIPS support in kernel                  [OK]
Checking for RSA private key (/etc/ipsec.secrets)     [OK]
Checking that pluto is running                        [OK]
DNS checks.
Looking for TXT in forward map: colossus              [OK]
Does the machine have at least one non-private address [OK]
```

Now, just restart Openswan:

```
# /etc/init.d/ipsec restart
```

You should now be able to connect to any other host that supports opportunistic encryption. But what if other hosts want to connect to you? To allow this, you'll need to create a TXT record for your machine in your reverse DNS zone:

```
# ipsec showhostkey --txt 192.168.0.64
; RSA 2192 bits   colossus   Tue Jan 13 03:02:07 2004
       IN     TXT     "X-IPsec-Server(10)=192.168.0.64" "
AQOR7rM7ZMBXu2ej/1vtzhNnMayZO1jwVHUyAIubTKpd/
PyTMogJBAdbb3IOxzGLaxadPGfiqPN2AQn76zLIsYFMJnoMbBTDY/2xK1X/
pWFRUUIHzJUqCBIijVWEMLNrIhdZbei1s5/
MgYIPaX2OUL+yAdxV4RUU3JJQhV7adVzQqEmdaNUnCjZOvZG6m4zv6dGROrVEZmJFP54v6WhckYf
qSkQu3zkctfFgzJ/rMTB6Y38yObyBg2HuWZMtWI"
"8VrTQqi7IGGHK+mWk+wSoXer3iFD7JxRTzPOxLk6ihAJMibtKna3j7QP9ZHGOnm7NZ/
L5M9VpK+Rfe+evUUMUTfAtSdlpus2BIeXGWcPfz6rw3O5H9"
```

Add this record to the reverse zone for your subnet, and other machines will be able to initiate encrypted connections with your machine. With opportunistic encryption in use, all traffic between the hosts will be encrypted automatically, protecting all services simultaneously. Pretty neat, huh?

HACK #96   Forward and Encrypt Traffic with SSH

Keep network traffic to arbitrary ports secure with SSH port forwarding.

In addition to providing remote shell access and command execution, OpenSSH can forward arbitrary TCP ports to the other end of your connection. This can be extremely handy for protecting email, web, or any other traffic that you need to keep private (at least, all the way to the other end of the tunnel).

ssh accomplishes local forwarding by binding to a local port, performing encryption, sending the encrypted data to the remote end of the *ssh* connection, and then decrypting it and sending it to the remote host and port you specify. Start an *ssh* tunnel with the -L (short for "local") switch:

```
# ssh -f -N -L 110:mailhost:110 user@mailhost
```

Naturally, substitute *user* with your username and `mailhost` with your mail server's name or IP address. Note that you will have to be root for this example, since you'll be binding to a privileged port (110, the POP3 port). You should also disable any locally running POP3 daemon (look in */etc/inetd.conf*); otherwise, it will get in the way.

Now, to encrypt all of your POP3 traffic, configure your mail client to connect to *localhost* port 110. It will happily talk to *mailhost* as if it were connected directly, except that the entire conversation will be encrypted. Alternatively, you could tell *ssh* to listen on a port above 1024 and eliminate the need to run it as root; however, you would have to configure your email client to also use this port, rather than port 110.

-f forks *ssh* into the background, and -N tells it not to actually run a command on the remote end, but just to do the forwarding. One interesting feature when using the -N switch is that you can still forward a port, even if you do not have a valid login shell on the remote server. However, for this to work you'll need to set up public-key authentication with the account beforehand.

If your *ssh* server supports it, you can also try the -C switch to turn on compression. This can significantly reduce the time it takes to download email. To speed up connections even more, try using the blowfish cipher, which is generally faster than 3des (the default). To use the blowfish cipher, type -c blowfish.

You can specify as many -L lines as you like when establishing the connection. To also forward outbound email traffic, try this:

```
# ssh -f -N -L 110:mailhost:110 -L 25:mailhost:25 user@mailhost
```

Now, set your outbound email host to *localhost*, and your email traffic will be encrypted as far as *mailhost*. Generally, this is useful only if the email is bound for an internal host or if you can't trust your local network connection (as is the case with most wireless networks). Obviously, once your email leaves *mailhost*, it will be transmitted in the clear, unless you've encrypted the message with a tool such as PGP or GPG [Hack #42].

If you're already logged into a remote host and need to forward a port quickly, try this:

1. Press Enter.
2. Type ~C (it doesn't echo).
3. You should be at an ssh> prompt; enter the -L line as you would from the command line.

For example:

```
rob@catlin:~$
rob@catlin:~$ ~C
ssh> -L8000:localhost:80
Forwarding port.
```

Your current shell will then forward local port 8000 to *catlin*'s port 80, as if you had entered it in the first place.

You can also allow other (remote) clients to connect to your forwarded port, with the -g switch. If you're logged into a remote gateway that serves as a network address translator for a private network, use a command like this:

```
$ ssh -f -g -N -L8000:localhost:80 10.42.4.6
```

This forwards all connections from the gateway's port 8000 to internal host 10.42.4.6's port 80. If the gateway has a live Internet address, this allows anyone from the Net to connect to the web server on 10.42.4.6 as if it were running on port 8000 of the gateway.

One last point worth mentioning is that the forwarded host doesn't have to be *localhost*; it can be any host that the machine you're connecting to can access directly. For example, to forward local port 5150 to a web server somewhere on an internal network, try this:

```
$ ssh -f -N -L5150:intranet.insider.nocat:80 gateway.nocat.net
```

Assuming that you're running a private domain called *.nocat*, and that *gateway.nocat.net* also has a connection to the private network, all traffic to port 5150 of the remote host will be obligingly forwarded to *intranet.insider. nocat:80*. The address *intranet.insider.nocat* doesn't have to resolve in DNS to the remote host; it isn't looked up until the connection is made to *gateway.nocat.net*, and then it's *gateway* that does the lookup. To securely browse that site from the remote host, try connecting to *http://localhost: 5150/*.

—*Rob Flickenger*

Automate Logins with SSH Client Keys

#97 Use SSH keys instead of password authentication to speed up and automate logins.

When you're an admin on more than a few machines, being able to navigate quickly to a shell on any given server is critical. Having to type `ssh my.server.com` (followed by a password) is not only tedious, but also breaks your concentration. Suddenly having to shift from "Where's the problem?" to "Getting there" and then back to "What's all this, then?" has led more than one admin to premature senility. It promotes the digital equivalent of "Why did I come into this room, anyway?"

At any rate, more effort spent logging into a machine means less effort spent solving problems. Fortunately, recent versions of SSH offer a secure alternative to endlessly entering passwords: public key exchange.

> The following examples assume you're using OpenSSH v3. 4p1 or later.

To use public keys with an SSH server, you'll first need to generate a public/private key pair:

```
$ ssh-keygen -t rsa
```

You can also use `-t dsa` for DSA keys, or `-t rsa1` if you're using protocol v1.

> Shame on you if you are using v1! There are well-known vulnerabilities in v1 of the SSH protocol. If you're using OpenSSH, you can disable v1 by modifying your *sshd_config* and making sure that the `Protocol` line only lists 2.

If at all possible, use RSA keys; though rare, there are some problems with DSA keys.

After you enter the command, you should see something like this:

```
Generating public/private rsa key pair.
Enter file in which to save the key (/home/rob/.ssh/id_rsa):
```

Just press Enter. It will then ask you for a passphrase; again, just press Enter twice (but read on for some caveats). Here's what the results should look like:

```
Enter passphrase (empty for no passphrase):
Enter same passphrase again:
Your identification has been saved in /home/rob/.ssh/id_rsa.
Your public key has been saved in /home/rob/.ssh/id_rsa.pub.
The key fingerprint is:
a6:5c:c3:eb:18:94:0b:06:a1:a6:29:58:fa:80:0a:bc rob@localhost
```

This creates two files: ~/.ssh/id_rsa and ~/.ssh/id_rsa.pub. To use this key pair on a server, try this:

```
$ cat .ssh/id_rsa.pub | ssh server \
"mkdir .ssh && chmod 0700 .ssh && cat > .ssh/authorized_keys2"
```

Of course, substitute your server name for *server*. Now, simply run ssh *server* and it should log you in automatically, without a password. And yes, it will use your shiny new public key for *scp*, too.

If this doesn't work for you, check your file permissions on both ~/.ssh/* and *server*:~/.ssh/*. Your private key (*id_rsa*) should be mode 0600 (and be present only on your local machine).

In addition, your home directory on the server will need to be mode 711or better. If it is group-writable, someone that belongs to the group that owns your home directory could remove ~/.ssh, even if ~/.ssh is not writable by that group. This might not seem obvious at first, but if he can do that, he can create his own ~/.ssh and an *authorized_keys2* file, which can contain whatever keys he wants. Luckily, the SSH daemon will catch this and deny public-key authentication until your permissions are fixed.

Some people consider the use of public keys a potential security risk. After all, an intruder just has to steal a copy of your private key to obtain access to your servers. While this is true, the same is certainly true of passwords.

Ask yourself, how many times a day do you enter a password to gain shell access to a machine (or *scp* a file)? How frequently is it the same password on many (or all) of those machines? Have you ever used that password in a way that might be questionable (on a web site, on a personal machine that isn't quite up-to-date, or possibly with an SSH client on a machine that you don't directly control)? If any of these possibilities sound familiar, consider that using an SSH key in the same setting would make it virtually impossible for an attacker to later gain unauthorized access (providing, of course, that you keep your private key safe).

Another way to balance ease of use with security is to use a passphrase on your key, but use the SSH agent to manage your key for you. When you start the agent, it will ask you for your passphrase once and cache it until you kill the agent. Some people even go so far as to store their SSH keys on removable media (such as USB keychains) and take their keys with them wherever they go. However you choose to use SSH keys, you'll almost certainly find that they're a very useful alternative to traditional passwords.

—*Rob Flickenger*

Use a Squid Proxy over SSH

#98   Secure your web traffic from prying eyes, and improve performance in the process.

squid (*http://www.squid-cache.org*) is normally used as an HTTP accelerator. It is a large, well-managed, full-featured caching HTTP proxy that is finding its way into many commercial web platforms. Best of all, *squid* is open source and freely available. Since it performs all of its magic on a single TCP port, *squid* is an ideal candidate for use with an SSH tunnel. This will not only help to secure your web browser when using wireless networks, but may even make it run faster.

First, choose a server on which to host your *squid* cache. Typically, this will be a Linux or BSD machine on your local wired network, although *squid* also runs in Windows, under Cygwin (*http://www.cygwin.com*). You want to have a fast connection to your cache, so choosing a *squid* cache at the other end of a dial-up connection is probably a bad idea (unless you enjoy simulating what the Internet was like in 1995). On a home network, the server you use for your *squid* cache is typically the same machine you use as a firewall or DNS server. Fortunately, *squid* isn't very demanding when it supports only a few simultaneous users, so it can happily share a box that runs other services.

Full *squid* installation instructions are beyond the scope of this hack, but configuration isn't especially difficult. Just be sure to check your access rules and set a password for the management interface. If you have trouble getting it to run, check out Jennifer Vesperman's "Installing and Configuring Squid" (*http://linux.oreillynet.com/pub/a/linux/2001/07/26/squid.html*).

When *squid* is installed and running, it binds to TCP port 3128 by default. Once you have it running, you should test it manually by setting your HTTP proxy to the server. For example, suppose your server is running *proxy.example.com*. In Mozilla, go to Preferences → Advanced → Proxies, as shown in Figure 10-1.

Enter proxy.example.com as the HTTP proxy host and 3128 for the port. Click OK, and try to load any web page. You should immediately see the page you requested. If you see an Access Denied error, look over the http_access lines in your *squid.conf*, and restart *squid* if necessary.

Once you are satisfied that you have a happy *squid*, you need only forward your connection to it over SSH. Set up a local listener on port 3128, forwarding to proxy.example.com:3128 like this:

```
rob@caligula:~$ ssh -L 3128:localhost:3128 proxy.example.com -f -N
```

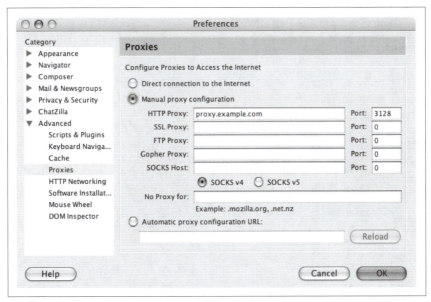

Figure 10-1. Testing squid using the HTTP Proxy field in Mozilla

This sets up an SSH tunnel and forks it into the background automatically. Next, change the HTTP proxy host in your browser to localhost, and reload your page. As long as your SSH tunnel is running, your web traffic will be encrypted all the way to *proxy.example.com*, where it is decrypted and sent onto the Internet.

The biggest advantage of this technique (compared to using the SSH SOCKS 4 proxy [Hack #99]) is that virtually all browsers support the use of HTTP proxies, while not every browser supports SOCKS 4. Also, if you are using Mac OS X, support for HTTP proxies is built into the OS itself. This means that every properly written application will use your proxy settings transparently.

Note that HTTP proxies have the same difficulties with DNS as SOCKS 4 proxies, so keep those points in mind when using your proxy. Typically, your *squid* proxy will be used from a local network, so you shouldn't run into the DNS schizophrenia issue. But your *squid* can theoretically run anywhere (even behind a remote firewall), so be sure to check out the notes on DNS in "Use SSH As a SOCKS Proxy" [Hack #99].

Running *squid* takes a little bit of preparation, but it can both secure and accelerate your web traffic when you're going wireless. *squid* will support as many simultaneous wireless users as you care to throw at it, so be sure to set it up for all of your regular wireless users, and keep your web traffic private.

—*Rob Flickenger*

Use SSH As a SOCKS Proxy

#99   Protect your web traffic using the basic VPN functionality built into SSH itself.

In the search for the perfect way to secure their wireless networks, many people overlook one of the most useful features of SSH: the -D switch. This simple little switch is buried near the bottom of the SSH manpage. Here is a direct quote from the manpage:

> -D *port*
>
> Specifies a local "dynamic" application-level port forwarding. This works by allocating a socket to listen to *port* on the local side, and whenever a connection is made to this port, the connection is forwarded over the secure channel, and the application protocol is then used to determine where to connect to from the remote machine. Currently the SOCKS 4 protocol is supported, and SSH will act as a SOCKS 4 server. Only root can forward privileged ports. Dynamic port forwardings can also be specified in the configuration file.

This turns out to be an insanely useful feature if you have software that is capable of using a SOCKS 4 proxy. It effectively gives you an instant encrypted proxy server to any machine to which you can SSH, and it does so without the need for further software on either your machine or the remote server.

Just as with SSH port forwarding [Hack #96], the -D switch binds to the specified local port, encrypts any traffic to that port, sends it down the tunnel, and decrypts it on the other side. For example, to set up a SOCKS 4 proxy from local port 8080 to *remote*, type the following:

```
rob@caligula:~$ ssh -D 8080 remote
```

That's all there is to it. Now you simply specify localhost:8080 as the SOCKS 4 proxy in your application, and all connections made by that application will be sent down the encrypted tunnel. For example, to set your SOCKS proxy in Mozilla, go to Preferences → Advanced → Proxies, as shown in Figure 10-2.

Select "Manual proxy configuration" and type in localhost as the SOCKS host. Enter the port number that you passed to the -D switch, and be sure to check the SOCKSv4 button.

Click OK, and you're finished. All of the traffic that Mozilla generates is now encrypted and appears to originate from the remote machine that you logged into with SSH. Anyone listening to your wireless traffic now sees a large volume of encrypted SSH traffic, but your actual data is well protected.

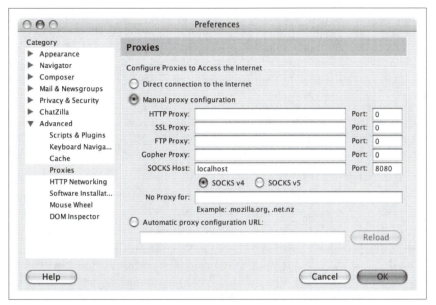

Figure 10-2. Proxy settings in Mozilla

One important point is that SOCKS 4 has no native support for DNS traffic. This has two important side effects to keep in mind when using it to secure your wireless transmissions.

First of all, DNS lookups are still sent in the clear. This means that anyone listening in can still see the names of sites that you browse to, although the actual URLs and data are obscured. This is rarely a security risk, but it is worth bearing in mind.

Second, you are still using a local DNS server, but your traffic originates from the remote end of the proxy. This can have interesting (and undesirable) side effects when attempting to access private network resources.

To illustrate the subtle problems that this can cause, consider a typical corporate network with a web server called *intranet.example.com*. This web server uses the private address 192.168.1.10 but is accessible from the Internet through the use of a forwarding firewall. The DNS server for *intranet. example.com* normally responds with different IP addresses depending on where the request comes from, perhaps using the views functionality in BIND 9. When coming from the Internet, you would normally access *intranet.example.com* with the IP address 208.201.239.36, which is actually the IP address of the outside of the corporate firewall.

Now, suppose that you are using the SOCKS proxy example just shown, and *remote* is actually a machine behind the corporate firewall. Your local

DNS server returns 208.201.239.36 as the IP address for *intranet.mybusiness. com* (since you are looking up the name from outside the firewall), but the HTTP request actually comes from *remote* and attempts to go to 208.201. 239.36. This is often forbidden by the firewall rules, because internal users are supposed to access the intranet by its internal IP address, 192.168.1.10. How can you work around this DNS schizophrenia?

One simple method to avoid this trouble is to make use of a local *hosts* file on your machine. Add an entry like this to */etc/hosts* (or the equivalent on your operating system):

```
192.168.1.10    intranet.example.com
```

In this manner, you can list any number of hosts that are reachable only from the inside of your corporate firewall. When you attempt to browse to one of those sites from your local machine through *remote* (via the SOCKS proxy), the local *hosts* file is consulted before DNS, so the private IP address is used. Since this request is actually made from *remote*, it finds its way to the internal server with no trouble. Likewise, responses arrive back at the SOCKS proxy on *remote*, are encrypted and forwarded over your SSH tunnel, and appear in your browser as if they came in from the Internet.

SOCKS 5 support is planned for an upcoming version of SSH, which will also make tunneled DNS resolution possible. This is particularly exciting for Mac OS X users, as there is support in the OS for SOCKS 5 proxies. Once SSH supports SOCKS 5, every native OS X application will automatically be able to take advantage of encrypting SSH SOCKS proxies. In the meantime, we'll just have to settle for encrypted HTTP proxies [Hack #98].

—Rob Flickenger

HACK 100   Encrypt and Tunnel Traffic with SSL

Use stunnel to add SSL encryption to any network service.

stunnel (http://www.stunnel.org) is a powerful and flexible program that, using SSL, can encrypt traffic to and from any TCP port in several different ways. *stunnel* can tunnel connections, much like SSH can, by providing a local port to connect to. It encrypts the traffic sent to this port, forwards it to a remote system, decrypts the traffic, and finally forwards it to a local port on that system. *stunnel* can also provide transparent SSL support for *inetd*-compatible services.

Building Stunnel

To install *stunnel*, simply run `./configure` from the directory that was created when you unpacked the archive file that you downloaded. Since *stunnel* requires OpenSSL (*http://www.openssl.org*), download and install that first if it is not already installed. If you would like to compile *stunnel* with TCP wrappers support or install OpenSSL in a nonstandard location, you'll probably want to make use of the `--with-tcp-wrappers` or `--with-ssl` command-line options for *configure*.

For example, the following command configures *stunnel* to include TCP wrapper support, using the OpenSSL installation under */opt*:

```
$ ./configure --with-tcp-wrappers --with-ssl=/opt/openssl
```

After the script runs, run make to actually compile *stunnel*. You will then be prompted for information to create a self-signed certificate. This self-signed certificate will be valid for only one year. If this is not what you want, you should create your own certificate and Certificate Authority [Hack #69].

With the older 3.x versions of *stunnel*, it was possible to configure all options from the command line. The newer 4.x versions make use of a configuration file, *stunnel.conf*. A sample configuration file can usually be found in */etc/stunnel/stunnel.conf-sample* or */usr/local/etc/stunnel/stunnel.conf-sample*.

Configuring stunnel

Let's take a look at the basic form of a configuration file used to forward a local port to a remote port with *stunnel*.

Here's the client side:

```
pid =
client = yes

[<server port>]
accept = <forwarded port>
connect = <remote address>:<server port>
```

And here's the server side:

```
cert = /etc/stunnel/stunnel.pem
pid =
client = no

[<forwarded port>]
accept = <server port>
connect = <forwarded port>
```

You can use the default configuration file or choose another file. If you want to use the default configuration file, you can start *stunnel* without any arguments. Otherwise, specify the configuration file as the first argument to *stunnel*.

With the above setup, a program will be able to connect to <forwarded port> on the client side. Then *stunnel* will encrypt the traffic it receives on this port and send it to <server port> on the remote system specified by <remote address>. On the remote system, *stunnel* will decrypt the traffic that it receives on this port and forward it to the program that is listening on <forwarded port> on the remote system.

Here's the format for the equivalent *ssh* port-forwarding command:

```
ssh -f -N -L <forwarded port>:<remote address>:<forwarded port> \
<remote address>
```

If you want to specify a process ID file, you can set the pid variable to whatever filename you wish. Leaving the pid variable in the configuration file without giving it a value causes *stunnel* to not create a PID file. However, if you leave out the pid variable completely, *stunnel* will try to create either */var/run/stunnel.pid* or */usr/local/var/run/stunnel.pid* (i.e., *$prefix/var/run/stunnel.pid*), depending on how you configured it at compile-time.

Encrypting Services

In addition to providing SSH-style port forwarding, *stunnel* can also be used to add SSL capabilities to *inetd*-style services that don't have native SSL functionality, such as email or other services.

Here's an *inetd.conf* entry for the Samba Web Administration Tool (SWAT):

```
swat stream tcp nowait.400 root /usr/local/samba/bin/swat swat
```

To add SSL support to SWAT, you first need to create a configuration file for *stunnel* to use. Call it *swat.conf* and put it in */etc/stunnel*:

```
cert = /etc/stunnel/swat.pem
exec = /usr/local/samba/bin/swat
execargs = swat
```

Modify the entry in *inetd.conf* to look like this:

```
swat stream tcp nowait.400 root /usr/sbin/stunnel stunnel \
  /etc/stunnel/swat.conf
```

Now, you can access SWAT securely with your favorite SSL-enabled web browser.

Alternatively, you can do away with *inetd* altogether and have *stunnel* listen for connections from clients and then spawn the service process itself. Create a configuration file with contents similar to these:

```
cert = /etc/stunnel/swat.pem

[swat]
accept = 901
exec = /usr/local/samba/bin/swat
execargs = swat
```

Then, start *stunnel* with the path to the configuration file:

```
# stunnel /etc/stunnel/swat.conf
```

In addition, you can start it at boot time by putting the previous command in your startup script (i.e., */etc/rc.local*).

stunnel is a powerful tool: not only can it forward connections through an encrypted tunnel, but it can also be used to add SSL capabilities to common services. This is especially nice when clients with SSL support for these services already exist. In this case, you can use *stunnel* solely on the server side, enabling encryption for the service with no need for the client to install any extra software.

 ## HACK 101 Tunnel Connections Inside HTTP

Break through draconian firewalls by using httptunnel.

If you've ever been on the road and found yourself in a place where the only connectivity to the outside world is through an incredibly restrictive firewall, you probably know the pain of trying to do anything other than sending and receiving email or basic web browsing.

Here's where *httptunnel* (*http://www.nocrew.org/software/httptunnel.html*) comes to the rescue. *httptunnel* is a program that allows you to tunnel arbitrary connections through the HTTP protocol to a remote host. This is especially useful in situations like the one mentioned earlier, when web access is allowed but all other services are denied.

Of course, you could just use any kind of tunneling software and configure it to use port 80, but where will that leave you if the firewall is actually a web proxy? This is roughly the same as an application-layer firewall and will accept only valid HTTP requests. Fortunately, *httptunnel* can deal with these as well.

To compile *httptunnel*, download the tarball and run ./configure and make:

```
$ tar xfz httptunnel-3.3.tar.gz
$ cd httptunnel-3.3
$ ./configure && make
```

Install it by running make install, which installs everything under */usr/local*. If you want to install it somewhere else, you can use the standard --prefix= option to the *configure* script.

The *httptunnel* client program is called *htc*, and the server is *hts*. Like stunnel [Hack #100], *httptunnel* can be used to listen on a local TCP port for connections, forward the traffic that it receives on this port to a remote server, and then decrypt and forward the traffic to another port outside of the tunnel.

Try tunneling an SSH connection over HTTP. On the server, run a command like this:

```
# hts -F localhost:22 80
```

Now, run a command like this on the client:

```
# htc -F 2222 colossus:80
```

In this case, *colossus* is the remote server and *htc* is listening on port 2222. You can use the standard port 22 if you aren't running a local *sshd*. If you're curious, you can verify that *htc* is now listening on port 2222 by using *lsof*:

```
# /usr/sbin/lsof -i | grep htc
htc      2323   root    6u  IPv4 0x02358a30      0t0   TCP *:2222 (LISTEN)
```

Now, try out the tunnel:

```
[andrew@kryten andrew]$ ssh -p 2222 localhost
andrew@localhost's password:
[andrew@colossus andrew]$
```

You can also forward connections to machines other than the one on which you're running *hts*. Just replace the localhost in the hts command with the remote host to which you want to forward.

For instance, to forward the connection to *example.com* instead of *colossus*, run this command:

```
# hts -F example.com:22 80
```

If you're curious to see what an SSH connection tunneled through the HTTP protocol looks like, you can take a look at it with a packet sniffer. Here's the initial portion of the TCP stream that is sent to the *httptunnel* server by the client:

```
POST /index.html?crap=1071364879 HTTP/1.1
Host: example.com:80
Content-Length: 102400
Connection: close

SSH-2.0-OpenSSH_3.6.1p1+CAN-2003-0693
```

If your tunnel needs to go through a web proxy, no additional configuration is needed as long as the proxy is transparent and does not require authentication. If the proxy is not transparent, you can specify it with the -P switch. Additionally, if you do need to authenticate with the proxy, you'll want to make use of the -A or --proxy-authorization options, which allow you to specify a username and password with which to authenticate.

Here's how to use these options:

```
# htc -P myproxy:8000 -A andrew:mypassword -F 22 colossus:80
```

If the port that the proxy listens on is the standard web proxy port (8080), you can just specify the proxy by using its IP address or hostname.

 ## Tunnel with VTun and SSH

Connect two networks using VTun and a single SSH connection.

VTun is a user-space tunnel server, allowing entire networks to be tunneled to each other using the *tun* universal tunnel kernel driver. An encrypted tunnel such as VTun allows roaming wireless clients to secure all of their IP traffic using strong encryption. It currently runs under Linux, BSD, and Mac OS X.

 The examples in this hack assume that you are using Linux.

The following procedure allows a host with a private IP address (10.42.4.6) to bring up a new tunnel interface with a real, live, routed IP address (208. 201.239.33) that works as expected, as if the private network weren't even there. You can accomplish this by bringing up the tunnel, dropping the default route, and then adding a new default route via the other end of the tunnel.

Here is the beginning, pretunneled network configuration:

```
root@client:~# ifconfig eth2
eth2 Link encap:Ethernet HWaddr 00:02:2D:2A:27:EA
inet addr:10.42.3.2 Bcast:10.42.3.63 Mask:255.255.255.192
UP BROADCAST RUNNING MULTICAST MTU:1500 Metric:1
RX packets:662 errors:0 dropped:0 overruns:0 frame:0
TX packets:733 errors:0 dropped:0 overruns:0 carrier:0
collisions:0 txqueuelen:100
RX bytes:105616 (103.1 Kb) TX bytes:74259 (72.5 Kb)
Interrupt:3 Base address:0x100

root@client:~# route
Kernel IP routing table
Destination Gateway Genmask Flags Metric Ref Use Iface
10.42.3.0 * 255.255.255.192 U 0 0 0 eth2
loopback * 255.0.0.0 U 0 0 0 lo
default 10.42.3.1 0.0.0.0 UG 0 0 0 eth2
```

As you can see, the local network is 10.42.3.0/26, the IP address is 10.42.3. 2, and the default gateway is 10.42.3.1. This gateway provides network address translation (NAT) to the Internet. Here's what the path to *yahoo. com* looks like:

```
root@client:~# traceroute -n yahoo.com
traceroute to yahoo.com (64.58.79.230), 30 hops max, 40 byte packets
1 10.42.3.1 2.848 ms 2.304 ms 2.915 ms
2 209.204.179.1 16.654 ms 16.052 ms 19.224 ms
3 208.201.224.194 20.112 ms 20.863 ms 18.238 ms
4 208.201.224.5 213.466 ms 338.259 ms 357.7 ms
5 206.24.221.217 20.743 ms 23.504 ms 24.192 ms
6 206.24.210.62 22.379 ms 30.948 ms 54.475 ms
7 206.24.226.104 94.263 ms 94.192 ms 91.825 ms
8 206.24.238.61 97.107 ms 91.005 ms 91.133 ms
9 206.24.238.26 95.443 ms 98.846 ms 100.055 ms
10 216.109.66.7 92.133 ms 97.419 ms 94.22 ms
11 216.33.98.19 99.491 ms 94.661 ms 100.002 ms
12 216.35.210.126 97.945 ms 93.608 ms 95.347 ms
13 64.58.77.41 98.607 ms 99.588 ms 97.816 ms
```

In this example, we are connecting to a tunnel server on the Internet at 208. 201.239.5. It has two spare live IP addresses (208.201.239.32 and 208.201. 239.33) to be used for tunneling. We'll refer to that machine as the *server* and our local machine as the *client*.

Configuring VTun

Now, let's get the tunnel running. First, load the *tun* driver on both machines:

```
# modprobe tun
```

It is worth noting that the *tun* driver will sometimes fail if the server and client kernel versions don't match. For best results, use a recent kernel (and the same version) on both machines.

On the server machine, save this file to */usr/local/etc/vtund.conf*:

```
options {
    port 5000;
    ifconfig /sbin/ifconfig;
    route /sbin/route;
    syslog auth;
}

default {
    compress no;
    speed 0;
```

```
}

home {
    type tun;
    proto tcp;
    stat yes;
    keepalive yes;

    pass sHHH; # Password is REQUIRED.

    up {
        ifconfig "%% 208.201.239.32 pointopoint 208.201.239.33";
        program /sbin/arp "-Ds 208.201.239.33 %% pub";
        program /sbin/arp "-Ds 208.201.239.33 eth0 pub";
        route "add -net 10.42.0.0/16 gw 208.201.239.33";
    };

    down {
        program /sbin/arp "-d 208.201.239.33 -i %%";
        program /sbin/arp "-d 208.201.239.33 -i eth0";
        route "del -net 10.42.0.0/16 gw 208.201.239.33";
    };
}
```

Launch the *vtund* server, like so:

```
root@server:~# vtund -s
```

Now, you'll need a *vtund.conf* file for the client side. Try this one, again in */usr/local/etc/vtund.conf*:

```
options {
    port 5000;
    ifconfig /sbin/ifconfig;
    route /sbin/route;
}

default {
    compress no;
    speed 0;
}

home {
    type tun;
    proto tcp;
    keepalive yes;

    pass sHHH; # Password is REQUIRED.

    up {
        ifconfig "%% 208.201.239.33 pointopoint 208.201.239.32 arp";
        route "add 208.201.239.5 gw 10.42.3.1";
        route "del default";
        route "add default gw 208.201.239.32";
```

```
    };

    down {
        route "del default";
        route "del 208.201.239.5 gw 10.42.3.1";
        route "add default gw 10.42.3.1";
    };
}
```

Testing VTun

Finally, it's time to test VTun by running this command on the client:

```
root@client:~# vtund -p home server
```

Presto! Not only do you have a tunnel up between the client and the server, but you also have a new default route via the other end of the tunnel. Take a look at what happens when you traceroute to *yahoo.com* with the tunnel in place:

```
root@client:~# traceroute -n yahoo.com
traceroute to yahoo.com (64.58.79.230), 30 hops max, 40 byte packets
1 208.201.239.32 24.368 ms 28.019 ms 19.114 ms
2 208.201.239.1 21.677 ms 22.644 ms 23.489 ms
3 208.201.224.194 20.41 ms 22.997 ms 23.788 ms
4 208.201.224.5 26.496 ms 23.8 ms 25.752 ms
5 206.24.221.217 26.174 ms 28.077 ms 26.344 ms
6 206.24.210.62 26.484 ms 27.851 ms 25.015 ms
7 206.24.226.103 104.22 ms 114.278 ms 108.575 ms
8 206.24.238.57 99.978 ms 99.028 ms 100.976 ms
9 206.24.238.26 103.749 ms 101.416 ms 101.09 ms
10 216.109.66.132 102.426 ms 104.222 ms 98.675 ms
11 216.33.98.19 99.985 ms 99.618 ms 103.827 ms
12 216.35.210.126 104.075 ms 103.247 ms 106.398 ms
13 64.58.77.41 107.219 ms 106.285 ms 101.169 ms
```

This means that any server processes running on the client are now fully available to the Internet, at IP address 208.201.239.33. This has all happened without making a single change (e.g., port forwarding) on the gateway 10.42.3.1.

Here's what the new tunnel interface looks like on the client:

```
root@client:~# ifconfig tun0
tun0 Link encap:Point-to-Point Protocol
inet addr:208.201.239.33 P-t-P:208.201.239.32 Mask:255.255.255.255
UP POINTOPOINT RUNNING MULTICAST MTU:1500 Metric:1
RX packets:39 errors:0 dropped:0 overruns:0 frame:0
TX packets:39 errors:0 dropped:0 overruns:0 carrier:0
collisions:0 txqueuelen:10
RX bytes:2220 (2.1 Kb) TX bytes:1560 (1.5 Kb)
```

And here's the updated routing table:

```
root@client:~# route
Kernel IP routing table
Destination Gateway Genmask Flags Metric Ref Use Iface
208.201.239.5 10.42.3.1 255.255.255.255 UGH 0 0 0 eth2
208.201.239.32 * 255.255.255.255 UH 0 0 0 tun0
10.42.3.0 * 255.255.255.192 U 0 0 0 eth2
10.42.4.0 * 255.255.255.192 U 0 0 0 eth0
loopback * 255.0.0.0 U 0 0 0 lo
default 208.201.239.32 0.0.0.0 UG 0 0 0 tun0
```

You'll need to keep a host route to the tunnel server's IP address via the old default gateway; otherwise, the tunnel traffic can't get out.

To bring down the tunnel, simply kill the *vtund* process on the client. This restores all network settings back to their original states.

Encrypting the Tunnel

This method works fine if you trust VTun to use strong encryption and to be free from remote exploits. Personally, I don't think you can be too paranoid when it comes to machines connected to the Internet. To use VTun over SSH (and therefore rely on the strong authentication and encryption that SSH provides), simply forward port 5000 on the client to the same port on the server:

```
root@client:~# ssh -f -N -c blowfish -C -L5000:localhost:5000 server
root@client:~# vtund -p home localhost
root@client:~# traceroute -n yahoo.com
traceroute to yahoo.com (64.58.79.230), 30 hops max, 40 byte packets
1 208.201.239.32 24.715 ms 31.713 ms 29.519 ms
2 208.201.239.1 28.389 ms 36.247 ms 28.879 ms
3 208.201.224.194 48.777 ms 28.602 ms 44.024 ms
4 208.201.224.5 38.788 ms 35.608 ms 35.72 ms
5 206.24.221.217 37.729 ms 38.821 ms 43.489 ms
6 206.24.210.62 39.577 ms 43.784 ms 34.711 ms
7 206.24.226.103 110.761 ms 111.246 ms 117.15 ms
8 206.24.238.57 112.569 ms 113.2 ms 111.773 ms
9 206.24.238.26 111.466 ms 123.051 ms 118.58 ms
10 216.109.66.132 113.79 ms 119.143 ms 109.934 ms
11 216.33.98.19 111.948 ms 117.959 ms 122.269 ms
12 216.35.210.126 113.472 ms 111.129 ms 118.079 ms
13 64.58.77.41 110.923 ms 110.733 ms 115.22 ms
```

To discourage connections to *vtund* on port 5000 of the server, add a Netfilter rule to drop connections from the outside world:

```
root@server:~# iptables -A INPUT -t filter -i eth0 \
-p tcp --dport 5000 -j DROP
```

This allows local connections to get through (since they use loopback) and therefore requires an SSH tunnel to the server before accepting a connection.

As you can see, VTun can be an extremely handy tool to have around. In addition to giving live IP addresses to machines behind a NAT device, you can effectively connect any two networks if you can obtain a single SSH connection between them (originating from either direction).

If your head is swimming from this VTun setup or you're feeling lazy and don't want to figure out what to change when setting up your own client's *vtund.conf* file, take a look at the automatic *vtund.conf* generator [Hack #103].

—*Rob Flickenger*

HACK 103 Generate VTun Configurations Automatically

Generate a vtund.conf file on the fly to match changing network conditions.

If you've just come from "Tunnel with VTun and SSH" [Hack #102], the following script will automatically generate a working *vtund.conf* file for the client side.

If you haven't read the previous hack (or if you've never used VTun), go back and read it before attempting to grok this bit of Perl. Essentially, it attempts to take the guesswork out of changing around the routing table on the client side by auto-detecting the default gateway and building *vtund.conf* accordingly.

The Code

Save this file as *vtundconf*, and run the script each time you use a new wireless network to generate an appropriate *vtund.conf* on the fly:

```
#!/usr/bin/perl -w
#
# vtund wrapper in need of a better name.
#
# (c)2002 Schuyler Erle & Rob Flickenger
#
################ CONFIGURATION

# If TunnelName is blank, the wrapper will look at @ARGV or $0.
#
# Config is TunnelName, LocalIP, RemoteIP, TunnelHost, TunnelPort, Secret
#
my $TunnelName = "";
my $Config     = q{
    home     208.201.239.33 208.201.239.32 208.201.239.5   5000    sHHH
    tunnel2   10.0.1.100      10.0.1.1       192.168.1.4     6001    foobar
};
```

```
################ MAIN PROGRAM BEGINS HERE

use POSIX 'tmpnam';
use IO::File;
use File::Basename;
use strict;

# Where to find things...
#
$ENV{PATH}   = "/bin:/usr/bin:/usr/local/bin:/sbin:/usr/sbin:/usr/local/
[RETURN]sbin";
my $IP_Match = '((?:\d{1,3}\.){3}\d{1,3})';        # match xxx.xxx.xxx.xxx
my $Ifconfig = "ifconfig -a";
my $Netstat = "netstat -rn";
my $Vtund   = "/bin/echo";
my $Debug   = 1;

# Load the template from the data section.
#
my $template = join( "", );

# Open a temp file -- adapted from Perl Cookbook, 1st Ed., sec. 7.5.
#
my ( $file, $name ) = ("", "");
$name = tmpnam()
  until $file = IO::File->new( $name, O_RDWR|O_CREAT|O_EXCL );
END { unlink( $name ) or warn "Can't remove temporary file $name!\n"; }

# If no TunnelName is specified, use the first thing on the command line,
# or if there isn't one, the basename of the script.
# This allows users to symlink different tunnel names to the same script.
#
$TunnelName ||= shift(@ARGV) || basename($0);
die "Can't determine tunnel config to use!\n" unless $TunnelName;

# Parse config.
#
my ($LocalIP, $RemoteIP, $TunnelHost, $TunnelPort, $Secret);
for (split(/\r*\n+/, $Config)) {
  my ($conf, @vars) = grep( $_ ne "", split( /\s+/ ));
  next if not $conf or $conf =~ /^\s*#/o; # skip blank lines, comments
  if ($conf eq $TunnelName) {
    ($LocalIP, $RemoteIP, $TunnelHost, $TunnelPort, $Secret) = @vars;
    last;
  }
}

die "Can't determine configuration for TunnelName '$TunnelName'!\n"
  unless $RemoteIP and $TunnelHost and $TunnelPort;

# Find the default gateway.
#
my ( $GatewayIP, $ExternalDevice );
```

```
for (qx{ $Netstat }) {
  # In both Linux and BSD, the gateway is the next thing on the line,
  # and the interface is the last.
  #
  if ( /^(?:0.0.0.0|default)\s+(\S+)\s+.*?(\S+)\s*$/o ) {
    $GatewayIP = $1;
    $ExternalDevice = $2;
    last;
  }
}

die "Can't determine default gateway!\n" unless $GatewayIP and
$ExternalDevice;

# Figure out the LocalIP and LocalNetwork.
#
my ( $LocalNetwork );
my ( $iface, $addr, $up, $network, $mask ) = "";

sub compute_netmask {
  ($addr, $mask) = @_;
  # We have to mask $addr with $mask because linux /sbin/route
  # complains if the network address doesn't match the netmask.
  #
  my @ip = split( /\./, $addr );
  my @mask = split( /\./, $mask );
  $ip[$_] = ($ip[$_] + 0) & ($mask[$_] + 0) for (0..$#ip);
  $addr = join(".", @ip);
  return $addr;
}

for (qx{ $Ifconfig }) {
  last unless defined $_;

  # If we got a new device, stash the previous one (if any).
  if ( /^([^\s:]+)/o ) {
    if ( $iface eq $ExternalDevice and $network and $up ) {
      $LocalNetwork = $network;
      last;
    }
    $iface = $1;
    $up = 0;
  }

  # Get the network mask for the current interface.
  if ( /addr:$IP_Match.*?mask:$IP_Match/io ) {
    # Linux style ifconfig.
    compute_netmask($1, $2);
    $network = "$addr netmask $mask";
  } elsif ( /inet $IP_Match.*?mask 0x([a-f0-9]{8})/io ) {
    # BSD style ifconfig.
    ($addr, $mask) = ($1, $2);
    $mask = join(".", map( hex $_, $mask =~ /(..)/gs ));
    compute_netmask($addr, $mask);
```

```
    $network = "$addr/$mask";
  }

  # Ignore interfaces that are loopback devices or aren't up.
  $iface = "" if /\bLOOPBACK\b/o;
  $up++    if /\bUP\b/o;
}

die "Can't determine local IP address!\n" unless $LocalIP and $LocalNetwork;

# Set OS dependent variables.
#
my ( $GW, $NET, $PTP );
if ( $^O eq "linux" ) {
  $GW = "gw"; $PTP = "pointopoint"; $NET = "-net";
} else {
  $GW = $PTP = $NET = "";
}

# Parse the config template.
#
$template =~ s/(\$\w+)/$1/gee;

# Write the temp file and execute vtund.
#
if ($Debug) {
  print $template;
} else {
  print $file $template;
  close $file;
  system("$Vtund $name");
}

_ _DATA_ _

options {
  port $TunnelPort;
  ifconfig /sbin/ifconfig;
  route /sbin/route;
}

default {
  compress no;
  speed 0;
}

# 'mytunnel' should really be `basename $0` or some such
# for automagic config selection
$TunnelName {
  type tun;
  proto tcp;
  keepalive yes;

  pass $Secret;
```

```
up {
  ifconfig "%% $LocalIP $PTP $RemoteIP arp";
  route "add $TunnelHost $GW $GatewayIP";
  route "delete default";
  route "add default $GW $RemoteIP";
  route "add $NET $LocalNetwork $GW $GatewayIP";
};

down {
  ifconfig "%% down";
  route "delete default";
  route "delete $TunnelHost $GW $GatewayIP";
  route "delete $NET $LocalNetwork";
  route "add default $GW $GatewayIP";
};
}
```

Running the Hack

To configure the script, take a look at its Configuration section. The first line of $Config contains the addresses, port, and secret used in "Tunnel with VTun and SSH" [Hack #102]. The second line simply serves as an example of how to add more.

To run the script, either call it as vtundconf home or set $TunnelName to the name of the tunnel you would like to be the default. Better yet, make symlinks to the script, like this:

```
# ln -s vtundconf home
# ln -s vtundconf tunnel2
```

Then, you can generate the appropriate *vtund.conf* by calling the symlink directly:

```
# vtundconf home > /usr/local/etc/vtund.conf
```

You might be wondering why anyone would go to all of the trouble of making a *vtund.conf*-generating script in the first place. Once you get the settings right, you'll never have to change them, right?

Well, usually, that's true. But consider the case of a Linux laptop that uses many different networks in the course of the day (say, a DSL line at home, Ethernet at work, and maybe a wireless connection at the local coffee shop). Running *vtundconf* once at each location will give you a working configuration instantly, even if your IP address and gateway are assigned by DHCP. This makes it easy to get up and running quickly with a live, routable IP address, regardless of the local network topology.

—Rob Flickenger

Create a Cross-Platform VPN

Use OpenVPN to easily tie together your networks.

Creating a VPN can be quite difficult, especially when dealing with clients using multiple platforms. Quite often, a single VPN implementation isn't available for all of them. As an administrator, you can be left trying to get different VPN implementations to operate on all the different platforms that you need to support, which can become a nightmare.

Luckily, someone has stepped in to fill the void in cross-platform VPN packages by writing OpenVPN (*http://openvpn.sourceforge.net*). OpenVPN supports Linux, Solaris, OpenBSD, FreeBSD, NetBSD, Mac OS X, and Windows 2000/XP. It achieves this by implementing all of the encryption, key-management, and connection-setup functionality in a user-space daemon, leaving the actual tunneling portion of the job to the host operating system.

To accomplish the tunneling, OpenVPN makes use of the host operating system's virtual TUN or TAP device. These devices export virtual network interfaces, which are then managed by the *openvpn* process to provide a point-to-point interface between the hosts participating in the VPN.

Instead of being sent and received by the virtual device, traffic is sent and received from a user-space program. Thus, when data is sent across the virtual device, it is relayed to the *openvpn* program, which then encrypts it and sends it to the *openvpn* process running on the remote end of the VPN link. When the data is received on the other end, the *openvpn* process decrypts it and relays it to the virtual device on that machine. It is then processed just like a packet being received on any other physical interface.

OpenVPN uses SSL and relies on the OpenSSL library (*http://www.openssl. org*) for encryption, authentication, and certificate verification functionality. Tunnels created with OpenVPN can either use preshared static keys or take advantage of TLS dynamic keying and digital certificates. Since OpenVPN makes use of OpenSSL, it can support any cipher that OpenSSL supports. The main advantage of this is that OpenVPN will be able to transparently support any new ciphers as they are added to the OpenSSL distribution.

Installing OpenVPN

If you're using a Windows-based operating system or Mac OS X, all you need to do is download the installer, run it, and configure OpenVPN. On all other platforms, you'll need to compile OpenVPN yourself. Before you compile and install OpenVPN, make sure that you have OpenSSL installed.

Installing the LZO compression library (*http://www.oberhumer.com/opensource/lzo/*) is also generally a good idea. Using LZO compression can make much more efficient use of your bandwidth, and it may even greatly improve performance in some circumstances.

To compile and install OpenVPN, download the tarball and type something similar to this:

```
$ tar xfz openvpn-2.0.7.tar.gz
$ cd openvpn-2.0.7
$ ./configure && make
```

If you installed the LZO libraries and header files somewhere other than */usr/lib* and */usr/include*, you will probably need to use the `--with-lzo-headers` and `--with-lzo-lib` *configure* script options.

For example, if you have installed LZO under the */usr/local* hierarchy, you'll want to run the *configure* script like this:

```
$ ./configure --with-lzo-headers=/usr/local/include \
--with-lzo-lib=/usr/local/lib
```

If the *configure* script cannot find the LZO libraries and headers, it will print out a warning that looks like this:

```
LZO library and headers not found.
LZO library available from http://www.oberhumer.com/opensource/lzo/
configure: error: Or try ./configure --disable-lzo
```

If the script does find the LZO libraries, you should see output on your terminal that is similar to this:

```
configure: checking for LZO Library and Header files...
checking lzo1x.h usability... yes
checking lzo1x.h presence... yes
checking for lzo1x.h... yes
checking for lzo1x_1_15_compress in -llzo... yes
```

Now that that's out of the way, you can install OpenVPN by running the usual make install. If you are running Solaris, you'll also need to install a TUN/TAP driver. The other Unix-based operating systems already include one, and the Windows and Mac OS installers will install the driver for you. You can get the source code to the Solaris driver from the SourceForge project page (*http://vtun.sourceforge.net/tun/*).

Testing OpenVPN

Once you have LZO, OpenSSL, the TUN/TAP driver, and OpenVPN installed, you can test everything by setting up a rudimentary VPN (that isn't so private) from the command line.

On machine A (*kryten* in this example), run a command similar to this one:

```
# openvpn --remote zul --dev tun0 --ifconfig 10.0.0.19 10.0.0.5
```

The command that you'll need to run on machine B (*zul*) is a lot like the previous command, except the arguments to --ifconfig are swapped:

```
# openvpn --remote kryten --dev tun0 --ifconfig 10.0.0.5 10.0.0.19
```

The first IP address is the local end of the tunnel, and the second is the remote end; this is why you need to swap the IP addresses on the other end. When running these commands, you should see a warning about not using encryption, as well as some status messages. Once OpenVPN starts, run ifconfig to verify that the point-to-point tunnel device has been set up:

```
[andrew@kryten andrew]$ /sbin/ifconfig tun0
tun0: flags=51<UP,POINTOPOINT,RUNNING> mtu 1300
        inet 10.0.0.19 --> 10.0.0.5 netmask 0xffffffff
```

Now, try pinging the remote machine, using its tunneled IP address:

```
[andrew@kryten andrew]$ ping -c 4 10.0.0.5
PING 10.0.0.5 (10.0.0.5): 56 data bytes
64 bytes from 10.0.0.5: icmp_seq=0 ttl=255 time=0.864 ms
64 bytes from 10.0.0.5: icmp_seq=1 ttl=255 time=1.012 ms
64 bytes from 10.0.0.5: icmp_seq=2 ttl=255 time=0.776 ms
64 bytes from 10.0.0.5: icmp_seq=3 ttl=255 time=0.825 ms

--- 10.0.0.5 ping statistics ---
4 packets transmitted, 4 packets received, 0% packet loss
round-trip min/avg/max = 0.776/0.869/1.012 ms
```

Creating Your Configuration

Now that you have verified that OpenVPN is working properly, it's time to create a configuration that's a little more useful in the real world. First, you will need to create SSL certificates [Hack #69] for each end of the connection. After you've done this, you'll need to create configuration files on your server and clients. For these examples, *zul* will be the gateway into the private network and *kryten* will be the external client.

The configuration file for *zul* will be stored in */etc/openvpn/openvpn.conf*. Here are the contents:

```
port 5000
dev tun0

tls-server
dh /etc/ssl/dh1024.pem
ca /etc/ssl/CA.crt
cert /etc/ssl/zul.crt
key /etc/ssl/private/zul.key
```

```
mode server
ifconfig 192.168.1.1 192.168.1.2
ifconfig-pool 192.168.1.4 192.168.1.255

push "route 192.168.0.0 255.255.255.0"
route 192.168.1.0 255.255.255.0

ping 10
ping-restart 120
push "ping 10"
push "ping-restart 60"

daemon
user _openvpn
group _openvpn
chroot /var/empty
writepid /var/run/openvpn.pid
verb 1
```

The port and dev options are used to specify what port to listen on and what
TUN device to use. The tls-server option enables TLS mode and specifies
that you want to designate this side of the connection as the server during
the TLS handshaking process. The dh option specifies the Diffie-Hellman
parameters to use during key exchange. These are encoded in a *.pem* file and
can be generated with the following openssl command:

```
# openssl dhparam -out dh1024.pem 1024
```

The next few configuration options deal with the SSL certificates. The ca
option specifies the Certificate Authority's public certificate, and the cert
option specifies the public certificate to use for this side of the connection.
Similarly, the key option specifies the private key that corresponds to the
public certificate.

The next option, server, tells OpenVPN to act as a multi-client UDP server.
This means that the server will dynamically allocate an IP address for any
VPN client that connects to it. The range that the server uses to allocate
these addresses is set with the ifconfig-pool option. However, as you're still
really using a TUN interface to send and receive traffic, you'll need to specify the addresses for each end of your TUN interface by using the ifconfig
option.

Next, set up routing between the VPN subnet and the rest of the network.
Set the route on the server with the route option, which takes a network
address and netmask as its arguments. Set the route on the client via the
push command, which lets you send configuration information to authenticated clients.

To help ensure that the VPN tunnel doesn't get dropped from any intervening firewalls that are doing stateful filtering, use the ping option. This causes OpenVPN to ping the remote host every *n* seconds so that the tunnel's entry in the firewall's state table does not time out. If the client or server doesn't receive a ping within 60 or 120 seconds, respectively, the ping-restart option will cause them to attempt to reconnect to each other.

Finishing up, tell OpenVPN to fork into the background by using the daemon option, drop its privileges to the *_openvpn* user and group with the user and group options, and tell it to chroot( ) to */var/empty* by using the chroot option.

On *kryten*, the following configuration file is used:

```
port 5000
dev tun0
remote zul
tls-client
ca /etc/ssl/CA.crt
cert /etc/ssl/kryten.crt
key /etc/ssl/private/kryten.key
pull
verb 1
```

The main differences in this configuration file are that the remote and tls-client options have been used. Other than that, *kryten*'s public and private keys are used instead of *zul*'s, and the pull option is used to request that the server push additional configuration information to the client. To turn on compression, add the comp-lzo option to the configuration files on both ends of the VPN.

Now, the only thing to worry about is firewalling. You'll want to allow traffic coming through your tun0 device, as well as UDP port 5000.

Finally, you are ready to run *openvpn* on both sides, using a command like this:

```
# openvpn --config /etc/openvpn.conf
```

Using OpenVPN and Windows

Setting up OpenVPN under Windows is even easier. Simply run the OpenVPN GUI installer (*http://openvpn.se/download.html*), and everything you need will be installed onto your system. This includes OpenSSL, LZO, the TUN/TAP driver, and OpenVPN itself. During the install process, you'll be prompted about what to install and about whether or not to hide the TUN/TAP interface so that it won't appear in your *Network Connections* folder, as shown in Figure 10-3.

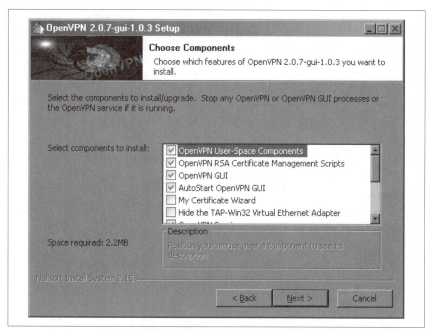

Figure 10-3. Choosing components to install with the OpenVPN GUI

Accepting the defaults should be okay in most situations. The Certificate Wizard is provided so that users can generate certificate requests to have their network administrators create certificates for them.

As part of the install process, files with the *.ovpn* extension are associated with OpenVPN. After the installation has completed, go into the *config* directory where you installed OpenVPN (e.g., *C:\Program Files\OpenVPN\config* if you accepted the defaults).

Now, create a file with an *.ovpn* extension and put your configuration settings in it. You'll need to put your certificate and key files into the *config* directory as well. You should now be able to connect to your VPN by clicking on the OpenVPN GUI System Tray icon.

Using OpenVPN with Mac OS X

With the aid of Tunnelblick (*http://www.tunnelblick.net*), installing OpenVPN under Mac OS X is just as easy as it is under Windows. Simply go to the Tunnelblick site and download the disk image appropriate for your version of Mac OS (Panther or Tiger). After you've opened the disk image, double-click on the *Tunnelblick-Complete.mpkg* package file. Once installation has completed, go to your *Applications* folder, find Tunnelblick, and launch it.

Tunnelblick will then prompt you to create a configuration file and open a window in which you can paste your settings. The file that you create here will be stored in *~/Library/openvpn*. After you've done this, copy your key and certificates to *~/Library/openvpn*.

You're almost done now. Locate the icon that looks like a tunnel in the right-most position of the menu bar, click it, and then click Connect. With luck, you should be connected to your VPN in moments.

> This hack should get you started using OpenVPN, but it has far too many configuration options to discuss here. Be sure to look at the OpenVPN web site for more information.

HACK 105   Tunnel PPP

Use PPP and SSH to create a secure VPN tunnel.

There are so many options to choose from when creating a VPN or tunneled connection that it's mind-boggling. You might not be aware that all the software you need to create a VPN—namely, PPP and SSH daemons—is probably already installed on your Unix machines.

If you used PPP back in the day to connect to the Internet over a dial-up connection, you might be wondering how the same PPP can operate over SSH. Well, when you used PPP in conjunction with a modem, it was talking to the modem through what the operating system presented as a TTY interface, which is, in short, a regular terminal device. The PPP daemon on your end sent its output to the TTY, and the operating system then sent it out via the modem; it then traveled across the telephone network until it reached the remote end, where the same thing happened in reverse.

The terminals on which you run shell commands (e.g., the console or an xterm) use pseudo-TTY interfaces, which are designed to operate similarly to TTYs. Because of this, PPP daemons can also operate over pseudo-TTYs. So, you can replace the serial TTYs with pseudo-TTYs, but you still need a way to connect the local pseudo-TTY to the remote one. Here's where SSH comes into the picture.

You can create the actual PPP connection in one quick command. For instance, if you want to use the IP address 10.1.1.20 for your local end of the connection and 10.1.1.1 on the remote end, run a command similar to this:

```
# /usr/sbin/pppd updetach noauth silent nodeflate \
pty "/usr/bin/ssh root@colossus /usr/sbin/pppd nodetach notty noauth" \
ipparam 10.1.1.20:10.1.1.1
root@colossus's password:
local  IP address 10.1.1.20
remote IP address 10.1.1.1
```

The first line of the command starts the *pppd* process on the local machine and tells it to fork into the background once the connection has been established (updetach). It also tells *pppd* to not do any authentication (noauth), because the SSH daemon already provides very strong authentication, and turns off deflate compression (nodeflate).

The second line of the command tells *pppd* to run a program and to communicate with it through the program's standard input and standard output. This is used to log into the remote machine and run a *pppd* process there. Finally, the last line specifies the local and remote IP addresses that are to be used for the PPP connection.

After the command returns you to the shell, you should be able to see a ppp interface in the output of ifconfig:

```
$ /sbin/ifconfig ppp0
ppp0      Link encap:Point-to-Point Protocol
          inet addr:10.1.1.20  P-t-P:10.1.1.1  Mask:255.255.255.255
          UP POINTOPOINT RUNNING NOARP MULTICAST  MTU:1500  Metric:1
          RX packets:58 errors:0 dropped:0 overruns:0 frame:0
          TX packets:50 errors:0 dropped:0 overruns:0 carrier:0
          collisions:0 txqueuelen:3
          RX bytes:5372 (5.2 Kb)  TX bytes:6131 (5.9 Kb)
```

Now, try pinging the remote end's IP address:

```
$ ping 10.1.1.1
PING 10.1.1.1 (10.1.1.1) 56(84) bytes of data.
64 bytes from 10.1.1.1: icmp_seq=1 ttl=64 time=4.56 ms
64 bytes from 10.1.1.1: icmp_seq=2 ttl=64 time=4.53 ms
64 bytes from 10.1.1.1: icmp_seq=3 ttl=64 time=5.45 ms
64 bytes from 10.1.1.1: icmp_seq=4 ttl=64 time=4.51 ms

--- 10.1.1.1 ping statistics ---
4 packets transmitted, 4 received, 0% packet loss, time 3025ms
rtt min/avg/max/mdev = 4.511/4.765/5.451/0.399 ms
```

And finally, the ultimate litmus test—actually using the tunnel for something other than ping:

```
$ ssh 10.1.1.1
The authenticity of host '10.1.1.1 (10.1.1.1)' can't be established.
RSA key fingerprint is 56:36:db:7a:02:8b:05:b2:4d:d4:d1:24:e9:4f:35:49.
Are you sure you want to continue connecting (yes/no)? yes
Warning: Permanently added '10.1.1.1' (RSA) to the list of known hosts.
andrew@10.1.1.1's password:
[andrew@colossus andrew]$
```

Before deciding to keep this setup, you might want to generate login keys to use with ssh [Hack #97], so that you don't need to type in a password each time. In addition, you might want to create a separate user for logging in on the remote machine and starting *pppd*. However, *pppd* needs to be started as root, so you'll have to make use of *sudo* [Hack #6]. Also, you can enable SSH's built-in compression by adding a -C to the ssh command. In some circumstances, SSH compression can greatly improve the speed of the link. Finally, to tear down the tunnel, simply kill the *ssh* process that *pppd* spawned.

Although it's ugly and might not be as stable and full of features as actual VPN implementations, the PPP and SSH combination can help you create an instant encrypted network without the need to install additional software.

See Also

- The section "Creating a VPN with PPP and SSH" in *Virtual Private Networks*, Second Edition, by Charlie Scott, Paul Wolfe, and Mike Erwin (O'Reilly)

Network Intrusion Detection
Hacks 106–120

One type of tool that's come to the forefront in network security in recent years is the network intrusion detection system (NIDS). These systems can be deployed on your network and monitor the traffic until they detect suspicious behavior, when they spring into action and notify you of what is going on. They are excellent tools to use in addition to your logs, since a network IDS can often spot an attack before it reaches the intended target or has a chance to end up in your logs.

Currently, there are two main types of NIDS. The first type detects intrusions by monitoring network traffic for specific byte patterns that are similar to known attacks. A NIDS that operates in this manner is known as a *signature-based* intrusion detection system. The other type of network IDS is a *statistical monitor*. These systems also monitor the traffic on the network, but instead of looking for a particular pattern or signature, they maintain a statistical history of the packets that pass through the network and report when they see a packet that falls outside of the normal network traffic pattern. NIDSs that employ this method are known as *anomaly-based* intrusion detection systems.

In this chapter, you'll learn how to set up Snort, a signature-based IDS. You'll also learn how to set up Snort with SPADE, which adds anomaly-detection capabilities to Snort, giving you the best of both worlds. This chapter also demonstrates how to set up several different applications that can help you to monitor and manage your NIDS once you have it deployed. In addition, you'll learn how to leverage Snort and ClamAV to scan your network traffic for viruses and prevent them from propagating.

Finally, you'll see how to set up a system that appears vulnerable to attackers, but is actually quietly waiting and monitoring everything it sees. These systems are called *honeypots*. The last few hacks will show you how to quickly and easily get a honeypot up and running, and how to monitor intruders that have been fooled and trapped by it.

Detect Intrusions with Snort

HACK 106

Use one of the most powerful (and free) network intrusion detection systems available to keep an eye on your network.

Monitoring your logs can take you only so far in detecting intrusions. If the logs are being generated by a service that has been compromised, welcome to one of the security admin's worst nightmares: you can no longer trust your logs. This is where network intrusion detection systems come into play: they can alert you to intrusion attempts, or even intrusions in progress.

The undisputed champion of open source NIDSs is Snort (*http://www.snort. org*). Some of the features that make Snort so powerful are its signature-based rule engine and its easy extensibility through plug-ins and preprocessors. These features allow you to extend Snort in any direction you need. Consequently, you don't have to depend on anyone else to provide you with rules when a new exploit comes to your attention: with a basic knowledge of TCP/IP, you can write your own rules quickly and easily. This is probably Snort's most important feature, since new attacks are invented and reported all the time. Additionally, Snort has a very flexible reporting mechanism that allows you to send alerts to a *syslogd*, flat files, or even a database.

Installing Snort

To compile and install a plain-vanilla version of Snort, download the latest version and unpack it. Run the *configure* script and then make:

```
$ ./configure && make
```

Then become root and run:

```
# make install
```

Note that all the headers and libraries for *libpcap* (*http://www.tcpdump.org*) and PCRE (*http://www.pcre.org*) must be installed before you start building Snort; otherwise, compilation will fail. Additionally, you might need to make use of the --with-libpcap-includes, --with-libpcre-includes, --with-libpcap-libraries, or --with-libpcre-libraries *configure* script options to tell the compiler where it can find the libraries and headers. However, you should need to do this only if you have installed the libraries and headers in a nonstandard location (i.e., somewhere other than the */usr* or */usr/local* hierarchy).

For example, if you have installed *libpcap* within the */opt* hierarchy, you would use this:

```
$ ./configure --with-libpcap-includes=/opt/include \
--with-libpcap-libraries=/opt/lib
```

Snort is capable of *flexible response*: the ability to respond to the host that has triggered one of its rules. To enable this functionality, you'll also need to use the --enable-flexresp option, which requires the *libnet* packet injection library (*http://www.packetfactory.net/projects/libnet/*). After ensuring that this package is installed on your system, you can use the --with-libnet-includes and --with-libnet-libraries switches to specify its location.

If you want to include support for sending alerts to a database, you will need to make use of either the --with-mysql, --with-postgresql, or --with-oracle option. To see the full list of *configure* script options, type ./configure --help.

Testing Snort

After you have installed Snort, test it out by using it in sniffer mode. You should immediately see some traffic:

```
# snort -evi eth0
Running in packet dump mode

Initializing Network Interface eth0

        --== Initializing Snort ==--
Initializing Output Plugins!
Decoding Ethernet on interface eth0

        --== Initialization Complete ==--

  ,,_      -*> Snort! <*-
 o"  )~    Version 2.4.4 (Build 28)
  ''''     By Martin Roesch & The Snort Team: http://www.snort.org/team.html
           (C) Copyright 1998-2005 Sourcefire Inc., et al.
  NOTE: Snort's default output has changed in version 2.4.1!
        The default logging mode is now PCAP, use "-K ascii" to activate
        the old default logging mode.

05/06-14:16:13.214265 0:C:29:C3:C8:3B -> 0:A:95:F5:F1:A5 type:0x800 len:0x92
192.168.0.43:22 -> 192.168.0.60:63126 TCP TTL:64 TOS:0x10 ID:29515 IpLen:20
DgmLen:132 DF
***AP*** Seq: 0x7FCD85CF  Ack: 0xA75EBFF2  Win: 0x9E8  TcpLen: 32
TCP Options (3) => NOP NOP TS: 486412346 1797431762
=+=+=+=+=+=+=+=+=+=+=+=+=+=+=+=+=+=+=+=+=+=+=+=+=+=+=+=+=+=+=+=+

05/06-14:16:13.252177 0:A:95:F5:F1:A5 -> 0:C:29:C3:C8:3B type:0x800 len:0x42
192.168.0.60:63126 -> 192.168.0.43:22 TCP TTL:64 TOS:0x10 ID:38015 IpLen:20
DgmLen:52 DF
***A**** Seq: 0xA75EBFF2  Ack: 0x7FCD861F  Win: 0xFFFF  TcpLen: 32
TCP Options (3) => NOP NOP TS: 1797431762 486412307
=+=+=+=+=+=+=+=+=+=+=+=+=+=+=+=+=+=+=+=+=+=+=+=+=+=+=+=+=+=+=+=+
```

Configuring Snort

The Snort source distribution provides some configuration files in the *etc* directory, but they are not installed when running `make install`. You can create a directory to hold these in */etc* or */usr/local/etc* and copy the pertinent files to it by running something similar to this:

```
# mkdir /usr/local/etc/snort && cp etc/[^Makefile]* /usr/local/etc/snort
```

You'll probably want to copy the *rules* directory to that location as well. Note that, as of Version 2.4.0, rules are not distributed with the source but can be downloaded from *http://www.snort.org/rules/*. Unregistered users have access to rulesets that are updated only with every major version release (e.g., 2.4.0, 2.5.0, etc.), whereas registered users can receive rulesets that trail the current rules offered to paying subscribers by five days. In addition, you can download community rules that are contributed by the OSS community to the Snort team.

Now, you need to edit the *snort.conf* file. Snort's sample *snort.conf* file lists a number of variables. Some are defined with default values, and all are accompanied by comments that make this section mostly self-explanatory. Of particular note, however, are these two variables:

```
var HOME_NET any
var EXTERNAL_NET any
```

`HOME_NET` specifies which IP address spaces should be considered local. The default is set so that any IP address is included as part of the home network. Networks can be specified using CIDR notation (i.e., *xxx.xxx.xxx.xxx/yy*). You can also specify multiple subnets and IP addresses by enclosing them in brackets and separating them with commas:

```
var HOME_NET [10.1.1.0/24,192.168.1.0/24]
```

To automatically set `HOME_NET` to the network address of a particular interface, set the variable to `$eth0_ADDRESS`. In this particular case, `$eth0_ADDRESS` sets it to the network address of *eth0*.

The `EXTERNAL_NET` variable allows you to explicitly specify IP addresses and networks that are not part of `HOME_NET`. Unless a subset of `HOME_NET` is considered hostile, you can just keep the default value, which is any.

The rest of the variables that deal with IP addresses or network ranges— `DNS_SERVERS`, `SMTP_SERVERS`, `HTTP_SERVERS`, `SQL_SERVERS`, and `TELNET_SERVERS`—are set to `$HOME_NET` by default. These variables are used within the ruleset that comes with the Snort distribution and can be used to fine-tune a rule's behavior. For instance, rules that deal with SMTP-related attack signatures use the `SMTP_SERVERS` variable to filter out traffic that isn't actually related to those rules. Fine-tuning with these variables leads not only to more relevant alerts and fewer false positives, but also to higher performance.

Another important variable is RULE_PATH, which is used later in the configuration file to include rulesets. The sample configuration file sets it to `../rules`, but to be compatible with the previous examples you should change it to `./rules`, since *snort.conf* and the *rules* directory are both in */usr/local/etc/snort*.

The next section in the configuration file allows you to configure Snort's built-in preprocessors. These do anything from reassembling fragmented packets to decoding HTTP traffic to detecting port scans. For most situations, the default configuration is sufficient. However, if you need to tweak any of these settings, the configuration file is fully documented with each preprocessor's options.

If you've compiled in database support, you'll probably want to enable the database output plug-in, which will cause Snort to store any alerts that it generates in your database. Enable this plug-in by putting lines similar to these in your configuration file:

```
output database: log, mysql, user=snort password=snortpass dbname=SNORT \
    host=dbserver
output database: alert mysql, user=snort password=snortpass dbname=SNORT \
    host=dbserver
```

The first line configures Snort to send any information generated by rules that specify the log action to the database. Likewise, the second line tells Snort to send any information generated by rules that specify the alert action to the database. For more information on the difference between the log and alert actions, see "Write Your Own Snort Rules" [Hack #110].

If you're going to use a database with Snort, you'll need to create a new database, and possibly a new database user account. The Snort source code's *schemas* directory includes scripts to create databases of the supported types: *create_mssql*, *create_mysql*, *create_oracle.sql*, and *create_postgresql*.

If you are using MySQL, you can create a database and then create the proper tables by running a command like this:

```
# mysql SNORT -p < ./schemas/create_mysql
```

This lets you easily organize your alerts and logs and enables you to take advantage of user-friendly systems that can be used to monitor your IDS, such as BASE [Hack #107].

The rest of the configuration file deals mostly with the rule signatures Snort will use when monitoring network traffic for intrusions. These rules are categorized and stored in separate files and are activated by using the include directive. For testing purposes (or on networks with light traffic) the default configuration is sufficient, but you should look over the rules and decide which rule categories you really need and which ones you don't.

Now that all of the hard configuration and setup work is out of the way, you should test your *snort.conf* file. You can do this by running something similar to the following command:

```
# snort -T -c /usr/local/etc/snort/snort.conf
```

Snort will report any errors that it finds and then exit. If there aren't any errors, run Snort with a command similar to this:

```
# snort -Dd -c /usr/local/etc/snort/snort.conf
```

Two of these flags, -d and -c, were used previously (to tell Snort to decode packet data and to use the specified configuration file, respectively). The -D flag tells Snort to print out some startup messages and then fork into the background.

Some other useful options are -u and -g, which let Snort drop its privileges and run under the user and group that you specify. These are especially useful with the -t option, which will chroot( ) Snort to the directory that you specify.

Now you should start to see logs appearing in */var/log/snort*, if you're not logging to a database. The *alerts* file is a text file that contains human-readable alerts generated by Snort. The *snort.log* files are *tcpdump* capture files containing the packets that triggered the alerts.

See Also

- Chapter 11, "Simple Intrusion Detection Techniques," in *Building Secure Servers with Linux*, by Michael D. Bauer (O'Reilly)

Keep Track of Alerts

HACK 107

Use BASE to make sense of your IDS logs.

Once you have set up Snort to log information to your database **[Hack #106]**, you might find it hard to cope with all the data that it generates. Very busy and high-profile sites can generate a huge number of Snort warnings that eventually need to be followed up on. One way to alleviate the problem is to install the Basic Analysis and Security Engine (BASE).

BASE (*http://secureideas.sourceforge.net*) is a web-based interface to Snort alert databases. It features the ability to search for alerts based on a variety of criteria, such as alert signature, time of detection, source and destination addresses and ports, as well as payload or flag values. BASE can display the packets that triggered the alerts and can decode their layer-3 and layer-4 information.

BASE also contains alert-management features that allow you to group alerts related to a specific incident, delete acknowledged or false-positive alerts, email alerts, or archive them to another database. It also provides many different statistics on the alerts in your database based on time, the sensor they were generated by, signature, and packet-related statistics such as protocol, address, or port.

To install BASE, you'll first need a web server and a working installation of PHP (e.g., Apache and mod_php), as well as a Snort installation that has been configured to log to a database (e.g., MySQL). You will also need a couple of PHP code libraries: ADODB (*http://adodb.sourceforge.net*) for database abstraction and PEAR::Image_Graph (*http://pear.veggerby.dk*) for graphics rendering.

After you have downloaded ADODB, unpack it into a suitable directory. You'll then need to install Image_Graph. Download the Image_Graph package and its dependencies, Image_Color and Image_Canvas, and then run the following commands:

```
# pear install Image_Color-1.0.2.tgz
install ok: Image_Color 1.0.2
# pear install Image_Canvas-0.3.0.tgz
install ok: Image_Canvas 0.3.0
# pear install Image_Graph-0.7.2.tgz
Optional dependencies:
package `Numbers_Roman' is recommended to utilize some features.
package `Numbers_Words' is recommended to utilize some features.
install ok: Image_Graph 0.7.2
```

Next, unpack BASE and rename the directory that was created (e.g., *base-1. 2.4*) to *base*. Then, change to the directory and copy the *base_conf.php.dist* file to *base_conf.php*. Now, edit that file to tell BASE where to find ADODB, as well as how to connect to your Snort database.

You can do this by changing these variables to similar values that fit your situation:

```
$DBlib_path = "../..adodb";
$DBtype = "mysql";
$alert_dbname = "SNORT";
$alert_host = "localhost";
$alert_port = "";
$alert_user="snort";
$alert_password = "snortpass";
```

This configuration tells BASE to look for the ADODB code in the *adodb* directory one level above the *base* directory. In addition, it tells BASE to connect to a MySQL database called *SNORT* that is running on the local machine, using the user *snort* with the password *snortpass*. Since it is connecting to a

MySQL server on the local machine, there is no need to specify a port number. If you want to connect to a database running on another system, you should specify 3389, which is the default port used by MySQL.

Additionally, you can configure an archive database for BASE using variables that are similar to the ones used to configure the alert database. You'll need to set the following variables to use BASE's archiving features:

```
$archive_dbname
$archive_host
$archive_port
$archive_user
$archive_password
```

You'll also need to set $archive_exists to 1.

Congratulations! You're finished mucking about in configuration files for the time being. Now, open a web browser and go to the URL that corresponds to the directory where you unpacked BASE. You should be greeted with the database setup page shown in Figure 11-1.

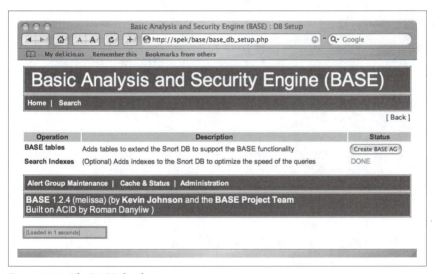

Figure 11-1. The BASE database setup page

Before you can use BASE, you must tell it to create some database tables for its own use. To do this, click the Create BASE AG button. You should see a screen confirming that the tables were created. In addition, you can have BASE create indexes for your events table if this was not done before. Indexes will greatly speed up queries as your events table grows, at the expense of using a little more disk space.

Once you are done with the setup screen, click the Home link to go to the main BASE page, shown in Figure 11-2.

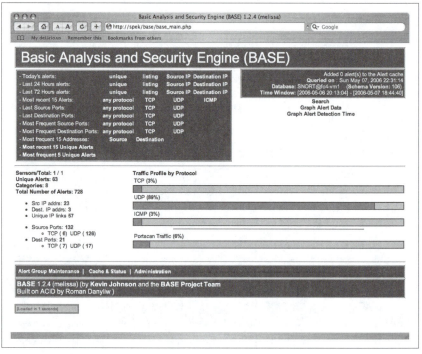

Figure 11-2. The BASE home page

BASE has a fairly intuitive user interface. The main table provides plenty of links to display many useful views of the database at a glance, such as lists of the source or destination IP addresses or ports associated with the alerts in your database.

HACK 108 Monitor Your IDS in Real Time

Use Sguil's advanced GUI to monitor and analyze IDS events in a timely manner.

One thing that's crucial when analyzing IDS events is the ability to correlate all your audit data from various sources, so you can determine the exact trigger for an alert and what actions should be taken. This could involve anything from simply querying a database for similar alerts to viewing TCP stream conversations. One tool to help facilitate this correlation is *Sguil* (*http://sguil.sourceforge.net*).

In case you're wondering, Sguil is pronounced "sgweel" (to rhyme with "squeal").

Sguil is a graphical analysis console written in Tcl/Tk that brings together the power of such tools as Ethereal (*http://www.ethereal.com*), TcpFlow (*http://www.circlemud.org/~jelson/software/tcpflow/*), and Snort's port scan and TCP stream decoding preprocessors into a single unified application, where it correlates all the data from each of these sources. Sguil uses a client/server model and is made up of three parts: a plug-in for Barnyard, a server (*sguild*), and a client (*sguil.tk*). Agents installed on each of your NIDS sensors report back information to the Sguil server. The server takes care of collecting and correlating all the data from the sensor agents and handles information and authentication requests from the GUI clients.

Before you begin using Sguil, you'll need to download the Sguil distribution from the project's web site and unpack it. This creates a directory that reflects the package and its version number (e.g., *sguil-0.6.1*).

Creating the Database

The first step in setting up Sguil is creating a MySQL database to store its information. You should also create a user that Sguil can use to access the database:

```
$ mysql -u root -p
Enter password:
Welcome to the MySQL monitor.  Commands end with ; or \g.
Your MySQL connection id is 546 to server version: 3.23.55

Type 'help;' or '\h' for help. Type '\c' to clear the buffer.

mysql> CREATE DATABASE SGUIL;
Query OK, 1 row affected (0.00 sec)

mysql> GRANT ALL PRIVILEGES ON SGUIL.* TO sguil IDENTIFIED BY 'sguilpass' \
WITH GRANT OPTION;
Query OK, 0 rows affected (0.06 sec)

mysql> FLUSH PRIVILEGES;
Query OK, 0 rows affected (0.06 sec)

mysql>
```

Now, you'll need to create Sguil's database tables. Locate the *create_sguildb. sql* file (it should be in the *server/sql_scripts* subdirectory of the directory that was created when you unpacked the Sguil distribution) and feed it as input to the mysql command, like this:

```
$ mysql -u root -p SGUIL < create_sguildb.sql
```

Setting Up the Server

sguild requires several Tcl packages in order to run. The first is *Tclx* (*http://tclx.sourceforge.net*), which is an extensions library for Tcl. The second is *mysqltcl* (*http://www.xdobry.de/mysqltcl/*). Both of these can be installed by running ./configure && make, and then becoming root and running make install.

You can verify that the packages were installed correctly by running the following commands:

```
$ tcl
tcl>package require Tclx
8.3
tcl>package require mysqltcl
3.02
tcl>
```

If you want to use SSL to encrypt the traffic between the GUI and the server, you will also need to install *tcltls* (*http://sourceforge.net/projects/tls/*). To verify that it was installed correctly, run this command:

```
$ tcl
tcl>package require tls
1.40
tcl>
```

Now, you'll need to configure *sguild*. First, create a directory suitable for holding its configuration files (e.g., */etc/sguild*):

```
# mkdir /etc/sguild
```

Then, copy *sguild.users*, *sguild.conf*, *sguild.queries*, *sguild.access*, and *autocat.conf* to the directory that you created:

```
# cd server
# cp autocat.conf sguild.conf sguild.queries \
  sguild.users sguild.access /etc/sguild
```

This assumes that you're in the directory that was created when you unpacked the *Sguil* distribution. You'll also want to copy the *sguild* script to somewhere more permanent, such as */usr/local/sbin* or something similar.

Now, edit *sguild.conf* to tell it how to access the database you created. If you used the database commands shown previously to create the database and user for Sguil, set these variables to the following values:

```
set DBNAME SGUIL
set DBPASS sguilpass
```

```
set DBHOST localhost
set DBPORT 3389
set DBUSER sguil
```

In addition, *sguild* requires access to the Snort rules used on each sensor so that it can correlate the different pieces of data it receives from the sensors. You can tell *sguild* where to look for these by setting the RULESDIR variable. For instance, the following line tells *sguild* to look for rules in */etc/snort/ rules*:

```
set RULESDIR /etc/snort/rules
```

However, *sguild* needs to find rules for each sensor that it monitors here, so this is really just the base directory for the rules. When looking up rules for a specific host, it looks in a directory corresponding to the hostname within the directory that you specify (e.g., *zul*'s rules will be in */etc/snort/rules/zul*).

To set where *sguild* archives the data it retrieves from sensors, change the LOCAL_LOG_DIR variable to something like the following:

```
set LOCAL_LOG_DIR /var/log/snort/archive
```

You'll also need to install *tcpflow* (*http://www.circlemud.org/~jelson/ software/tcpflow/*) and *p0f* (*http://www.stearns.org/p0f/*) on the host on which you decide to run *sguild*. Once you've done that, set their locations so that *sguild* can find the programs using the TCPFLOW and P0F_PATH variables:

```
set TCPFLOW "/usr/bin/tcpflow"
set P0F_PATH "/usr/sbin/p0f"
```

If you want to use SSL to encrypt *sguild*'s traffic (which you should), you'll now need to create an SSL certificate/key pair [Hack #69]. After you've done that, move them to */etc/sguild/certs* and make sure they're named *sguild.key* and *sguild.pem*.

Next, you'll need to add users for accessing *sguild* from the Sguil GUI:

```
# sguild -adduser andrew
Please enter a passwd for andrew:
Retype passwd:
User 'andrew' added successfully
```

You can test out the server at this point by connecting to it with the GUI client. All you need to do is edit the *sguil.conf* file and change the SERVERHOST variable to point to the machine on which *sguild* is installed. In addition, if you want to use SSL, you'll need to change the following variables to values similar to these:

```
set OPENSSL 1
set TLS_PATH /usr/lib/tls1.4/libtls1.4.so
```

Now, test out the client and server by running *sguil.tk*. After a moment, you should see a login window, as shown in Figure 11-3.

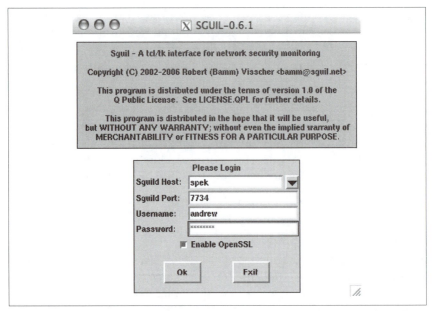

Figure 11-3. The Sguil login dialog

Enter the information that you used when you created the user and click OK. You should then see the dialog shown in Figure 11-4.

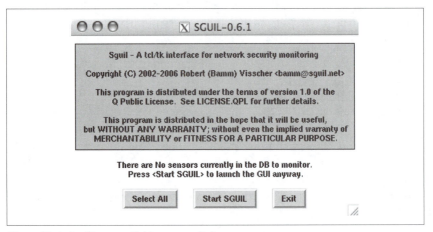

Figure 11-4. Sguil's no available sensors dialog

Since you won't have any sensors to monitor yet, click Exit.

Installing a Sensor

Setting up a sensor involves installing a patched version of Snort that uses modified versions of the *portscan* and *stream4* preprocessors. You'll also need to patch Barnyard to use Sguil's special output plug-in. Sguil's sensor agent script will then collect data from Snort and Barnyard and forward it to *sguild*.

Patching Snort. To set up a Sguil sensor, you'll need to patch your Snort source code. You can find the patches you need in the *sensor/snort_mods/2_1* subdirectory of the Sguil source distribution. Now, change to the directory that contains the Snort source code, go to the *src/preprocessors* subdirectory, and patch *spp_portscan.c* and *spp_stream4.c*:

```
$ cd ~/snort-2.4.4/src/preprocessors
$ patch spp_portscan.c < \
~/sguil-0.6.1/sensor/snort_mods/2_1/spp_portscan_sguil.patch
patching file spp_portscan.c
Hunk #4 succeeded at 1252 (offset 2 lines).
Hunk #6 succeeded at 1285 (offset 2 lines).
Hunk #8 succeeded at 1416 (offset 2 lines).
$ patch spp_stream4.c < \
~/sguil-0.6.1/sensor/snort_mods/2_1/spp_stream4_sguil.patch
patching file spp_stream4.c
Hunk #1 succeeded at 72 with fuzz 1 (offset 39 lines).
Hunk #3 succeeded at 197 (offset 47 lines).
Hunk #4 succeeded at 254 with fuzz 2 (offset 32 lines).
Hunk #5 succeeded at 300 (offset -12 lines).
Hunk #6 succeeded at 421 (offset 46 lines).
Hunk #7 succeeded at 419 with fuzz 2 (offset -8 lines).
Hunk #8 succeeded at 1069 with fuzz 1 (offset 82 lines).
Hunk #9 succeeded at 1117 (offset 14 lines).
Hunk #10 succeeded at 3609 (offset 296 lines).
Hunk #11 succeeded at 3361 (offset 14 lines).
Hunk #12 succeeded at 4002 (offset 327 lines).
```

Compile Snort [Hack #106] as you normally would. After you've done that, edit your *snort.conf* and enable the *portscan* and *stream4* preprocessors:

```
preprocessor portscan: $HOME_NET 4 3 /var/log/snort/portscans gw-ext0
preprocessor stream4: detect_scans, disable_evasion_alerts, keepstats db \
   /var/log/snort/ssn_logs
```

The first line enables the *portscan* preprocessor and tells it to trigger a portscan alert if connections to four different ports are received from the same host within a three-second interval. Next, it specifies that the *portscan* preprocessor will keep its logs in */var/log/snort/portscans*. The last field on the line is the name of the sensor. The second line enables the *stream4* preprocessor, directs it to detect stealth port scans, and tells it not to alert on overlapping TCP datagrams. It also tells the *stream4* preprocessor to keep its logs in */var/log/snort/ssn_logs*.

You'll also need to set up Snort to use its unified output format, so that you can use Barnyard to handle logging of Snort's alert and log events:

```
output alert_unified: filename snort.alert, limit 128
output log_unified: filename snort.log, limit 128
```

Next, create a crontab entry for the *log_packets.sh* script that comes with Sguil. This script starts an instance of Snort solely to log packets. This crontab line will have the script restart the Snort logging instance every hour:

```
00 0-23/1 * * * /usr/local/bin/log_packets.sh restart
```

Edit the variables at the beginning of the script, changing them to suit your needs. These variables tell the script where to find the Snort binary (SNORT_PATH), where to have Snort log packets to (LOG_DIR), which interface to sniff on (INTERFACE), and which command-line options to use (OPTIONS).

Pay special attention to the OPTIONS variable, where you can tell Snort what user and group to run as; the default won't work unless you've created a *sguil* user and group. In addition, you can specify what traffic to not log by setting the FILTER variable to a BPF (i.e., *tcpdump*-style) filter. You should also configure the sensor's name by setting the HOSTNAME variable.

Patching Barnyard. Next, compile and install Barnyard [Hack #116]. You'll need to patch it, which you can do by running these commands:

```
$ cd ~/barnyard-0.2.0
$ cp ~/sguil-0.6.1/sensor/barnyard_mods/configure.in .
$ ./autojunk.sh
$ cd src/output-plugins/
$ cp ~/sguil-0.6.1/sensor/barnyard_mods/op_* .
$ patch op_plugbase.c < op_plugbase.c.patch
```

After you've done that, run the *configure* script with the --enable-tcl option in addition to any other options that you want to use. Then, run make from the current directory; when that completes, change to the top-level directory of the source distribution and run make install. To configure Barnyard to use the Sguil output plug-in, add this line to your *barnyard.conf* file:

```
output sguil
```

Now, you can start Barnyard as you would normally.

Finishing Up

Finally, you'll need to set up Sguil's sensor agent script, *sensor_agent.tcl*, which you'll find in the *sensor* directory of the source distribution. Before running the script, you'll need to edit several variables in its configuration file, *sensor_agent.conf*, to fit your situation. For example:

```
set SERVER_HOST localhost
set SERVER_PORT 7736
set HOSTNAME gw-ext0
set LOGDIR /var/log/snort
```

Now that everything's set up, create a user to run *sguild* under and start it like this:

```
$ sguild -O /usr/lib/tls1.4/libtls1.4.so
```

Make sure that the argument to -O points to the location of *libtls* on your system, or, if you're not using SSL, omit the -O /usr/lib/tls1.4/libtls1.4. so portion of the command.

Now, start the sensor agent by running a command like the following:

```
$ sensor_agent.tcl -o -O /usr/lib/tls1.4/libtls1.4.so
```

As with the daemon, omit the command-line options if you don't want to use SSL encryption. However, using it is recommended.

Getting Sguil running isn't trivial, but it is well worth the effort. Once it's in place, Sguil will provide you with a very good overview of precisely what is happening on your network. Sguil presents data from a bunch of sources simultaneously, giving you a good view of the big picture that is sometimes impossible to see when simply looking at your NIDS logs.

HACK 109   Manage a Sensor Network

Use SnortCenter's easy-to-use web interface to manage your NIDS sensors.

Managing an IDS sensor and keeping track of the alerts it generates can be a daunting task, and it's even more difficult when you're dealing with multiple sensors. One way to unify all your IDS-management tasks into a single application is to use *SnortCenter* (*http://sourceforge.net/projects/snortcenter2/*), a management system for Snort.

SnortCenter is comprised of a web-based console and sensor agents that run on each machine in your NIDS infrastructure. It lets you unify all of your management and monitoring duties into one program, which can help you get your work done quickly. SnortCenter has its own user authentication scheme, and it supports encrypted communication between the web-based management console and the individual sensor agents. This enables you to update multiple sensors with new Snort rules or create new rules of your own and push them to your sensors securely.

SnortCenter also allows you to start and stop your sensors remotely through its management interface. To help you monitor the alerts from your sensors, SnortCenter can integrate with BASE [Hack #107].

To set up SnortCenter, you'll first need to install the management console on a web server that has both PHP support and access to a MySQL database server where SnortCenter can store its configuration database. To install the management console, download the distribution from its Source-Forge project page and unpack it:

```
# tar xfz snortcenter-console-3-31-05.tar.gz
```

This will create a directory containing SnortCenter's PHP scripts, graphics, and SQL schemas. Now, copy the contents of the directory to a suitable location within your web server's document root using commands like the following:

```
# cp -R snortcenter-release /var/www/html
# mv snortcenter-release snortcenter
```

Installing the Prerequisites

To enable SnortCenter to communicate with your database, you'll also need to install ADODB (*http://adodb.sourceforge.net*), a PHP package that provides database abstraction functionality. After you've downloaded the ADODB code, unpack it to a location where CGI scripts can access it.

Next, install *curl* (*http://curl.haxx.se*). Download the source distribution and unpack it. Run ./configure && make, and then become root and run make install. (Alternatively, *curl* might be available with your operating system: Red Hat has a *curl* RPM, and *BSD includes it in the ports tree.)

Setting Up the Console

After that's out of the way, you'll need to edit SnortCenter's *config.php* file (e.g., */var/www/html/snortcenter/config.php*) and change these variables to similar values that fit your situation:

```
$DBlib_path = "../../adodb/";
$curl_path = "/usr/bin";
$DBtype = "mysql";
$DB_dbname    = "SNORTCENTER";
$DB_host      = "localhost";
$DB_port      = "";
$DB_user      = "snortcenter";
$DB_password = "snortcenterpass";
$hidden_key_num =1823701983719312;
```

This configuration tells SnortCenter to look for the ADODB code in the *adodb* directory two directory levels above the one containing SnortCenter. In addition, it tells SnortCenter to connect to a MySQL database called *SNORTCENTER* that is running on the local machine as the user *snortcenter* with the password *snortcenterpass*.

Since it is connecting to a MySQL server on the local machine, there is no need to specify a port. If you want to connect to a database running on another system, you should specify 3389, which is the default port used by MySQL. Set $hidden_key_num to a random number. It is used to make sure only your console can talk to your SnortCenter agents, and vice-versa.

After you're done editing *config.php*, you'll need to create the database and user you specified and set the proper password:

```
$ mysql -u root -p mysql
Enter password:
Welcome to the MySQL monitor.  Commands end with ; or \g.
Your MySQL connection id is 72 to server version: 4.1.16

Type 'help;' or '\h' for help. Type '\c' to clear the buffer.

mysql> create database SNORTCENTER;
Query OK, 1 row affected (0.01 sec)

mysql> GRANT SELECT,INSERT,UPDATE,DELETE ON SNORTCENTER.* TO \
snortcenter@localhost IDENTIFIED BY 'snortcenterpass';
Query OK, 0 rows affected (0.00 sec)

mysql> FLUSH PRIVILEGES;
Query OK, 0 rows affected (0.02 sec)

mysql> exit
Bye
```

Then, create the database tables:

```
$ mysql -u root -p SNORTCENTER < snortcenter_db.mysql
```

Now, use your web browser to load the URL corresponding to where you installed it. The first time SnortCenter loads, it will connect to the database that you specified and create the required database tables. After the page has loaded, you should see something similar to Figure 11-5.

The page should refresh after a few moments and you should see the login page shown in Figure 11-6.

Enter the default login/password *admin*/change and then click the Login button. You should see a page similar to Figure 11-7.

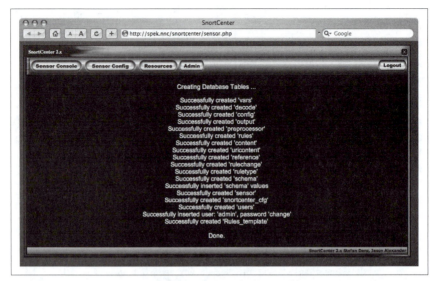

Figure 11-5. Automatic creation of SnortCenter database tables

Figure 11-6. The SnortCenter login page

Now that you know that the management console has been installed successfully, you can move on to installing the agent. But first, you should change the password for the *admin* account. Choose Admin → User Administration → View Users to bring up the user listing page shown in Figure 11-8.

Clicking the icon to the left of the username should bring you to a page similar to Figure 11-9, where you can edit the *admin* account's information (including the password).

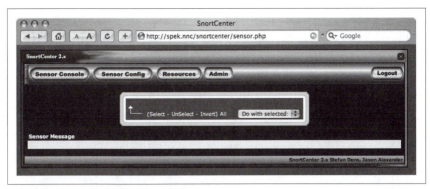

Figure 11-7. The initial SnortCenter main page

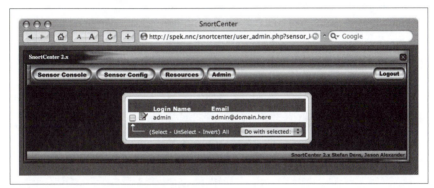

Figure 11-8. SnortCenter's user listing page

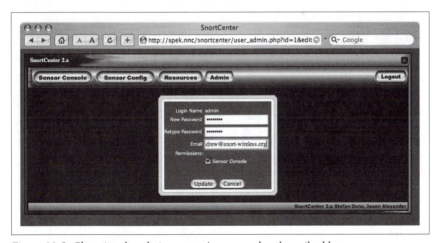

Figure 11-9. Changing the admin account's password and email address

Setting Up an Agent

Now you can go on to set up your sensor agents (really, I'm serious this time).

SnortCenter's sensor agents are written in Perl and require the `Net::SSLeay` module to communicate with the management console through a secure channel. If you have Perl's CPAN module installed, you can install `Net::SSLeay` easily by running the following command:

```
# perl -MCPAN -e "install Net::SSLeay"
```

To install the sensor code, you'll first need to unpack it:

```
# tar xfz /tmp/snortcenter-agent-v1.0-RC1.tar.gz
```

This will create a directory called *sensor* containing all of the sensor agent code. Copy that directory to a suitable permanent location. For example:

```
# cp -R sensor /usr/local/snortcenter
```

Finally, run the sensor agent's setup script:

```
# sh setup.sh
*****************************************************************************
*  Welcome to the SnortCenter Sensor Agent setup script, version 1.0 RC1  *
*****************************************************************************

Installing Sensor in /usr/local/snortcenter ...

*****************************************************************************
The Sensor Agent uses separate directories for configuration files and log
files.
Unless you want to place them in another directory, you can just accept the
defaults.

Config file directory [/usr/local/snortcenter/conf]:
```

This script will prompt you for several pieces of information, such as the sensor agent's configuration file and log directories, the full path to the *perl* binary (e.g., */usr/bin/perl*), and the location of your *snort* binary and rules. It will also ask you questions about your operating system, what port and IP address you want the sensor agent to listen on (the default is TCP port 2525), and what IP addresses are allowed to connect to the agent (e.g., the IP address of the SnortCenter console).

You'll be asked to set a login and password that the management console will use for logging into the agent, and during the setup process a self-signed certificate will be copied to *conf/sensor.pem* for the agent to use when communicating with the console. Alternatively, you can create a signed certificate [Hack #69] and use that. Once the certificate is in place, open *conf/miniserv.conf* and change the line that says `ssl=0` to say `ssl=1`.

After SnortCenter has prompted you for all the information it needs, it will start the sensor agent on the port and IP address specified in the configuration file. You can now test out the sensor agent by accessing it with your web browser (be sure to use *https* instead of *http*).

After entering the login information contained in the setup script, you should see the direct console page shown in Figure 11-10.

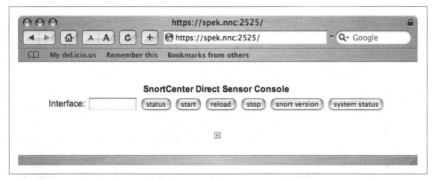

Figure 11-10. The sensor agent direct console page

Adding an Agent to the Console

Now, you can go back to the main management console and add the sensor to it. Log in and select Add Sensor from the Sensor Console menu. You should see the dialog shown in Figure 11-11.

Figure 11-11. Adding a sensor agent

Fill in the information you used when running the setup script and click the Save button. When the next page loads, the sensor you just added should appear in the sensor list. You can push a basic configuration to the sensor by opening the Admin menu, selecting the Import/Update Rules item, and choosing Update from Internet.

Go back to the sensor list by clicking View Sensors in the Sensor Consoles menu, and then click the Push hyperlink for the sensor. To start Snort on that particular sensor, click the Start link. After Snort has started on the sensor, SnortCenter's sensor list should look similar to Figure 11-12.

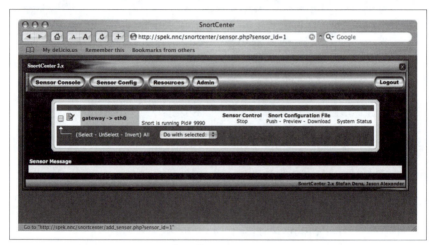

Figure 11-12. SnortCenter's sensor list after starting a sensor

You can now configure your sensor by using the Sensor Config and Resources menus. Once you've created a configuration you're satisfied with, you can push it to your sensor(s) by going back to the sensor list and selecting Push.

HACK 110 Write Your Own Snort Rules

Customize Snort for your own needs quickly and easily by leveraging its flexible rule engine and language.

One of the best features of Snort [Hack #106] is its rule engine and language. Snort's rule engine provides an extensive language that enables you to write your own rules, allowing you to extend it to meet the needs of your network.

A Snort rule can be broken down into two basic parts: the rule header and options for the rule. The rule header contains the action to perform, the protocol that the rule applies to, and the source and destination addresses and ports. The rule options allow you to create a descriptive message to associate with the rule, as well as check a variety of other packet attributes by making use of Snort's extensive library of plug-ins.

Rule Basics

Here's the general form of a Snort rule:

```
action proto src_ip src_port direction dst_ip dst_port (options)
```

When a packet comes in, its source and destination IP addresses and ports are compared to the rules in the ruleset. If any of the rules is applicable to the packet, its options are then compared to the packet. If all of these comparisons return a match, the specified action is taken.

Actions. Snort provides several built-in actions you can use when crafting your rules. To simply log the packet that matches a rule, use the log action. The alert action generates an alert using the method specified in your configuration file or on the command line, in addition to logging the packet.

One nice feature is that you can establish very general rules and then create exceptions by writing rules that use the pass action. This works especially well when you are using the rules distributed with Snort but are getting frequent false positives for some of them. If it's not a security risk to ignore them, you can simply write pass rules that will exclude the packets in question.

The last two built-in rule actions, activate and dynamic, are used together to dynamically modify Snort's ruleset at runtime. Rules that use the dynamic action are just like log rules, except they will be considered only after they have been enabled by an activate rule. To determine what dynamic rules to enable once an activate rule has been triggered, Snort enforces the use of the activates and activated_by rule options. In addition, dynamic rules are required to specify a count option so that Snort can limit how many packets the rules will record.

For instance, if you want to start recording packets after an exploit of an SSH daemon on 192.168.1.21 has been noticed, use a couple of rules similar to these:

```
activate tcp any any -> 192.168.1.21 22 (content:"/bin/sh"; activates:1; \
  msg:"Possible SSH buffer overflow"; )
dynamic tcp any any -> 192.168.1.21 22 (activated_by:1; count:100;)
```

These two rules aren't completely foolproof, but if someone were to run an exploit with shell code against an SSH daemon, it would most likely send the string */bin/sh* in the clear in order to spawn a shell on the system being attacked.

In addition, since SSH is encrypted, strings like that wouldn't be sent to the daemon under normal circumstances. Once the first rule is triggered, it will activate the second one, which will record 100 packets and then stop. This is useful, since you might be able to catch the intruder downloading or installing a rootkit within those first few packets, and recording them will help you to analyze the compromised system much more quickly.

You can also define custom rule actions, in addition to Snort's built-in actions. This is done with the ruletype keyword:

```
ruletype redalert
{
    type alert
    output alert_syslog: LOG_AUTH LOG_ALERT
    output database: log, mysql, user=snort dbname=snort host=localhost
}
```

This custom rule action tells Snort that it behaves like the alert rule action, but specifies that the alerts should be sent to the *syslog* daemon, while the packets will be logged to a database. When defining a custom action, you can use any of Snort's output plug-ins, just as you would if you were configuring them as your primary output method.

Protocols. Snort's detection engine supports several protocols. The proto field is used to specify the protocol to which your rule applies. Valid values for this field are ip, icmp, tcp, and udp.

IP addresses. The next fields in a Snort rule are used to specify the source and destination IP addresses and ports of the packet, as well as the direction in which the packet is traveling. Snort can accept a single IP address or a list of addresses. When specifying a list of IP address, you should separate each one with a comma and then enclose the list within square brackets, like this:

```
[192.168.1.1,192.168.1.45,10.1.1.24]
```

When doing this, be careful not to use any whitespace. You can also specify ranges of IP addresses using CIDR notation, or even include CIDR ranges within lists. Snort also allows you to apply the logical NOT operator (!) to an IP address or CIDR range to specify that the rule should match all but that address or range of addresses.

Ports. As with IP addresses, Snort can accept single ports as well as ranges. To specify a range, use a colon character to separate the lower bound from the upper bound. For example, if you want to specify all ports from 1 to 1024, do it like this:

```
1:1024
```

You can also apply the NOT operator to a port, and you can specify a range of ports without an upper or lower bound.

For instance, if you want to examine only ports greater than 1024, do it this way:

```
1024:
```

Similarly, you can specify ports less than 1024 by doing this:

```
:1024
```

If you do not care about the IP address or port, you can simply specify any.

Moving on, the direction field is used to tell Snort which are the source IP address and port and which are the destination. In earlier versions of Snort, you could use either -> or <- to specify the direction. However, the <- operator has been removed, since you can make either one equivalent to the other by just switching the IP addresses and port numbers. Snort does have another direction operator in addition to ->, though. Specifying <> as the direction tells Snort that you want the rule to apply bidirectionally. This is especially useful when using log rules or dynamic rules, since it enables you to log both sides of the TCP stream rather than just one.

Options

The next part of the rule includes the options. This part lets you specify many other attributes to check against. Each option is implemented through a Snort plug-in. When a rule that specifies an option is triggered, Snort runs through the option's corresponding plug-in to perform the check against the packet. Snort has over 40 plug-ins—too many to cover in detail in this hack—but we will look at some of the more useful ones.

Adding human-readable messages. The most useful option is msg. This option allows you to specify a custom message that will be logged in the alert when a packet matching the rule is detected. Without it, most alerts wouldn't make much sense at first glance. This option takes a string enclosed in quotes as its argument.

For example, this specifies a logical message whenever Snort notices any traffic that is sent from 192.168.1.35:

```
alert tcp 192.168.1.35 any -> any any (msg:"Traffic from 192.168.1.35";)
```

Be sure not to include any escaped quotes within the string. Snort's parser is a simple one and does not support escaping characters.

Inspecting packet content. Another useful option is `content`, which allows you to search a packet for a sequence of characters or hexadecimal values. If you are searching for a string, you can just put it in quotes; to specify a case-insensitive search, add `nocase;` to the end of all your options. If you are looking for a sequence of hexadecimal digits, you must enclose them in | characters. For example, this rule will trigger when the digit `0x90` is spotted in a packet's data payload:

```
alert tcp any any -> any any (msg:"Possible exploit"; content:"|90|";)
```

This digit is the hexadecimal equivalent of the NOP instruction on the x86 architecture and is often seen in exploit code because it can be used to make buffer overflow exploits easier to write.

The `offset` and `depth` options can be used in conjunction with the `content` option to limit the searched portion of the data payload to a specific range of bytes. For example, if you want to limit content matches for NOP instructions to between bytes 40 and 75 of the data portion of a packet, you can modify the previously shown rule to look like this:

```
alert tcp any any -> any any (msg:"Possible exploit"; content:"|90|"; \
    offset:40; depth:75;)
```

You can also match against packets that do not contain the specified sequence by prefixing it with a !.

Another thing you might want to check is the size of a packet's data payload. Many shell code payloads can be large compared to the normal amount of data carried in a packet sent to a particular service. You can check the size of a packet's data payload by using the `dsize` option. This option takes a number as an argument. In addition, you can specify an upper bound by using the < operator, or you can choose a lower bound by using the > operator. Upper and lower bounds can be expressed with <>. For example, the following line modifies the previous rule to match only if the data payload's size is greater than 6000 bytes, in addition to the other options criteria:

```
alert tcp any any -> any any (msg:"Possible exploit"; content:"|90|"; \
    offset:40; depth:75; dsize: >6000;)
```

Matching TCP flags. To check the TCP flags of a packet, Snort provides the `flags` option. This option is especially useful for detecting port scans that employ various invalid flag combinations.

For example, this rule will detect when the SYN and FIN flags are set at the same time:

```
alert any any -> any any (flags:SF,12; msg:"Possible SYN FIN scan";)
```

Valid flags are S for SYN, F for FIN, R for RST, P for PSH, A for ACK, and U for URG. In addition, Snort lets you check the values of the two reserved flag bits. You can specify these by using either 1 or 2. You can also match packets that have no flags set by using 0. The flags option will accept several operators. You can prepend either a +, *, or ! to the flags, to match on all the flags plus any others, any of the flags, or only if none of the flags are set, respectively.

Thresholding

In practice, you might find that some of your rules are a bit noisy and trigger alerts too often to be useful. A way to overcome this is to use Snort's thresholding feature. This feature allows you to specify a minimum number of times a rule needs to be matched for a particular IP address before it actually generates an alert, or limit the number of alerts a rule can generate during an arbitrary interval of time.

You can use thresholding in two different ways.

Thresholding by signature ID. You can specify a threshold for a rule separately by referencing its ID. Threshold statements take the following form and are usually put in *threshold.conf* (located in the same directory as your *snort.conf*):

```
threshold gen_id <generator ID>, sig_id <signature ID>, \
  type <limit | threshold | both>, \
  track <by_src | by_dest>, count <n>, seconds <m>
```

The <generator ID> is the portion of Snort that generates the alert you want to threshold. This is used to track which preprocessor an alert came from. Since all alerts for signatures are generated by Snort's signature engine, this should always be set to 1. The <signature ID> corresponds to the signature's ID. This, of course, means that you'll need to specify IDs when writing your own rules. This is done with the sid option. You'll also want to specify the rule's revision with the rev option.

For example, here's a rule that we looked at before, but with sid and rev options added:

```
alert tcp any any -> any any (msg:"Possible  exploit"; content:"|90|"; \
  offset:40; depth:75; dsize: >6000; sid:1000001; rev:1;)
```

Note that only signature IDs greater than one million can be used for local rules.

When specifying thresholds, you can choose between three types. `limit` thresholds cause an alert to be generated up until the signature has been matched a set number of times (specified with the `count` option) during the chosen interval (specified with the `seconds` parameter). The `threshold` type is used to prevent an alert from being generated unless the signature has been matched at least `count` times during the specified time interval. Specifying `both` as the type produces a mixture of the two techniques: it will cause one alert to be generated only after `count` has been reached during the specified time period. To indicate whether the thresholding should apply to the source or destination IP address, use `by_src` or `by_dest`, respectively.

Thresholding with rule options. The other way to use thresholding is to include the thresholding parameters in the rule itself. For instance, if someone were to actually send a bunch of packets toward your IDS with the SYN and FIN flags set, the previously shown rule that would match them would generate far too many alerts to be useful. So, let's add some thresholding to it:

```
alert any any -> any any (flags:SF,12; msg:"Possible SYN FIN scan"; \
    threshold: type both, track by_dest, count 100, seconds 60)
```

Now, the alert will trigger only once every minute for each IP address that it sees receiving at least 100 SYN/FIN packets during that time period.

Suppression

If you find that a rule is still too noisy, you can disable it either altogether or for specific IP addresses by using Snort's suppression feature. Suppression statements take the following form and are usually also kept in *threshold.conf*:

```
suppress gen_id <generator ID>, sig_id <sid>, [track <by_src | by_dest>,
ip[/mask]]
```

The IDs are specified just like in a threshold statement; however, the `track` and `ip` parameters can be omitted to completely suppress alerts generated by the signature. Use them if you want to limit the suppression to a specific source or destination IP address (or range of addresses). Ranges of IP addresses and networks can be entered in CIDR format.

One of the best features of Snort is that it provides many plug-ins that can be used in the *options* field of a rule. The options discussed here should get you off to a good start. However, if you want to write more complex rules, consult Snort's excellent rule documentation, which contains full descriptions and examples for each of Snort's rule options. The Snort User's Manual is available at *http://www.snort.org/docs/writing_rules/*.

Prevent and Contain Intrusions with Snort_inline

Install Snort_inline on your firewall to contain intrusions, or stop them as they're happening.

Wouldn't it be nice if your NIDS could not only detect intrusions, but also do something about them? It would be great if it could actually stop an intrusion occurring on the host that was being attacked, but the next best thing would be to block the network traffic propagating the attack. One tool that can do this for you is *Snort_inline*, which has been integrated into the main Snort source tree as of Snort 2.3.0.

Snort_inline allows Snort to read data from the Linux kernel's Netfilter queue, which enables Snort to effectively integrate itself with the firewall. This allows it not only to detect intrusions, but also to decide whether to drop packets or to forward them to another host (using *libnet*). This, of course, requires that your kernel be compiled with IP queue support, either statically or as a module.

You can see if you have the module by running a command like this:

```
$ locate ip_queue.ko
/lib/modules/2.6.16/kernel/net/ipv4/netfilter/ip_queue.ko
```

In this case, the output shows that the module is available. If it isn't, check to see whether the file */proc/net/ip_queue* exists. If you can't find the module, but that file exists, it means IP queue support is compiled into your kernel statically. If neither file exists, you'll need to enable IP queue support in your kernel and recompile.

Snort_inline also requires *libipq*, a library that comes with Netfilter and is used by applications to communicate with Netfilter's queue. You can check to see if it's installed on your system by running this command:

```
$ locate libipq
/usr/include/libipq.h
/lib/libipq.a
```

If you don't see output similar to this, chances are that you don't have *libipq* installed. You can install it by downloading the *iptables* source from the Netfilter distribution site (*http://www.netfilter.org*). For instructions on compiling it, refer to "Fool Remote Operating System Detection Software" **[Hack #65]**. After compilation is finished, run make install-devel, since *libipq* is not installed by default.

You might encounter an error that looks like this:

```
Extensions found: IPv4:dccp IPv4:recent IPv4:string IPv6:REJECT
cc -O2 -Wall -Wunused -I/usr/src/kernels/2.6.14/include -Iinclude/ -
DIPTABLES_VERSION=\"1.3.5\"  -fPIC -o extensions/libipt_ah_sh.o -c
extensions/libipt_ah.c
```

```
In file included from /usr/src/kernels/2.6.14/include/linux/netfilter_ipv4.
h:8,
                 from /usr/src/kernels/2.6.14/include/linux/netfilter_ipv4/
ip_tables.h:26,
                 from include/libiptc/libiptc.h:6,
                 from include/iptables.h:5,
                 from extensions/libipt_ah.c:8:
/usr/src/kernels/2.6.14/include/linux/config.h:6:2: error: #error including
kernel header in userspace; use the glibc headers instead!
make: *** [extensions/libipt_ah_sh.o] Error 1
```

If you do, you'll need to edit the *config.h* file mentioned in the error message (e.g., */usr/src/kernels/2.6.14/include/linux/config.h* in this example) and comment out the line that begins with #error by adding two slashes at the start of the line.

In addition to IP queue support and the *libipq* package, you'll need the *libnet* packet injection library (*http://www.packetfactory.net/projects/libnet/*). Simply download the source distribution, unpack it, run ./configure && make, and then become root and run make install.

Now that all the prerequisites are out of the way, you can compile *Snort_inline*. First, download and unpack the source distribution and change to the directory that is created. Then, run this command:

```
$ ./configure --enable-inline && make
```

You can use any options to *configure* that you'd normally use with Snort, since at its heart *Snort_inline* is still Snort.

Don't be alarmed if your compile aborts with the following error:

```
gcc -DHAVE_CONFIG_H -I. -I. -I../.. -I../.. -I../../src -I../../src/sfutil -
I/usr/include/pcap -I../../src/output-plugins -I../../src/detection-plugins
-I../../src/preprocessors -I../../src/preprocessors/flow -I../../src/
preprocessors/portscan  -I../../src/preprocessors/flow/int-snort  -I../../
src/preprocessors/HttpInspect/include  -I/usr/include  -g -O2 -Wall -DGIDS -
D_BSD_SOURCE -D__BSD_SOURCE -D__FAVOR_BSD -DHAVE_NET_ETHERNET_H -DLIBNET_
LIL_ENDIAN -c spo_alert_fast.c
In file included from /usr/include/linux/netfilter_ipv4/ip_queue.h:10,
                 from /usr/local/include/libipq.h:37,
                 from ../../src/inline.h:8,
                 from ../../src/snort.h:36,
                 from spo_alert_fast.c:51:
/usr/include/linux/if.h:59: error: redefinition of 'struct ifmap'
/usr/include/linux/if.h:77: error: redefinition of 'struct ifreq'
/usr/include/linux/if.h:126: error: redefinition of 'struct ifconf'
spo_alert_fast.c: In function 'AlertFastInit':
spo_alert_fast.c:124: warning: pointer targets in passing argument 1 of
'ParseAlertFastArgs' differ in signedness
make[3]: *** [spo_alert_fast.o] Error 1
make[3]: Leaving directory `/tmp/snort-2.4.4/src/output-plugins'
make[2]: *** [all-recursive] Error 1
```

```
make[2]: Leaving directory `/tmp/snort-2.4.4/src'
make[1]: *** [all-recursive] Error 1
make[1]: Leaving directory `/tmp/snort-2.4.4'
make: *** [all] Error 2
```

This error is caused by the kernel headers in */usr/include/linux* being out of sync with the headers of the kernel for which you're building Netfilter. To fix this, create a symbolic link from the */include/linux* directory in the kernel source tree to */usr/include/linux*:

```
# cd /usr/include
# mv linux linux.orig
# ln -s /usr/src/kernels/2.6.14/include/linux .
```

You can then restart the compilation from where it left off by simply typing make, or, if you're paranoid, you can use this command to completely start over:

```
$ make clean && make
```

After compilation has finished, become root and type make install.

You can now configure *Snort_inline* just as you would configure Snort regularly [Hack #106]. However, it's recommended that you run a separate instance of Snort if you want alerting and use *Snort_inline* solely for setting firewall rules.

In addition to modifying Snort to capture packets from Netfilter rather than *libpcap*, the *Snort_inline* patch adds three new rule types—drop, sdrop, and reject—as well as a new rule option. The drop rule type drops the packet that triggered the rule without notifying the sending host, much like the iptables DROP target, and logs that it has done so. The sdrop rule type is similar, except that it drops the packet silently, with no log entry to inform you. Using the reject rule type blocks the offending packet but notifies the sending host with either a TCP RST or an ICMP port unreachable message, depending on whether the packet that triggered the rule used the TCP or UDP protocol, respectively.

The new rule option added by *Snort_inline* allows you to replace arbitrary content within a packet with whatever you choose. The only restriction is that the replacement byte stream must be the same length as the original. This is implemented with the replace rule option, which is used in conjunction with the content rule option to select what is to be replaced.

To run *Snort_inline*, start it just as you would start Snort. If you want to use it in inline mode, though, use its -Q command-line switch, which tells *Snort_inline* to use IP queues rather than *libpcap* to gather packets. In this case, you'll also need to configure the kernel to send the packets to the IP queues before starting *Snort_inline*. This is done with the `iptables` command:

```
# iptables -F
# iptables -A INPUT -j QUEUE
# iptables -A OUTPUT -j QUEUE
# iptables -A FORWARD -j QUEUE
```

This pushes all traffic going in, out, and through the machine into an IP queue from which *Snort_inline* will read its packets. You can then start snort (just don't forget to use the -Q option):

```
# snort -Qvc /etc/snort/snort_inline.conf
```

If you're using a version that isn't from Snort.org, substitute `snort_inline` for snort.

If you're administering the machine remotely, you'll probably want to start snort before enabling the QUEUE targets, since it's snort that will actually pass the packets back and forth. Otherwise, your remote logins will be dropped as soon as you put the `iptables` rules in place. To be extra cautious, have your QUEUE target rules ignore packets coming from a certain IP address or range of addresses.

HACK 112 Automatically Firewall Attackers with SnortSam

Use SnortSam to prevent intrusions by putting dynamic firewall rules in place to stop in-progress attacks.

An alternative to running Snort on your firewall and having it activate filtering rules on the machine it's running on [Hack #111] is to have Snort communicate which filtering rules should be put in place when an intrusion is detected on an external firewall. To do this, you can use *SnortSam* (*http://www.snortsam.net*).

SnortSam is made up of two components: a Snort plug-in and a daemon. It uses Snort's plug-in architecture and extends Snort with the ability to communicate with a remote firewall, which then dynamically applies filtering rules to stop attacks that are in progress. Unlike *Snort_inline*, which is highly dependent on Linux, SnortSam supports a wide variety of firewalls, such as Check Point's FireWall-1, various Cisco firewalls, NetScreen, Firebox, OpenBSD's PF, and Linux's *ipchains* and *iptables* interfaces to Netfilter.

Installing SnortSam

To set up SnortSam, first download the source distribution and then unpack it. After you've done that, go into the directory it created and run this command:

```
$ sh makesnortsam.sh
```

This will build the *snortsam* binary, which you can then copy to a suitable place in your path (e.g., */usr/bin* or */usr/local/bin*).

Now, download the patch for Snort, which you can get from the same site as SnortSam. After you've done that, unpack it:

```
$ tar xvfz snortsam-patch.tar.gz
patchsnort.sh
patchsnort.sh.asc
snortpatch8
snortpatch8.asc
snortpatch9
snortpatch9.asc
snortpatchb
snortpatchb.asc
```

Next, run patchsnort.sh and specify the directory where you're keeping Snort's source:

```
$ patchsnort.sh snort-2.4.4
Patching Snort version 2.x...
patching file spo_alert_fwsam.c
patching file spo_alert_fwsam.h
patching file twofish.c
patching file twofish.h
rm: cannot remove `spo_alert_fwsam.?.orig': No such file or directory
rm: cannot remove `twofish.?.orig': No such file or directory
patching file plugbase.c
Hunk #1 succeeded at 114 with fuzz 2 (offset 4 lines).
Hunk #2 succeeded at 588 with fuzz 2 (offset 13 lines).
patching file plugin_enum.h
Hunk #1 succeeded at 37 with fuzz 1.
Patching Makefiles...
Done
```

Finally, compile Snort [Hack #106] as you would normally, except run the following commands before running ./configure:

```
$ aclocal
$ autoheader
$ automake --add-missing
$ autoconf
```

Configuring SnortSam

Before running SnortSam, you must create a configuration file for it. Snort-Sam's configuration syntax is pretty easy to use, but there are quite a few options, so only a subset of the available ones will be discussed here.

One useful option is accept, which lets you tell SnortSam what Snort sensors are allowed to connect to it. This option can take a CIDR-format address range, a hostname, or a single IP address. You can optionally specify a password as well. If you don't specify a password, the one specified by the defaultkey option is used.

For example, if you want to allow all hosts from the network 192.168.1.0/24 with the password *qwijybo*, you can put a line like this in your configuration file:

```
accept 192.168.1.0/24, qwijybo
```

To specify multiple hosts or network address ranges, you can use multiple accept entries.

Another useful option is dontblock, which enables you to construct a whitelist of hosts and networks that SnortSam will not block under any circumstances. This option takes hostnames, single IP addresses, and CIDR address ranges; you can also use multiple dontblock entries, just as you can with accept.

To improve SnortSam's performance, you might want to use the skipinterval option, which lets you tell SnortSam how long to skip identical blocking requests before it resumes applying rules for that request. This ensures that SnortSam isn't constantly requesting the firewall to block the same IP address and port over and over again. The skipinterval option takes a single number as its argument, specifying how many seconds to wait.

You'll probably want to keep tabs on what SnortSam's doing, since you're allowing it to modify your firewall's rules. One way is to use the logfile option, which will cause SnortSam to log events such as program starts, blocking and unblocking requests, and any errors that were encountered. This option takes a single argument: the filename to which the logs will be written. The log file that you specify will be created in */var/log*.

A couple of other useful options are daemon and bindip. The daemon option simply tells SnortSam to fork into the background and run as a daemon; it does not take any arguments. The bindip option allows you to specify which IP address to listen on, which is useful when the machine that SnortSam is running on has multiple addresses available.

For instance, if you want SnortSam to listen on only 192.168.1.15, use a line like this:

```
bindip 192.168.1.15
```

You can also change the port that SnortSam listens on (898, by default) with the port option.

After you're done with SnortSam's options, you'll need to tell it what kind of firewall to communicate with and how to do it. For example, to use Snort-Sam with a Check Point firewall, you can specify either the fwexec or fwsam keywords. Use fwexec when you want to run SnortSam on the host that the firewall is installed on, and use fwsam when you want to communicate with a remote firewall. The fwexec keyword takes the full pathname to the *fw* executable as its only argument, whereas the fwsam keyword uses the hostname or IP address of the firewall.

In addition, you'll need to modify the *fwopsec.conf* file on your firewall to include the following line:

```
sam_server port 1813
```

To use *SnortSam* with a PIX firewall, you'll need to use the pix keyword and specify the IP address of the firewall as well as the telnet and enable mode passwords:

```
pix 192.16.1.2 telnetpw enablepw
```

Or, if your firewall is set up to do user authentication, you can use *user/ password* in place of the telnet password.

If you want to use SnortSam with OpenBSD's PF or Linux's *iptables*, you'll need to use the pf or iptables keywords. For basic usage, all you need to do is specify the interface on which to block packets.

To configure the Snort side of things, you'll need to add the alert_fwsam output plug-in to the output plug-ins that you're already using. This plug-in takes a hostname and an optional port to connect to, along with a password. If SnortSam is using the default port, you don't need to specify the port here:

```
output alert_fwsam: firewall/mypassword firewall2:1025/mypassword
```

Notice that you can list multiple instances of SnortSam to send block requests to by separating them with whitespace.

You should modify any rules that you want to trigger a firewall rule to use the fwsam rule option. This option takes as its arguments what to block, and how long the block should be in effect. To block the source of the packet that caused the alert, use src; to block the destination, use dst. If you want to block both, use either. For the duration, you can use a number along with a modifier specifying what unit it's in (i.e., seconds, minutes, hours, days, weeks, months, or years), or you can use 0 to specify an indefinite period of time.

For instance, to block the source address of the packet that triggered a rule for five minutes, you could add this to your rule options:

```
fwsam: src, 5 minutes;
```

Now that everything is configured, start SnortSam by running a command similar to this:

```
# snortsam /usr/local/etc/snortsam.conf
```

Of course, you'll need to substitute the full path to your configuration file if it's not *usr/local/etc/snortsam.conf*. As for Snort, just start it as you normally would.

See Also

- For more information on using SnortSam with other types of firewalls, be sure to check out the *README* files included with the source distribution

- "Prevent and Contain Intrusions with Snort_inline" [Hack #111] discusses installing *Snort_inline* on your firewall

HACK 113 Detect Anomalous Behavior

Detect attacks and intrusions by monitoring your network for abnormal traffic, regardless of the actual content.

Most NIDSs monitor the network for specific signatures of attacks and trigger alerts when one is spotted on the network. Another means of detecting intrusions is to generate a statistical baseline of the traffic on the network and flag any traffic that doesn't fit the statistical norms. One intrusion detection system of this type is the Statistical Packet Anomaly Detection Engine (SPADE).

SPADE is actually a modified version of Snort that extends its functionality into the realm of anomaly-based intrusion detection. The SPADE preprocessor uses Snort to monitor the network and constructs a probability table based on the traffic that it sees. It then uses this table to generate an anomaly score of between 0 and 1 for each packet (0 is definitely normal, and 1 is a definite anomaly).

Installing SPADE is easy. Just download the pre-patched source distribution, which includes the Snort and SPADE source code, unpack it, and change into the directory that it created. Now compile and install Snort [Hack #106] as you normally would.

Once you've done that, you'll need to configure Snort to use SPADE. You have two choices here: you can set it up to use only SPADE functionality or to use normal Snort functionality along with SPADE. For the former, you can use the *spade.conf* file located in the SPADE source distribution as a starting point.

Most of the defaults are fine. However, you will need to set the SPADEDIR variable to a place where Snort has read and write access:

```
var SPADEDIR /var/log/snort/spade
```

SPADE will keep various logs and checkpointing information here so that it does not lose its probability table whenever Snort is restarted.

It is also important that you tell SPADE what network is your *home* network. You can do this by using a line similar to this one in your configuration file:

```
preprocessor spade-homenet: 192.168.1.0/24
```

You can specify multiple networks by separating them with commas and enclosing the list in square brackets.

If you want to run Snort with SPADE and traditional Snort functionality, you can just include your *spade.conf* in your *snort.conf* with a line like this:

```
include spade.conf
```

Run Snort just as you did before. SPADE will now send its output to any of the output plug-ins that you have configured when it detects anomalous behavior. This is triggered when a given packet's anomaly score is in the range .8 to .9 (it depends on the type of packet). Any alerts generated by SPADE will be prefixed with Spade: and will include a description of the packet's deviant behavior and its anomaly score.

Automatically Update Snort's Rules
Keep your Snort rules up-to-date with Oinkmaster.

If you have only a handful of IDS sensors, keeping your Snort rules up-to-date is a fairly quick and easy process. However, as the number of sensors grows, it can become more difficult. Luckily, you can automatically update your Snort rules with *Oinkmaster (http://oinkmaster.sourceforge.net/news.shtml)*.

Oinkmaster is a Perl script that does much more than just download new Snort signatures. It will also modify the newly downloaded signatures according to rules that you specify or selectively disable them, which is useful when you've modified the standard Snort rules to fit your environment more closely or have disabled a rule that was reporting too many false positives.

To install Oinkmaster, simply download the source distribution and unpack it. Then, copy the *oinkmaster.pl* file from the directory that it created to some suitable place on your system. In addition, you'll need to copy the *oinkmaster.conf* file to either */etc* or */usr/local/etc*. The *oinkmaster.conf* file that comes with the source distribution is full of comments explaining all the minute options that you can configure.

Oinkmaster is most useful for when you want to update your rules but have a set of rules that you don't want enabled and that are already commented out in your current Snort rules. To have Oinkmaster automatically disable these rules, use the `disablesid` directive with the Snort rule IDs (separated by commas) that you want disabled when your rules are updated.

For instance, if you get a lot of ICMP unreachable datagrams on your network, you might have decided that you don't want to receive alerts when Snort detects this type of traffic and commented out the following rule in your *icmp.rules* file:

```
#alert icmp any any -> any any (msg:"ICMP Destination Unreachable
(Communication Administratively Prohibited)"; itype: 3; icode: 13; sid:485;
classtype:misc-activity; rev:2;)
```

This is only one rule, so it's easy to remember to go back and comment it out again after updating your rules, but this can become quite a chore when you've done the same thing with several dozen other rules. If you use Oinkmaster, putting the following line in your *oinkmaster.conf* file will disable the preceding rule after Oinkmaster has updated your rules with the newest ones available from Snort.org:

```
disablesid 485
```

Then, when you want to update your rules, run *oinkmaster.pl* and tell it where you'd like the updated rules to be placed:

```
# oinkmaster.pl -o /etc/snort/rules
/oinkmaster.pl -o /usr/local/etc/snort/rules
Loading /usr/local/etc/oinkmaster.conf
Downloading file from http://www.snort.org/pub-bin/downloads.cgi/Download/
comm_rules/Community-Rules-2.4.tar.gz... done.
Archive successfully downloaded, unpacking... done.
Downloading file from http://www.bleedingsnort.com/bleeding.rules.tar.gz...
done.
Archive successfully downloaded, unpacking... done.
Setting up rules structures... done.
Processing downloaded rules... disabled 0, enabled 0, modified 0, total=1912
Setting up rules structures... done.
Comparing new files to the old ones... done.
Updating local rules files... done.

[***] Results from Oinkmaster started 20060511 20:21:18 [***]

[*] Rules modifications: [*]
    None.

[*] Non-rule line modifications: [*]
    None.
```

[+] Added files (consider updating your snort.conf to include them if
needed): [+]

```
       -> bleeding-attack_response.rules
       -> bleeding-dos.rules
       -> bleeding-drop-BLOCK.rules
       -> bleeding-drop.rules
       -> bleeding-dshield-BLOCK.rules
       -> bleeding-dshield.rules
       -> bleeding-exploit.rules
       -> bleeding-game.rules
       -> bleeding-inappropriate.rules
       -> bleeding-malware.rules
       -> bleeding-p2p.rules
       -> bleeding-policy.rules
       -> bleeding-scan.rules
       -> bleeding-sid-msg.map
       -> bleeding-virus.rules
       -> bleeding-web.rules
       -> bleeding.conf
       -> bleeding.rules
       -> community-bot.rules
       -> community-dos.rules
       -> community-exploit.rules
       -> community-ftp.rules
       -> community-game.rules
       -> community-icmp.rules
       -> community-imap.rules
       -> community-inappropriate.rules
       -> community-mail-client.rules
       -> community-misc.rules
       -> community-nntp.rules
       -> community-oracle.rules
       -> community-sid-msg.map
       -> community-sip.rules
       -> community-smtp.rules
       -> community-sql-injection.rules
       -> community-virus.rules
       -> community-web-attacks.rules
       -> community-web-cgi.rules
       -> community-web-client.rules
       -> community-web-dos.rules
       -> community-web-iis.rules
       -> community-web-misc.rules
       -> community-web-php.rules
```

You've now updated the rules from BleedingSnort.com, a community site
used for disseminating Snort signatures, and the community rules maintained by Snort.org. If you also want to have Oinkmaster automatically
update Sourcefire VRT Certified Rules (see *http://www.snort.org/rules/*), you
can add a line like this to your *oinkmaster.conf* file:

```
url = http://www.snort.org/pub-bin/oinkmaster.cgi/ \
    5f6e64e16258a2f94dd7e7b0ef4e5c59cf4216a3/snortrules-snapshot-2.4.tar.gz
```

Replace the long substring that looks like an SHA1 hash with the code you received when registering for access to the rules.

Now, just add a crontab entry to run Oinkmaster regularly and to restart Snort when it's finished updating the rules, and you'll always be up-to-date on the most current Snort signatures. And, as a plus, you won't have to remember which rules to disable ever again.

HACK 115 Create a Distributed Stealth Sensor Network

Keep your IDS sensors safe from attack, while still giving yourself access to their data.

Your IDS sensors are the early warning system that can both alert you to an attack and provide needed evidence for investigating a break-in after one has occurred. You should take extra care to protect them and the data that they collect. One way to do this is to run your IDS sensors in *stealth mode*.

To do this, simply don't configure an IP address for the interface from which your IDS software will be collecting data:

```
# tcpdump -i eth1
tcpdump: bind: Network is down
# ifconfig eth1 up promisc
# ifconfig eth1
eth1      Link encap:Ethernet  HWaddr 00:DE:AD:BE:EF:00
          UP BROADCAST PROMISC MULTICAST  MTU:1500  Metric:1
          RX packets:0 errors:0 dropped:0 overruns:0 frame:0
          TX packets:0 errors:0 dropped:0 overruns:0 carrier:0
          collisions:0 txqueuelen:100
          RX bytes:0 (0.0 b)  TX bytes:0 (0.0 b)
          Interrupt:11 Base address:0x1c80

# /usr/sbin/tcpdump -i eth1
tcpdump: WARNING: eth1: no IPv4 address assigned
tcpdump: listening on eth1
```

After you've put up the interface, just start your IDS. It will run as normal, but since there is no way to directly access the machine, it will be very difficult to attack.

However, like any potential attackers, you will also be unable to access the machine remotely. Therefore, if you want to manage the sensor remotely, you'll need to put in a second network interface. Of course, if you did this and hooked it up to the same network that the IDS sensor was monitoring, it would totally defeat the purpose of running the other interface without an IP address. To keep the traffic isolated, you should create a separate network for managing the IDS sensors. Attach this network to one that is remotely accessible, and then firewall it heavily.

Another approach is to access the box using an alternate channel, such as a serial port connected to another machine that does have a network connection. Just run a console on the serial port, and take care to heavily secure the second machine. You could also connect a modem (remember those?) to an unlisted phone number or, better yet, an unlisted extension on your office's private branch exchange. Depending on your situation, simply using the console for access may be the simplest and most secure method.

Which method to use for remote access is a choice you'll have to make by weighing the value of increased security against the inconvenience of jumping through hoops to access the machine. Security nearly always involves a trade-off between convenience and confidence.

HACK 116 Use Snort in High-Performance Environments with Barnyard

Decouple Snort's output stage so it can keep pace with the packets.

By itself, Snort is fine for monitoring small networks or networks with low amounts of traffic, but it does not scale very well without some additional help. The problem is not with Snort's detection engine itself, but rather stems from the fact that Snort is a single-threaded application. Because of this, whenever an alert or log event is triggered, Snort must first send the alert or log entry to its final destination before it can go back to looking at the incoming data stream.

This isn't such a big deal if you're just having Snort write to a file, but it can become a problem if you are logging to a database because Snort will have to wait a relatively long time for the database insert to complete. This problem, of course, is exacerbated when you're having Snort log to a remote database server.

Barnyard (*http://www.snort.org/dl/barnyard/*) was written to solve this problem. Functionally, Barnyard is the equivalent of Snort's output plug-ins all rolled into one program, with a frontend for reading in files that Snort generates and then sending them to the same database or other destination that you would normally have Snort log to. The only draw back to Barnyard is its limited database support: Barnyard supports only MySQL and PostgreSQL, whereas Snort supports MySQL, PostgreSQL, Oracle, and ODBC outputs.

Installation

After downloading Barnyard and unpacking it, change to the directory it created and run its *configure* script:

```
$ ./configure --enable-mysql
```

This will enable MySQL support when Barnyard is compiled. If you've installed your MySQL libraries and include files in a nonstandard place (i.e., somewhere other than the the the */usr* or */usr/local* hierarchy), you'll probably need to add the `--with-mysql-includes` and `--with-mysql-libraries` command-line options. If you're using Postgres, you'll need to use `--enable-postgres`. Likewise, use `--with-postgres-includes` and `--with-postgres-libraries` to specify where Postgres's headers and libraries are located.

After you're done with the *configure* script, you can compile Barnyard by running make. When it finishes compiling, install it by becoming root and running make install.

Configuring Snort

Before you use Barnyard, you'll need to configure Snort to use its unified output format. This is a binary format that includes both the alert information and the data for the packet that triggered the alert, and it is the only type of input that Barnyard will understand.

To configure Snort to use the unified output format for both alert and log events, add lines similar to these to your Snort configuration (e.g., */etc/snort/snort.conf* or */usr/local/etc/snort/snort.conf*):

```
output alert_unified: filename snort.alert, limit 128
output log_unified: filename snort.log, limit 128
```

The filenames specified here are the basenames for the files to which Snort will write its alert and log event information. When it writes a file, it will append the current Unix timestamp to the end of the basename. These lines also specify that the size of these files will be limited to 128 MB.

Configuring Barnyard

Now, you'll need to create a configuration file for use with Barnyard. To run Barnyard in daemon mode and have it automatically fork itself into the background, add this line to your configuration file:

```
config daemon
```

If you're going to be logging to a database for use with BASE [Hack #107], you'll also want to add two lines similar to these:

```
config hostname: colossus
config interface: eth0
```

These two lines should be set to the name of the machine on which you're running Barnyard and the interface from which Snort is reading packets.

Note that Barnyard can process only one type of unified log at a time. So, if you want it to process both alert and log events, you'll need to run an instance of Barnyard for each type.

All that's left to configure is where Barnyard will send the data. If you want to use Snort's fast alert mode to generate single-line abbreviated alerts, use the alert_fast output plug-in:

```
output alert_fast: fast_alerts.log
```

Or, if you want Barnyard to generate ASCII packet dumps of the data contained in the unified logs, use a line like this:

```
output log_dump: ascii_dump.log
```

To have Barnyard output to your *syslog* daemon, you can use the alert_syslog plug-in just like you would in your *snort.conf*. For instance, if you want to send data to the local *syslogd* and use the auth facility and the alert log level, use a line like this:

```
output alert_syslog: LOG_AUTH LOG_ALERT
```

Or, if you want to send to a remote *syslog* daemon, use a line similar to this:

```
output alert_syslog: hostname=loghost, LOG_AUTH LOG_ALERT
```

You can also have Barnyard create Pcap-formatted files from the data in the unified logs. This is useful for analyzing the data later in tools such as Ethereal. To do this, use the log_pcap plug-in:

```
output log_pcap: alerts.pcap
```

Finally, you can also have Barnyard output to a database by using the alert_acid_db plug-in for logging alert events and the log_acid_db plug-in for capturing log events.

For instance, this line would send alerts to the *SNORT* MySQL database running on *dbserver* using the username *snort*:

```
output alert_acid_db: mysql, sensor_id 1, database SNORT, server dbserver, \
    user snort, password snortpw, detail full
```

The sensor_id is the one BASE assigned to the particular instance of Snort that is gathering the data. You can find what sensor ID to use by clicking on the Sensors link on BASE's front page [Hack #107], which will show you a list of the sensors that are currently logging to BASE.

The log_acid_db plug-in is similar:

```
output log_acid_db: mysql, sensor_id 1, database SNORT, server dbserver, \
    user snort, password snortpw, detail full
```

Testing Barnyard

You can start Barnyard by simply using a command similar to the following, if Snort's configuration files are stored in */etc/snort* and Snort is set to keep its logs in */var/log/snort*:

```
# barnyard -f snort.alert
```

You should then see new records in your database's events table.

Of course, this assumes that you used `snort.alert` when configuring Snort's `alert_unified` plug-in. If your Snort configuration files aren't stored in */etc/snort*, you can specify the locations of all the files that Barnyard needs to access by running a command similar to this one:

```
# barnyard -c /usr/local/etc/snort/barnyard.conf -f snort.alert
```

This tells Barnyard where to find all the files it needs if they are in */usr/local/etc/snort*, since it will automatically look for the *sid-msg.map* and *gen-msg.map* files in the same directory as the Barnyard configuration file. If you're using a directory other than */var/log/snort* to store Snort's logs, you can specify it with the `-d` option, and Barnyard will look for input files there.

Congratulations. With Barnyard running, you should be able to handle much larger volumes of traffic without dropping log entries or missing a single packet.

HACK 117 Detect and Prevent Web Application Intrusions

Protect your web server and dynamic content from intrusions.

Network intrusion detection systems are well suited to detecting intrusions that utilize common protocols and services, such as those used by web applications. However, due to the complexity of these applications and the variety of attacks they are vulnerable to, it can be difficult to detect and prevent intrusions without generating many false positives. This is especially true for web applications that use SSL, since this requires you to jump through hoops to enable the NIDS to actually get access to the unencrypted traffic coming to and from the web server.

One way to get around these issues is to integrate the intrusion detection system into the web server itself. This is just what mod_security (*http://www.modsecurity.org*) does for the popular Apache (*http://www.apache.org*) web server.

mod_security, as the name suggests, is a module for the Apache web server that is meant to increase its security by providing facilities for filtering requests and performing arbitrary actions based on user-specified rules. In addition, mod_security performs various sanity checks that normalize the requests that the web server receives. With the proper filtering rules, mod_security can defeat directory traversal, cross-site scripting, SQL injection, and buffer overflow attacks.

Installing mod_security

To install mod_security, download and unpack the source distribution. If you want to install it as a DSO (i.e., a module), you can do so easily with the *apxs* utility. First, change to the directory appropriate for the version of Apache that you are using: *apache1* or *apache2*. Then, run a command like this:

```
# apxs -cia mod_security.c
```

This compiles mod_security and configures Apache to load it at startup. If you want to statically compile mod_security, you will have to rebuild Apache. If you are using Apache 1.x, you can compile it statically by copying *mod_security.c* to the *src/modules/extra* directory in the Apache source tree. Then, when you run Apache's *configure* script, use these command-line switches:

```
--activate-module=src/modules/extra/mod_security
--enable-module=security
```

For Apache 2.x, copy *mod_security.c* from the *apache2* directory to the *modules/proxy* directory in the Apache 2.x source tree. Then, use these command-line switches when running the *configure* script:

```
--enable-security
--with-module=proxy:mod_security.c
```

Enabling and Configuring mod_security

Once you've installed mod_security, you'll need to enable it. You can do this by putting the following lines in your *httpd.conf* file:

```
<IfModule mod_security.c>
    SecFilterEngine On
</IfModule>
```

This enables the request normalization features of mod_security for all requests made to the web server. When mod_security is enabled, it intercepts all requests coming into the web server and performs several checks on them before passing the requests through any user-defined filters and finally either servicing or denying them.

During these sanity checks, mod_security converts several types of evasive character sequences to their more commonly used equivalent forms. For example, it transforms the character sequences // and /./ to /, and on

Windows, it converts the \ character to /. It also decodes any URL-encoded characters.

In addition to these checks, you can configure mod_security to scan the payload of POST method requests and to validate URL and Unicode encoding within requests. To enable these features, add these lines to your *httpd.conf*:

```
SecFilterScanPOST On
SecFilterCheckURLEncoding On
SecFilterCheckUnicodeEncoding On
```

URL encoding allows someone making a request to encode characters by using hexadecimal values, which use the numbers 0 through 9 and the letters A through F, prefixed by the % character. When URL-encoding validation is enabled, mod_security simply ensures that any URL-encoded characters don't violate the hexadecimal numbering system. Similarly, when performing Unicode validation, mod_security ensures that the string seen by the web server in fulfilling the request is a valid Unicode string. Unicode validation is useful if your web server is running on an operating system that supports Unicode or your web application makes use of it.

To avoid buffer overflow exploits, you can also limit the range of bytes that are allowed in request strings. For instance, to allow only printable characters (and not ones that might show up in exploit shell code), add a line like this to your *httpd.conf* file:

```
SecFilterForceByteRange 32 126
```

Creating Filters

You can create user-defined filters with either the SecFilter or the SecFilterSelective keyword. Use SecFilter to search just the query string, or use SecFilterSelective if you would like to filter requests based on the value of an internal web server variable. Both of these filtering keywords can accept regular expressions.

Let's look at a few filtering rules can help prevent some common attacks.

This rule filters out requests that contain the character sequence ../:

```
SecFilter "\.\./"
```

Even though the web server will interpret the ../ correctly and disallow access if it ends up resolving to something outside of its document root, that might not be the case for scripts or applications that are on your server. This rule prevents such requests from being processed.

Cross-site scripting (XSS) attacks are invoked by inserting HTML or JavaScript into an existing page so that other users will execute it. Such attacks can be used to read a user's session cookie and gain full control of that user's information. You can prevent these attacks by having mod_security filter out requests that contain JavaScript.

To disallow JavaScript in requests, use a rule like this:

```
SecFilter "<[[:space:]]*script"
```

However, there are many other ways in which JavaScript can be inserted into a request. It is safer to simply disallow HTML, which can be done by using this rule:

```
SecFilter "<.+>"
```

SQL injection attacks are similar to XSS attacks, except in this case attackers modify variables that are used for SQL queries in a way that enables them to execute arbitrary SQL commands.

This rule prevents SQL injection in a cookie called sessionid:

```
SecFilterSelective COOKIE_sessionid "!^(|[0-9]{1,9})$"
```

If a sessionid cookie is present, the request can proceed only if the cookie contains one to nine digits.

This rule requires HTTP_USER_AGENT and HTTP_HOST headers in every request:

```
SecFilterSelective "HTTP_USER_AGENT|HTTP_HOST" "^$"
```

You can search on multiple variables by separating each variable in the list with a | character. Attackers often investigate using simple tools (even telnet) and don't send all headers, as browsers do. Such requests can be rejected, logged, and monitored.

This rule rejects file uploads:

```
SecFilterSelective "HTTP_CONTENT_TYPE" multipart/form-data
```

This is a simple but effective protection, rejecting requests based on the content type used for file upload.

Again, manual requests frequently do not include all HTTP headers. This rule logs requests without an Accept header, so you can examine them later:

```
SecFilterSelective "HTTP_ACCEPT" "^$" log,pass
```

The Keep-Alive header is another good candidate. Notice that in addition to the variable and search string this rule contains the keywords log and pass, which specify the actions to take if a request matches the rule. In this case, any requests that match will be logged to Apache's error log, and then the request will go on for further processing by the web server. If you do not specify an action for a filter rule, the default action will be used.

You can specify the default action like this:

```
SecFilterDefaultAction "deny,log,status:500"
```

If you set this as the default action, the web server will deny all requests that match filter rules and that do not specify a custom action. These requests will be logged and then redirected to an HTTP 500 status page, which will inform the client that an internal server error occurred. Other possible actions include `allow`, which is similar to `pass` but stops other filters from being tried; `redirect`, which redirects the client to an arbitrary URL; `exec`, which executes an external binary or script; and `chain`, which allows you to effectively AND rules together.

In addition to filtering, `mod_security` provides extensive auditing features, allowing you to keep logs of all the requests sent to the server. To turn on audit logging, add lines similar to these to your *httpd.conf*:

```
SecAuditEngine On
SecAuditLog logs/audit_log
```

Bear in mind, though, that this option can generate quite a lot of data very quickly. To log only requests that trigger a filter rule, set the `SecAuditEngine` variable to `RelevantOnly`. Alternatively, you can set this variable to `DynamicOrRelevant`, which will log requests for dynamic content as well as requests that trigger a filter rule.

As with most other Apache configuration directives, you can enclose `mod_security` configuration directives within a `<Location>` tag to specify individual configurations for specific scripts or directory hierarchies.

For more examples of useful `mod_security` rules, be sure to look at *modsecurity-rules-current.tar.gz*, which is available from the `mod_security` download page and includes an extensive list of rules that can be included in your Apache configuration using the `Include` directive.

`mod_security` is a powerful tool for protecting your web applications, but it should not take the place of actually validating input in your application or other secure coding practices. If possible, it is best to use a tool such as `mod_security` in addition to employing such methods.

See Also

- "Introducing mod_security": *http://www.onlamp.com/pub/a/apache/2003/11/26/mod_security.html*
- Mod_security Reference Manual v1.7.4: *http://www.modsecurity.org/documentation/modsecurity-apache/1.9.3/modsecurity-manual.pdf*

Scan Network Traffic for Viruses

Use Snort and ClamAV to detect viruses as they cross your network.

Much focus in recent years has been given to email attachments as an avenue for viruses and worms to infiltrate a network. The Melissa and I Love You viruses are infamous examples. You can easily set up a system to scan your users' email for such things [Hack #74], but there are many more vectors for virus propagation, such as web pages, IRC, IM file transfers... there's really no limit. So, how do you scan for viruses and prevent them from propagating over those services?

One way is to modify Snort using the useful ClamAV [Hack #74] patch, which integrates the two packages. The patch adds a *clamav* preprocessor to Snort that monitors network traffic and uses the ClamAV engine to scan it for viruses. When ClamAV matches a virus definition, it generates a Snort alert. Even better, you can use this functionality with *Snort_inline* [Hack #111] to actually drop the traffic containing the viral payload before it can propagate.

Patching Snort

To get started, download the ClamAV patch (*http://www.bleedingsnort.com/cgi-bin/viewcvs.cgi/snort-clamav/?root=Snort-Clamav*) that's appropriate for the version of Snort you're using. Then, change to the directory into which you've unpacked the Snort source code and apply the patch:

```
$ cd snort-2.4.3
$ patch -p1 < ../snort-2.4.3-clamonly.diff
$ find . -name \*.rej
```

You'll then need to regenerate all of the files used by the build system. Do so by running the following command:

```
$ libtoolize -f && aclocal -I ./m4 && autoheader && automake && autoconf
```

Notice that there are a few more options for the *configure* script now:

```
$ ./configure --help | grep -i clam
  --enable-clamav          Enable the clamav preprocessor
  --with-clamav-includes=DIR  clamav include directory
  --with-clamav-defdir=DIR   clamav virusdefinitions directory
```

Run *configure* with all three of these options, in addition to any others that you want to use. If you've installed ClamAV in its default location, you'll want to use */usr/local/include* and */usr/local/share/clamav* for the --with-clamav-includes and --with-clamav-defdir options, respectively. After the *configure* script has finished, type make to start compiling.

Configuring the Preprocessor

Once the build has finished, install Snort as normal. Enable the *clamav* preprocessor by editing your Snort configuration file and adding a `preprocessor clamav` directive.

> Make sure you enable the *clamav* preprocessor *after* enabling the *stream4_reassemble* preprocessor in your configuration file; otherwise, the *clamav* preprocessor might miss some viral payloads that span multiple IP datagrams or arrive out of order. Also be sure to put it before the directive enabling the *http_inspect* preprocessor.

The *clamav* preprocessor has several options that you can use to specify which ports to scan for viral traffic, which direction of a TCP stream to scan, what to do in inline mode if a virus is found, and a few other miscellaneous things. To specify options, put a colon after the preprocessor name (e.g., `clamav:`) and list the options separated by commas. The examples shown here are complete `preprocessor` directives. When you edit your configuration file, you should combine all of the options you want to use into one `preprocessor clamav` line.

Ports to scan. By default, ClamAV scans only ports 21, 25, 80, 81, 110, 119, 139, 143, and 445 for viral payloads. To add ports, use the `ports` option followed by a space-delimited list of the ports to include. You can also exclude a port from being scanned by using the `!` operator. This is especially useful when you're using the `all` keyword, which specifies all ports for scanning.

For instance, you might want to scan all ports, except for some that usually carry encrypted traffic:

```
preprocessor clamav: ports all !22 !443 !993 !995
```

Direction to scan. For TCP streams, you can opt to scan traffic going to the client, to the server, or in either direction. By default ClamAV scans both directions, but if you want to scan only traffic going to clients, to lessen the load on your IDS, you can use the `toclientonly` option:

```
preprocessor clamav: toclientonly
```

Alternatively, if you feel that viruses being sent to your servers is a bigger issue, you can use the `toserveronly` option.

Blocking propagation. Determining when viruses are loose on your network is very different from being able to proactively block them. When using Snort in inline mode with the *clamav* preprocessor, it's possible to automatically stop a viral payload from reaching its destination. The only thing in question is which method to use. If you want Snort to silently drop any packets in which it detects a viral payload, use the action-drop option. If you want to perform a TCP reset instead, use the action-reset option:

```
preprocessor clamav: action-reset
```

Miscellaneous options. If the location of the virus definitions (specified when running *configure* with --with-clamav-defdir) has changed since you compiled Snort, you can use the dbdir option to specify the new location. The preprocessor also allows you to specify how often to reload the virus definitions with the dbreload-time option. This defaults to 600 seconds, but you'll probably want to change it to a longer time period (for example, 86400 seconds if you update your virus definitions once a day).

The following directive specifies */opt/clamav/share* as the directory to read virus definitions from and indicates that they should be reloaded once per day:

```
preprocessor clamav: dbdir /opt/clamav/share, dbreload-time 86400
```

To increase the preprocessor's reliability, you can use the file-descriptor-mode option, which causes it to write packet payloads to a file before scanning them. Otherwise, it holds them in memory when doing the scanning. When this option is enabled, the payloads are written to */tmp* by default. If you want to change this, use the descriptor-temp-dir option. The following directive tells Clam AV to write payloads to */var/tmp/clamav* before scanning them for viral content:

```
preprocessor clamav: file-descriptor-mode, descriptor-temp-dir /var/tmp/
clamav
```

Bear in mind, however, that the file-descriptor-mode option can reduce performance significantly, since the preprocessor is constantly writing to disk. To alleviate this problem, use a memory-based filesystem. For instance, in Linux you can create a 256MB filesystem that is backed by memory at */var/tmp/clamav* by running the following command:

```
# mount -t tmpfs tmpfs /var/tmp/clamav -o size=256M
```

Of course, you should make sure you have plenty of RAM to do this.

Similarly, under FreeBSD, you can add the following lines to */etc/rc.conf* to cause */tmp* to use the Virtual Memory Manager (VMM) for storage rather than a disk:

```
tmpmfs="YES"
tmpsize="256m"
```

After you've done that, reboot to let the change take effect.

Trying It Out

Once you've configured the preprocessor, start Snort as you normally would. If you didn't use the -q command-line option, which suppresses output, you should see some lines similar to these, signifying that the *clamav* preprocessor was loaded properly:

```
ClamAV config:
    Ports: 0 1 2 3 4 5 6 7 8 9 10 11 12 13 14 15 16 17 18 19 20 ...
    Virus definitions dir: '/usr/local/share/clamav'
    Virus DB reload time: '86400'
    Scan only traffic to the client
    File descriptor scanning mode: Enabled, using cl_scandesc
    Directory for tempfiles (file descriptor mode): '/tmp'
```

As a quick test, you can use Netcat (*http://www.vulnwatch.org/netcat/*) on another system to have it send one of the ClamAV test files to a system that is visible to your IDS sensor. Do so by running something like this on the server:

```
$ nc -l 65535 < clam.cab
```

Of course, make sure to use a port that you're actually monitoring for viruses. Then, use Netcat on the client system to connect to it. Once the client system connects and is sent the test file, you should see Snort generate an alert similar to this:

```
06/24-00:30:45.562228  [**] [125:1:1] (spp_clamav) Virus Found: ClamAV-Test-
File [**] {TCP} 192.168.0.62:65535 -> 192.168.0.40:65129
```

Now that you have it working, you can deploy the *clamav* preprocessor across all of your Snort sensors. Doing so will give you a heads-up on any viruses that might be propagating across your network and give you time to take action before any outbreaks get too serious.

Simulate a Network of Vulnerable Hosts

HACK #119

Use honeyd to fool would-be attackers into chasing ghosts.

As the saying goes, you'll attract more flies with honey than with vinegar. (I've never understood that saying; who wants to attract flies, anyway?) A *honeypot* is used to attract the "flies" of the Internet: script kiddies and hacker wannabes who have nothing better to do with their time than scan for vulnerable hosts and try to attack them. A honeypot does this by pretending to be a server running vulnerable services, while in fact collecting information about the attackers who think themselves so clever.

Whether you want to simulate one or one thousand vulnerable network hosts, *honeyd* (*http://www.honeyd.org*) makes the job as simple as editing a configuration file and running a daemon. The *honeyd* daemon can simulate thousands of hosts simultaneously and lets you configure what operating system each host will appear as when scanned with operating-system-detection tools such as Nmap [Hack #66].

Each system that *honeyd* simulates will appear to be a fully functioning node on the network. Besides simply creating hosts that respond to pings and traceroutes, *honeyd* also lets you configure what services each host appears to be running. You can either use simple scripts to emulate a given service or have *honeyd* act as a proxy and forward requests to another host for servicing.

Compiling honeyd

As a daemon that has extensive capabilities in mimicking other daemons, *honeyd* has several prerequisites you'll need to install before building the daemon itself:

- *libevent (http://www.monkey.org/~provos/libevent/)*
- *libdnet (http://libdnet.sourceforge.net)*
- *libpcap (http://www.tcpdump.org)*
- PCRE (*http://www.pcre.org*)
- Readline (*http://cnswww.cns.cwru.edu/php/chet/readline/rltop.html*)
- Zlib (*http://www.zlib.net*)
- Python (*http://www.python.org*)

libpcap, PCRE, Readline, Zlib, and Python should be available with most Linux and BSD flavors. You can easily install any of these prerequisites by downloading and unpacking them, running ./configure && make, and then running make install as root.

After you've installed the libraries, install *honeyd* the same way. Then, copy the service emulation scripts from the source distribution to somewhere more permanent (e.g., */usr/local/share/honeyd/scripts*). Only a few scripts come with *honeyd* itself, but additional service emulation scripts are available on *honeyd*'s contributions page (*http://www.honeyd.org/contrib.php*).

Configuring honeyd

Once you've installed *honeyd*, you'll need to create a configuration file that defines the types of operating systems and services *honeyd* will emulate and the IP addresses to which *honeyd* will respond. First, create some operating system templates:

```
### Windows computers
create windows-web
set windows-web personality "Microsoft Windows Millennium Edition (Me),
Windows 2000 Professional or Advanced Server, or Windows XP"
```

```
set windows-web  default tcp action reset
set windows-web default udp action reset
set windows-web default icmp action open
add windows-web tcp port 80 "perl scripts/win2k/iisemulator-0.95
/iisemul8.pl"
add windows-web tcp port 139 open
add windows-web tcp port 137 open
add windows-web tcp port 5900 "sh scripts/win2k/vnc.sh"
add windows-web udp port 137 open
add windows-web udp port 135 open

create windows-xchng
set windows-xchng personality "Microsoft Windows Millennium Edition (Me),
Windows 2000 Professional or Advanced Server, or Windows XP"
set windows-xchng default tcp action reset
set windows-xchng default udp action reset
set windows-xchng default icmp action open
add windows-xchng tcp port 25 "sh scripts/win2k/exchange-smtp.sh"
add windows-xchng tcp port 110 "sh scripts/win2k/exchange-pop3.sh"
add windows-xchng tcp port 119 "sh scripts/win2k/exchange-nntp.sh"
add windows-xchng tcp port 143 "sh scripts/win2k/exchange-imap.sh"
add windows-xchng tcp port 5900 "sh scripts/win2k/vnc.sh"
add windows-xchng tcp port 139 open
add windows-xchng tcp port 137 open
add windows-xchng udp port 137 open
add windows-xchng udp port 135 open

### Solaris
create sol-mail
set sol-mail personality "Sun Solaris 9"
set sol-mail default tcp action reset
set sol-mail default udp action reset
set sol-mail default icmp action open
add sol-mail tcp port 110 "sh scripts/pop3.sh"
add sol-mail tcp port 25 "sh scripts/smtp.pl"
add sol-mail tcp port 22 open
add sol-mail tcp port 143 open
add sol-mail tcp port 993 open
```

Then bind them to the IP addresses that you want to use:

```
bind 192.168.0.210 windows-web
bind 192.168.0.211 windows-xchng
bind 192.168.0.212 sol-mail
```

Save this configuration file in a good place (e.g., */usr/local/share/honeyd/honeyd.conf*).

Instead of configuring IP aliases on your NIC for each IP address listed in your configuration file, you can use *arpd* (*http://www.honeyd.org/tools.php*) to respond to the IP addresses. You can install *arpd* by running ./configure && make and then make install as root. However, if you're using a recent version of GCC, you might encounter the following error:

```
arpd.c: In function 'arpd_lookup':
arpd.c:285: error: syntax error before string constant
arpd.c:294: error: syntax error before string constant
arpd.c:297: error: syntax error before string constant
arpd.c: In function 'arpd_recv_cb':
arpd.c:426: error: syntax error before string constant
make: *** [arpd.o] Error 1
```

This is because, as of Version 3.4 of the compiler, it's no longer possible to concatenate __FUNCTION__ with other strings. To fix this problem, see *http://seclists.org/lists/honeypots/2005/Jul-Sep/0035.html* for a patch to *arpd.c*.

Running honeyd

After you have installed *arpd* and *honeyd*, you can start them:

```
# arpd 192.168.0.210-192.168.0.212
# cd /usr/local/share/honeyd
# honeyd -p nmap.prints -x xprobe2.conf -a nmap.assoc -0 pf.os -f honeyd.
conf
honeyd[5861]: started with -p nmap.prints -x xprobe2.conf -a nmap.assoc -0
pf.os -f
honeyd.conf
honeyd[5861]: listening on eth0: (arp or ip proto 47 or (ip )) and not ether
src
00:0c:29:e2:2b:c1
Honeyd starting as background process
```

The most recent version of *honeyd* now includes a built-in web server, which lets you view the current status of your honeynet as well as its configuration, as shown in Figure 11-13.

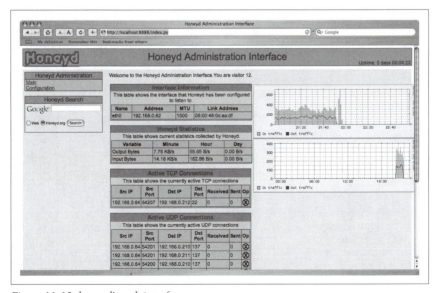

Figure 11-13. honeyd's web interface

The web interface allows you to view active TCP and UDP connections along with bandwidth statistics for your honeynet. In addition, you can view the settings for the different virtual hosts you have configured. If you don't want to use the web interface, you can use the --disable-webserver option when starting *honeyd*.

Testing honeyd

Now, try running Nmap on the IP addresses that *honeyd* is handling:

```
# nmap -sS -sU -O 192.168.0.210-212

Starting nmap 3.70 ( http://www.insecure.org/nmap/ ) at 2006-05-06 15:45 MDT
Interesting ports on 192.168.0.210:
(The 3132 ports scanned but not shown below are in state: closed)
PORT       STATE         SERVICE
80/tcp     open          http
135/udp    open|filtered msrpc
137/tcp    open          netbios-ns
137/udp    open|filtered netbios-ns
139/tcp    open          netbios-ssn
5900/tcp   open          vnc
MAC Address: 08:00:46:0C:AA:DF (Sony)
Device type: general purpose
Running: Microsoft Windows 95/98/ME|NT/2K/XP
OS details: Microsoft Windows Millennium Edition (Me), Windows 2000
Professional or Advanced Server, or Windows XP

Interesting ports on 192.168.0.211:
(The 3129 ports scanned but not shown below are in state: closed)
PORT       STATE         SERVICE
25/tcp     open          smtp
110/tcp    open          pop3
119/tcp    open          nntp
135/udp    open|filtered msrpc
137/tcp    open          netbios-ns
137/udp    open|filtered netbios-ns
139/tcp    open          netbios-ssn
143/tcp    open          imap
5900/tcp   open          vnc
MAC Address: 08:00:46:0C:AA:DF (Sony)
Device type: general purpose
Running: Microsoft Windows 95/98/ME|NT/2K/XP
OS details: Microsoft Windows Millennium Edition (Me), Windows 2000
Professional or Advanced Server, or Windows XP

Interesting ports on 192.168.0.212:
(The 3133 ports scanned but not shown below are in state: closed)
PORT    STATE SERVICE
22/tcp  open  ssh
25/tcp  open  smtp
```

```
110/tcp open   pop3
143/tcp open   imap
993/tcp open   imaps
MAC Address: 08:00:46:0C:AA:DF (Sony)
Device type: general purpose
Running: Sun Solaris 9
OS details: Sun Solaris 9
Uptime 0.080 days (since Sat May  6 13:50:40 2006)
```

You can certainly see that *honeyd* fools Nmap. You'll notice that the MAC address reported for each host is the same as the network interface of the host on which *honeyd* is being run, though, which is a dead giveaway that something fishy is going on. This can be fixed by assigning a MAC address to each of the host templates in the configuration file:

```
create sol-mail
set sol-mail personality "Sun Solaris 9"
set sol-mail ethernet "08:00:20:23:45:EE"
set sol-mail default tcp action reset
set sol-mail default udp action reset
set sol-mail default icmp action open
add sol-mail tcp port 110 "sh scripts/pop3.sh"
add sol-mail tcp port 25 "sh scripts/smtp.pl"
add sol-mail tcp port 22 open
add sol-mail tcp port 143 open
add sol-mail tcp port 993 open
```

Now, run Nmap again:

```
# nmap -sS -sU -O 192.168.0.212

Starting nmap 3.70 ( http://www.insecure.org/nmap/ ) at 2006-05-06 15:52 MDT
Interesting ports on 192.168.0.212:
(The 3133 ports scanned but not shown below are in state: closed)
PORT    STATE SERVICE
22/tcp  open  ssh
25/tcp  open  smtp
110/tcp open  pop3
143/tcp open  imap
993/tcp open  imaps
MAC Address: 08:00:20:F9:6A:F3 (SUN Microsystems)
Device type: general purpose
Running: Sun Solaris 9
OS details: Sun Solaris 9
Uptime 0.023 days (since Sat May  6 15:18:57 2006)

Nmap run completed -- 1 IP address (1 host up) scanned in 7.394 seconds
```

One thing to note is that if you specify a MAC address for a host template, you do not need to have *arpd* answering ARP requests for the IP address associated with it. *honeyd* will handle this for you.

Simulate a Network of Vulnerable Hosts

Everything has appeared to be realistic so far, but what happens when you try to access one of the services that are purportedly running? Try connecting to port 25 of the fake Windows mail server:

```
$ telnet 192.168.0.211 25
Trying 192.168.0.11...
Connected to 192.168.0.11.
Escape character is '^]'.
220 bps-pc9.local.mynet Microsoft ESMTP MAIL Service, Version: 5.0.2195.5329
ready at
Mon Jan 12 12:55:04 MST 2004
EHLO kryten
250-bps-pc9.local.mynet Hello [kryten]
250-TURN
250-ATRN
250-SIZE
250-ETRN
250-PIPELINING
250-DSN
250-ENHANCEDSTATUSCODES
250-8bitmime
250-BINARYMIME
250-CHUNKING
250-VRᴦY
250-X-EXPS GSSAPI NTLM LOGIN
250-X-EXPS=LOGIN
250-AUTH GSSAPI NTLM LOGIN
250-AUTH=LOGIN
250-X-LINK2STATE
250-XEXCH50}
250 OK
```

Pretty effective at first glance, isn't it? If you'd like to specify some real services for attackers to play with, you can use the proxy keyword to forward any port to a port on another machine. For example, the following line will forward SSH requests from our imaginary Linux host to the machine at 192.168.0.100:

```
add linux tcp port 22 proxy 192.168.0.100:22
```

Proxying works especially well when utilizing honeypots created from full-blown systems. This enables you to create a handful of dedicated honeypot machines and then set up *honeyd* to act as a frontend to them. The end result is that you appear to have more vulnerable systems than you actually have, and you can monitor any intruder's activities in more detail in the richer user environment.

In addition to running the service emulation scripts, *honeyd* can limit inbound or outbound bandwidth, or even slow down access to a particular service. This can be used to tie up spammers' resources, by holding open an apparently open mail relay. The possibilities provided by *honeyd* are limited only by your imagination and the time you're willing to spend building your virtual fly-catching network.

Record Honeypot Activity

Keep track of everything that happens on your honeypot.

Once an attacker has fallen prey to your honeypot and gained access to it, it is critical that you monitor all activity on that machine. By monitoring every tiny bit of activity on your honeypot, you can not only learn the intentions of your uninvited guest, but often also learn about new techniques for compromising a system as the intruder tries to gain further access. Besides, if you're not interested in what attackers are trying to do, why run a honeypot at all?

One of the most effective methods for tracking every packet and keystroke is to use a kernel-based monitoring tool. This way, you can monitor nearly everything that attackers do on your honeypot, even if they use encryption to protect their data or network connections. One powerful package for monitoring a honeypot at the kernel level is *Sebek* (*http://www.honeynet.org/tools/sebek/*).

Sebek is a loadable kernel module for the Linux, Solaris, BSD, and Windows operating systems that intercepts key system calls in the kernel and monitors them for interesting information. It then transmits the data to a listening server, hiding the presence of the transmissions from the local system.

Installing the Linux Client

To build the kernel modules on Linux, first make sure that the *build* directory within your *modules* directory points to the source code of the kernel for which you want to compile the modules:

```
$ ls -lad /lib/modules/2.6.16/build
lrwxrwxrwx  1 root root 47 Apr 10 22:55 /lib/modules/2.6.16/build -> ../../.
./usr/src/linux-2.6.16
```

Then, run the usual ./configure command. Alternatively, you can build Sebek for another version of the kernel by adding the --with-kernel-dir switch and specifying a directory containing the kernel source code:

```
$ ./configure --with-kernel-dir=/usr/src/linux-2.6.11
```

Note, however, that if you specify an alternative version of the kernel, you'll need to have the kernel source at the specified location configured and set up. Run the following commands from within the directory containing the kernel source to do this:

```
$ make oldconfig
$ make prepare
```

Now that all of that is out of the way, run ./configure and then make. The latter will generate a tarball containing the kernel modules and an installer script. Copy this archive to your honeypot to complete the installation.

Here's what's inside:

```
$ tar tfz sebek-lin26-3.1.2b-bin.tar.gz
sebek-lin26-3.1.2b-bin/
sebek-lin26-3.1.2b-bin/parameters.sh
sebek-lin26-3.1.2b-bin/sbk_install.sh
sebek-lin26-3.1.2b-bin/README
sebek-lin26-3.1.2b-bin/sbk.ko
```

Before installing the modules on your honeypot, you'll need to edit the *sbk_install.sh* script and modify three variables that tell *sebek.ko* where to send the information that it collects: DESTINATION_MAC, DESTINATION_IP, and DESTINATION_PORT. These should all be set to point to the Sebek server that you will build in a moment. If the server is on a different subnet, set DESTINATION_MAC to your router's MAC address.

Additionally, you can optionally configure the source port that Sebek uses by setting SOURCE_PORT. Make sure to use the same DESTINATION_PORT for all honeypots that you'll be operating. You'll also need to set INTERFACE to the interface that should be used to send data to DESTINATION_IP.

Set the MAGIC_VAL variable to the same value on all your honeypots. This variable, in conjunction with DESTINATION_PORT, hides traffic from other honeypots you are operating.

If you want Sebek to collect only keystrokes from your honeypot, you can set the KEYSTROKE_ONLY variable to 1. The SOCKET_TRACKING and WRITE_TRACKING variables also control what Sebek records. If the former is set to 1, Sebek will collect information on socket usage. If the latter is enabled, Sebek will track all write operations. This can be quite a lot of activity, so it's recommended that you leave this variable at its default setting: -- disabled.

Once you're satisfied with your configuration, set the TESTING variable to 0. This will cause Sebek to hide itself once it's loaded into the kernel.

Now, run the install script on your honeypot:

```
# ./sbk_install.sh
Installing Sebek:
  358887816.o installed successfully
```

The *358887816.o* file contains the contents of *sebek.ko*. The new filename is randomly generated at compile-time in order to obscure its presence from intruders, who might try to detect its presence by examining kernel memory directly. Alternatively, you can set the MODULE_NAME variable in *sbk_install.sh* to a name of your choosing. Once Sebek is installed, be sure to remove the archive and installation files. The presence of these files on a system is a pretty clear indication that it is a honeypot and could tip off intruders.

Setting Up the Server

There are two ways to collect the data from a system running Sebek. The simplest is to run the Sebek server, which will sniff for the information and automatically extract it for you. If you prefer to collect the data manually, you can use a sniffer and later use Sebek's data extraction utility to pull the information out of your packet dumps.

To install the server, download the source distribution from the project page, unpack it, and go into the directory that it created. Then, run this command:

```
$ ./configure && make
```

After compilation has finished, become root and run make install. This will install *sbk_extract*, *sbk_ks_log.pl*, and *sbk_upload.pl*. To extract information sent from a honeypot, use *sbk_extract*. You can run it in sniffer mode by using the -i and -p options to specify which interface to listen on and which destination port to look for, respectively.

If you want to process packets that have already been captured using a packet capture tool, use the -f option to specify the location of the packet dump file. *sbk_extract* also gives the option of running in a chroot( ) jail: simply use the -c option and specify a directory to chroot( ) to. It's recommended that you do this when collecting data in the wild because of the chance (however remote it may be) that an intruder could exploit an unknown vulnerability in *sbk_extract* by sending specially crafted data.

Once you've extracted the data, you can use *sbk_ks_log.pl* to display the attacker's keystrokes. It's also possible to monitor keystrokes in real time, by piping the output of *sbk_extract* into *sbk_ks_log.pl*:

```
# ./sbk_extract -c /var/empty -i eth0 -p 65000 | ./sbk_ks_log.pl
 monitoring eth0: looking for UDP dst port 65000
192.168.0.43 2006/05/04 05:12:48  record 362 recieved 1 lost 0 (0.00
percent)
[2006-05-04 01:38:48 Host:192.168.0.43 UID:0 PID:9958 FD:0 INO:4 COM:bash
]#cat /etc/shadow
192.168.0.43 2006/05/04 05:13:50  record 539 recieved 177 lost 0 (0.00
percent)
```

Installing the Windows Client

Installing the Sebek client under Windows is much more straightforward, especially when using the precompiled binaries (*http://www.savidtech.com/ sebek/latest/*), which walk you through the installation process via wizards.

After you've downloaded and unpacked the *.zip* archive, run the included *Setup.exe* program, which installs *Sebek.sys*. By default, the wizard will install it into *C:\Windows\system32\drivers*, but the wizard allows you to change this location.

Once *Sebek.sys* has been installed, you can configure it by launching *Configuration Wizard.exe*. Here, you can specify all of the parameters that were specified in *sbk_install.sh* (see "Installing the Linux Client"). In the first step of this process, you'll need to tell the wizard where you installed *Sebek. sys*. Then, click the Next button to bring up the dialog shown in Figure 11-14.

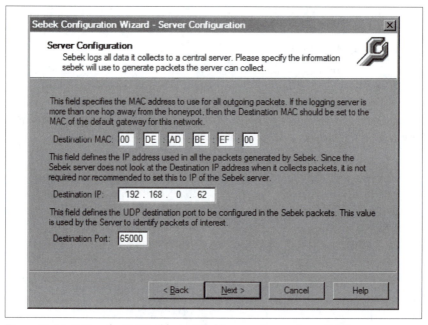

Figure 11-14. Setting the MAC address, IP address, and port of your Sebek server

The fields in Figure 11-14 correspond to the DESTINATION_MAC, DESTINATION_ IP, and DESTINATION_PORT variables in *sbk_install.sh*. In the next step, you'll need to input a magic value. The configuration wizard thoughtfully includes the ability to randomly generate this number for you; simply click the Random Value button, as shown in Figure 11-15.

After you've done that, click Next and select the network adapter that will be used to send data to your Sebek server.

So far, the entire configuration process has pretty much corresponded with variables used in setting up Sebek under Linux. The only difference is the next screen, shown in Figure 11-16.

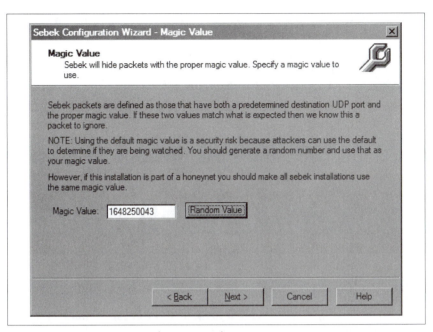

Figure 11-15. Generating a random magic value

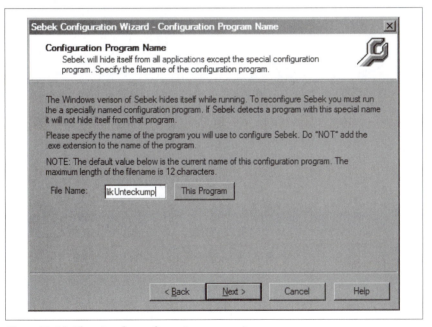

Figure 11-16. Choosing the configuration program's name

What if you want to reconfigure Sebek at some point? You can run the configuration wizard again, but what's to stop intruders from using it to disable Sebek after they've compromised the system? This screen helps you to make it a lot harder for someone to do that by allowing only programs with a certain name to alter Sebek's configuration. By default, this name is the first 12 characters of the filename you used to launch the current instance of the configuration wizard (e.g., *Configuration*, if you didn't rename it). At this point, it's best to use a random password generator to generate a filename. Then, rename *Configuration Wizard.exe* to the randomly generated name and keep it in a safe place (i.e., not on a system running Sebek).

After you've done this, click Next, and you're finished. After you reboot the system, it will begin sending data to your Sebek server.

Sebek also has an optional web interface called Walleye, which allows you to analyze the collected data easily. In addition to logged keystrokes, the web interface can extract files that have been uploaded to the honeypot. Walleye is part of the Roo Honeywall CD-ROM distribution, a hardened Fedora Core 3-based Linux distribution designed with honeynet data collection and analysis in mind. More information about it can be found at *http://www.honeynet.org/tools/cdrom/*.

## CHAPTER TWELVE

Recovery and Response
Hacks 121–125

Incident recovery and response is a broad topic, and there are many opinions on the proper methods to use and actions to take once an intrusion has been discovered. Just as the debate rages on regarding *vi* versus *emacs*, Linux versus Windows, and BSD versus everything else, there is much debate in the computer forensics crowd on the "clean shutdown" versus "pull the plug" argument. Whole books have been written on recovering from and responding to incidents. There are many things to consider when doing so, and the procedures you should use are far from well defined.

With this in mind, this chapter is not meant to be a guide on what to do when you first discover an incident, but it does show you how to perform tasks that you might decide to undertake in the event of a successful intrusion. By reading this chapter, you will learn how to properly create a filesystem image to use for forensic investigation of an incident, methods for verifying that files on your system haven't been tampered with, and some ideas on how to quickly track down the owner of an IP address.

HACK
121

Image Mounted Filesystems
Make a bit-for-bit copy of your system's disk for forensic analysis.

Before you format and reinstall the operating system on a recently compromised machine, you should take the time to make duplicates of all the data stored on the system. Having an exact copy of the contents of the system is not only invaluable for investigating a break-in, but might also be necessary for pursuing any future legal actions. Before you begin, you should make sure that your *md5sum*, *dd*, and *fdisk* binaries are not compromised.

But hang on a second. Once you start wondering about the integrity of your system, where do you stop? Hidden processes could be running, waiting for the root user to log in on the console and ready to remove all evidence of the break-in. Likewise, there could be scripts installed to run at shutdown to clean up log entries and delete any incriminating files.

Once you've determined that it is likely that a machine has been compromised, you might want to simply power down the machine (yes, just switch it off!) and boot from alternate media, such as a Knoppix boot CD (*http://www.knoppix.org*) or another hard drive that has a known good copy of the operating system. That way, you can be absolutely sure that you are starting the system from a known state, eliminating the possibility of hidden processes that could taint your data before you can copy it.

The downside to this procedure is that it will destroy any evidence of running programs or data stored on a RAM disk. However, chances are good that the intruder has installed other backdoors that will survive a reboot, and these changes will most certainly be saved to the disk.

To make a bit-for-bit copy of your disk, use the dd command. But first, generate a checksum for the disk so that you can check your copy against the disk contents, to ensure that it is indeed an exact copy.

To generate a checksum for the partition you want to image (in this example, the second partition of the first IDE disk on a Linux system), run this command:

```
# md5sum /dev/hda2 > /tmp/hda2.md5
```

It's wise to use other types of hashes as well, such as SHA1 or RMD160, if you have commands to generate them. You can usually do this with the sha1sum and rmd160 commands.

Now that that's out of the way, it's time to make an image of the disk:

```
# dd if=/dev/hda of=/tmp/hda.img
```

Note that you will need enough space in */tmp* to hold a copy of the entire */dev/hda* hard drive. This means that */tmp* shouldn't be a RAM disk and should not be stored on */dev/hda*. Write it to another hard disk altogether.

Why do you want to image the whole disk? If you image just a partition, it is not an exact copy of what is on the disk. An attacker could store information outside of the partition, and this information wouldn't be copied if you just imaged the partition itself. In any case, you can always reconstruct a partition image as long as you have an image of the entire disk.

To create separate partition images, though, you'll need some more information. Run fdisk to get the offsets and sizes for each partition in sectors. To get the sectors offsets for the partition, run this command:

```
# fdisk -l -u /dev/hda
Disk /dev/hda: 4294 MB, 4294967296 bytes
```

```
255 heads, 63 sectors/track, 522 cylinders, total 8388608 sectors
Units = sectors of 1 * 512 = 512 bytes

   Device Boot    Start       End   Blocks  Id  System
/dev/hda1    *       63    208844   104391  83  Linux
/dev/hda2         208845   7341704  3566430 83  Linux
/dev/hda3        7341705   8385929  522112+ 82  Linux swap
```

Be sure to save this information for future reference.

Now, create an image file for the second partition:

```
# dd if=hda.img of=hda2.img bs=512 skip=208845 count=$[7341704-208845]
7132859+0 records in
7132859+0 records out
```

Note that the count parameter does some shell math for you: the size of the partition is the location of the last block (7341704) minus the location of the first block (208845). Be sure that the bs parameter matches the block size reported by fdisk (usually 512, but it's best to check it when you run fdisk).

Finally, generate a checksum of the image file and then compare it against the original one you created:

```
# md5sum hda2.img > /tmp/hda2.img.md5 && diff /tmp/hda2.md5 /tmp/hda2.img.md5
```

The checksum for the image matches that of the actual partition exactly, so you know you have a good copy. Now, you can rebuild the original machine and look through the contents of the copy at your leisure.

HACK 122 Verify File Integrity and Find Compromised Files

Use Tripwire to alert you to compromised files or verify file integrity in the event of a compromise.

One tool that can help you detect intrusions on a host and also ascertain what happened after the fact is *Tripwire* (*http://sourceforge.net/projects/tripwire*). Tripwire is part of a class of tools known as *file integrity checkers*, which can detect the presence of important changed files on your systems. This is desirable because intruders who have gained access to a system often install what's known as a rootkit [Hack #124], in an attempt to both cover their tracks and maintain access to the system.

A rootkit usually accomplishes these goals by modifying key operating system utilities such as *ps*, *ls*, and other programs that could give away the presence of a backdoor program. This usually means that the rootkit patches these programs to not report that a certain process is active or that certain files exist on the system. Attackers might also modify the system's MD5 checksum program (e.g., *md5* or *md5sum*) to report correct checksums for all the binaries that they have replaced. Since using MD5 checksums is usually one of the primary ways to verify whether a file has been modified, it should be clear that another measure is sorely needed.

This is where Tripwire comes in handy. It stores a snapshot of your files in a known state, so you can periodically compare the files against the snapshot to discover discrepancies. With this snapshot, Tripwire can track changes in a file's size, inode number, permissions, or other attributes, such as the file's contents. To top it all off, Tripwire encrypts and signs its own files, so it can detect if it has been compromised itself.

Tripwire is driven by two main components: a *policy* and a *database*. The policy lists all the files and directories that Tripwire should snapshot, along with rules for identifying violations (i.e., unexpected changes). For example, a simple policy might treat any changes in */root*, */sbin*, */bin*, and */lib* as violations. The Tripwire database contains the snapshot itself, created by evaluating the policy against your filesystems. Once setup is complete, you can compare filesystems against the snapshot at any time, and Tripwire will report any discrepancies.

Along with the policy and database, Tripwire has configuration settings, stored in a file that controls global aspects of its behavior. For example, the configuration specifies the locations of the database, policy file, and *tripwire* executable.

Tripwire uses two cryptographic keys to protect its files. The *site key* protects the policy file and the configuration file, and the *local key* protects the database and generated reports. Multiple machines with the same policy and configuration can share a site key, but each machine must have its own local key for its database and reports.

One caveat with Tripwire is that its batch-oriented method of integrity checking gives intruders a window of opportunity to modify a file after it has been legitimately modified and before the next integrity check has been run. Tripwire flags the modified file, but you'll probably expect that (because you know that the file has been modified) and dismiss the flag as indicating a legitimate change to the file. For this reason, it is best to update your Tripwire snapshot as often as possible. Failing that, you should note the exact time that you modify any file that is being monitored, so you can compare it with the modification time that Tripwire reports.

Building and Installing Tripwire

Tripwire is available with the latest versions of Fedora and as a port on FreeBSD. If you're not running either of those, you'll need to compile it from source. To compile Tripwire, download the source package and unpack it. Next, check whether you have a symbolic link from *usr/bin/ gmake* to */usr/bin/make*. If you don't have such a link, create one.

> Operating systems outside the world of Linux don't always come with GNU make, so Tripwire explicitly looks for gmake, but this is simply called make on most Linux systems.

Another thing to check for is a full set of subdirectories in */usr/share/man*. Tripwire will need to place manpages in *man4*, *man5*, and *man8*. On systems where these are missing, the installer will create files named after those directories, rather than creating directories and placing the appropriate files within them. For instance, the installer will create a file called */usr/man/ man4* instead of a directory of the same name containing the appropriate manual pages.

Change your working directory to the Tripwire source's root directory (e.g., *./tripwire-2.3.1-2*), and read the *README* and *INSTALL* files. Both are brief but important.

Finally, change to the source tree's *src* directory (e.g., *./tripwire-2.3.1-2/src*) and make any necessary changes to the variable definitions in *src/Makefile*. Be sure to verify that the appropriate SYSPRE definition is uncommented (SYSPRE = i686-pc-linux, SYSPRE = sparc-linux, etc.).

Now, you're ready to compile. While still in Tripwire's *src* directory, enter this command:

```
$ make release
```

After compilation has finished, run these commands:

```
$ cd ..
$ cp ./install/install.cfg .
$ cp ./intall/install.sh
```

Open *install.cfg* in your favorite text editor to fine-tune the configuration variables. While the default paths are probably fine, you should at the very least examine the Mail Options section, which is where you initially tell Tripwire how to route its logs. Note that you can change these settings later.

If you set TWMAILMETHOD=SENDMAIL and specify a value for TWMAILPROGRAM, Tripwire will use the specified local mailer (*sendmail* by default) to deliver its reports to a local user or group. If instead you set TWMAILMETHOD=SMTP and specify values for TWSMTPHOST and TWSMTPPORT, Tripwire will mail its reports to an external email address via the specified SMTP server and port.

Once you are done editing *install.cfg*, it's time to install Tripwire. While still in the root directory of the Tripwire source distribution, enter the following command:

```
# sh ./install.sh
```

You will be prompted for site and local passwords: the site password protects Tripwire's configuration and policy files, whereas the local password protects Tripwire's databases and reports. This allows the use of a single policy across multiple hosts, to centralize control of Tripwire policies but distribute responsibility for database management and report generation.

If you do not plan to use Tripwire across multiple hosts with shared policies, there's nothing wrong with setting the site and local Tripwire passwords on a given system to the same string. In either case, choose a strong passphrase that contains some combination of upper- and lowercase letters, punctuation (which can include whitespace), and numerals.

Configuring Tripwire

Installing Tripwire (whether via binary package or source build) creates a default configuration file: */etc/tripwire/tw.cfg*. You can't edit this file because it's an encrypted binary, but for your convenience, a clear-text version of it, *twcfg.txt*, should also reside in */etc/tripwire*. If it does not, you can create the text version with this command:

```
# twadmin --print-cfgfile > /etc/tripwire/twcfg.txt
```

You can edit this file to make changes to the settings you used when installing Tripwire, and you can change the location where Tripwire will look for its database by setting the DBFILE variable. One interesting use of this variable is to set it to a directory within the */mnt* directory hierarchy. Then, after the database has been created you can copy it to a CD-ROM and remount it there whenever you need to perform integrity checks.

After you are done editing the configuration file, encrypt it again by running this command:

```
# twadmin --create-cfgfile --site-keyfile ./site.key twcfg.txt
```

You should also remove the *twcfg.txt* file.

You can then initialize Tripwire's database by running this command:

```
# tripwire --init
```

Since this uses the default policy file that Tripwire installed, you will probably see errors related to files and directories not being found. These errors are nonfatal, and the database will finish initializing. If you want to get rid of these errors, you can edit the policy and remove the files that were reported as missing.

First, you'll need to decrypt the policy file into an editable plain-text format:

```
# twadmin --print-polfile > twpol.txt
```

Then, comment out any files that were reported as missing. You should also look through the file and determine whether any files that you would like to catalog are absent. For instance, you will probably want to monitor all SUID files on your system [Hack #2]. Tripwire's policy-file language can allow for far more complex constructs than simply listing one file per line; read the twpolicy(4) manpage for more information if you'd like to use some of these features.

After you've updated your policy, you'll also need to update Tripwire's database:

```
# tripwire --update-policy twpol.txt
```

Day-to-Day Use

To perform checks against your database, run this command:

```
# tripwire --check
```

This prints a report to the screen and leaves a copy of it in */var/lib/tripwire/report*. If you want Tripwire to automatically email the report to the configured recipients, add --email-report to the end of the command. You can view the reports by running twprint:

```
# twprint --print-report --twrfile \
/var/lib/tripwire/report/colossus-20040102-205528.twr
```

Finally, to reconcile changes that Tripwire reports with its database, you can run a command similar to this one:

```
# tripwire --update --twrfile \
/var/lib/tripwire/report/colossus-20040102-205528.twr
```

You can and should schedule Tripwire to run its checks as regularly as possible. In addition to keeping your database in a safe place, such as on a CD-ROM, you'll want to make backup copies of your configuration, policy, and keys. Otherwise, you will not be able to perform an integrity check in the event that someone (malicious or not) deletes them.

See Also

- twpolicy(4)
- The section "Using Tripwire" in *Linux Server Security*, Second Edition, by Michael D. Bauer (O'Reilly)

Find Compromised Packages

123

Verify operating system managed files with your system's package management system.

So, you've had a compromise and you need to figure out which files (if any) the intruder modified, but you didn't install Tripwire? Well, all is not lost if your distribution uses a package management system.

While not as powerful as Tripwire, package management systems can be useful for finding to what degree a system has been compromised. They usually keep MD5 signatures for all the files the package has installed. You can use this functionality to check the packages on a system against its signature database.

Using RPM

To verify a single package on a system that uses RPM, run this command:

```
# rpm -V package
```

If the intruder modified any binaries, it's likely that the ps command was one of them. Use these commands to check its signature:

```
# which ps
/bin/ps
# rpm -V `rpm -qf /bin/ps`
S.5....T    /bin/ps
```

Here, the S, 5, and T show us that the file's size, checksum, and modification time have changed since it was installed—not good at all. Note that only files that do not match the information contained in the package database will result in output.

To verify all packages on the system, use the usual rpm option that specifies all packages, -a:

```
# rpm -Va
S.5....T    /bin/ps
S.5....T c /etc/pam.d/system-auth
S.5....T c /etc/security/access.conf
S.5....T c /etc/pam.d/login
S.5....T c /etc/rc.d/rc.local
S.5....T c /etc/sysconfig/pcmcia
.......T c /etc/libuser.conf
S.5....T c /etc/ldap.conf
.......T c /etc/mail/sendmail.cf
S.5....T c /etc/sysconfig/rhn/up2date-uuid
.......T c /etc/yp.conf
S.5....T   /usr/bin/md5sum
.......T c /etc/krb5.conf
```

There are other options you can use to limit what gets checked on each file. Some of the more useful ones are -nouser, -nogroup, -nomtime, and -nomode, which can eliminate a lot of the output that results from configuration files that you've modified.

Note that you'll probably want to redirect the output to a file, unless you narrow down what gets checked by using the command-line options. Running rpm -Va without any options can result in quite a lot of output from modified configuration files and such.

This is all well and good, but it ignores the possibility that an intruder has compromised key system binaries and might have compromised the RPM database as well. If this is the case, you can still use RPM, but you'll need to obtain the file the package was installed from in order to verify the installed files against it.

The worst-case scenario is that the *rpm* binary itself has been compromised. It can be difficult to be certain of this unless you boot from alternate media, as mentioned in "Image Mounted Filesystems" [Hack #121]. If this is the case, you should locate a safe *rpm* binary to use for verifying the packages.

First, find the name of the package that owns the file:

```
# rpm -qf filename
```

Then, locate that package from your distribution media, or download it from the Internet. After doing so, verify the installed files against what's in the package using this command:

```
# rpm -Vp package file
```

Using Other Package Managers

Under systems that use Debian's packaging system, you can use the debsums command to achieve mostly the same results. Run this to verify all packages installed on the system:

```
# debsums -ac
```

Or, if you want to verify them against packages stored on distribution media, you can use the following command instead:

```
# debsums -cagp path_to_packages
```

Under FreeBSD, you can use the -g option with pkg_info to verify the checksums of files that have been installed via a package:

```
$ pkg_info -g jpeg-6b_1
Information for jpeg-6b_1:

Mismatched Checksums:
```

```
/usr/local/bin/cjpeg fails the original MD5 checksum
/usr/local/bin/djpeg fails the original MD5 checksum
/usr/local/bin/jpegtran fails the original MD5 checksum
/usr/local/bin/rdjpgcom fails the original MD5 checksum
/usr/local/bin/wrjpgcom fails the original MD5 checksum
/usr/local/lib/libjpeg.a fails the original MD5 checksum
/usr/local/lib/libjpeg.so.9 fails the original MD5 checksum
```

To do this for all packages, run a command like this:

```
$ pkg_info -g `pkg_info | awk '{print $1}'`
```

Package managers can be used for quite a number of useful things, including verifying the integrity of system binaries. However, you shouldn't rely on them for this purpose. If possible, you should use a tool such as Tripwire [Hack #122] or AIDE (*http://sourceforge.net/projects/aide*).

HACK 124   Scan for Rootkits
Use chkrootkit to determine the extent of a compromise.

If you suspect that you have a compromised system, it is a good idea to check for a *rootkit*, which is a collection of programs that intruders often install after they have compromised the root account of a system. These programs help the intruders clean up their tracks and provide access back into the system.

Rootkits sometimes leave processes running to allow the intruder to return easily and without the system administrator's knowledge. This means that the rootkit needs to modify some of the system's binaries (such as *ps*, *ls*, and *netstat*) in order to not give away the backdoor processes that the intruder has put in place. Unfortunately, there are so many different rootkits that it would be far too time-consuming to learn the intricacies of each one and look for them manually. Thankfully, scripts like *chkrootkit* (*http://www.chkrootkit.org*) will do the job for you automatically.

The main *chkrootkit* script calls various C programs to perform all of the tests it carries out. In addition to detecting over 50 different rootkits, *chkrootkit* detects network interfaces that are in promiscuous mode, altered *lastlog* files, and altered *wtmp* files. These files contain times and dates when users have logged on and off the system, so if they have been altered, this is evidence of an intruder. *chkrootkit* also performs tests to detect kernel-module-based rootkits.

It isn't a good idea to install *chkrootkit* on your system and simply run it periodically, since an attacker might simply find the installation and change it so that it doesn't detect his presence. A better idea is to compile it and put it on removable or read-only media. To compile *chkrootkit*, download the source package and extract it. Then, go into the directory that it created and run the make sense command.

Running *chkrootkit* is as simple as typing ./chkrootkit from the directory in which it was built. When you do this, it will print each test that it performs and the result of the test:

```
# ./chkrootkit
ROOTDIR is `/'
Checking `amd'... not found
Checking `basename'... not infected
Checking `biff'... not found
Checking `chfn'... not infected
Checking `chsh'... not infected
Checking `cron'... not infected
Checking `date'... not infected
Checking `du'... not infected
Checking `dirname'... not infected
Checking `echo'... not infected
Checking `egrep'... not infected
Checking `env'... not infected
Checking `find'... not infected
Checking `fingerd'... not found
Checking `gpm'... not infected
Checking `grep'... not infected
Checking `hdparm'... not infected
Checking `su'... not infected
...
```

That's not very interesting, because the machine hasn't been infected (yet). In contrast, here's some output from a machine that has been infected by a simple rootkit that replaces system binaries with versions that have been modified to hide the intruder's presence:

```
ROOTDIR is `/'
Checking `amd'... not found
Checking `basename'... not infected
Checking `biff'... not found
Checking `chfn'... not infected
Checking `chsh'... not infected
Checking `cron'... not infected
Checking `date'... not infected
Checking `du'... not infected
Checking `dirname'... not infected
Checking `echo'... not infected
Checking `egrep'... not infected
Checking `env'... not infected
Checking `find'... not infected
Checking `fingerd'... not found
Checking `gpm'... not infected
Checking `grep'... not infected
Checking `hdparm'... not infected
```

```
Checking `su'... not infected
Checking `ifconfig'... INFECTED
Checking `inetd'... not tested
Checking `inetdconf'... not found
Checking `identd'... not found
Checking `init'... not infected
...
```

As you can see, the ifconfig command has been replaced. This is because it's possible for a system administrator to easily see if a sniffer is active by running the ifconfig command and checking to see if it shows the network interface in promiscuous mode.

More sophisticated rootkits insert code into the kernel to subvert key system calls in order to hide an intruder's activities. If you see something similar to the following, it means a rootkit that uses loadable kernel modules (LKMs) to do this has been installed on the system:

```
Checking `lkm'... You have      1 process hidden for readdir command
You have     1 process hidden for ps command
chkproc: Warning: Possible LKM Trojan installed
```

chkrootkit can also be run on disks mounted in another machine; just specify the mount point for the partition with the -r option, like this:

```
# ./chkrootkit -r /mnt/hda2_image
```

Also, since chkrootkit depends on several system binaries, you might want to verify them before running the script (using the Tripwire [Hack #122] or RPM [Hack #123] methods). These binaries are awk, cut, egrep, find, head, id, ls, netstat, ps, strings, sed, and uname. If you have known good backup copies of these binaries, you can specify the path to them instead by using the -p option. For instance, if you copied them to a CD-ROM and then mounted it under /mnt/cdrom, use a command like this:

```
# ./chkrootkit -p /mnt/cdrom
```

You can also add multiple paths by separating each one with a colon (:).

Alternatively, instead of maintaining a separate copy of each of these binaries, you can simply keep a statically compiled copy of BusyBox (http://www.busybox.net) handy. Intended for embedded systems, BusyBox can perform the functions of over 200 common binaries, and it does so using a very tiny binary with symlinks. A floppy, CD, or USB keychain (with the read-only switch enabled) with chkrootkit and a static BusyBox installed can be a quick and handy tool for checking the integrity of your system.

Find the Owner of a Network

125 Track down network contacts using WHOIS databases.

Looking through your IDS logs, you've seen some strange traffic coming from another network across the Internet. When you look up the IP address in DNS, it resolves as something like *dhcp-103.badguydomain.com*. Whom do you contact to help track down the person who sent this traffic?

Getting DNS Information

You're probably already aware that you can use the whois command to find out contact information for owners of Internet domain names. If you haven't used whois, it's as simple as typing, well, "whois":

```
$ whois badguydomain.com
Registrant:
    Dewey Cheatum

    Registered through: GoDaddy.com
    Domain Name: BADGUYDOMAIN.COM

    Domain servers in listed order:
        PARK13.SECURESERVER.NET
        PARK14.SECURESERVER.NET
    For complete domain details go to:
    http://whois.godaddy.com
```

Unfortunately, this whois entry isn't as helpful as it might be. Normally, administrative and technical contacts are listed, complete with a phone number and email and snail mail addresses. Evidently, *godaddy.com* has a policy of releasing this information only through its web interface, apparently to cut down on spam harvesters. But if the registrant's name is listed as "Dewey Cheatum," how accurate do you think the rest of this domain record is likely to be? Although domain registrants are "required" to give legitimate information when setting up domains, I can tell you from experience that using whois in this way is actually only a great way to track down *honest* people.

Since this approach doesn't get you anywhere, what other options do you have? Well, you can use the whois command again, this time using it to query the number registry for the IP address block containing the offending address.

Getting Netblock Information

Number registries are entities with which owners of large blocks of IP addresses must register, and they are split up according to geographic region. The main difficulty is picking the correct registry to query. The WHOIS server for the American Registry for Internet Numbers (ARIN) is generally the best bet; it tells you the correct registry to query if the IP address is not found in its own database.

With that in mind, let's try out a query using the offending IP address:

```
# whois -h whois.arin.net 208.201.239.103
[Querying whois.arin.net]
[whois.arin.net]
Final results obtained from whois.arin.net.
Results:
UUNET Technologies, Inc. UUNET1996B (NET-208-192-0-0-1)
                                    208.192.0.0 - 208.255.255.255
SONIC.NET, INC. UU-208-201-224 (NET-208-201-224-0-1)
                                    208.201.224.0 - 208.201.255.255

# ARIN WHOIS database, last updated 2004-01-18 19:15
# Enter ? for additional hints on searching ARIN's WHOIS database.
```

Our query returned multiple results, which will happen sometimes when an owner of a larger IP block has delegated a sub-block to another party. In this case, UUNET has delegated a sub-block to Sonic.net.

Now we'll run a query with Sonic.net's handle:

```
# whois -h whois.arin.net NET-208-201-224-0-1
Checking server [whois.arin.net]
Results:

OrgName:    SONIC.NET, INC.
OrgID:      SNIC
Address:    2260 Apollo Way
City:       Santa Rosa
StateProv:  CA
PostalCode: 95407
Country:    US

ReferralServer: rwhois://whois.sonic.net:43

NetRange:   208.201.224.0 - 208.201.255.255
CIDR:       208.201.224.0/19
NetName:    UU-208-201-224
NetHandle:  NET-208-201-224-0-1
Parent:     NET-208-192-0-0-1
NetType:    Reallocated
Comment:
RegDate:    1996-09-12
Updated:    2002-08-23
```

```
OrgTechHandle: NETWO144-ARIN
OrgTechName:   Network Operations
OrgTechPhone:  +1-707-522-1000
OrgTechEmail:  noc@sonic.net

# ARIN WHOIS database, last updated 2004-01-18 19:15
# Enter ? for additional hints on searching ARIN's WHOIS database.
```

From the output, you can see that we have a contact listed with a phone number and email address. This information is most likely for the ISP that serves the miscreant who is causing the trouble. Now, you have a solid contact who should know exactly who is behind *badguydomain.com*. You can let them know about the suspicious traffic you're seeing and get the situation resolved.

Incidentally, you might have trouble using whois if you are querying some of the new top-level domains (TLDs), such as *.us*, *.biz*, *.info*, and so on. One great shortcut for automatically finding the proper WHOIS server is to use the GeekTools Whois Proxy (*http://geektools.com/tools.php*). It automatically forwards your request to the proper WHOIS server, based on the TLD you are requesting. I specify an alias such as this in my *.profile* to always use the GeekTools proxy:

```
alias whois='whois -h whois.geektools.com'
```

Now, when I run whois from the command line, I don't need to remember the address of a single WHOIS server. The folks at GeekTools have a bunch of other nifty tools to make sysadmin tasks easier, too. Check them out at *http://geektools.com*.

—Rob Flickenger

Index

Symbols

< > (direction operator), in Snort
 rules, 373
* flag matching in Snort rules, 375
| character
 enclosing hexadecimal vales in Snort
 rules, 374
 logical OR operator, 44
 searching on multiple variables, 395
! (logical NOT) operator, 44
 applied to IP address or CIDR range
 in Snort rules, 372
 matching flags in Snort rules, 375
+ operator, TCP flag matching in Snort
 rules, 375

Numbers

802.1X, 240
 configuring your AP, 243

A

A (address) records, 175
ac command (process accounting), 272
Accept header, logging requests
 without, 395
accept option, SnortSam, 381
access point (AP), configuring for
 802.1X with PEAP, 243
access.conf file (pam_access
 module), 43

ACLs (access control lists), 5–8
 grsecurity, 29, 34
 setting, modifying, and removing, 7
 Windows event logs, securing, 73
actions, Snort rules, 371
 defining custom, 372
activate and dynamic actions, Snort
 rules, 371
Active Directory environment
 configuration information for your
 CA, 218
 using Group Policy to configure
 Automatic Updates, 63–66
active responses (OSSEC HIDS), 279
Address Resolution Protocol (see ARP)
address space layouts, randomization
 with grsecurity, 32
address spoofing
 preventing for internal addresses with
 PacketFilter, 126
 (see also ARP; spoofing)
administrative roles, delegating, 11
ADODB (PHP code library), 354, 364
agents, OSSEC HIDS
 adding, 275–277
 installing Windows agent, 277
AIDE, 422
alerts
 generated by Spade, 385
 generating to test OSSEC HIDS, 277
 IDS sensor, tracking, 363
 Snort NIDS, 352, 390
 tracking, 353

We'd like to hear your suggestions for improving our indexes. Send email to *index@oreilly.com*.

B

N

R

race conditions in /tmp
  preventing exploitation of, 30
  prevention with grsecurity, 28
racoon program, 306–309
  client configuration, 307
  configuring on the client, 306
  gateway configuration, 307
  starting at boot, 307
  using x.509 certificates for
    authentication, 308
RADIUS server
  IP address, substituting for NVRAM
    variable, 243
  setting up FreeRADIUS, 241
  use by 802.1X networks, 241
ranges of IP addresses, scanning with
  nmap, 195
raw I/O, removing ability for, 10
rc.conf file, starting jails automatically at
  boot, 22
Readline, 401
records, DNS, 174–176
recovery agents (EFS on Windows), 81
  backing up keys, 85
  restoring EFS keys, 84
recovery (see incident recovery and
  response)
Red Hat Linux, AutoRPM, 56
referrer field, checking with
  SpoofGuard, 104
Registry
  disabling default shares, 78
  Memory Management key,
    editing, 88
regular expressions for swatch tool, 265
reject rule, Snort_inline, 379
Remote Access Dial-In User Service (see
  RADIUS server)
remote machines (Windows), scanning
  for system updates, 61
remote procedure calls (RPCs), email
  notifications sent by, 136
Remote PwdHash, 106
replace rule option, Snort_inline, 379
request normalization features, mod_
  security, 393
resolving hostnames to IP addresses with
  DNS queries through Tor, 96
resource limits, enforcing, 54

response (see incident recovery and
  response)
responses, active (OSSEC HIDS), 279
return option (PacketFilter), 124
roaming user profiles, backing up EFS
  certificates and key pairs, 82
Roo Honeywall CD-ROM
  distribution, 412
root access, selectively granting, 11
root CA, 214
root privileges
  administrative role delegation
    and, 11
  effective UID (EUID) of 0, 19
  Linux, modifying capabilities for, 10
  services not needing, 21
root user, running nmap as, 195
root-exploitable programs, checking
  for, 3
rootkits, 415
  scanning for, 422–424
    code inserted into kernel, 424
round-robin database (see RRDtool)
rpcapd, remote monitoring
  with, 297–300
RPCs (remote procedure calls), email
  notifications sent by, 136
RPM
  AutoRPM for system updates, 56
  finding compromised packages, 420
RRDtool, 291–293
  hourly graphs of data, 292
  multiple servers on a single
    graph, 293
RSS feeds, tracking network
  vulnerabilities, 234
rssh, 46–49
  configuring to use chroot( ), 47
  supported services, 49
rules
  CORE FORCE, 144
  egress filtering, 150
  Netfilter
    examples, 119
    ordering, 120
    saving all, 121
  PacketFilter
    DNS server, 127
    filtering rules, 126
    scrub rules, 125
    traffic normalization, 125

T

tables of IP addresses (PacketFilter), 123
Tcl packages, required for Sguil, 358
tcltls package, 358
Tclx package, 358
TCP
    general packet form in test.conf
        file, 152
    packet flags, checking with
        Snort, 374
    support by syslog-ng, 267
tcpdump, 305, 309
TcpFlow, 357, 359
TCP/IP
    blocking ports, 138
    disguising stack to prevent remote
        OS detection, 190
temporary files folder, encrypting on
        Windows, 79
Terminal.app, 113
terminals, specifying in pam_time
        configuration file, 45
thresholding (Snort rules), 375
    including parameters in the rule, 376
throttle action, swatch, 266
Thunderbird, 107–112
    Enigmail extension
        public/private key pair, 109–111
        sending/receiving encrypted
            email, 111
    setting up, 107
time
    connect time for users,
        analyzing, 272
    restricting access by, 44–46
    synchronizing on network
        systems, 207–209
time.conf file, 44
timeouts (SSH sessions), setting to guard
        against ARP spoof
        attacks, 149
timeperiods.cfg file (Nagios), 290
tinydns program, 172–176
    authoritative DNS records, 174
    user accounts, 173
TLDs (top-level domains), querying with
        whois, 427

TLS (Transport Layer Security)
    EAP/TLS, 241
    setting up for SMTP, 161
    using TLS-enabled SMTP with
        Qmail, 163
    VPN connections, 342
Tor (Onion Router), 91–95
    blocking user access, 156–157
    testing, web page, 94
    tor-resolve program, 96
    tunneling SSH through, 95
    using with Privoxy, 93
ToS (Type-of-Service) field in IP
        header, 152
traffic analysis, evading on the
        Internet, 91–94
traffic normalization rules
        (PacketFilter), 125
trampoline functions, 33
Transport Layer Security (see TLS)
trends on the network,
        graphing, 291–293
Tripwire, 415–419
    compiling from source, 416
    configuration file, editing, 418
    configuration settings, 416
    configuration variables,
        fine-tuning, 417
    cryptographic keys that protect its
        files, 416
    database, 416
    database, updating, 419
    day-to-day use, 419
    installing, 418
    policy, 416
    policy file, decrypting and
        editing, 419
    stored snapshots of files, 416
    subdirectories, 417
    vulnerability to file modification by
        intruders, 416
Trojan horses
    distribution in software, 13
    inability of Windows Firewall to
        protect against, 129
    ports used, 137
    preventing in common directories, 3
TrueCrypt, 96–100

Wireless Vulnerabilities and Exploits
project, 235
wl0_wpa_psk NVRAM variable, 240
WPA (WiFi Protected Access), 236
802,1X, 241
configuring AP to support, 243
WPA2, 241
configuring AP to support, 243
WPA-PSK, 240
write action, swatch, 265
WRT54G wireless routers, 237
downloading OpenWRT firmware
image, 237
WSH (Windows Script Host), 77
wtmp files (altered), detection by
chkrootkit, 422

X

X11
Nessus client, 198
preventing server from listening on
TCP port, 18
x.509 certificates
authentication on FreeBSD IPsec
connection, 308
authentication on OpenBSD IPsec
connection, 312
XML, output from nmap, 196
XSS (cross-site scripting) attacks, 394

Y

yum program, 57

Z

Zlib, 92, 401
zone transfers, restricting for DNS
servers, 171

Colophon

The image on the cover of *Network Security Hacks*, Second Edition, is barbed wire. The type of barbed wire pictured in the cover image was patented by Joseph Glidden in 1874. Glidden improved on earlier attempts at manufacturing wire fencing by fashioning sharp barbs, spacing them along a smooth wire, and then twisting another wire around the first to hold the barbs in place. Advertised as "cheaper than dirt and stronger than steel," barbed wire was immediately adopted by farmers in the American west as a way to control their herds. The days of free-roaming cattle and cowboys were soon numbered, but battles over barbs were fought both in court and on the ranch. Opponents called barbed wire "the Devil's rope," and the Cole Porter song "Don't Fence Me In" mourned this change in the western landscape. Barbed wire was here to stay, though—in addition to agricultural use, it has become a ubiquitous component of warfare and is a common feature of high-security areas such as prisons.

The cover image is a photograph from *gettyimages.com*. The cover font is Adobe ITC Garamond. The text font is Linotype Birka; the heading font is Adobe Helvetica Neue Condensed; and the code font is LucasFont's TheSans Mono Condensed.

Better than e-books

Buy *Network Security Hacks*, 2nd Edition, and access the digital edition FREE on Safari for 45 days.

Go to www.oreilly.com/go/safarienabled and type in coupon code C6K9-A3AJ-TEYH-61JM-136S

Search
thousands of top tech books

Download
whole chapters

Cut and Paste
code examples

Find
answers fast

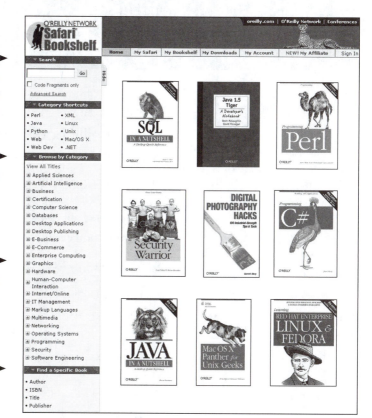

Search Safari! The premier electronic reference library for programmers and IT professionals.